US History in 15 Photographs

History in 15

This pioneering new series offers lively perspectives on regional and global histories. Adopting an innovative thematic approach, each title is structured around 15 items, concepts, or sources through which the history of a particular region, or the entire world, can be illuminated. From food to films, from cities to songs, this series brings history into focus for students and interested readers.

These approachable books use a consistent set of themes or sources as a lens through which to view the broader history, transforming how the reader understands these items while imparting critical lessons about historical context and analysis. For example, a book on US History in 15 Foods would use 15 foods to examine the history of the nation, covering key topics and themes in US history.

Series Editor: Laura A. Belmonte (Virginia Tech, USA)

Editorial Board:
Maria Montoya, NYU-Shanghai, China
Kyle Longley, Chapman University, USA
Anne Foster, Indiana State University, USA
Julia Irwin, University of South Florida, USA
Fabian Hilfrich, University of Edinburgh, UK
Justin Hart, Texas Tech, USA
Kelly Shannon, Florida Atlantic University, USA
Holly M. Karibo, Oklahoma State University, USA
Ellen Hartigan O'Connor, UC-Davis, USA
Andrew Rotter, Colgate University, USA

Published:

US History in 15 Foods, Anna Zeide

A History of Canada in 15 Moments, Jeff Keshen and Raymond B. Blake

Forthcoming:

Global History in 15 Epidemics, Andrew Robarts

Queer History in 15 Lives, Laura A. Belmonte

Scottish History in 15 Violent Crimes: Gender, Society and the Law, Louise Heren

Global History in 15 Latin American Foods, Elizabeth Newman

Atlantic History in 15 Slave Revolts: Resistance, Rebellion and Abolition from Below, Christian Høgsbjerg

South Asian History in 15 Films, Talat Ahmed

Global History in 15 Disasters: Urban Catastrophes and Reconstruction since 18th Century, Pierre Purseigle

US History in 15 Photographs

1865 to the 21st century

**EDITED BY REBECCA S. WINGO
AND LAUREN TILTON**

BLOOMSBURY ACADEMIC
LONDON • NEW YORK • OXFORD • NEW DELHI • SYDNEY

BLOOMSBURY ACADEMIC
Bloomsbury Publishing Plc, 50 Bedford Square, London, WC1B 3DP, UK
Bloomsbury Publishing Inc, 1359 Broadway, New York, NY 10018, USA
Bloomsbury Publishing Ireland, 29 Earlsfort Terrace, Dublin 2, D02 AY28, Ireland

BLOOMSBURY, BLOOMSBURY ACADEMIC and the Diana logo are trademarks of
Bloomsbury Publishing Plc

First published in Great Britain 2026

A catalogue record for this book is available from the British Library.

A catalog record for this book is available from the Library of Congress.

ISBN: HB: 978-1-3504-6338-7
         PB: 978-1-3504-6337-0
       ePDF: 978-1-3504-6340-0
      eBook: 978-1-3504-6339-4

Series: History in 15

Typeset by Integra Software Services Pvt. Ltd.
Printed and bound in Great Britain

For product safety related questions contact productsafety@bloomsbury.com.

To find out more about our authors and books visit www.bloomsbury.com
and sign up for our newsletters.

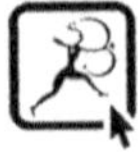

Online resources to accompany this book are available at https://bloomsbury.pub/
us-history-in-15-photographs. If you experience any problems, please contact
Bloomsbury at: onlineresources@bloomsbury.com.

Contents

List of Figures ix
Acknowledgments xii

There's More to It Than Meets the Eye 1
By Rebecca S. Wingo and Lauren Tilton

Reading Photographs Like a Historian 19
By Rebecca S. Wingo and Lauren Tilton

1 Veiled History: Confederate Memorialization and the Politics of Race and Place after Emancipation 33
By Julian Maxwell Hayter

2 Regarding Sovereign History as Incomplete: The Cherokee Outlet Land Opening Photographs 49
By Laura Wexler

3 Owned to Landowner: Black Homesteaders in the West 63
By Jacob K. Friefeld

4 Illuminating the Kodak Girl: Style and Marketing in the Gilded Age 79
By Shannon Perich

5 Native American Women and the Politics of Portraiture at the Turn of the Twentieth Century 97
By Cathleen D. Cahill

6 The Interwar Period (1918–39): Internationalism in the Pacific 113
By Courtney Sato

7 Complicating the Legacy of Dorothea Lange's Photography 131
By Linda Gordon

8 Framing a Fractured System: The Bracero Program through Leonard Nadel's Lens 147
By Mireya Loza

9 Race and the Space Race: Cold War Computing at NASA 161
By Nabeel Siddiqui and Thomas Haigh

10 Tear Down, Rise Up: Redevelopment and Revolts in American Cities 179
By Ann Pfau, David Hochfelder, and Stacy Sewell

11 They Don't Own Us: Harlan County, the Brookside Coal Strike, and the Forgotten History of the Working Class 195
By Grace Elizabeth Hale

12 "Very Strong Women You Don't Mess With": The Section 504 Disability Rights Protest 207
By Scot Danforth

13 *Documerica*: Picturing Pollution in the 1970s 223
By Lauren Tilton and Mia Lazar

14 The *Enola Gay* and the Culture Wars 237
By Rebecca S. Wingo

15 Selfie as Self-Love: Coyote Park's Decolonizing of Photography 255
By Ace Lehner

Works Cited 270
Index 297

Figures

1.1 Four African Americans helping raise a statue of Confederate General Robert E. Lee just prior to its unveiling in Richmond, Virginia, on May 29, 1890. Courtesy of the Robert A. Lancaster, Jr. Photograph Collection, The Valentine 32

2.1 Two photographs by William S. Prettyman documenting the "Land Rush" for formerly Cherokee lands in present-day Oklahoma, September 16, 1893. An estimated 100,000 people participated in the land run on the Cherokee Strip. Courtesy of Cowan's Auctions, Wikimedia Commons 48

3.1 The Shores family in front of their home near Westerville, Nebraska, in 1887. Photo by Solomon D. Butcher. Courtesy of the Nebraska State Historical Society 62

4.1 A real photo postcard of Kodak Girl, "Jane," 1909. Courtesy of the Photographic History Collection, Smithsonian's National Museum of American History 78

4.2 *Self-portrait (A New Woman)*, 1896. Photo by Frances Benjamin Johnston, in her Washington, DC, studio. Courtesy of the Prints and Photographs Division, Library of Congress 89

5.1 Three portraits of Marie Bottineau Baldwin, originally published in *The Washington Times*, August 3, 1914. Digitized by Chronicling America. Courtesy of the Library of Congress 96

5.2 Portrait of Marie Bottineau Baldwin seated with loose braids, ca. 1914. Courtesy of the Prints and Photographs Division, Library of Congress 105

6.1 Acting Consul General Komaji Takeuchi's tea in honor of the delegates from the Pan-Pacific Women's Conference, August 7, 1928. Photo by Yew Char. Courtesy of the Hocken Collections Uare Taoka o Hākena, University of Otago 112

6.2 A full "Society" page about the Pan-Pacific Women's Association conference in Vancouver, Canada, 1937. The article showcases some of the members' calling cards. "When East Meets West," *The Vancouver Sun*, July 10, 1937. Material republished with the express permission of *The Vancouver Sun*, a division of Postmedia Network, Inc 120

7.1 Dorothea Lange's most iconic photograph, commonly referred to as *Migrant Mother*, depicting pea pickers in Nipomo, California, March 1936. Photo by Dorothea Lange. Courtesy of the Prints and Photographs Division, Library of Congress 130

7.2 *Filipinos Cutting Lettuce*. Salinas, California, June 1935. Photo by Dorothea Lange. Courtesy of the Prints and Photographs Division, Library of Congress 136

7.3 *Dust Storm. It Was Conditions of This Sort Which Forced Many Farmers to Abandon the Area*. New Mexico, April 1935. Photo by Dorothea Lange. Courtesy of the Prints and Photographs Division, Library of Congress 138

7.4 *Negro Girl Working in the Fields*. The Mississippi Delta, July 1936. Photo by Dorothea Lange. Courtesy of the Prints and Photographs Division, Library of Congress 139

8.1   *Braceros Sprayed with DDT at the Hidalgo Texas Processing Center*, 1956. Photo by Leonard Nadel. Courtesy of the Archives Center, Smithsonian's National Museum of American History 146

9.1   Portrait of Melba Roy Mouton, head of a group of "human computers" tracking Echo satellites at NASA, 1964. Courtesy of the National Air & Space Administration, Wikimedia Commons 160

10.1   Robert and Ethel Mather inside their apartment, Albany, New York, February 28, 1963. Photo by Harold Furlong. Courtesy of the New York State Archives 178

11.1   *Brookside Women's Club Picket*, 1973. Photo by Earl Dotter. Courtesy of Earl Dotter 194

12.1   Disability rights advocates Kitty Cone, Judy Heumann, Eunice Fiorito, and American Sign Language interpreter Jadine Murello on stage at a Section 504 protest rally in Lafayette Square. Washington, DC, April 26, 1977. Photo by HolLynn D'Lil. Courtesy of Getty Images 206

13.1   *Chemical Plants on Shore Are Considered Prime Source of Pollution*. Lake Charles, Louisiana, June 1972. Photo by Marc St. Gil for Documerica. Courtesy of the National Archives & Records Administration 222

14.1   Demonstrators protesting the Smithsonian National Air and Space Museum's *Enola Gay* exhibit at the Steven F. Udvar-Hazy Center. Chantilly, Virginia, December 15, 2003. Photo by Joyce Naltchayan Boghosian. Courtesy of Getty Images 236

15.1   Instagram post by Coyote Park on October 10, 2022. Photos by Coyote Park. Courtesy of author, with permission from Coyote Park 254

Acknowledgments

We extend our heartfelt gratitude to all the contributors who joined us on this project. Thank you for responding to our suggestions and revisions with such humor and grace. It has been a pleasure to think and learn with you. Our thanks also go to the scholars who, while unable to contribute, offered their encouragement and support.

Our sincere appreciation goes to our team at Bloomsbury. To our editor, Maddie Smith, thank you for your support and patience as we repeatedly blew past our deadlines, and for arranging such outstanding and generous peer reviewers. To our assistant editors, Megan Harris and Niamh Coffey, thank you for your guidance and attention to detail. Last but not least, many thanks to Laura Belmonte for inviting us to the series.

It would not have been possible to publish a book with this many photographs without the funding support of the University of Cincinnati's Department of History. To both of our universities, we appreciate the time that enabled us to think, create, learn, and share cutting-edge research that supports our personal and institutional missions of engaging communities with the insights of the past. The University of Richmond's commitment to innovative liberal arts teaching, along with the University of Cincinnati's commitment to inclusive excellence, played a central role.

Finally, we are grateful to the family, friends, mentors, and colleagues who were by our side. Lauren's interest in photography is deeply indebted to her mentors, Grace Hale and Laura Wexler. She is overjoyed to share the same intellectual space on these pages. She also wants to thank Rebecca Wingo for including her in the project and for the opportunity to collaborate with such a brilliant public historian. Wingo is just grateful that Lauren agreed to co-edit this volume in the first place. Lauren's strengths in visual culture provided cover for any of Wingo's shortcomings. This would be a very different (much worse) book without her insights.

Asking someone to co-edit a book is the academic equivalent of "hey, let's start a band!" We are happy to report that we are still friends. We hope that you enjoy this volume as much as we enjoyed creating it.

There's More to It Than Meets the Eye

By Rebecca S. Wingo and Lauren Tilton

Glossary: Camera Obscura, Daguerreotype, Dry Plate, Lithography, Negatives, Photojournalism, Pictorialism, Positives, Punctum, That-Has-Been, Wet Plate

What is the last photograph you took?
What kind of camera did you use?
Why did you take the picture?
Did you filter it? Crop it?
Did you share it?

From news to social media, photography is a ubiquitous presence in nearly every aspect of our digital lives. As of 2024, 91 percent of Americans own smartphones.[1] Apps with easy-to-use editing features enable us to crop and filter our pictures and even remove photobombers in the background. The ease with which we can quickly capture a moment in time has fundamentally reshaped the way we remember. Instead of observing our present, our attention is often divided between the moment and our desire to record it.

Psychologists debate whether our ability to constantly photograph our lives is enhancing or deteriorating our recall.[2] Our memories record not just images but also sensations—such as smell, temperature, and emotion—but only if we are paying attention. One reason we may be forgetting more is due to a phenomenon called "cognitive offloading." We are literally outsourcing our memory to digital technology, freeing our brains from the burden of recall.[3] Take phone numbers, for instance. Do you have any memorized, or do you rely on the contact list in your smartphone?

Allowing our phones to remember for us is neither good nor bad. Instead, technology offers us a choice. On the one hand, fully immersing ourselves in a moment free of other distractions makes our memories more vivid. On the other hand, taking pictures forms a visual record of our lives, allowing us to share those memories with people who were not there. There are drawbacks and benefits to both. Some studies show that taking photos to share them removes us from the experience and even makes our brains more likely to remember them from a third-person perspective; others show that photos are useful memory tools for slowing dementia.[4]

In one experiment, Linda Henkel invited two groups of participants on a guided tour of an art museum. She instructed one group to photograph all the objects on the tour with their smartphones and the other to photograph only specific objects by zooming in on particular parts. When asked later, the first group experienced less recall about the objects and even struggled to remember their location in the museum. Far from an indictment of the smartphone, Henkel's findings suggest that by actively paying attention, we can eliminate what she calls "the photo-taking-impairment effect."[5]

We hope this book achieves a similar goal by demonstrating how to pause, look closely, and interpret photography—both historic and contemporary. Cameras, smartphones, laptops, and tablets have given each of us the ability to produce an unlimited quantity of photographs. Still, that ubiquity has also turned many of us into passive consumers. How often do we take the time to interrogate a photograph and notice not only what we're seeing but also what we're *not* seeing? Historians—notoriously reliant on written texts—are among the worst offenders. We tend to forget that photographs are *visual* texts worthy of study and investigation. Instead, we often include them as illustrations of our existing arguments rather than using them to deepen or challenge our arguments. Our volume shifts this gaze by reading photographs as primary sources vital to our analysis and understanding of American history.

This book spans the history of the United States from 1865 to the present. Colleges and universities use this periodization to divide US history into two sections: pre- and post-Civil War. (Some historians prefer to use the end of Reconstruction in 1877 as the dividing line.) The problem with periodization is that it suggests there is a linearity to history, a timeline with firm boundaries around what is past and what is present. In our first chapter, for example, Julian Hayter discusses a monument to Robert E. Lee and the Confederacy in Richmond, Virginia. But the story does not begin with the Civil War, nor does it end with the monument's unveiling in 1890, or even 130 years later when the statue was removed following Black Lives Matter protests. For all our emphasis on dates and change over time, understanding history is a process that often defies time.

Understanding photography is a process, too. Just because we can all be photographers does not mean that we are magically imbued with the ability to read photography. We must choose to zoom in—to be active, not passive, consumers. To begin, it is essential to understand the origins of photography and how photographic technology and its use have reciprocally shaped the trajectory of American society.

Picture This

Photography as we recognize it today dates back to the early 1800s. The **camera obscura**, an instrument that projects images, dates back farther to at least 500 BC and forms the foundation for modern photography. The oldest surviving photograph is *View from the Window at Le Gras* by Joseph Nicéphore Niépce (ca. 1826). Compared to the smartphone in your pocket, Niépce's process was incredibly complicated. He washed a pewter plate with light-sensitive petroleum tar dissolved in lavender oil, set a camera obscura in a window, and exposed the projected image onto the plate. Estimates of exposure time vary from eight hours to several days.

Like Niépce, the men who invented modern photography were chemists. In 1839, fellow Frenchman Louis Daguerre revolutionized the world when he released instructions for the **daguerreotype**, the first widely adopted method for producing fixed images. Instead of pewter, Daguerre used a copper plate coated with silver iodide and developed the image with mercury fumes. Exposure time ranged from three to fifteen minutes, making it possible to photograph people for the first time if they sat very still. From its earliest days, people understood this technological innovation as a powerful tool for self-representation and identity formation. Early African American daguerreotypists, such as James P. Ball, Glenalvin Goodridge, and Augustus Washington, opened studios and democratized access to portraiture by taking portraits of both white and Black Americans. More than equal opportunity photographers, these men were abolitionists, businessmen, politicians, and teachers.[6]

The collodion **wet plate** process replaced the daguerreotype, reducing both the cost and the time required for the entire process to fifteen minutes. The most common variants were the ambrotype (1850s), which used a glass plate, and the tintype (1860s), which used a translucent iron plate. Like the daguerreotype, the challenge with these methods was that they were not replicable. Analogous to the Polaroid instant camera, the photos were **positives** developed directly onto the surface of the plate. To make a copy, photographers would have to make a photograph of the photograph.

Photographic **negatives**, also invented around 1850, allowed photographers to produce limitless copies by shining light through a glass plate onto photosensitive paper. These early negatives also relied on the wet plate process. Rather inconveniently, the silver nitrate emulsion used on the plates could become unstable and potentially explosive if it dried before processing. This kept many professional photographers tethered to their studios, though some intrepid photographers converted tents and wagons into portable studios and darkrooms.

In the 1870s, photography transformed once again with the introduction of the gelatin **dry plate** negative process (which would not explode), opening the field to amateur photographers. Dry plates could be prepared ahead of time and developed at the photographer's leisure. The same technology could be applied to other light-sensitive surfaces, such as nitrocellulose film.

George Eastman, the founder of Kodak, capitalized on this new demographic by patenting the world's first flexible roll film. Kodak's original camera came preloaded with a 100-exposure roll and cost $25, a price affordable for the more affluent amateur. For another $10, users sent the entire camera back to the company's headquarters in New York, and Kodak sent back the negatives, the prints, and the camera reloaded with a new roll of film. Kodak released its most affordable camera, the "Brownie," in 1900, setting the price at $1. Virtually anyone could be a photographer. Newer, faster, better camera technologies developed over the twentieth century continued to democratize photography and expand the field to amateur photographers.

But the camera is an imperfect tool. Everything from its technical features, the type of film, and the printing process influences the creation and perception of an image. While vacationers played with cheap cameras and sent black-and-white real photo postcards to friends and family, researchers experimented with new film techniques to capture the world in full color.[7] The Lumière brothers, renowned for their pioneering advances in cinematography, played a significant role in the development of color photography. They marketed the Autochrome Lumière to the public in 1907, but their method relied on an additive color process. Kodachrome, a color-reversal film utilizing a subtractive color process, was introduced to the market in 1935 with great success.

Kodak film earned acclaim for its ability to replicate color as seen in the world, but issues arose due to the technical calibrations the company suggested for photo labs. Kodak notoriously controlled its entire imaging process. They produced and sold the printers to photo labs, and they standardized the colors using "Shirley Cards," depicting a white woman model with bright colors and soft contrast. Lab technicians calibrated their printers to her shadows, colors, and skin tone. Although competitors later offered drugstores a wider variety of color baselines (think Pantone versus the CYMK standard in home printers), Shirley Cards had set a precedent for basing all color calibration on whiteness. Although Kodak began incorporating non-white models in the 1970s, photography and the motion picture industry are still reckoning with Shirley's legacy to this day.[8]

Debates over photography's gaze persist as digital technologies have raised new concerns about the truthfulness of images. Companies such as Canon, Nikon, and Sony competed for dominance of the SLR market at the turn of the twenty-first century, marketing cameras that used digital sensors and memory cards instead of film. Software tools like Adobe Photoshop, which placed digital editing control in consumers' hands, led to new questions and concerns about manipulation. Advancements in computing increasingly put the editorial power inside the camera itself. Embedded processors, data storage, and touch screens turned popular models such as the Canon 5D and Mark series into mini-computers.

The power to take a picture now extends well beyond a single-function camera, most notably with the development of multi-function phones. In 1997, French tech entrepreneur Philippe Kahn pioneered wireless image circulation when he used his cell phone to share a photo of his newborn daughter with over 2,000 people.[9] "I wanted to create a twenty-first-century version of a Polaroid picture," he explained.[10] Companies such as Sharp, Nokia, and the game-changing Apple iPhone launched a digital flurry of instant photos. In addition to other groundbreaking advances in device size, memory size, and pixel density, smartphones continue to push forward photographic innovation and challenge photography's legacy. In 2024, after over a decade of research, the Chinese company TECNO released a smartphone with AI-powered "Universal Tone" imaging technology to rectify skin-tone bias. Focusing on markets in South Asia, Africa, and the Middle East, TECNO's Universal Tone is "reimagining imaging technology with diversity at its core."[11]

The speed with which camera technology changed since Niépce and Daguerre is hard to fathom. In less than 200 years, photography transformed from a cost-prohibitive science experiment into a habit. We can now capture moments both candid and planned in a fraction of a second and instantaneously distribute them to global audiences with the tap of a button.

We can no longer imagine a world without photography, but what has the pervasiveness of photography done for our ability to "read" the images we see?

The Camera Never Lies

Photography today encompasses an alphabet soup of genres, from art and astrophotography to wedding and wildlife photography. These specializations developed in tandem with advances in camera technology as photographers pushed the limits of their equipment. Sports photography, for example, did not professionalize until the 1920s, when companies began marketing cameras with a shutter speed of 1/1,000th of a second. (By way of comparison, a daguerreotype camera had a shutter speed of around 1,000 seconds—though it technically used a lens cap, not a shutter—and the Brownie was fixed at 1/40th of a second.) Given the nature of this book, most of the photographs fall into the genres of historical documentary and/or art.

However, photography's origins in empirical science give the false impression that photographs are indeed documentary representations of objective and observable facts or genuine moments from the past. This impression stems from photography's indexical nature. It records light reflecting off a subject and back through the lens to create a direct account of what stands before the camera. Fundamentally different from artistic *representations* of reality, photographs are *actual traces of reality* itself. Roland Barthes, a French philosopher and scholar of photography, termed this indexical quality "**that-has-been**."[12]

Photographs may harness light to illuminate the past and imbue it with a physicality, but where there is light, there are shadows. Lewis Hine, a sociologist and photographer, is credited with the popular phrase "the camera never lies." Less often do we hear his complete sentence: "While photographs may not lie, liars may photograph."[13] The camera is not a neutral tool, and photographers are not neutral users. Pictures are snippets of a past reality, easily manipulated, enhanced, exaggerated, or distorted. While historical photographs carry the weight of Barthes' "that-has-been" quality, we can only fully understand them when we accept that they are creations and recreations of realities made by imperfect people with their own agendas and biases.

Over time, photographers have harnessed the camera's power for both good and ill, either reinforcing or challenging the beliefs of American society. Three early adopters of photography were documentarians (best understood today as photojournalists), the US government, and artists. As soon as Daguerre released his process to the public, photographers began documenting historical moments and important people. When the Mexican-American War broke out in 1846, for instance, daguerreotypists were on hand to create portraits of important military leaders, street scenes, and battlefields.

Daguerreotypes had limited reach. They are relatively small (a "full plate" measured 6.5 × 8.5 inches, slightly more than half the size of a standard sheet of paper) and not reproducible. In order to share them widely, printers relied on a print-making process invented in the late 1700s called **lithography**. Artists would draw scenes from photographs by hand on flat pieces of stone or metal, then treat the surface with chemicals that made specific parts of the images receptive or repellent to ink. They would often embellish the lithographs with artistic flourishes to make their rendering of the photograph more appealing. For the first few decades of photography, more people saw unreliable artistic interpretations than actual photographs.

Although the first American newspaper to print a photograph using the halftone process would not appear until 1880, historians often credit the evolution of American **photojournalism** to Mathew Brady and his team of Civil War photographers.[14] Originally a studio photographer in New York City, Brady asked President Abraham Lincoln for permission to follow soldiers to the battlefields and document the war. Artists converted many of Brady's images into printable woodcuts for the widely read magazine *Harper's Weekly*, which created a sensation by bringing the war front to the home front for the first time.

There is a direct line from Brady's *The Dead of Antietam* (1862) to other iconic war photographs, such as *Napalm Girl* (1972) from the Vietnam War and *Tank Man* (1989) from Tiananmen Square. However, photographing war—like sports photography—required a shutter speed that was unavailable to Brady during the Civil War. Many of his "action" photographs were staged reenactments. He altered others by repositioning the bodies of the deceased and rearranging background objects to create a more captivating picture. His manipulation of the scene to convey the horrors of war was also a manipulation of his viewers, one designed to provoke a visceral response.[15]

Around the same time, the US government embraced the camera as a tool of empire. In the 1860s, the government hired photographers to join geographic and geologic surveys of the American West. They depicted an untamed wilderness that not only cropped Indigenous peoples off the land, but also buttressed the idea of Manifest Destiny by depicting a vacant region ripe for settlement. As Americans spread westward, photographers portrayed Indigenous peoples as primitive and savage, and made the visual case for bringing "civilization" to the West.[16] Around the turn of the century, anthropologists reinforced these ideas even further by photographing the head size and facial features of Black and Indigenous peoples to "scientifically" measure their racial and intellectual inferiority.[17] However, as Cathleen Cahill demonstrates in her chapter on activist Marie Bottineau Baldwin, Indigenous peoples often challenged this power dynamic by strategically producing and deploying their own photography.

As Bottineau Baldwin knew, portraiture and self-representation are potent ways to assert or control one's identity. For example, President Lincoln was a rather "ungainly-looking fellow." When he sat for a studio portrait, the photographer—Brady himself!—suggested he pull up his shirt collar to shorten his neck to make him appear more dignified and youthful. Lincoln credited his victory in 1860 to Brady's photograph.[18] Likewise, President Franklin D. Roosevelt carefully controlled his appearance in photographs to hide the fact that he was primarily confined to a wheelchair. He did so to exude the power Americans expected from a leader in the highest public office.[19] More recently, President Barack Obama tapped into social media and selfie culture to make him more relatable to America's youth.[20] And who can forget the time Beyoncé's publicist asked *Buzzfeed* to remove several "unflattering" photos from her Superbowl performance because they didn't fit with her brand?[21]

The art of photographic portraiture borrowed heavily from the aesthetics and composition honed by generations of artists trained in the Western art tradition. (You'll learn more about this in the chapters by Shannon Perich and Ace Lehner.) In the 1880s, a movement called **pictorialism** emerged to a rather cold reception from the art community. Pictorialists asserted that, despite the medium's newness, photography was a form of art. Unlike Brady and the photojournalists who focused on realistic documentation, pictorialists believed that the value of the photograph lie in the ways the photographer effectively mimicked popular painting styles rather than in the actual content. They softened the lighting and focus and even manipulated the negatives by drawing on the surface or sanding them to produce different effects.[22]

Not everyone celebrated when companies like Kodak put cameras in the hands of everyday Americans. Pictorialists such as Alfred Stieglitz and Group f/64 drew distinctions between professional art photography and amateurism, while the art world continued to fortify the gates against photography at all. In 1935, cultural critic Walter Benjamin argued that the reproducibility of photography destroyed the "aura" of traditional artworks. Art was singular, he argued, unique in its presence and authenticity, and in the ritual value that came from art, existing as a one-of-a-kind object in a specific time and place.[23] However, democratization and reproduction are integral to photography's cultural and social influence. For example, many Americans know what Leonardo da Vinci's *Mona Lisa* looks like—not because we've all been to the Louvre but because we've seen a photograph of the painting. Benjamin is correct that the experience of a reproduction is not the same as viewing art in person. Similar to the way that art photography forced the definition of art to expand, photographic reproduction liberated it from its elitist confines.

Pictorialism and other photographic art movements continued to proliferate, and by the turn of the century, many emerging photojournalists were well-entrenched and trained in those rich artistic traditions. However, instead of staying inside the controlled conditions of a studio, they took their craft to the streets. They leveraged their camerawork into a mechanism for reform and produced impactful visual arguments capable of swaying public opinion. Barthes called the ability of photographs to pierce or even wound us the "**punctum**."[24] Photography's direct relationship to reality can deeply move its audience and produce enormous societal change.

One of the first photographers to use pictures in this manner was Jacob Riis, a Danish-American social reformer in New York City. Appalled by the squalid living conditions people endured in New York's tenements in the 1880s, Riis documented the urban poor and published a photographic exposé called *How the Other Half Lives*. He challenged the government's apathy by appealing to the public's sympathy, which ultimately resulted in national housing reform.[25] Riis' camerawork inspired future generations of reformers, including Lewis Hine, whose documentation of child labor and poor working conditions in the early twentieth century hastened America's first child labor laws.[26]

These photographers were so successful in effecting change that the US government once again embraced the camera as a tool (this time in service to social reform rather than empire). During the Great Depression, the Farm Security Administration (FSA) dispatched numerous photographers to document the everyday lives of rural Americans. In a relatively progressive move, they hired women photographers like Dorothea Lange (Linda Gordon's chapter expands on Lange's legacy) and African American photographers like Gordon Parks.

Parks enjoyed a prolific artistic career as a filmmaker, writer, and photographer. He became the first Black photographer on staff at *Life* magazine in the 1950s and also photographed for other high-profile publications, including *Vogue*. Following in the footsteps of Riis and Hine, Parks took up the twin causes of poverty and civil rights. He explained, "I picked up a camera because it was my choice of weapons against what I hated most about the universe: racism, intolerance, poverty."[27] Inspired by the work of Lange, Parks, and other FSA photographers, the government commissioned a similar project called *Documerica* in the 1970s to advocate for environmental protection (as Lauren Tilton and Mia Lazar explore in their chapter).

In a conversation with Black Panther Party member Eldridge Cleaver, Parks once said, "You have a 45mm automatic pistol on your lap, and I have a 35mm camera on my lap, and my weapon is just as powerful as yours."[28] Like Cleaver's gun and Parks' camera, the language of photography is loaded. We *shoot* pictures and make *headshots* for work. Photographers *capture* images, and the people in them are often referred to as *subjects*. Amateur cameras requiring little mechanical knowledge are called *point-and-shoot* cameras. Even the widely used social media platform Snapchat is a play on the word *snapshot*. One of the first movie cameras invented in 1882 was called the *chronophotographic gun*. Housed in the body of a rifle, it used revolver technology to produce twelve photographs per second with the squeeze of a trigger. Photoactivists recommend that we change our language. Instead of *taking* photographs during *photoshoots*, could we not "make" them in "photo sessions"?[29]

Photography is laden with biases of all sorts, from the technology that undergirds it to the people who use and consume it. Photographers crop people or objects out of a frame or manipulate the people and objects within the frame to create a more compelling visual argument. The technology in our cameras today even allows us to erase unwanted figures from the background—albeit rather benignly—so we can make it appear that we were the only ones on that mountaintop, beachfront, or wherever. America's latest generation has grown up in a world where self-presentation and photographic manipulation are so commonplace that they are *almost* unworthy of comment.

Reading photography is not a passive or superficial act. As many media theorists remind us, historical contexts are as important as our modern contexts. As viewers, our interpretations are more than reflections of our perspectives; they are active choices we make to accept or challenge the perspectives presented to us. A war photograph, for instance, evokes vastly different responses from the standpoints of the aggressor or victim, or the political positionality of the viewer.[30]

Reading photography is also intimate and multi-sensorial. In cultural critic Susan Sontag's foundational essay collection *On Photography* (1977), she wrote, "all photographs are *memento mori*. To take a photograph is to participate in another person's (or thing's) mortality, vulnerability, mutability. Precisely by slicing out this moment and freezing it, all photographs testify to time's relentless melt."[31] Visual theorist Tina Campt similarly urges us to not just *read* photographs but to *listen* with all our senses. She builds on Barthes' "punctum," arguing that photography's haptic qualities—the visceral ways photographs emotionally and physically touch, engage, and resonate with viewers—deserve careful exploration as they communicate far beyond their literal content.[32]

By looking, listening, and feeling, we can read with and against the grain of the world represented within and beyond the frame—and in times both historic and modern—to see what the photographer wants us to see *and* what we want to see.

Framing the Book

Our volume is designed to expand our understanding of different periods in American history following the Civil War. American history is often reduced to a few essential eras or events, but these Big Moments™ hardly account for the expansiveness of the American experience. While we welcome all curious readers, this book is designed for the college classroom and a typical fifteen-week semester, and our chapters intentionally *correspond with* and *respond to* common periodizations.

The photographs in this volume originate from various sources, including archives, newspapers, and social media. A few of the photographs have experienced some measure of virality either at the time they were made or later through media circulation, but the majority will be unfamiliar. We hope they prompt you to deepen your understanding of American history and rethink what you already know.

We open in the immediate aftermath of the Civil War. Julian Hayter situates us in the American South by documenting how city boosters in Richmond, Virginia, blended urban planning and segregation by funding a two-story monument to Confederate "heroes." Laura Wexler then takes us westward to former Cherokee lands in Oklahoma where white Americans competed for land claims, and journalists competed for the best photograph. Jacob Friefeld complicates the tension between American expansion and Indigenous dispossession by using a family portrait of African American homesteaders in Nebraska seeking freedom from the Jim Crow South. Offering another angle on late nineteenth-century capitalism, Shannon Perich uses a "Kodak Girl" real photo postcard to demonstrate how the democratization of the camera intersects with gender, consumerism, and leisure.

Bringing us firmly into the early twentieth century, Cathleen Cahill examines how activist Marie Bottineau Baldwin (Turtle Mountain Chippewa and French) used photography to play with existing stereotypes of Indigenous peoples and advocate for women's suffrage. For the interwar years, Courtney Sato centers a women's philanthropic organization in the Pacific to shift our focus from nationalism to internationalism, from Europe to Asia, and from portraits to group photography. Next, Linda Gordon extends Dorothea Lange's Depression-era photography beyond *Migrant Mother* (which remains one of the most iconic photographs of the twentieth century) by showcasing Lange's photographs of Black and Filipino laborers, among others.

Turning to life during and after the Second World War, Mireya Loza draws our attention to braceros, millions of legal Mexican migrant workers contracted by the United States to support the nation's wartime food economy and agribusiness. The Second World War also spurred technological innovations that proved crucial to America's power during the Cold War and the Space Race. Nabeel Siddiqui and Thomas Haigh illuminate the brilliance and ingenuity of African American women working at NASA as "human computers" through a portrait of Melba Roy Mouton.

The next chapters expand the discussion of the rapid cultural and social changes that characterized the 1960s and 1970s. Ann Pfau, David Hotchfelder, and Stacy Sewell prompt us to consider the human cost of urban renewal and modernization by using a photographic survey documenting future sites of destruction in Albany, New York, that left underserved citizens displaced and homeless. Grace Hale turns to rural America through a photograph of Appalachian women picketing against deadly working conditions in corporate coal mines, inviting us to expand our understanding of the vital role women played in labor movements. Scot Danforth brings to light a lesser-known aspect of the civil rights struggles by focusing on the women activists who pioneered the disability rights movement and compelled the Carter administration to enforce accessibility laws. Mia Lazar and Lauren Tilton then examine the Environmental Protection Agency's newly created photography unit, Documerica, to discuss how the environmental movement of the 1970s sought to preserve the air, water, and land on which the future of the nation relies.

The final chapters bring us into more contemporary histories. The Reagan Era, which followed the counterculture and liberation movements of the 1960s and 1970s, fanned the flames of what would become the Culture Wars. Rebecca Wingo uses a photograph of the *Enola Gay* (the plane that dropped the atomic bomb on Hiroshima) to detail a battle waged in the exhibit halls of the Smithsonian Institution as Americans debated the memory of the Second World War in the 1990s. Finally, Ace Lehner turns to a form of photography that animates our daily lives: the selfie. They analyze how the trans community has leveraged social media into a critical site for self-representation, identity formation, and political expression.

Photo Finish

We can only speculate about what Louis Daguerre would think of today's glut of photography, but he would certainly sympathize with the precarity wrought by rapidly changing technology. His invention was relatively short-lived compared to popular companies like Polaroid and Kodak. Still, even these photography behemoths struggled to keep pace with market changes in the Information Age. Polaroid declared bankruptcy in 2001. Kodak followed in 2012. Their downfalls were bellwethers for the difficulties ahead.

Following bankruptcy, Kodak tried (and failed) several ventures, including a smartphone, a tablet, and two cryptocurrencies. Ironically, their current success still hinges on film, and they remain one of the largest suppliers to the motion picture industry. In the 1980s, Polaroid attempted to pivot from film to magnetic data storage in floppy disks, but they were unable to compete with tech giants like IBM. Polaroid experienced a brief commercial boost in 2003 after Outkast released their chart-topping hit "Hey Ya," which encouraged listeners to "shake it like a Polaroid picture."[33] Akin to the surge of vinyl sales in direct defiance of music streaming services like Spotify, Polaroid's instant cameras still resonate with nostalgic collectors and hipster hobbyists who defy photography-driven social media platforms like Instagram and Tumblr.

The authors and photographs in this book offer lessons about the past, but they also provide valuable insights into our present. Becoming as active in our photographic consumption as we are in our production requires us to pay attention—to zoom in, as the participants in Henkel's museum study did. Reading photography requires the curiosity to ask questions about the content included *and* excluded from the frame, the motivation of the photographer *and* subject, the intended *and* unintended audience.

Equally important are questions about who preserved the photograph and why. Many of us are active contributors to massive digital photography collections. We do so almost by instinct or reflex. In 2024, 78 percent of adults under the age of thirty used Instagram (compared to 15 percent of adults aged above sixty-five who just don't like what all these new-fangled gadgets are doing to kids these days).[34] Yet, many of us are not aware of what we are consenting to when we share and post. According to Meta, Instagram's parent company, when users post on their platform, they grant Meta "a non-exclusive, transferable, sub-licensable, royalty-free, worldwide license to: host, use, distribute, modify, run, copy, publicly perform or display, translate, and create derivative works of any information, data, and other content."[35] In other words, Meta owns their users' content.

Think of it this way: future historians could one day pay Meta for the right to mine Instagram for a collection of essays much like this one. We can see it now: *US History in 15 Instagram Posts* ... But since its launch in 2010, Instagram users have shared billions of photographs—who could choose just fifteen? Given the rapid pace of change in digital technology, it is unlikely that the platforms we use today will remain in use for the next generation ... So we're *mostly* kidding.

However, it does raise questions about where all this photographic content will end up and who will have access to it. People often say that digital content never truly disappears and that what we post today may come back to haunt us in a decade or two. While that may be true for Beyoncé, digital ephemerality holds a different meaning for the everyday person. The misperception that our digital content will always be available and in the form in which we created it does a disservice to the field of archival preservation—and to the archivists who have retained the records for the images in this volume.

The photographs in this book exist because someone chose to create them and someone else decided to preserve them. We choose to highlight them as another vantage point into American history.

How many photographs are on your smartphone?
How many are worth saving for the future?
How will you save them?

Notes

1   Pew Research Center, "Mobile Fact Sheet," November 13, 2024.

2   Brian Resnick, "What Smartphone Photography Is Doing to Our Memories," *Vox*, March 28, 2018. Last accessed March 12, 2025, https://www.vox.com/science-and-health/2018/3/28/17054848/smartphones-photos-memory-research-psychology-attention.

3   Nathaniel Barr, Gordon Pennycook, Jennifer A. Stolz, and Jonathan A. Fugelsang, "The Brain in Your Pocket: Evidence That Smartphones Are Used to Supplant Thinking," *Computers in Human Behavior* 48 (July 2015): 473–80.

4   Deborah Stone, "How Images Can Help Dementia Sufferers Engage with Life," *Psychology Today*, May 13, 2021; and Alixandra Barasch, Gal Zauberman, and Kristin Diehl, "How the Intention to Share Can Undermine Enjoyment: Photo-Taking Goals and Evaluation of Experiences," *Journal of Consumer Research* 44, no. 6 (April 2018): 1220–37.

5   Linda A. Henkel, "Point-and-Shoot Memories: The Influence of Taking Photos on Memory for a Museum Tour," *Psychological Science* 25, no. 2 (2013): 401.

6   Sophia Alvarez Boyd, "Smithsonian Acquires Rare Antique Portraits by First Black Photographers," *NPR's Weekend Edition Sunday*, August 29, 2021. Last accessed March 20, 2025, https://www.npr.org/sections/pictureshow/2021/08/29/1031703142/smithsonian-acquires-rare-antique-portraits-from-first-black-photographers; David Kindy, "New Collection of Portraits Presents the Diversity of 19th-Century American Photography," *Smithsonian Magazine*, August 17, 2021. Last accessed March 20, 2025, https://www.smithsonianmag.com/smithsonian-institution/trove-new-portrait-photographs-presents-rarely-seen-diversity-19th-century-america-180978456/; "Photography," Smithsonian American Art Museum. Last accessed March 20, 2025, https://americanart.si.edu/art/highlights/photography.

7   Lynda Klich and Benjamin Weiss, *Real Photo Postcards: Pictures of a Changing Nation* (MFA Publications, 2022).

8   Mandalit del Barco, "How Kodak's Shirley Cards Set Photography's Skin-Tone Standard," *NPR Morning Edition,* November 13, 2014. Last accessed March 19, 2025, https://www.npr.org/2014/11/13/363517842/for-decades-kodak-s-shirley-cards-set-photography-s-skin-tone-standard.

9   Bob Parks, "The Big Picture," *Wired* 8, no. 10 (October 2000). Last accessed March 20, 2025, https://web.archive.org/web/20060326205210/http://www.wired.com/wired/archive/8.10/kahn.html

10   Samantha Murphy, "Meet the Man behind the Very First Camera Phone," *Mashable*, March 6, 2012. Last accessed March 20, 2025, https://mashable.com/archive/philippe-kahn-camera-phone

11   Geoff Harris, "Love the Skin You're In: How TECNO Is Beating Skin-Tone Bias in Phone Cameras," *Amateur Photographer*, November 15, 2024. Last accessed March 20, 2025, https://amateurphotographer.com/latest/photo-news/how-tecno-is-beating-skin-tone-bias-in-phone-cameras.

12 Roland Barthes, *Camera Lucida: Reflections on Photography* (Hill and Wang, 1981), 77.

13 Lewis W. Hine, "Social Photography," in *Classic Essays on Photography*, ed. Alan Trachtenburg (Leete's Island Books, 1980), 111.

14 This newspaper was the March 4, 1880 edition of *The Daily Graphic* in New York City. For more on Mathew Brady and early photojournalism, see Alan Trachtenburg, *Reading American Photographs: Images as History, Mathew Brady to Walker Evans* (Hill & Wang, 1989).

15 Trachtenburg, *Reading American Photographs*, 73–4.

16 Toby Jurovics, *Framing the West: The Survey Photographs of Timothy H. O'Sullivan* (Smithsonian American Art Museum, 2010).

17 See Daniel Steinbach and Robert S.G. Fletcher, "Photography, Colonialism, and War: Five Exposures," *War & Society* (February 2025): 1–8; Alessandra Link, "Editing for Expansion: Railroad Photography, Native Americans, and the American West, 1860–1880," *Western Historical Quarterly* 50, no. 3 (Autumn 2019): 281–313; Nicole Dawn Strathman, *Through a Native Lens: American Indian Photography* (University of Oklahoma Press, 2020); and Laura Wexler, *Tender Violence: Domestic Visions in an Age of U.S. Imperialism* (University of North Carolina Press, 2000).

18 PBS Digital Studios, "Did This Photo Make Lincoln President?" *The Bigger Picture with Vincent Brown*, August 9, 2022. Last accessed March 15, 2025, https://www.pbs.org/video/did-this-photo-make-lincoln-president-perejr/.

19 Davis W. Houck and Amos Kiewe, *FDR's Body Politics: The Rhetoric of Disability* (Texas A&M University Press, 2003).

20 James E. Katz, Michael Barris, and Anshul Jain, *The Social Media President: Barack Obama and the Politics of Digital Engagement* (Palgrave Macmillan, 2013).

21 Nesta McGregor, "Beyonce and Other Stars Struggle to Control Their Image," *BBC News*, February 7, 2013. Last accessed March 17, 2025, https://www.bbc.com/news/newsbeat-21373659.

22 Mary Street Alinder, *Group F.64: Edward Weston, Ansel Adams, Imogen Cunningham, and the Community of Artists Who Revolutionized American Photography* (Bloomsbury, 2014).

23 Walter Benjamin, "Work of Art in the Age of Mechanical Reproduction," in *Illuminations: Essays and Reflections*, ed. Hannah Arendt and trans. Harry Zohn (Schocken Books, 1968), 217–52.

24 Barthes, *Camera Lucida*, 42.

25 Jacob Riis, *How the Other Half Lives: Studies among the Tenements of New York* (Charles Scribner's Sons, 1890); Tom Buk-Swienty, *The Other Half: The Life of Jacob Riis and the World of Immigrant America* (W.W. Norton, 2008); and Bonnie Yochelson and Daniel Czitrom, *Rediscovering Jacob Riis: Exposure Journalism and Photography in Turn-of-the-Century New York* (University of Chicago Press, 2007).

26 Russell Freedman, *Kids at Work: Lewis Hine and the Crusade against Child Labor* (Clarion Books, 1994); and Alexander Nemerov, *Soulmaker: The Times of Lewis Hine* (Princeton University Press, 2016).

27   Belle Hutton, "'The Camera Could Be a Weapon': Gordon Parks on the Power of Photography," *AnOther*, July 1, 2020. Last accessed March 20, 2025, https://www.anothermag.com/art-photography/12638/gordon-parks-quotes-of-note-exhibition-alison-jacques-gallery-life-magazine. See also The Gordon Parks Foundation: https://www.gordonparksfoundation.org/.

28   Hutton, "The Camera Could Be a Weapon."

29   See Teju Cole, "When the Camera Was a Weapon of Imperialism (And When It Still Is.)," *New York Times*, February 6, 2019. Last accessed March 17, 2025, https://www.nytimes.com/2019/02/06/magazine/when-the-camera-was-a-weapon-of-imperialism-and-when-it-still-is.html; and Jessica Czarnecki, "Decolonizing the Language of Photography," *Photographers without Borders*, June 29, 2021. Last accessed March 17, 2025, https://www.photographerswithoutborders.org/online-magazine/decolonizing-the-language-of-photography.

30   For more, see Stuart Hall, ed., *Representation: Cultural Representation and Signifying Practices* (SAGE Publications, 1997), 13–74; and W.J.T. Mitchell, *What Do Pictures Want?: The Lives and Loves of Images* (University of Chicago Press, 2005).

31   Susan Sontag, *On Photography* (Farrar, Straus and Giroux, 1977).

32   Tina M. Campt, *Listening to Images* (Duke University Press, 2017).

33   Disclaimer: shaking a Polaroid picture may cause distortion of the image.

34   Pew Research Center, "Americans' Social Media Use," January 31, 2024.

35   Meta, "Meta Platform Terms: 2. Intellectual Property Rights." Last accessed March 18, 2025, https://developers.facebook.com/terms#intellectualproperty rights.

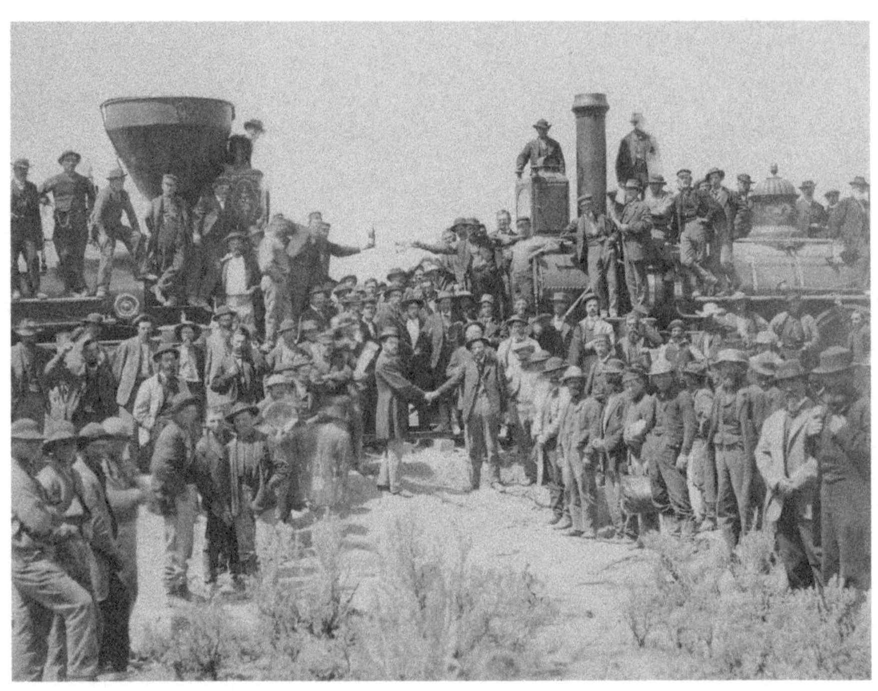

East and West Shaking Hands at Laying of Last Rail, *May 10, 1869. Photo by Andrew J. Russell. Courtesy of Yale University Libraries, Wikimedia Commons.*

Reading Photographs Like a Historian

By Rebecca S. Wingo and Lauren Tilton

Glossary: Collection, Composition, Finding Aid, Metadata, Primary Sources, Provenance, Public Domain, Secondary Sources

People say that a picture is worth a thousand words, and it is true that photographs can bring the past to life in ways that words cannot. They can tell evocative stories about moments both big and small, and historians rarely read photographs in isolation. We untangle numerous threads to weave the stories back together. This guide will help you read photography like a historian. We offer three general steps:

1 **INFORM**

2 **OBSERVE**

3 **INTERPRET**

We walk you through these steps by analyzing Andrew J. Russell's *East and West Shaking Hands at Laying of Last Rail*. A close reading of Russell's iconic photograph provides a lens into the distinction between *illustrating* history with photography and *illuminating* photography in history.

While we follow these steps in sequence for this guide, we often go back and forth between them in practice. The exact order is less important than the ways of analyzing a photograph that each step offers.

Inform

The photographs in this volume come from archival collections, historical societies, museums, newspapers, postcards, private collections, and social media. The source of the photograph often dictates the amount of information available. For example, a photo from a family photo album may only have a handwritten note or date on the back.

Finding Photographs

Archives are one of the best places to find photographs because they often have **provenance**, or verifiable information about the image's origin and how the archive acquired it. Individual photographs are usually one document in a larger **collection** that may include other visual or written texts. Archivists develop useful **finding aids** that describe the content in a collection. They also create **metadata**, including details like the date, photographer, format, size, subject tags, and other relevant information.

Ask ...

- Who took the photograph? When and where was it made?

- Where does the photograph come from?

- Who owns the photograph now and why? Are there any restrictions on its use?

- What other clues does the metadata reveal about the context or purpose?

East and West Shaking Hands

This famous photograph documented the Golden Spike Ceremony at Promontory Summit in Utah Territory on May 10, 1869. There, two railroad companies working from the east and west united to create the country's first transcontinental railroad.

East and West Shaking Hands is preserved in multiple archives around the country. This version is from the Collection of Western Americana in the Beinecke Rare Book and Manuscript Library at Yale University, and it aligns with the library's mission to collect materials related to the history of Western expansion, imperialism, and migration.[1] We chose the Beinecke because their version is in the **public domain**, meaning Yale has no restrictions on its use or publication. They also do not charge a fee to download the photo with a high enough resolution for printing in a physical book.

Part of an archivist's job is to process the collections and provide information to help us understand when, where, and why this photo was made. According to Mary Caldera, the archivist who authored the finding aid, the photo is one of over 200 black-and-white photographs created by Andrew J. Russell between

1864 and 1869 to chronicle the construction of the Union Pacific Railroad. Caldera explains that Russell was not some random photographer who just so happened to be in the right place at the right time. Instead, Union Pacific commissioned Russell for the project, which prompts questions about his objectivity.[2]

In addition to *East and West Shaking Hands*, Russell's photos also include "laborers, military personnel, housing, living and work conditions." They are stored in four large portfolios, each measuring approximately 11 × 14 inches, purchased from the Union Pacific Railroad Company sometime before 1996.[3]

Captions

While not all photographs have captions, others have formal or informal captions, and some have official titles. Captions often inform (or even bias) our first impression, which makes the source of the caption as crucial as the caption itself. While the photographer typically provides the first caption, it can change in publication. Tracking changes to the captions offers valuable insights into how the photograph was interpreted or used over time.

Ask ...

- Is the caption formal or informal? Who wrote it?

- How does the caption inform what you see?

- Has the photo ever been published or republished? Did the caption change?

East and West Shaking Hands

All the titles associated with Russell's photographs at the Beinecke are transcriptions from handwritten captions on the back of each image.[4] Captions derived in this manner are a remarkable find, and in most cases, it is fine to stop there. But the Golden Spike Ceremony was highly publicized, and the photo now has a nickname.

Union Pacific did not originally plan to publish the photos, but Russell wanted to bring the rugged western landscape into the parlors of people back east. He believed that a book would "interest all classes of people [and] excite the admiration of all reflecting minds." The result was a multi-volume series titled *The Great West Illustrated in a Series of Photographic Views*.[5] The volumes benefited both parties. Russell gained notoriety, and Union Pacific had a ready-made advertisement for the commercial promise of the West— now accessible by rail.

The title *East and West Shaking Hands at Laying of Last Rail* is a clever play on words. It draws the reader's attention to two serious-looking men (Samuel Montague and Grenville Dodge, the chief engineers for the Central Pacific and Union Pacific) symbolically shaking hands in the center of the photograph.[6] It also figuratively conveys the enormity of uniting the country's transportation system.

Since its publication, people have shifted their focus away from the handshake to the action unfolding above. Two men lean out of the engines, reaching to each other with bottles of champagne. After the conductors inched their trains toward one another, they christened them by breaking bottles of champagne. Russell's photo is now nicknamed the "The Champagne Photo," which not only changes where we look first but also the tone of the photograph. Instead of a Very Serious Historical Moment™, we now see a Very Serious Historical Party™. Russell's original caption may have more effectively communicated the importance of the day, but perhaps the modern nickname more accurately reflects its mood.

Observe

Digital cameras today enable people to make a boundless number of photographs in rapid succession. Photographers in the past didn't have this luxury. The materials to develop and reproduce photographs were costly and slow. Every frame—and everything in the frame—counted. Considering the technology available—from the apparatus that created the photo to how the photo is circulated—informs our analysis. Now that you've examined the information about the photograph, it's time to analyze the information in the photograph.

Composition

Photographers compose their pictures in the same way that creative writers compose their essays. The photographer's **composition** (the visual elements in a photograph) can determine what we see and how we feel. For example, the *focal point* is the area where our eyes naturally gravitate, and the *angle* or *perspective* affect how we respond. An angle below the subject makes it appear larger. Similarly, a bird's eye view creates a feeling of detachment, whereas a close-up establishes an intimate connection. To help, we made a handy chart defining common elements photographers use in their composition.

Common Visual Elements	
Brightness	Distribution of light and overall exposure
Color	Harmonic/disharmonic relationships between hues
Contrast	Differences between brightness, color, and tone
Cropping	How tight or loose the framing appears
Depth of Field	Areas in sharper focus versus blurred
Focal Point	Area of visual dominance
Framing	Everything included or excluded in the visual boundaries
Layering	Foreground, middle ground, and background
Leading Lines	Visual pathways that guide the reader's eye
Movement	Implied motion through blur or frozen action
Perspective	Viewpoint and angle of observation
Positive/Negative Space	Balance/imbalance between filled areas and empty space
Repetition	Recurring elements that create rhythms or patterns
Rule of Thirds	Placement of the subject in an imaginary grid
Scale	Relational size between objects in the frame
Symmetry/ Asymmetry	Intentional balance or imbalance
Texture	Different visual "feel" that suggests a tactile surface
Tone	Mood created by the range of light and shadow

Ask …

- What kind of photo is this? (This could be architectural, documentary, portraiture, landscape, streetscape, or a selfie, among others.)

- Where is the focal point?

- What is the setting? Is it candid or posed? Action or staged?

- What is the photographer's angle or perspective, and how does it affect the image?

- Who was the intended audience? The unintended audience?

East and West Shaking Hands

In this group portrait, the composition is visually balanced, with people evenly divided down the middle of the frame where the trains meet. The men stand at a three-quarters angle to form an upside-down "V" using their bodies to guide the eye toward the handshake. Given the context, we can assume that the people on the left are from the Central Pacific in the west, and the people on the right are from the Union Pacific in the east. Russell photographed the group from a slightly below-the-angle perspective, using a view that added to the grandeur of both the people and the trains.

We know that Russell used a single-view camera with a wet-plate process, which required the crowd to remain still for several minutes. As a result, a few of the more fidgety men appear blurry. Russell couldn't let the negative dry, so he would have rushed the glass slide back to his makeshift darkroom (a wagon covered in black fabric).[7] Because he only had one chance at this photo, we know that everyone and everything is carefully posed. In other words, the chief engineers are holding hands more than they're shaking them, and the men with the champagne bottles probably had really tired arms.

Inside the Frame

Reading all the details, large and small, offers clues to the meaning of the image. People's clothes and accessories may indicate their professions, economic status, or other aspects of their daily lives. Objects in the frame tell a story about material culture. Signs and logos can offer insights into aspects like consumerism and political beliefs. A good method is to start by resisting the focal point. Look instead at the minor subjects in the foreground and background. Then, divide the photo into a grid and examine each section individually.

Ask …

- What are the photograph's main and minor subjects?

- If there are people, what are they wearing? What are they doing, and what does their body language convey?

- Are there textual clues, such as signs or logos? What do they tell you?

- What objects are present? How are they integrated into the scene?

East and West Shaking Hands

The two main subjects are the people and trains. Beyond the crowd, the background is a cloudless sky, and the foreground is covered in dirt and sagebrush.

By our count, there are over 100 people in the picture, and they all appear to be white men. Most look directly toward the camera with neutral facial expressions, which is understandable given the long exposure time. Their body language conveys some of the celebratory mood. Several of the men tip their hats, others have cigars hanging from their mouths, and there is the champagne, of course.

The men are crammed into the frame on both the ground and every available ledge on the trains. The metal was probably warm from the May sun, but not so hot they couldn't lean against it. They dressed nicely for the photograph, donning coats, hats, and vests. One man even has a crisp white shirt. If they were among the laborers who built the railroads, they cleaned up for the photo.

The trains seamlessly merge into the portrait. The crowds mostly obscure them, but some interesting details still grab our attention. For example, the Central Pacific's headlight appears to have ornate (possibly gilded) detailing, and the Union Pacific's sand dome has a mural. (Side note: don't know what a sand dome is? Neither did we. We don't know anything about trains, so we had to look up the parts of a historic steam locomotive. It's part of the process.)

Interpret

History is not straightforward enough to capture in a single photograph, so historians often compare the known information from a visual text with written documentation to develop a fuller picture. As we do with written texts, we situate photographs within the broader history of the region, nation, or world. Because we cannot always believe what we see, contextualization allows us to deepen our understanding of everything leading up to the photograph, the moment it was made, and the events that unfolded afterward.

The Photographer

Photographer *and* photograph are both critical components. When known, we can dig into the photographer's background for context clues and information about the motivation behind the image. For instance, a photographer-for-hire serves their benefactor, whereas a photojournalist serves their newspaper. The photographer's positionality shapes how they frame their images.

Ask ...

- What is the photographer's background?

- Is the photographer's motivation to make the photograph known? How does it shape the photograph?

- Is the photo similar or different to others they made, and why?

East and West Shaking Hands

Andrew J. Russell was a painter who transitioned into photography during the Civil War. He worked for the Union Army alongside Mathew Brady, the famed Civil War photographer, to document the war. The two other photographers also hired for the ceremony are hidden from Russell's view. Yet Russell's image is the one that defines the day. We'll never truly know why his photo was more popular, but we can hazard a guess that the success of his book cemented his image in our collective memory and that the whimsy of the champagne captured (and continues to capture) Americans' imagination.

Primary and Secondary Research

Primary and secondary sources are the bread and butter of historical evidence. They shape the direction of our interpretation. **Primary sources** include photographs as well as documents, objects, and other evidence created during the period of study. Close analysis of primary sources offers an extended lens into the period. **Secondary sources** are generally books or articles that analyze and interpret primary sources. Reading other scholars' work gives us an idea of what has already been said about the topic and the ways they interpreted the period—potentially even through the same image. Situating ourselves in these sources helps us understand how we can contribute something new.

Ask ...

- What other primary documents are associated with the collection, and how do they expand your understanding?

- What other repositories have information about your topic?

- What historical events influence the scene in the photograph?

- Who has already written about the topic and/or photo, and what do they say?

East and West Shaking Hands

For this photo, we would start by examining all the photos in Russell's portfolios to place *East and West Shaking Hands* in conversation with his larger corpus. We would compare portfolios to *The Great West Illustrated* to see which ones were published and if Russell modified any of the captions. We would also check if Yale had other holdings about Russell or the railroads. (Spoilers: they do, including a cool lithograph of *East and West Shaking Hands* from 1873.)[8] Then, we would explore other archives with material about Russell or the transcontinentals, and compare Russell's work to photos made for Central Pacific.

There isn't enough room in this guide to provide a comprehensive synthesis of all the secondary sources about the transcontinental railroad (and we're already breaking the rules by sneaking you this extra photo). We understand that this might make you sad, so we cited some outstanding scholars who wrote about how the transcontinentals shaped our national economy, informed labor rights, influenced immigration, and intensified the dispossession of Native lands in this endnote right here →.[9]

But we can give you some contextual teasers. The idea for a transcontinental railroad emerged in the 1840s. Northern and Southern legislators debated the routes, but all opposition to a northern route disappeared after the South seceded in 1861. The Union saw the potential in railroads for expediting westward expansion and allowing them to quickly mobilize their troops.[10]

Congress passed the Pacific Railroad Act in 1862 to subsidize the nation's first transcontinental railroad. Union Pacific headed west from Omaha, Nebraska, and Central Pacific headed east from Sacramento, California. The line spanned 1,900 miles. Union Pacific constructed more than 1,000 miles of the route over the vastness of the Great Plains and the Rocky Mountains. Central Pacific constructed 690 miles by blasting their way through the Sierra Nevada Mountains.

As for the Golden Spike Ceremony itself, it was the first-ever attempt at a live national broadcast. David Hewes, an enthusiastic and rich supporter of the transcontinental, proposed (and funded) using a commemorative golden spike to complete the line. Gold is a soft metal, so the 17.6-karat, copper-alloy spike created by a foundry in San Francisco was completely ceremonial. To up the ante, Hewes also devised a plan to broadcast the ceremony. With the help of a telegraph operator, they rigged the golden spike with wire so each hammer strike would transmit to stations across the country.

One of the Central Pacific's most prominent investors, Leland Stanford (yes—the namesake of Stanford University), was selected to drive the spike into a predrilled hole. With an equally ceremonial silver hammer and a tangle of telegraph wires, Stanford took his first swing. He missed. He missed again. Then Hewes took a swing. He missed, too. They gave up. The telegraph operator eventually just tapped out the word "DONE."

There were ultimately four transcontinentals, and the United States paid the railroad companies with cash and land. These were certainly engineering marvels that reduced a six-month trip across the country to one week, but railroads were not the only story unfolding in the American West. Railroad tycoons used unethical means to build small empires and turn large profits, and they quickly earned the nickname "robber barons." The labor camps that cropped up along the routes became dens of iniquity full of drinking, gambling, violence, and sex trafficking. Once complete, the transcontinentals accelerated America's industrial revolution and deepened the nation's reliance on capitalism.

The railroad also brought many thousands of settlers onto Indigenous lands. Tensions between Native Americans, settlers, and the government resulted in both treaties and warfare with detrimental implications for the sovereign rights of Native nations. Railroads had numerous other harmful effects, including lasting consequences for species such as the American bison and the disruption of the fragile ecosystems on the Great Plains.

Outside the Frame

Understanding photography also requires thinking outside the box. Photography is a decision to frame a particular moment in a particular way, and thinking about what is right outside the frame asks us to consider the unobservable and unseen.

Ask ...

- What occurred in the moments right before and after the photo was made?

- What other activities or people might be beyond the frame?

- Who or what are you *not* seeing?

East and West Shaking Hands

Russell's photo would suggest that only about 100 people—specifically white men—attended the ceremony, but records estimate that there were many hundreds, if not thousands, of people. Among them were laborers and their families, who only exist now in the unknown scene unfolding beyond the frame.

Based on the research, we do have an idea of who those people could be. It took six years to construct the transcontinental railroad, and the demand for skilled laborers made it a lucrative job for recent immigrants. Immigrants were a good deal for the companies, too, because the companies paid them less money.

Union Pacific hired over 8,000 laborers, including immigrants from Ireland, Germany, and Italy; Civil War veterans; and enslaved (and after 1865, formerly enslaved) peoples. Central Pacific recruited approximately 12,000 Chinese immigrants. Between the explosives needed to blast tunnels through the Sierra Nevadas, rockslides, and avalanches, these men performed hazardous work with little to no labor protections. Chinese laborers went on strike in June 1867, demanding the same rights as their white counterparts, including equal pay, equal hours, and company lodging and food. Immigrant labor built America's infrastructure, yet the Chinese especially faced hostility and discrimination within American society.

Over time, the view of the transcontinental through Russell's lens became our collective view, but we don't have to stop looking when we reach the boundaries of his frame. As *East and West Shaking Hands* shows us, history is complicated and can be simultaneously troubling and amusing.

Reading photography can be an equally messy process. The stories the scholars tell in the chapters that follow are unique to them, reflections of where they choose to focus or refocus. They use photography to understand, change, and challenge our picture(s) of the past.

As you set out on your own sleuthing adventure, where will you focus? What kind of stories will you tell?

Notes

1 "Yale Collection of Western Americana," Beinecke Rare Book & Manuscript Library, Yale University Libraries, 2025. Last accessed June 9, 2025, https://beinecke.library.yale.edu/collections/curatorial-areas/yale-collection-western-americana.

2 Mary A. Caldera, "Guide to the Andrew J. Russell Photographs Taken during Construction of the Union Pacific Railroad," Beinecke Rare Book & Manuscript Library, Yale University, April 2025, 3–4. Last accessed June 5, 2025, https://ead-pdfs.library.yale.edu/13771.pdf.

3 Caldera, "Guide to the Andrew J. Russell Photographs," 3.

4 Caldera, "Guide to the Andrew J. Russell Photographs," 4.

5 Andrew J. Russell, *The Great West Illustrated in a Series of Photographic Views across the Continent Taken along the Line of the Union Pacific Railroad West from Omaha, Nebraska* (Union Pacific Railroad Company, 1869), preface.

6 Golden Spike National Historic Park Utah, "Andrew J. Russell," National Park Service, April 29, 2025. Last accessed June 9, 2025, https://www.nps.gov/gosp/learn/historyculture/a-moment-in-time.htm.

7   William D. Pattison, "The Pacific Railroad Rediscovered," *Geographical Review* 52, no. 1 (January 1962): 28.

8   "The East and West," *Crofutts Trans-Continental Tourist's Guide* (The American News Company, 1873). Made available by the Beinecke Rare Book and Manuscript Library, Yale University. Last accessed June 8, 2025, https://collections.library.yale.edu/catalog/2032119/.

9   David Haward Bain, *Empire Express: Building the First Transcontinental Railroad* (Penguin Publishing Group, 2000); Gordon H. Chang, *Ghosts of Gold Mountain: The Epic Story of the Chinese Who Built the Transcontinental Railroad* (Houghton Mifflin Harcourt, 2019); Jeffrey Marcos Garcilazo, *Traqueros: Mexican Railroad Workers in the United States, 1870 to 1930* (University of North Texas Press, 2012); Manu Karuka, *Empire's Tracks: Indigenous Nations, Chinese Workers, and the Transcontinental Railroad* (University of California Press, 2019); and Richard White, *Railroaded: The Transcontinentals and the Making of Modern America* (W.W. Norton, 2012).

10   William Thomas argues that building out northern lines and destroying railroads in the South played a huge role in the outcome of the war. See William G. Thomas, *The Iron Way: Railroads, the Civil War, and the Making of Modern America* (Yale University Press, 2011).

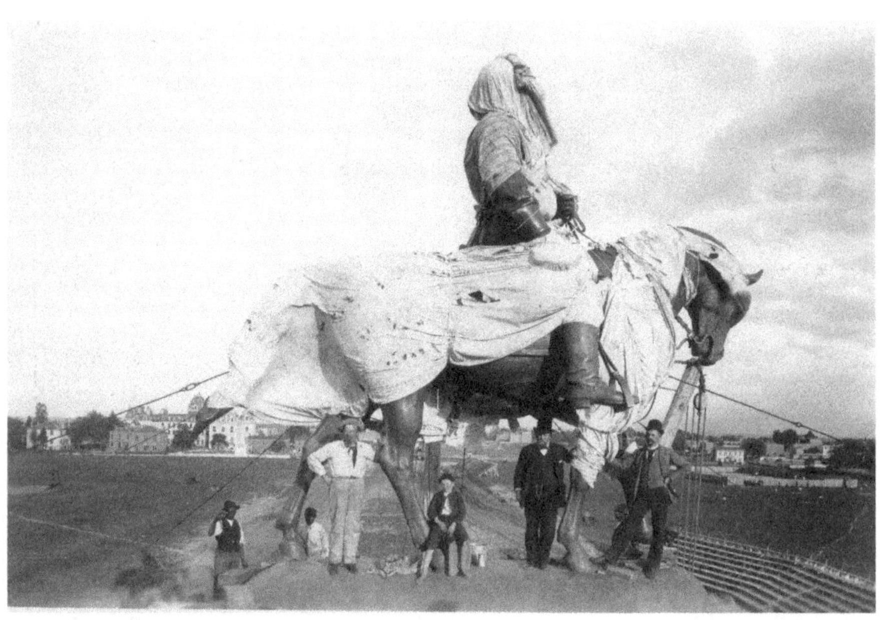

FIGURE 1.1 *Four African Americans helping raise a statue of Confederate General Robert E. Lee just prior to its unveiling in Richmond, Virginia, on May 29, 1890. Courtesy of the Robert A. Lancaster, Jr. Photograph Collection, The Valentine.*

1

Veiled History: Confederate Memorialization and the Politics of Race and Place after Emancipation

By Julian Maxwell Hayter

The **Reconstruction** Era (1865–77) was designed to reintegrate Southern states into the American Union and enforce African Americans' constitutional liberties established through the Thirteenth, Fourteenth, and Fifteenth Amendments. However, Southern states stripped Black citizens of these rights—first by upholding the customary practices of racial segregation and then by codifying them through series of laws commonly referred to as "**Jim Crow**" laws. The Supreme Court upheld the legality of segregation in the *Plessy v. Ferguson* (1896) case, creating a "separate but equal" precedent that intensified racial divides in both public and private life in the early twentieth century.

As White Southerners used the letter of the law to reclaim control over Southern life, they also set out to retell the story of the antebellum South, slavery, and the Confederacy. Known as the **Lost Cause**, Southerners portrayed slavery as a benign institution and the Confederacy as heroic. They embedded these historically revisionist ideas in everything from textbooks to the landscape as they memorialized and celebrated the Confederacy and its leaders. This chapter explores the ways Confederate memorialization in Richmond, Virginia, is inseparable from early twentieth-century urban history. Here, locals used Confederate statuary to implement **City Beautiful** plans, not just to modernize Richmond but also to cement over a century of residential segregation.

Suggested Topics: African American History, Commemoration and Memorialization, Reconstruction, Urban Studies

Glossary: City Beautiful Movement, Jim Crow, Lost Cause, Mason-Dixon Line, Racial Zoning Laws, Reconstruction, Reconstruction Amendments, Restrictive Covenants, White Flight

> The Negro was in the Northern processions on Decoration Day and in Southern ones, if only to carry buckets of ice-water. He put up the Lee Monument, and should the time come, will be there to take it down.
>
> —John Mitchell, Jr., *Richmond Planet,* 1890[1]

In June of 2020, protesters removed several statues of colonial and confederate monuments in Richmond, Virginia. The "de-monumentalization" of the former capital of the Confederacy began on June 9, when a diverse group of demonstrators yanked a statue honoring Christopher Columbus from its pedestal and dumped it into a local lake. The following evening, protestors turned their attention toward Monument Avenue—a street in the heart of the city originally named for five imposing statues honoring confederate leaders. They graffitied and pulled down a statue of Jefferson Davis, president of the Confederacy. Roughly one month later, the City of Richmond, under orders of then-mayor and African American, Levar Stoney, removed three more statues to confederates on Monument Avenue—the Matthew Maury, Stonewall Jackson, and J. E. B. Stuart monuments.[2] One monument, however, remained—a 60-foot tall, 12-ton statue honoring Confederate General Robert E. Lee.

After the initial protests, it took Richmond over a year to remove the Lee monument.[3] During that year, artists and activists transformed the Lee monument into a Black Lives Matter (BLM) shrine. *The New York Times* called the memorial "the most powerful piece of protest art in American life since World War II." The reimagining of the Lee monument was an immediate response to the murder of George Floyd by police in Minneapolis, Minnesota.[4] Yet, the statue's transformation was part of a much larger movement—a movement to reconsider not just the legacy of the Confederacy and Jim Crow segregation, but how we tell American history. Virginia's then-governor, Ralph Northam, hired an African American contractor, Devon Henry, to remove the Lee statue—just as John Mitchell, Jr. presaged in 1890. Devon Henry Enterprises removed the Lee monument September 8, 2021—a little over 131 years after the monument's unveiling on May 29, 1890.[5]

The South may have lost the American Civil War, but it won the peace afterward.[6] Few things better symbolize that victory than amateur photographer Robert Alexander Lancaster, Jr.'s photo of the Lee monument just prior to its unveiling. From 1865 to 1877, the United States entered a transformative era commonly referred to as **Reconstruction**. During this period, the fractured government attempted to heal by rebuilding the region from the ashes of war, emancipating enslaved peoples, facilitating Black citizenship, and extending them the right to vote. For over a century after the Civil War, Southerners responded by stripping African Americans of their constitutional liberties and reorganizing the Black labor force, heralding in the **Jim Crow** Era characterized by violence and segregation. The background of Lancaster's photo documents the labor of four African Americans working to erect the Lee statue, which exemplifies a paradox that has characterized Southern life from the outset: nowhere were white and Black citizens closer together, yet further apart than beneath the **Mason-Dixon Line**. Here we see African Americans working with white men to install a statue paying homage to a slaveowner that seceded from the United States and led an insurrection in defense of the slave system.[7] Much has been made of Reconstruction's demise and the racial apartheid that characterized post-bellum Southern life.[8] We also know a great deal about how African Americans met these challenges.[9]

Lancaster's photo depicts another story that Americans know less about—the relationship between confederate statuary, historical revisionism, and residential racial segregation. On the one hand, it is impossible to separate the Lancaster photo from the Lost Cause of the Confederacy. The Lee statue, and confederate iconography more generally, was primarily part of a larger effort to absolve the South of the sins of slavery and the Confederacy from treason. In fact, Lancaster was himself professionally affiliated with an organization that helped spearhead these ideals, the Virginia Historical Society. On the other hand, by the mid-twentieth century, segregationist politicians and profiteers not only used the power vested in state and local governments to secure their own political and economic power but also often used confederate statuary to consecrate exclusively white neighborhoods that forbid Black residents from owning, or even renting, homes. In this way, the events portrayed in the Lancaster photo cannot be separated from the ways historical actors inscribed their biases on American cities.

(Un)Reconstructed

Photography, like art, is a product of historical context. It reflects a time and place that is beyond repeating. Yet cameras—and the people who use them—are not neutral devices. The photography of the segregated South is no exception to this rule. In photographing the Lee monument Robert Lancaster helped to weaponize and glorify a history that not only sought to retell the story of the South but cement the legacy of the Lost Cause in public memory and public space. In this way, Lancaster's photo is a reflection of the spirit of the time—a time in which Southern whites ushered in an era of racial apartheid and their elites resolved retell the history of the South to make sense of and control the present.

The 26-year-old Richmond native took this photo of the Lee monument just prior to the unveiling ceremony in May of 1890. While Lancaster worked professionally as an insurance agent, he was best known in the commonwealth as the secretary and decades-long treasurer of one of America's oldest historical societies, the Virginia Historical Society, and editor for the *Virginia Magazine of History and Biography*.[10] An amateur historian and photographer, Lancaster authored *Historic Virginia Homes and Churches* in 1915, one of the first illustrated volumes of Virginia's historical sites.[11] This book emerged from his own private collection and the encouragement of his friends. While the photo of the Lee monument did not appear in the book and we know little of the equipment he used, he likely took the photo out of personal interest. Lancaster spent a considerable amount of time using photography to document his version of Virginia's history.[12]

Reconstruction had long faded when Lancaster took the photo of the Lee statue. For a brief period, Washington (especially, Radical Republicans) defended Black freedom, citizenship, and male suffrage. Collectively referred to as the **Reconstruction Amendments**, the Thirteenth (1865) abolished slavery, except as punishment for crime; the Fourteenth (1868) secured Black citizenship; and the Fifteenth (1870) secured Black male suffrage. Formerly enslaved people overcame enormous challenges to meet these promises. African Americans not only forged their own communities, organizations, and institutions across the American South, they also assumed political and economic leadership roles. Nearly 80 percent of recently emancipated Black men who were of age registered to vote. During Reconstruction, sixteen African Americans served in the US Congress (two in the US Senate). According to Eric Foner, Reconstruction's modern leading historian, roughly 2,000 African Americans held lesser political positions throughout the South.[13]

Yet, white Americans perceived Black freedom as a threat to their own and intensified their resistance.[14] White Southerners met Black men's demands for full citizenship with what is commonly referred to as Southern Redemption. Southern Democrats, their paramilitary organizations (namely the Ku Klux Klan, White Leagues, and Red Shirts), and white Southerners more generally attempted to redeem the South by stripping African Americans of their newly found freedoms.[15] By the late 1800s, the Supreme Court agreed, rubberstamping the South's segregationist prerogatives/policies in *Plessy v. Ferguson* (1896). *Plessy* held that racially segregated facilities did not violate the Fourteenth Amendment. Segregation and "separate but equal" lasted until 1954, when the Supreme Court struck down Jim Crowism in a case called *Brown v. Board of Education* (1954).[16]

Confederate memorialization was integral to Southern redemption and segregation. Remembrance of Lee began immediately after his death on October 12, 1870. The Lee monument was the brainchild of former confederates Jubal Early and John Mosby, and the women of the Hollywood Memorial Association who led the way in memorializing fallen confederate soldiers at Richmond Hollywood Cemetery and later formed the Ladies' Lee Monument Association.[17] It took twenty years for the men's and women's associations to decide on an equestrian statue designed by French sculptor Marius Jean Antonin Mercié. Another French sculptor, Paul Pujol, designed the statue's 40-foot base. Paid for by a collection of private funds raised by women's and men's confederate associations, the statue cost roughly $2 million in today's money.[18] Experts estimate that well over 100,000 people attended the unveiling ceremony on May 29, 1890.[19]

The focus on Lee was in keeping with the revisionist history that surfaced after the Civil War. Southerners spent the latter portions of the late nineteenth and early twentieth centuries rewriting and putting a positive spin on the history of the antebellum South and slavery. Jubal Early (along with Lee's nephew, Fitzhugh Lee) became one of the South's foremost confederate apologists. Early not only wrote extensively about vindicating the South but also helped create the Southern Historical Society in 1869 with the explicit intent of doing so.[20] Early's intervention into collective memory eventually grew into one of the most successful misinformation campaigns in recent history.

White historical societies, including the Virginia Historical Society, were essential to crafting what became known as the **Lost Cause**, and elite white women were often at the vanguard of this movement.[21] The Lost Cause held six central tenants that have made their way into modern Southern mythology: (1) that slavery was a benign institution, Black people were faithful slaves, and slaveowners were benevolent paternalists; (2) that the Civil War was about states' rights rather than slavery; (3) that the Confederacy was destined to lose because the North had more resources and men; (4) that the Confederacy was a "heroic and saintly" effort to maintain the Southern way of life; (5) that Lee was the ultimate Christian soldier and Southern gentleman; and (6) that Southern women "were loyal to the Confederate cause and sanctified by the sacrifice of their loved ones."[22] Lee, who argued against the creation of confederate war monuments on the grounds that it would "keep open the sores of war" and sow disunity, became the ultimate symbol of Southern heroism.[23]

Still, Lee became an essential icon for the Lost Cause. Even twenty years after his death, Lee's legacy—accurate or not—is what drew the throngs of onlookers including Lancaster and countless other photographers to the statue's unveiling.[24] In time, women such as Mildred Lewis Rutherford (the historian general of the United Daughters of the Confederacy known as "Miss Millie"), the Sons of Confederate Veterans, and the United Confederate Veterans established the Rutherford History Committee in Atlanta, Georgia, in 1919.[25] The intent? To absolve the South of treason, venerate the Confederacy by embedding the Lost Cause into textbooks, and ultimately defend white supremacy.

Confederate apologists waged one of the most successful textbook and book-banning campaigns in American history. Rutherford and the committee eventually published a 23-page pamphlet, *A Measuring Rod to Test Textbooks, and Reference Books in Schools, Colleges, and Libraries*. It set a standard. *A Measuring Rod* urged Southerners to not only ignore historical sources but also ban books that portrayed the Confederacy as dishonorable. Rutherford and others advised librarians, teachers, and professors to:

> Reject a textbook that does not give the principles for which the South fought in 1861 and does not clearly outline the interferences with the rights *guaranteed to* the South by the Constitution, and which caused secession.
>
> Reject a book that calls the Confederate soldier a traitor or rebel, and the war a rebellion.
>
> Reject a book that says the South fought to hold her slaves.
>
> Reject a text-book that glorifies Abraham Lincoln and vilifies Jefferson Davis, unless a truthful cause can be found for such glorification or vilification before 1865.
>
> Reject a book that speaks of the slaveholder as of the South as cruel and unjust to his slaves.
>
> Reject a textbook that omits to tell of the South's heroes and their deeds.[26]

During the early 1900s, Southern historical societies leaned on Jim Crow legislatures to embed Lost Cause ideals into school textbooks, where they remained for most of the twentieth century.

Southerners—and Texans in particular—have exercised a disproportionate influence on the teaching of American history. With over 5 million children, Texas is one of the largest textbook consumers. Publishers have generally chosen to bow to the whitewashing mandated by the Texas State Board of Education, claiming that publishing two versions of their textbooks (one for Texas, and one for everyone else) is too expensive.[27] As a result, generations of Americans learned Lost Cause mythologies in which enslaved people were often referred to as "indentured servants" and taught that "Northern aggression" caused the Civil War. In 2011, the PEW Research Center asked Americans what caused the Civil War. Forty-eight percent of respondents said the Civil War was mainly waged over states' rights, while only 38 percent believed that slavery was a foundational cause.[28] Locally, in 2018 Virginia's own *Richmond Times-Dispatch*, once an avid supporter of the Lost Cause, found that many Lost Cause talking points were not phased out of the commonwealth's history textbooks until the late twentieth century.[29]

Historians know better now. Rather than mythologizing about the past, experts have spent the last several decades analyzing *actual* sources. Take for instance the claim that the Civil War was about states' rights rather than slavery. Historians generally agree that slavery, more than any other issue, brought on the war. They looked to Southerners' own secession proceedings to prove their point.[30] The findings revealed that Southerners had a vested interest in portraying the Confederacy as patriotic and slavery as benign because they feared being punished for treason! The very treason that undergirded many of the speeches they made prior to secession.

Historians also know that enslaved peoples continually challenged the notion that they were contented—often daily and occasionally in violent and revolutionary ways.[31] Nowhere was this truer than during the Civil War itself. "This yearning for freedom," civil rights activist and scholar W. E. B. Du Bois held, "found its climax during the American Civil War where slaves increasingly ran away, took up arms against their masters, and intentionally sabotaged and disrupted global cotton production. These actions were not accidents. They were a form of politics."[32] Du Bois was then, and is still now, one of the foremost historians of the Reconstruction Era.

Rather than face the possibility that Black Americans had their own ideas about liberty, white Southerners fabricated beliefs to not only rationalize slavery but the racial order that emerged upon its abolition.[33]

City Beautiful

Racial considerations and the Lost Cause also shaped early twentieth-century urban reforms. As American cities expanded rapidly in the early 1900s, Southern cities very intentionally sanctified growing segregated spaces with confederate memorials and monuments.[34] The greatest surge in constructing confederate iconography occurred between 1890 and 1920 during a time characterized by intensifying racial turmoil and growing celebrations honoring Civil War veterans.[35] Southern cities placed the majority of monuments on courthouse grounds and other official sites, providing not-so-subtle visual cues about who the courts and public spaces were there to serve. Richmond was the only city in the United States to dedicate an entire street, Monument

Avenue, to confederate monuments. This street is implicated in the urban reforms of the early 1900s.

In the late nineteenth and early twentieth centuries, Americans reimagined cities by trying to improve living conditions. By the early 1900s, America's urban population began to eclipse the rural population. Industrialization, urban density, poor sanitation, environmental degradation, failing infrastructure, and poor planning led progressive reformers and urban planners to think more intently on how cities *should be* organized. Nothing exemplified this new philosophical approach to urban reforms like the **City Beautiful movement** (sometimes referred to as the City Functional movement).[36] Architects and planners set out alleviate the strain of urban life by creating places of refuge within cities (i.e., parks, lakes, botanical gardens, grand promenades, etc.). They endeavored to make cities attractive and well-organized by creating more efficient paths for the increasing number of people and other forms traffic. City Beautiful designs smartened cities by merging the built and natural environments. Planners and developers often carved out large, natural spaces and adorned them with monumental structures.

While integrating more greenspace into cities can hardly be condemned in theory, there were also less benevolent intentions behind these plans as people brought their biases to bear on urbanism. Planners often used these spaces as a barrier between wealthier residents and poor (i.e., Black) residents in slums. In fact, contemporaries believed that these beautification efforts prioritized creating idyllic landscapes for the wealthy at the expense of addressing urban vulnerability and poverty.[37] In Southern cities (and in Northern cities too), these spaces were almost exclusively designed to shield wealthy whites from African American communities.[38]

In Richmond, developers used the Lee monument to purposefully facilitate what might be called the first wave of **White Flight**. The city's planners did this by very specifically designating beautification efforts to venerate the Confederacy. Monument Avenue, an expansive, late nineteenth-century promenade forged in the spirit of the City Beautiful movement, is located just adjacent to Richmond's African American community on the other side of Broad Street. It became, in time, a veritable Maginot Line between Richmond's Black community on the North and East sides, and the white community on the city's West End. This history, while lesser known, is inextricably linked not just to the rise of Jim Crow segregation but to the long and tortured history of residential racial discrimination and confederate memorialization.

Consider what Lancaster's photo does not show—namely the lack of urban development around the Lee statue. Monument Avenue was (and continues to be) one of Richmond's wealthiest neighborhoods. Yet, up until the Civil War, the area surrounding the Lee monument was farmland. The Lee statue was part of an expansionist plan, crafted by local landowners and politicians to lure wealthy white people into a suburb with natural space and public art. The owner of that land, Otway Allen, eventually transformed the area into an exclusive neighborhood of *nouveau riche* Richmonders—his family got rich in the process too. Although the houses appear small nestled in the background of Lancaster's photograph, these residents built grand mansions, eclipsed only by the Lee statue itself.[39]

The wealthy development that emerged around the cloaked statue captured in Lancaster's photo reflects a much larger movement in America's urban history—the creation and maintenance of urban spaces that legally (or customarily) forbade integration. Well before its installation in 1890, Virginia's governor Fitzhugh Lee not only refused to build the Lee statue on the capitol grounds but also openly advocated for its placement on Monument Avenue as a "plain business proposal."[40] The wealthy residents around the Lee statue on Monument Avenue led the way for white elites in other cities in their use of racial zoning laws and restrictive housing covenants to maintain the exclusivity and racial homogeny of their neighborhood.

Restrictive covenants are contractual agreements or clauses in a housing deeds/leases that limit what owners can do with their property. For decades, white Americans successfully used them to prevent minorities from moving into residential (often suburban) neighborhoods.[41] The written language embedded in Monument Avenue deeds was clear: "No lots can ever be sold or rented in Monument Avenue Park to any person of African descent."[42] The visual language embedded in Lancaster's photograph conveys this too. The four white men who pose for Lancaster on the pedestal are literally elevated above the four Black men. On the left, one man shields his eyes from the sun, while the other stands partially shaded by the statue. On the right, two more men blend into the background of Lancaster's frame, their heads barely visible behind the horse's front leg. In essence, these four Black men helped erect a monument to their own exclusion.

In 1911, the City of Richmond was second only to Baltimore, Maryland in adopting America's first **racial zoning laws**.[43] After emancipation, racial segregation in housing patterns was often a matter of custom. Around the turn of the century, however, segregationists began to use the letter of the law to relegate Black communities to the urban margins. These exclusionary zoning laws place restrictions on the types of homes and commercial buildings that can be built in a particular neighborhood. In time, Southerners applied racial restrictions to these laws too. Racial zoning further precluded neighborhood integration (decades before the practice of redlining), keeping Monument Avenue exclusively white for most of the twentieth century.[44] It was also instrumental in consigning African American communities to the most undesirable and dangerous sections of America's cities—often near factories, city waste facilities, flood-prone areas, and in time, heavily concreted spaces.

In this way, the Lee monument and the creation of Monument Avenue are inextricably linked to over a century of Lost Cause rhetoric, fear-based and exclusionary architecture and commemoration, and the legacy of the deep residential discrimination infused throughout urban planning. The protests that occurred during the spring and summer of 2020 were not merely about toppling colonial and confederate statuary. These demonstrations drew attention to America's long, drawn-out struggle against the forces of racial restrictions, and the ways Southerners weaponized history and public space in the name of white supremacy.

Discussion Questions

1   Take a closer look at the photograph. What else do you see? Are there intentional or unintentional visual cues that highlight racial and economic divisions?

2   What does the story of Confederate memorialization tell us about the craft of writing history? Are there parallels in contemporary America to the ways that Confederate apologists wrote history?

3   What is the role of art in public space? What does the placement of Confederate monuments in American cities tell us about the intentions of historical actors?

4   Explore the "Whose Heritage?" interactive map from the Southern Poverty Law Center (https://www.splcenter.org/whose-heritage-map/). What counts as a Confederate monument? What conclusions can you draw from the distribution of Confederate monuments across the country?

Further Resources

Hayter, Julian Maxwell. "Redlining Is Only Part of the Story." *Bunk History*, October 5, 2022. https://www.bunkhistory.org/resources/redlining.

Internet Archive. "Address Delivered Buy Mildred Lewis Rutherford, Historian General United Daughters of the Confederacy." 1914. https://archive.org/details/addressdelivered03ruth/mode/2up.

Southern Poverty Law Center. "Whose Heritage? Public Symbols of the Confederacy." February 1, 2019. https://www.splcenter.org/resources/reports/whose-heritage-public-symbols-confederacy-3/.

Notes

1   "John Mitchell, Jr.," *Richmond Planet,* June 7, 1890. John Mitchell, Jr. was the president of the National Afro-American Press Association and editor of the *Richmond Planet.* Often referred to as "The Fighting Editor," Mitchell

was also a prominent civil rights activist, politician, and banker. For more on John Mitchell, Jr., see Ann Field Alexander, *Race Man: The Rise and Fall of the "Fighting Editor," John Mitchell, Jr.* (University of Virginia Press, 2002).

2 For visual depictions and history on Monument Avenue, see *On Monument Avenue* by the American Civil War Museum. Last accessed March 28, 2025, https://onmonumentave.com/onlineexhibits.

3 The Commonwealth of Virginia owned the Lee statue, while the City of Richmond controlled the other four statues. In early twentieth century, Virginia's general assembly resolved that Confederate statues were considered war memorials and disallowed their removal without an explicit mandate from the General Assembly. In other words, cities and localities like Richmond did not have control over the removal of monuments without approval from the state. After Virginia's Democratic Party gained the majority in 2019, the General Assembly reversed the mandate and gave cities and localities the ability to control and/or remove monuments without approval from the state's governing body.

4 Thad Williamson, Julian M. Hayter, and Amy L. Howard, *The Making of Twentieth Century Richmond: Politics, Policy, and Governance 1988–2016* (University of North Carolina Press, 2024).

5 Matt Stevens, "For a Black Man Hired to Undo a Confederate Legacy, It Has Not Been Easy," *New York Times*, April 17, 2022.

6 This saying is attributed to W.E.B. Du Bois and his general observations about the fall of Reconstruction and the rise of Jim Crow. See W.E.B. Du Bois, *Black Reconstruction in America, 1860–1880* (Free Press, 1998); and Eric Foner, *Reconstruction Updated Edition: America's Unfinished Journey, 1863–1877* (Harper Perennial Modern Classics, 2014).

7 For more on Lee, see Alan T. Nolan, *Lee Considered: General Robert E. Lee and Civil War History* (University of North Carolina Press, 1996).

8 Heather Cox Richardson, *How the South Won the Civil War: Oligarchy, Democracy, and the Continuing Fight for the Soul of America* (Oxford University Press, 2022).

9 Thomas C. Holt, *The Movement: The African American Struggle for Civil Rights* (Oxford University Press, 2021).

10 The Virginia Historical Society was established in 1831 and has since rebranded as the Virginia Museum of History and Culture. See also, "Mr. Lancaster, Historical Club, Dies," *Richmond Times-Dispatch*, August 27, 1940.

11 Robert A. Lancaster, *Historic Virginia Homes and Churches* (Lippincott, 1915).

12 "Mr. Lancaster, Historical Club, Dies."

13 Eric Foner, "Rooted in Reconstruction: The First Wave of Black Congressmen," *The Nation*, October 15, 2008. Last accessed March 30, 2025, https://www.thenation.com/article/archive/rooted-reconstruction-first-wave-black-congressmen/.

14 Edward L. Ayers, "How the Enemies of Reconstruction Created Reconstruction," in *Reconstruction and the Arc of Racial (in)Justice*, ed. Julian M. Hayter and George R. Goethals (Edward Elgar Publishing, 2018).

15 Foner, "Rooted in Reconstruction."

16 For more on *Plessy* and the road to *Brown,* see Gordon Andrews, *Undoing Plessy: Charles Hamilton Houston, Race, Labor, and the Law, 1895–1950* (Cambridge Scholars Publishing, 2014).

17 For more on Reconstruction, see Du Bois, *Black Reconstruction in America;* and Foner, *Reconstruction Updated Edition.*

18 Dave Brumfield, "A Monument Avenue Mystery," *Richmond Magazine,* December 3, 2017. Last accessed March 30, 2025, https://richmondmagazine.com/news/sunday-story/a-monument-avenue-mystery/.

19 Kevin M. Levin, "Richmond's Confederate Monuments Were Used to Sell a Segregated Neighborhood," *The Atlantic,* June 11, 2020. Last accessed March 30, 2025, https://www.theatlantic.com/ideas/archive/2020/06/its-not-just-the-monuments/612940/. For the history of Monument Avenue, see Sarah Shields Driggs, Richard Guy Wilson, and Robert P. Winthrop, *Richmond's Monument Avenue* (University of North Carolina Press, 2001).

20 For more on Early and the Lost Cause, see Gary W. Gallagher and Alan T. Nolan, *The Myth of the Lost Cause and Civil War History* (Indiana University Press, 2000).

21 Karen L. Cox, *Dixie's Daughters: The United Daughters of the Confederacy and the Preservation of Confederate Culture* (University Press of Florida, 2019); and Caroline Janney, *Burying the Dead but Not the Past: Ladies' Memorial Associations and the Lost Cause* (University of North Carolina Press, 2008).

22 For more on The Lost Cause, see Caroline Janney, "The Lost Cause," *Encyclopedia Virginia,* Virginia Humanities, December 2020. Last accessed March 30, 2025, https://encyclopediavirginia.org/entries/lost-cause-the/.

23 Lisa Desjardins, "Robert E. Lee Opposed Confederate Monuments," *PBS News,* August 15, 2017. Last accessed April 2, 2025, https://www.pbs.org/newshour/nation/robert-e-lee-opposed-confederate-monuments.

24 Robert E. Lee to Thomas L. Rosser, December 13, 1866. Lee Papers, University of Virginia Archives.

25 Sarah H. Case, "The Historical Ideology of Mildred Lewis Rutherford: A Confederate Historian's New South Creed," *The Journal of Southern History* 68, no. 3 (August 2002): 599–628.

26 Mildred Lewis Rutherford, *A Measuring Rod to Test Textbooks, and Reference Books in Schools, Colleges, and Libraries* (United Confederate Veterans, 1920), 5.

27 For more on the intersections of textbooks and politics, see Dana Goldstein, "Two States. Eight Textbooks. Two American Stories," *New York Times,* January 12, 2020. Last accessed April 2, 2025, https://www.nytimes.com/interactive/2020/01/12/us/texas-vs-california-history-textbooks.html; and Rob Alex Fitt, "Conservative Activists in Texas Have Shaped the History All American Children Learn," *Washington Post,* October 19, 2020. Last accessed April 2, 2025, https://www.washingtonpost.com/outlook/2020/10/19/conservative-activists-texas-have-shaped-history-all-american-children-learn/.

28 Pew Research Center, *Civil War at 150: Still Relevant, Still Divisive,* April 8, 2011. Last accessed March 28, 2025, https://www.pewresearch.org/politics/2011/04/08/civil-war-at-150-still-relevant-still-divisive/.

29　Rex Springston, "Happy Slaves? The Peculiar Story of Three Virginia School Textbooks," *Richmond Times-Dispatch*, April 15, 2018. Last accessed March 29, 2025, https://richmond.com/news/local/happy-slaves-the-peculiar-story-of-three-virginia-school-textbooks/article_47e79d49-eac8-575d-ac9d-1c6fce52328f.html.

30　Edward L. Ayers, *What Caused the Civil War?: Reflections on the South and Southern History* (W.W. Norton, 2006).

31　For more on slave resistance, see John Hope Franklin and Loren Schweninger, *Runaway Slaves: Rebels on the Plantation* (Oxford University Press, 2000). For more on portrayals of slavery as benign, see Micki McElya, *Clinging to Mammy: The Faithful Slave in Twentieth Century American* (Harvard University Press, 2007).

32　Guy Emerson Mount, "When Slaves Go on Strike: Du Bois's Black Reconstruction 80 Years Later," *African American Intellectual History Society*, December 28, 2015. Last accessed March 31, 2025, https://www.aaihs.org/when-slaves-go-on-strike/.

33　For more on how historians have come to terms with the Lost Cause, see Adam H. Domby, *The False Cause: Fraud, Fabrication, and White Supremacy in Confederate Memory* (University of Virginia Press, 2020).

34　On the history on the history of urbanization in the United States, see Lisa Krissoff Boehm and Steven H. Corey, *America's Urban History* (Routledge, 2023).

35　Southern Poverty Law Center, "Whose Heritage? Public Symbols of the Confederacy," February 1, 2019. Last accessed March 30, 2025, https://www.splcenter.org/resources/reports/whose-heritage-public-symbols-confederacy/#findings.

36　The City Beautiful movement gained traction in the United States during and after the 1890s and lasted until automobiles demanded a new approach to urban planning. For more on urbanization in the United States, see Eric Mumford, *Designing the Modern City: Urbanism since 1850* (Yale University Press, 2018). For more about Urban Renewal in the 1950s and 1960s, see Chapter 10.

37　For more on the relationship between urban planning and race, see Howard Gillette, Jr., *Between Justice and Beauty: Race, Planning, and the Failure of Urban Policy in Washington, D.C.* (University of Pennsylvania Press, 2011).

38　Gillette, *Between Justice and Beauty*.

39　Laura Byrd Earle, "Richmond's Monument Avenue: Memorializing the Lost Cause," *The Valentine*, October 6, 2023. Last accessed March 31, 2025, https://thevalentine.org/explore/richmond-stories/featured-stories/richmonds-monument-avenue-memorializing-the-lost-cause-myth/.

40　The Court forbade these covenants in the case called *Buchanan v. Warley* (1917). Real estate agents and homeowners kept up the practice, however. For more on housing discrimination, see Julian Maxwell Hayter, "Confederate Monuments Are about Maintaining White Supremacy," *The Washington Post*, July 27, 2017. Last accessed March 28, 2025, https://www.

washingtonpost.com/news/made-by-history/wp/2017/07/27/confederate-monuments-are-about-maintaining-white-supremacy/.

41 On restrictive covenants, see Richard R.W. Brooks and Carol M. Rose, *Saving the Neighborhood: Racially Restrictive Covenants, Law, and Social Norms* (Harvard University Press, 2013).

42 Levin, "Richmond's Confederate Monuments."

43 Christopher Silver, "The Racial Origins of Zoning," in *Urban Planning and the African American Community: In the Shadows*, ed. June Manning Thomas and Marsha Ritzdorf (Sage Publications, 1997).

44 For more on the long history of housing discrimination and redlining, see Julian Maxwell Hayter, "Redlining Is Only Part of the Story," *Bunk History*, October 5, 2022. Last accessed March 30, 2025, https://www.bunkhistory.org/resources/redlining.

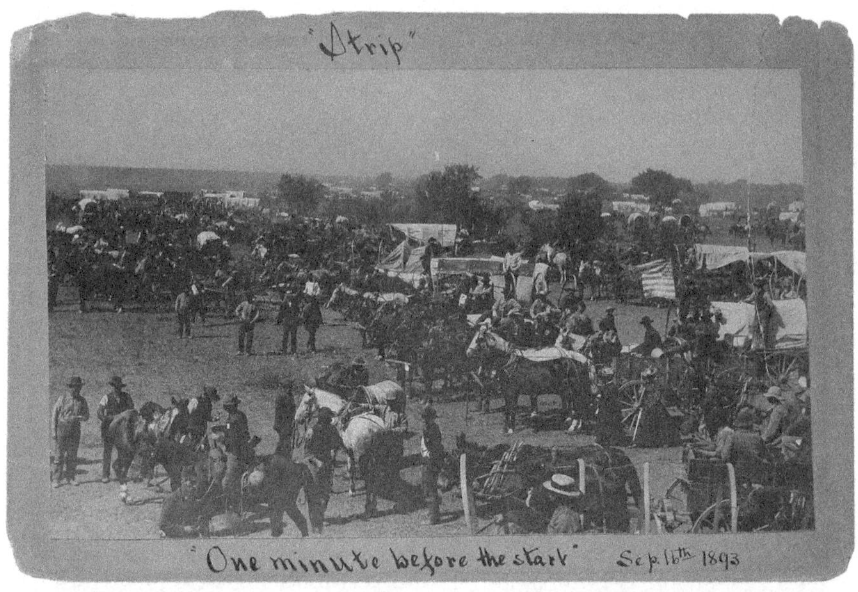

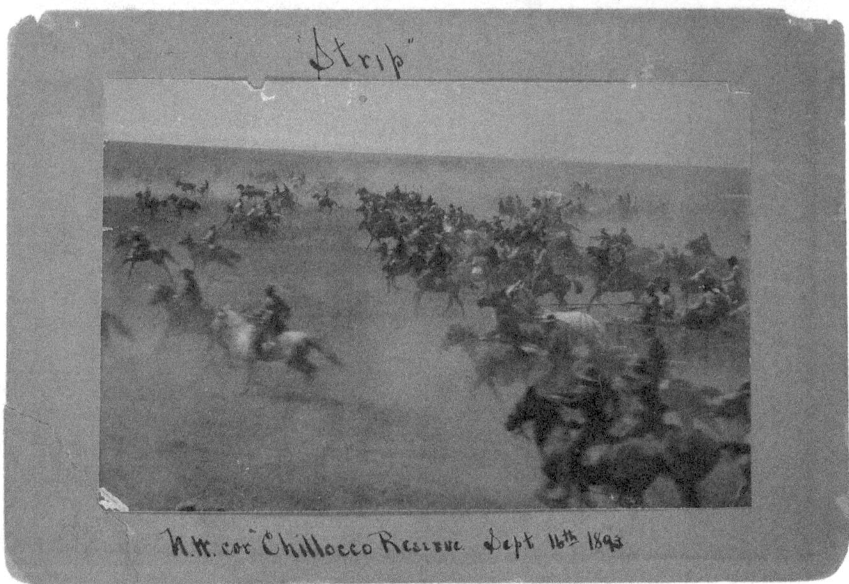

FIGURE 2.1 *Two photographs by William S. Prettyman documenting the "Land Rush" for formerly Cherokee lands in present-day Oklahoma, September 16, 1893. An estimated 100,000 people participated in the land run on the Cherokee Strip. Courtesy of Cowan's Auctions, Wikimedia Commons.*

2

Regarding Sovereign History as Incomplete: The Cherokee Outlet Land Opening Photographs

By Laura Wexler

Following the Civil War, Americans looked West for new economic opportunities. Settlers plowed up the native grass root systems that held down the topsoil and replaced them with wheat. Buffalo hunters decimated bison herds to meet the demand for hides in industrializing cities back east. Congress approved the formation of nine new states between 1865 and 1900, but settlement did not occur on vacant lands. The government established hundreds of Indian reservations during the "Reservation Era" (1851–91), reducing tribal landholdings to 138 million acres.

In Indian Territory (present-day Oklahoma), **"Boomers"** pressured the government to open Indian lands. Although Oklahoma did not become a state until 1907, the government slowly chipped away at Indian Territory. The first **"Land Rush"** occurred on Creek and Seminole lands in 1889. This chapter chronicles the 1893 run for the "Cherokee Outlet" (6 million acres previously guaranteed through the Treaty of New Echota) and one man's photographic innovation that changed the nature of photojournalism. Americans' desire for Indian lands was never satiated, and by 1934, only 48 million acres of Indian Country remained.

Suggested Topics: American West, Indigenous History, Westward Expansion

Glossary: Boomer/Sooner, Cartes de Visite, Indian Removal Act, Land Rush, Manifest Destiny, Photojournalism

In September 1893, an enterprising 35-year-old white photographer named William S. Prettyman nourished a secret plan. He quietly hired several carpenters to build a three-story-high wooden platform overlooking the starting line of the Cherokee Outlet Land Opening in Arkansas City, Kansas, which was set to commence at the sound of a gunshot on September 16, precisely at noon.

Prettyman was innovating a stop motion strategy reminiscent of Eadweard Muybridge's acclaimed experiment with photographs taken by a series of cameras set up along a track whose shutters were tripped by the hooves of a galloping horse. Muybridge's wildly successful project was undertaken roughly a decade earlier to prove what the eye could not see—that at one point in the gallop all four legs of a horse were off the ground. Prettyman planned to position multiple cameramen on the scaffold and instruct them to "squeeze the bulbs of their camera at two-second intervals as soon as the race began."[1] They would capture novel sequential images of the drama from above as the horses and wagons rushed past. Prettyman had already photographed "Sooner" encampments of would-be settlers awaiting the start of the 1889 Land Rush. But compared to the free-for-all that followed, his photographs of those anticipatory encampments were deceptively static. This time, Prettyman sought more spectacular pictures of the frenzy.

Prettyman kept himself at a distance from the carpenters so that no one would associate him with the construction. Even the carpenters did not know the purpose of the structure they were building. He wanted to keep reporters and other photographers from guessing his idea as long as possible. And indeed, when at the last minute he did appear, some tried to buy spaces on his platform for themselves, but he turned their offers down. Serial birds-eye images of the Cherokee Outlet Land Opening were to be exclusively his.

The carpenters succeeded in getting the wooden structure up and mounting four separate cameras in time. Prettyman, by then himself openly visible up on the platform, gave orders for four separate operators to prepare and make one glass plate exposure each, at two second intervals at the start of the race. One of the four photographs failed and the image was subsequently discarded, but the other three have come down to us just as Prettyman wished, as historical markers of "this epic event," to use the language of the Cherokee Strip Museum.

The photographs of the Cherokee Outlet Land Rush document things both visible and unseen. The concept of America as the land of opportunity often hinges on the opportunity for land. Inside the frame are throngs of white settlers literally racing for the chance to stake their claims. Far outside the frame are the Cherokees, on whose land those Sooners built their futures. The "settlement" of the American West was predicated on the unsettlement of Native nations. The very existence of these photographs is the result of ingenuity and photographic innovation, and they document an important moment in the professionalization of **photojournalism**. But while Prettyman's photographs celebrate a moment of opportunity in American history, they also document an American tragedy.

Manifest Photography

Prettyman was likely counting on selling *cartes de visite*, cabinet cards, and stereographs of photographs of the Cherokee Outlet Land Opening to Western tourists and to collectors back East, and maybe also even to local participants, many of whom would have been eager to display a record of this life-changing event in the albums they kept at home. It was a consumer market he knew well. As a newly divorced twenty-something photographer's apprentice recently arrived in Kansas from Princess Anne County, Maryland, where he had left his former wife and their two young daughters behind, he first started picturing Indians by making portraits of an Osage group who visited his studio. Photographing Indians in town further inspired him to show them "in their natural state of living before civilization took them off their land."[2]

To accomplish this, Prettyman made yearly expeditions throughout Indian Territory disguised as a hunter to avoid harassment from US Army soldiers patrolling the border of the Reserve. He worked from a mobile studio of his own design, devised from a covered buggy pulled by oxen, and he reported photographing Ponca, Otoe, Iowa, Sac, Cheyenne, Shawnee, Cherokee, and Potawatomi. Prettyman even made a self-portrait wearing his disguise, standing in a field with this equipment along with his assistant beside the Cimarron River, as both an advertisement and a souvenir. By the time he built his platform in 1893, he had been supplying white people's hunger for images that conveyed the nation's progress in "civilizing" Native people for over a decade. It is said that he made well over 10,000 photographs chiefly of Indians and settlers during his career as a photographer.[3]

By situating multiple cameras close to and above the starting line and timing the exposure intervals so precisely, Prettyman also managed to convey, perhaps more vividly than he even anticipated, not only the individual drama of this form of settlement but a momentous "just before" and "just after" slice of national transformation. The fourth and largest of seven Oklahoma land rushes organized by the US government, the Cherokee Outlet Land Opening was intended to mark a decisive end to the generations-long struggle of Indigenous nations to retain tribal sovereignty and keep possession of their lands out of white settler hands. President Grover Cleveland himself shot the pistol that kicked off the Cherokee Strip Land Rush (as it has since become known).

As well as opening literally millions of acres of Indigenous land to white settlement, the post-Civil War land rushes simultaneously inaugurated a new era of accommodation for the tribes who had been resettled on that land after the **Indian Removal Act** forced them from their traditional homelands in the southeastern United States, the traumatic displacement known to the Cherokee as the Trail of Tears. A number of these peoples, enslavers themselves, had previously allied with the Confederacy and were additionally required in that defeat to renegotiate their treaties. Thus, although the western lands had been conveyed to them for "as long as grass shall grow and water flow" by the very same federal government now setting the region on the path to US statehood by retracting their claim to it, multitudes of white Americans, immigrants, and African Americans felt little compunction to dampen their schemes to occupy it themselves as ranchers, farmers, merchants, miners, or railroad companies.[4] For the Native peoples losing their lands, this lack of respect was an existential threat.

The sensational words that Prettyman incised on some of his photographic negatives of the Ponca, Otoe, Iowa, Sac, Cheyenne, Shawnee, Cherokee, and Potawatomi he photographed, such as "half breed" and "plural marriage," show that he accepted and even amplified the ambient racism of his time and his milieu. The **Sooner**, or **Boomer**, movement which encouraged thousands to homestead on Indian land before it was legally available, fascinated him as well. Succeeding despite its illegality, it reinforced the white supremacist belief that Indian removal was an inevitable and progressive step and "civilization" *would* "[take] them off their land," and sooner rather than later.[5]

Prettyman's photographs record a transformative moment of American history in motion: the white supremacist nation at the cusp of significant expansion as US "Manifest Destiny" surged ahead and its Indigenous populations subsided. His project condenses into one compact set of images a historical process of devaluation, dispossession, deceit, desire, and denial that was ordinarily more diffusely represented. This achievement was appreciated by his contemporaries, who baptized him "The Father of News Photography," in its honor.

And the images still have much to tell us about the history of the United States. They are, for example, particularly revealing of the social hierarchies that shaped the moment. The first thing to notice, although it is rarely commented upon, is that Native Americans are not in the pictures. We know that virtually no individuals from the local tribes were there because Indians were the only group barred from participating in the United States land rushes, and in that way reclaiming the land from which they had been removed. The photographs thus also represent the desire for a sovereign white man's gaze. Simply, by focusing on themselves in photographs, they removed the Indians and their point of view.

Documenting the Land Rush

The earliest of Prettyman's iconic images of the Cherokee Outlet Opening depicts a tense assembly of non-Native men in Arkansas City, Kansas, jostling for places in the front row just minutes before the starting gun was fired. After considerable contemplation, one begins to recognize that some of the horses, wagons, and human figures in this first picture reappear in the subsequent two images. The caption reads: "Land Opening, 1893. Lining up in Arkansas City, Ks. One of three photos Prettyman and his associates made, before the race started. In a few minutes he joined the race, leaving picture taking to his associates. The first use of a high platform to take the picture known."

The second photograph was made just after the gun went off and catches the comparatively organized beginning of the race. It shows moving horses, all mounted now and running in a row, pulling ahead of the slower clump of horse-drawn wagons. If one has studied the prior image, one recognizes elements that have changed position. A white horse, previously unmounted, is especially striking as it charges forward with its rider. But members of the community could recognize even more, including the man on that horse. The local people were known to one another by name. The caption reads: "1893 Cherokee Outlet. Photo 2 of 3. John Sherwood is on the white horse. Elias McClenny is ahead of John. Fred McClenny is just behind John. High noon September 16, 1893, taken by one of Prettyman's associates." This exercise in identification suggests that the formation of the foremost group in the photographs that raced together from the starting gun was neither haphazard nor sudden; rather, its members likely planned to participate together, and perhaps to claim neighboring land.

This individuality distinguishes them from the third image, which shows how the initial formation swiftly devolved into a highly disorganized stampede as more than an estimated 100,000 aspirants—now no longer just people already known to one another—competed on foot, on bicycle, on horseback, in buggies and wagons, and even by jumping off moving trains, to stake roughly 50,000 claims to over 6 million acres of formerly Cherokee grazing land. Streaming past the cameras too quickly for the large format glass plate technology to register an image that was even approximately in focus, the main thing legible now is speed. The caption reads: "Two second later another associate took this picture. The slower wagons have replaced the horses in this view. The picture was considered too burred at the time to use. September 16, 1893. Credited to Cunningham."

However, the three most famous photographs taken from the platform at the moment the race began are in fact part of a larger set of images made *before* the race, which contain information that is not available elsewhere. To most viewers, recognizable elements disappear with the dusty blur of the third picture. But if one has studied one of the *prior* photographs made from the platform *before* the famous three, one may easily discern that a wagon that was originally at rest, with two women standing at its side, is later racing past at the bottom front of the frame. This raises the historically important question of whether women were active participants in the Cherokee Strip Land Opening among the vast majority of men, or if they got themselves out of the way just before the races began and only joined their menfolk later at the claim.

Land rushes were physically very violent occasions in which people were often hurt or even killed. The fact that there are women at the scene at all is fascinating, and the fact that there are not photographs that focus on them suggests how much is lost when sovereign history is only male and white. Homesteading women were very proud of their fortitude and the sometimes-significant farming and financial success they achieved. Several wrote powerful memoirs of the experience.[6] How valuable it would be if Prettyman had thought to make even a single image that concentrated on their presence at the race. That he didn't speaks volumes about this world.

Furthermore, comparing the many extant versions of the second image, which became the iconic one, with one another raises another interesting point. In most reproductions, the white horse and rider are the visual and emotional focus, intensified by the row of dark furiously galloping horses just behind them. But in some of the images it is possible to see the hats and upper bodies of another line of men along the bottom of the frame, a row of witnesses and reporters apparently standing behind some kind of barrier or fence. These men would also be standing below Prettyman's viewing structure. Among them must be some of the journalists who had begged to buy a position on the platform and whom he had denied. There is a second kind of race that is documented in this picture, not for land but for the prestige of photography. It shows how Prettyman fought for and won his reputation as a "picture man."

And finally, expanding our attention even further out to the rest of the set beyond the three tightly timed images uncovers an astonishing component: Prettyman's picture of his own claim! The image shows what the caption reads: "The horse, the claim, the virgin prairie in the Cherokee Outlet moments [*sic*] after the great race began. The claim was Prettyman's, as was the horse." If this is indeed a picture, as stated, of the initial moments of the race that

Prettyman did make himself that day, it is something of a puzzle how he got his camera equipment there through the dense and jostling crowd in order to take it. But Prettyman was, once again, not working in a vacuum and he was very well prepared. As Prettyman biographer Andrew G. Shupe has written:

> His special knowledge of the territory, [w]as a result of his many ventures into the Tribal Territories to take photographs of the Tribesmen and their life-style and of the Oklahoma Territory Land run in 1889, and [he] had several locations in mind. It has been said that during the race his horse stumbled into a Badger hole which broke one stirrup and threw him from the horse. Cowboy friends 'picketed' his horse and he was able to continue the race for land.[7]

Prettyman and his partner, Charles Hunt, each staked claims of 160 acres four miles south of Blackwell. The distance from the starting line to where Prettyman staked his claim was about 20 miles over prairie land, and they probably covered that distance in a little over one hour.

In other words, because of the years he had spent photographing Indian families, Prettyman knew precisely where he was going, and had stationed assistants in the field just as he had on the platform. His "cowboy friends" helped him with his horse after it stumbled and threw him off, and he rode another in tandem with Hunt to stake desirable neighboring claims just four miles from the newly founded town of Blackwell, Oklahoma, where he would soon serve two terms as mayor. Likely one of the photographers he employed followed him to photograph the scene.

Prettyman protected this claim from other settlers and from claim jumpers for the full required year by living on it, until he sold it to "a Dr. Padon in Blackwell, for whom one of the streets in Blackwell was named," and moved into town himself. Remarried, he built a family and a thriving photography practice of his own, and became the business entrepreneur he long had aspired to be. He helped to bring electricity, railroads, building codes, and running water to the town. Additionally, a civic presence, he served as president of the Board of Trade, president of the School Board, and trustee of the Baptist State College. Finally, in 1905, his photography having served his purposes, William Prettyman sold his photographic studio along with all his photographs and his real estate, and moved to Los Angeles, California, where he owned and ran a pharmacy with one of his three sons.[8]

This final anecdote reveals how Prettyman transmuted his knowledge of the territory gained over years of summer expeditions making photographs of the Indigenous populations in their own home places into a real estate advantage when the time was right, as "he had several locations [for his claim] in mind."[9] The thousands of ostensibly empathic pictures he made of local Native peoples simply cannot be divorced from this instrumental, long practiced, predatory gaze.

Framing and Reframing History

With Prettyman's accomplishment was registered not only a signal turn in US history but also, as the famous Oklahoma historian Muriel H. Wright remarked, "a particularly valuable landmark in news photography."[10] Vintage prints of the Prettyman photographs taken on this occasion are now owned by collectors and museums around the world, and contemporary prints and posters, and even a jigsaw puzzle with the second of Prettyman's land rush photographs on its face, are also currently for sale. The most iconic one of the three photographs, usually called *The Race*, is "among the most celebrated images of their time."[11] For decades it was used in American History textbooks—including the one I used in high school—to illustrate the chapter on "The Opening of the West." Despite protests lodged by Native families, Prettyman's pictures still guide fourth graders in the Oklahoma public schools who every year are required to stage a Land Rush reenactment, complete with costumes, covered wagons, sound effects, and a celebratory class picnic at the end.[12]

William Prettyman is remembered, a biographer writes, as a "journalistic and documentary rather than a 'pictorial'" photographer, which sets him off against Edward S. Curtis, whose often-critiqued campaign to make a photographic record of "the vanishing race" commenced shortly after this event.[13] However, as we have seen, after delivering his cameras to the platform and instructing his assistants about how to make them, and instead of taking photographs of the race himself that day Prettyman climbed back down and himself joined the rush for land. A seemingly objective panorama cited as a technical and intellectual landmark in the history of the evolution of news photography, the photographic record he secured was in fact no such a thing. Rather, Prettyman's participation reveals the perpetrator perspective shaping these pictures. They were conceived by, designed by, delegated by—and very likely they even depict—not an unbiased reporter but a specific man with a particular history whose personal enrichment at the expense of the destruction of an Indigenous world seemed to him virtually within grasp. Even the much-criticized Curtis was not interested in acquiring the impounded property of his ostensibly "vanishing" photographic subjects. Insofar as American history textbooks continue to center the history and memory of the Cherokee Strip Land Rush through Prettyman's lens, just that far does his gaze produce us as accomplices to its naturalizing force.

The *meaning* of a photograph is never as secure as its makers intend. The interpretation of photography is collaboratively produced over time by all of those who participate in the photographic event, including the photographer, the photographed persons, and its viewers at the time and later. As Ariella Azoulay, Wendy Ewald, Susan Meiselas, Leigh Raiford, and I have emphasized in our recent book, *Collaboration: A Potential History of Photography* (2023), photography preserves sovereign history as incomplete. "Using different forms of violence, sovereign power draws borders, destroys worlds, announces new beginnings and determines who is allowed to stay or enter, thus turning others' claims incompatible." But, at the same time, "these claims, inscribed in photographs, are being used to question the normalization of what was achieved with violence and declared irreversible, and to show that what was taken from others left scars that cannot be erased but can still be redressed."[14]

One is hard-pressed to think of a more sovereign American history than the story of the Cherokee Strip Land Rush as told from the government's triumphalist perspective. The land rush—a term invented by the US government especially for its Oklahoma land appropriation policy—is presented as the natural outcome of the western movement of American "civilization," which was the final (inevitable) nail in the coffin of Native claims to the continent. And yet because Prettyman's images, concretizing the abstraction of "American civilization," have survived beyond their moment of creation, they also introduce an opportunity to examine in how American history is told.

Native Americans developed their own perspectives on this historical period. In the years that culminated in Prettyman's 1893 images, they organized and sent delegations to Washington, DC, to protest the abrogation of treaty rights and lobby for medical, agricultural, cultural, and educational resources for their communities. Many of these delegations were photographed in the capitol and, as Nicole Dawn Strathman has shown in *Through a Native Lens*, their members often controlled the ways that photographers portrayed them.[15] Prominent Native American activists like Chief Red Cloud Oglala, Zitkala-Ša, and Sara Winnemucca also used photographs advantageously to parry and refashion the expectations of their white interlocutors.[16] It is well-known that in the government Indian boarding schools of the period, photography was a tool of the dominant culture which wished "to kill the Indian and save the man," as stated by Captain Richard Henry Pratt. But simultaneously there were opportunities for resistance, and, perhaps most consequentially, for the students to access instruction in camera clubs and use the tool for themselves.

How can we access these perspectives? We might consider, for example, the Cherokee Strip Land Rush photographs from the point of view of someone like Florence Owens Thompson, the woman who became the *Migrant Mother* in Dorothea Lange's iconic 1936 portrait for the Farm Security Administration.[17] Thompson was Cherokee, born on a reservation in Oklahoma near Tahlequah, the capital of the Cherokee Nation, on September 1, 1903, almost exactly twenty years after the Cherokee Strip Land Rush. She would have absorbed the pressures of white settler expansion and feared mistreatment or even persecution by the Federal government. Thompson would have known that Native children could legally be kidnapped and sent to Indian boarding schools where they were kept for many years from returning home, and many even died. When a woman who said she was from the federal government walked toward her and her children, carrying a large camera and saying she wanted to help, what did she think? Do Prettyman's photographs help us at all to imagine, and thereby begin to research, the knowledge behind the way she looks back out at Lange?

Although it was deemed desirable at the time to make and preserve these photographs as mementos showing American settler-colonialism literally in action, the Prettyman pictures have the potential to signify quite differently, revealing the scars. Renowned Salish artist Jaune Quick-To-See-Smith has brilliantly materialized that shift in point of view by flipping the orientation of US maps, and collaging photographs over them as her own personal wayfinding. Her series of *Memory Maps* turns photographs like Prettyman's of the Oklahoma Land Rushes inside out to claim and exhibit the personhood they overlook.[18]

But perhaps even the Prettyman photographs themselves suggest ways of addressing the disaster of the deliberate destruction of an entire living world. *Because* they exist *as* they exist, each image offers access, by comparison to others, to viewpoints that are ordinarily missing from their frames but yet may be conjured for inspirations of justice and repair.

Discussion Questions

1   The entirety of what is now the United States was once Indian land. What nations are native to where you live? Where are they located now?

2   A key principle to professional journalism is "journalistic objectivity," but as in any other professional field, journalists make choices about what information or voices to include or exclude. What role does photography play in journalism today? How do the framing choices and captions change, challenge, or enhance your interpretation of the images?

Further Resources

Native Land Digital. https://native-land.ca/.
Naegle, Rebecca, host. "This Land" (podcast). *Crooked Media*, June 3, 2019.
  https://crooked.com/podcast/this-land-episode-1-the-case/.

Notes

1   Kristine Schmucker, "Picture Man: William S. Prettyman," Harvey County
    Historical Museum (blog), September 15, 2017. Last accessed March 11,
    2025, https://hchm.org/picture-man-william-s-prettyman/.

2   Schmucker, "Picture Man."

3   Schmucker, "Picture Man."

4   The phrase "as long as the grass shall grow and the water flow" comes
    from President Andrew Jackson's removal orders for the Choctaws and
    Chickasaws. Variations appear in eight treaties with southeastern nations.
    For more, see Claudio Saunt, *Unworthy Republic: The Dispossession of
    Native Americans and the Road to Indian Territory* (W.W. Norton, 2020).

5   Schmucker, "Picture Man."

6   For accounts of women homesteaders in their own words, see Rachel Calof
    with J. Sanford Rikoon, ed., *Rachel Calof's Story: Jewish Homesteader on
    the Northern Plains* (Indiana University Press, 1995); Edith Eudora Kohl, *Land
    of the Burnt Thigh* (Minnesota Historical Society Press, 2008); and Elinore
    Pruitt Stewart, *Letters of a Woman Homesteader* (Open Road Media, 2020).

7   Andrew G. Shupe, "William Sheldon Prettyman: Mayor of Blackwell—Indian
    Photographer," *Rootsweb*, inactive but archived by the Internet Archive. Last
    accessed March 11, 2025, https://web.archive.org/web/20001007032119/
    http://www.rootsweb.com/~okkay/prettyman.htm.

8   Shupe, "William Sheldon Prettyman."

9   Shupe, "William Sheldon Prettyman."

10 John R. Lovett, "Prettyman, William S. (1858-1933)," *The Encyclopedia of
    Oklahoma* (Oklahoma Historical Society). Last accessed March 11, 2025,
    https://www.okhistory.org/publications/enc/entry?entry=PR010.

11 Schmucker, "Picture Man."

12 Oklahoma City banned the practice in their school districts in 2014, but
    the land run reenactments persist across the state. See Tim Willert,
    "Oklahoma City Public Schools Seeks 'Respectful' Alternative to Land
    Run Reenactments," *The Oklahoman*, December 23, 2014. Last accessed
    March 11, 2025, https://www.oklahoman.com/story/news/local/oklahoma-
    city/2014/12/23/oklahoma-city-public-schools-seeks-respectful-alternative-to-
    land-run-re-enactments/60776375007/; and Chuck Hoskin, Jr., "Teach Kids
    about the Oklahoma Land Run, but Don't Glorify It," *Native News Online*,
    April 28, 2024. Last accessed March 11, 2025, https://nativenewsonline.net/
    opinion/teach-kids-about-the-oklahoma-land-run-but-don-t-glorify-it.

13 Schmucker, "Picture Man." For more on Edward Curtis' campaign to document Native Americans, see Lee Allen, "Smudging the Colonizer's Lens: Artists Challenge Old Imagery with 'Regarding Curtis'," *Indian Country Today*, November 29, 2014. Last Accessed March 11, 2025, https://ictnews.org/archive/smudging-the-colonizers-lens-artists-challenge-old-imagery-with-regarding-curtis.

14 Ariella Aïsha Azoulay, Wendy Ewald, Susan Meiselas, Leigh Raiford, and Laura Wexler, *Collaboration: A Potential History of Photography* (Thames & Hudson, 2023).

15 Nicole Dawn Strathman, *Through a Native Lens: American Indian Photography* (University of Oklahoma Press, 2020).

16 For more on how Native activists deployed their own self-presentation, see Cathleen Cahill's essay in Chapter 5, and Phil Deloria, *Indians in Unexpected Places* (University of Kansas Press, 2004).

17 For more on Dorothea Lange and *Migrant Mother*, see Linda Gordon's essay in Chapter 7.

18 Laura Phipps and Neal Ambrose-Smith, *Jaune Quick-to-See Smith* (Whitney Museum of American Art, 2023).

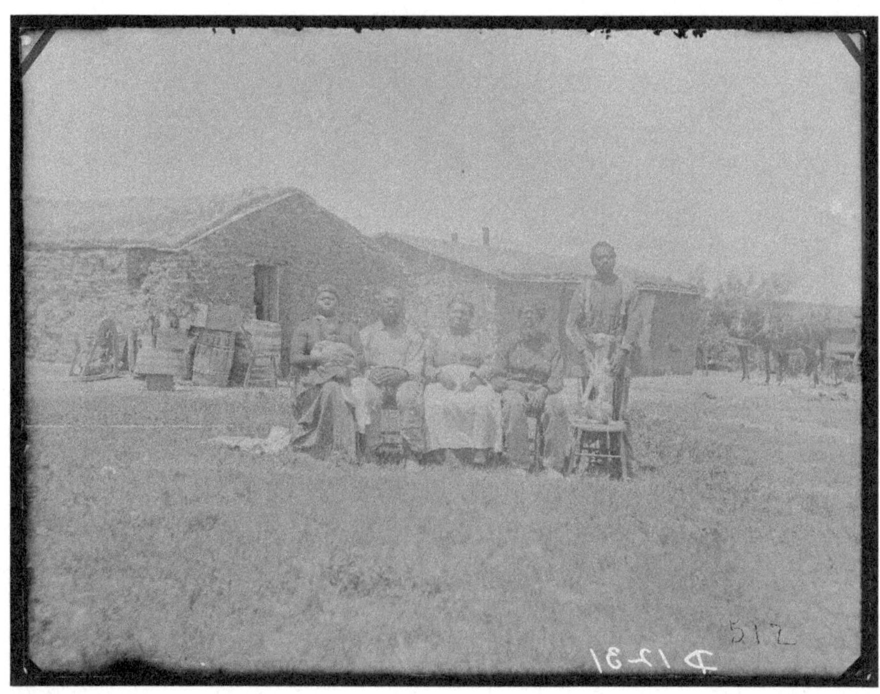

FIGURE 3.1 *The Shores family in front of their home near Westerville, Nebraska, in 1887. Photo by Solomon D. Butcher. Courtesy of the Nebraska State Historical Society.*

3

Owned to Landowner: Black Homesteaders in the West

By Jacob K. Friefeld

Between the 1910s and 1970s, approximately 6 million African Americans migrated from the American South to escape the racial violence that accompanied Jim Crow laws. During the **First Great Migration** (1910s–1940s), African Americans took advantage of industrial job vacancies in cities across the North and Midwest produced by America's participation in the First World War and a declining European immigrant population. The Second World War opened opportunities in cities along the Pacific Coast, prompting the **Second Great Migration** (1940s–1970s). There, Black Americans faced intense housing discrimination that set the foundation for generations of racial and economic disparities, as we will learn in Chapter 11.

But not all African Americans fleeing the South for new opportunities migrated between 1910 and 1970, and not all moved to urban centers. Like the white homesteaders described in Chapter 3, African Americans took advantage of the government's offer for free land in the American West through the **Homestead Act of 1862**. As many as 15,000 African Americans migrated from the South to newly opened lands in the American West. The following account of the Shores and Speese families prompts us to consider different routes to freedom and reconsider what we think we know about who settled the American West.

Suggested Topics: African American History, Agriculture, American West, Great Migration, Labor History, Westward Expansion

Glossary: Agrarian Vision, General Land Office, Great Migration, Homestead Act (1862), Prove Up, Reconstruction, Sharecropping, Sod

The Shores family poses in front of their home in 1887. The work on the farm is never done, and their clothes suggest they might have been interrupted while at their chores. They look well-fed and healthy—their hard work has paid off. Minerva, with her infant on her lap, stares at the camera, perhaps happy about these moments of rest sitting for Solomon Butcher, the traveling photographer.

To the twenty-first-century eye, this photo might look bleak. Homemade structures stand behind the Shores family with farm and household equipment stacked with barrels near one wall. One of the buildings is their home; the other could be a barn, or a second home for Minerva Shores and her husband Reverend Marks (left). A single house would be cramped to share with Rachel and Jerry Shores, Minerva's parents, and their son Jim, but not an altogether unusual living arrangement for the 1880s.

This may look like poverty, but the Shores family is doing quite well. The horses photobombing in the background speak to this. Horses required cash on hand to purchase, each costing the equivalent of over $2,000 in 2025, adjusted for inflation. They provided transportation and lent their strength (literal horsepower) to work on the farm, both plowing and hauling. The horses pull double-duty in the photograph, they fill background space for the photographer, and they also show off the Shores' wealth. Whatever the reason for their inclusion, it suggests life was good. Jim Shores thinks so as he injects whimsy into the photo, propping up the family dog in the chair like a person. The pooch looks on with a smile.[1]

Without looking carefully, you might assume this is a family of freedpeople in the post-Civil War South. After all, 90 percent of Black Americans lived in the South in the 1880s. But then we look closely. At first the houses seemed to be made of brick, but now you realize they aren't ordinary bricks. They're Nebraska bricks, a construction material commonly known as **sod**.[2]

The Shores migrated from the South to Nebraska as homesteaders, or settlers who received free land from the government. The Nebraska landscape is nothing like the South, and the Shores family was likely shocked by the endless prairie that stretched to the horizon. The grasslands meant there was little timber to build their home. The Shores set to work like countless other settlers, building their house from sod, or prairie soil held together by a root system so robust that you could cut it into hard bricks.[3]

Why did the Shores family leave everything familiar to build a house from the very ground on which they stood, ground that had until recently belonged to the Pawnee Nation? How many other Black Southerners followed in the Shores' footsteps, and how does their presence in Great Plains change our ideas about homesteaders and who settled the US West? To answer these questions, we need to travel back in time and visit North Carolina.

Carolina to Indiana

Jerry Shores's migration story actually begins with his half-brother, Moses Speese. In 1872, Speese lay in a wagon hiding underneath a pile of hay. He probably itched from the touch of the hay and perhaps second-guessed his decision. This must have seemed a bitter turn of events. As he lay in the wagon he might have thought about his father, Moses Shores, who had been born into slavery in 1795.

Moses Shores had known his own bitterness and showed resilience in the face of it. His first wife, Fanny Shores, along with his son, Jerry Shores, had been sold away to another plantation. He emerged from what must have been a chasm of grief to marry again. His new wife, Hannah Webb, gave birth to Moses Speese, taking the last name of his enslaver.

Like other Black Americans, Moses Speese, his father, and half-brother Jerry Shores had celebrated in 1865. What had seemed impossible a decade ago had come to pass—American chattel slavery was dead. Abraham Lincoln's 1863 Emancipation Proclamation that announced the freedom of enslaved people in rebel territory had transformed the Union Army into an agent of liberty as it marched through the South. The Thirteenth and Fourteenth Amendments followed, destroying slavery and widening the circle of citizenship to include the formerly enslaved. It was a new birth of freedom. It was a time for celebration.

Freedpeople hoped that through **Reconstruction** the federal government would redistribute land confiscated from the traitors who had fought for the Confederacy. In an agricultural society, land meant opportunity and Black Southerners pinned their hopes on becoming landowners. Landowning would provide a pathway to economic freedom, but President Andrew Johnson betrayed America's new Black citizens and returned most confiscated land to the treasonous rebels. The best land would remain with white Southerners.[4]

Without land reform, the sweet fruit of new liberty turned to ash in Moses Speese's mouth. After the war, he turned to what he knew best, farming. But the exploitative system of **sharecropping** and debt peonage ensnared him. As a sharecropper, Speese lived on and farmed a white landowner's land. He paid his rent as a share of the crop after harvest. He soon found himself in debt because he gave up precious income in crop yields each year. He also purchased supplies, equipment, food, and the very clothes on his back on credit at the white landowner's store. White landowners had fashioned a new system of domination forged by the chains of debt and dependence.

Speese wanted to take his family and leave behind this life of debt, but the landowner forbade them to leave as long as they remained indebted. So there Speese hid under a pile of hay in a friendly neighbor's wagon, an escape tactic similar to those used by the enslaved prior to emancipation. The wagon would spirit him aboard a northbound train to Indiana. There he would catch his breath and wait for his wife and children to join. He would also be joined by his father, Moses Shores, and half-brother, Jerry.

Indiana marked only a waypoint on a longer journey. The Speese and Shores families had heard of an opportunity to secure their dream of landownership—the Homestead Act.[5]

Homesteading the Plains

When the Emancipation Proclamation went into effect on January 1, 1863, so did the Homestead Act. For years, a coalition of Northern politicians had tried to pass a law that offered American citizens free land in the country's western territories. The federal government during the country's early history looked to the sale of western lands to raise money. Thomas Jefferson's **agrarian vision** foresaw an "Empire of Liberty" that would stretch common (white) men on farmland across the continent, but early expansion models privileged revenue over speedy settlement.

Northern politicians supported free land policy through a homestead act rather than cash sales for a variety of reasons. Some wanted to see western territories populated and become states, others hoped to stop the spread of slavery, others wanted to accelerate Indian removal, and still others hoped to provide an opportunity for independence in the West to working-class men in eastern cities. Southern lawmakers saw free land policy as a plot to fill the West with Northerners and exclude slavery from the region. They blocked attempts to pass a homestead act, but in 1860, a free land bill successfully passed through the chambers of Congress. President James Buchanan, a Southern sympathizer, vetoed the bill. When Abraham Lincoln took office in 1861, Congress moved quickly to pass the Homestead Act, and Lincoln signed it into law.[6]

The Homestead Act of 1862 allowed any American citizen over the age of twenty-one (or any immigrant declaring their intent to become a citizen) to claim up to 160 acres of land (equivalent to about 120 American football fields!). Homesteaders, as they were called, could "**prove up**," or gain full title to their land, if they settled on that land for five years, built a house, cultivated crops, and built other improvements like fences, wells, barns, and chicken coops. Americans and immigrants could gain a farm for hard work and a small filing fee.[7]

From Indiana, Moses Speese and Jerry Shores went west to homestead in Nebraska. Their 85-year-old father Moses Shores, now reunited with first wife Fanny after the death of his second and third wives, stayed behind in Indiana. Jerry Shores strode into the land office in Grand Island, Nebraska (which was neither grand nor an island) on October 11, 1882, to file a claim on 162 acres of land near Westerville. He attested that he was "the head of the family, over 21 years of age, and a citizen of the United States." That simple statement, so routine for many white homesteaders, must have been emotional for Shores, who was born enslaved. Now he claimed land with the full rights of citizenship. He marked his homestead application with an X, unable to sign his name, and he went off to improve his land.[8]

Shores filed his claim in October, too late in the season to plant any crops, so he didn't rush to move his family onto the land. They had been living farther east in Seward County, about thirty miles outside Nebraska's capital of Lincoln, and they could stay there until the next growing season. In April 1883, Jerry and Rachel Shores moved with their three children onto their claim, and Jerry began to build their home of sod.

The process was grueling. When many families arrived on their homesteads, they first built their houses as partial dugouts. That is, they dug the floor of their home into the soil so the surrounding high ground could serve as walls or at least the stable beginnings of walls. The Shores home is not a dugout. Jerry Shores likely started building his home by clearing the prairie grass that grew from the sod that would become bricks. Then, he got busy cutting sod. For this, he needed a special plow that cut deep slits into the soil, leaving it intact as bricks, rather than breaking and tossing it as a normal plow would.[9] Though it was tough work, it served the Shores family twice over. As Jerry peeled up the earth to build his home, he simultaneously primed his first field for planting.

Shores laid the heavy sod in overlapping layers as more traditional bricklayers would, cutting the sod into manageable sizes to lighten his load. A woman homesteading in Montana remembered trying to help build her sod house but found that "to lift a single sod was beyond the strength of one woman." This was backbreaking labor. Once Shores laid the walls, he added wooden supports and placed sod over them. Wood was scarce on the plains, and Shores needed to make certain the beams he fashioned would be strong enough to withstand the weight of the sod after the first spring rain. Even then, sod roofs didn't always protect homesteaders. One homesteader recalled that "during a rainstorm there was but one dry spot in the room," but the moisture wasn't nearly as bad as the "snakes that suddenly darted out of the little round holes in the walls."[10]

Sod house living was rustic, but regardless of the outward appearance of their homestead, the Shores family wasn't impoverished. While some surrounding homesteaders lived more affluently, others lived in true poverty. Rachel Calof, who moved from Russia to the United States for an arranged marriage to a homesteader, remembered living in a house with her in-laws who had created a private space for Calof and her husband consisting of "a pit ... scooped out in the center of the dirt floor." The Shores' soddy (as locals referred to sod houses) was a dream by comparison.[11]

The Shores family lived in their first sod house for three years. They built it quickly to keep them sheltered for the early years of their homesteading experience, but by 1886 the family readied themselves to move into a new home. No doubt built in much the same way as the first, the second house measured 18 by 32 feet with a board floor (a luxury not many could afford), three doors and four windows. They furnished the space with a table, four chairs, and three beds.[12]

When Solomon Butcher arrived to take their photo, they pulled all four chairs out of the house to sit proudly in front of their home. Posing with furniture from inside the home is typical of the homestead photography genre. Homesteaders intentionally incorporated prized possessions like pianos and tables in the frame to convey and redefine what affluence looked like on America's frontier. Our modern-day assumptions about what wealth and poverty look like can cloud our judgment when reading homestead photography. A closer reading reveals that the Shores used their belongings to assert their place in civilized American society. The chairs indicate not only that their home had ample space for a dining table but also that they had enough to afford matching chairs. Before sitting for Butcher in those same chairs, the Shores took the time to hitch their horses to their wagon to further exhibit their success.

The chairs and wagon aren't the only clues to the Shores family's hard work. Along with their two homes, they built a sod stable, dug a well with a pump, and planted fruit trees. Shores also cultivated twenty-five acres of corn and other grain. He plowed those acres with four plows likely pulled by the four horses he owned. Five head of cattle, thirty hogs, and a flock of chickens rounded out the Shores family's wealth by 1889 when they were ready to prove up their claim.

On February 22, 1889, Shores announced in the local newspaper, as required by law, that he intended to prove up—the announcement appeared in the paper for five consecutive weeks. In his announcement, Shores included a list of four witnesses who could confirm he had fulfilled the requirements of the Homestead Act. Two of those witnesses formally testified on his behalf in a sworn affidavit at the land office. This was the most delicate moment in the homesteading process. If Shores's witnesses betrayed him, the land office official would reject his claim, and Shores would lose his years of investment on the land.[13]

Picking the right witnesses was important, especially for Black Americans living in a new place. Shores listed four white men, Alexander McEwen, John Welsh, Bem S. Wood, and Fabias D. Mills, as his witnesses. Shores notably didn't list his half-brother Moses as a witness. This is a testament to the relationships Shores had built with his white neighbors. It also indicates that Shores suspected a white man's testimony might be worth more than that of a Black man in the 1880s.

When he entered the land office on April 2, 1889, to prove up, McEwen and Welsh joined him. McEwen was a 33-year-old farmer of Scottish ancestry who had immigrated to the United States from Canada in 1865. He homesteaded land a mile from Shores and visited the family about once a month. McEwen and Shores developed a neighborly rapport, likely providing useful assistance on each other's farms. Welsh was likewise a farmer with ancestry in the British Isles. Welsh arrived in the United States from Ireland in 1858 in his late teens, joining the millions of Irish who emigrated to the United States trying to escape oppression and famine in their homeland. Like McEwen, Welsh homesteaded about one mile from Shores and visited the family nearly every month.[14]

Shores gave his own testimony too, and listed his improvements. Either he or the land office clerk added values to each improvement—sod house, $100; sod stable, $100; hog pen, $10; 75 acres of cultivation, $300. His witnesses didn't betray him. McEwen and Welsh confirmed everything Shores had built during his time on the land. Shores proved up his homestead with improvements worth nearly $700, the equivalent of $24,000 in 2025.[15]

A proved-up homestead wasn't just a way for the United States to populate the land with settlers or merely an opportunity for the homesteader. A homestead was taxable land. The land could be borrowed against—it was a financial instrument in the growing capitalist economy tied to Gilded Age banks in urban areas. This value, the land as a commodity, is what made the land so attractive for the US government to wrest from Natives to begin with, and Indian dispossession reveals the central paradox of the Homestead Act. While the federal government offered free land so more Americans might share in the nation's wealth, that offer relied on taking Native land and limiting Native peoples' access to that same wealth. Each value listed next to Shores's improvements in his homestead documents forced him to triangulate himself in this capitalist economy built, in part, on Native removal—an economy in which he had not long ago been a commodity himself.[16]

When Shores returned to his land from the Grand Island land office, a journey of over 70 miles, he might have relished those first few steps on *his* property. He, who had once been owned, now owned land. Not only did he own land but he had also created a prosperous farm—he grasped freedom in the Great Plains, not just for himself but for his descendants as well.

Moses Speese homesteaded nearby and did just as well. Speese proved up his homestead on May 24, 1889, calling Samuel Steward and William Thornton (both white) as witnesses. Like Shores, he'd built a sod house for his family with a lumber floor and roof and acquired an impressive 5 horses, 11 cows, and 140 hogs. Managing his livestock while planting tens of acres of corn and wheat each season must have been arduous, but he did it. He also dug a well on his property and added a windmill. His windmill was no ordinary windmill, but a first-of-its kind Halladay Standard self-regulating windmill—not only did it stop pumping water once it filled the tank but it also used the counterweight to adjust the surface area of the sails to withstand high winds. The Halladay was likely the envy of the township. Speese proved up, and, like Shores, completed his journey from owned to landowner.[17]

Toward the Sunset

Free from the rigged sharecropper system, Jerry Shores and Moses Speese became prosperous on the Nebraska plains. It was a great boon when a photographer, rare in rural Nebraska in the 1880s, arrived and offered to photograph them.

The man behind the camera was an eccentric young Illinoisan named Solomon Butcher. Butcher arrived in Nebraska with his father to homestead in 1880. Like Shores, he immediately got to work building a sod house. Butcher remembered that "my first experience in sod laying consisted principally in wearing out my hands and patience." Despite his frustration with the hard labor, Butcher filed his own claim after accompanying his father on a trip back to Illinois to collect his mother and brother. He lasted only two weeks before giving up.[18]

After a stint in Minnesota, he returned to Nebraska a married man. With no home of their own, the newlyweds lived with his father while Butcher worked as a teacher, saving enough to acquire land and purchase photographic equipment. He got busy building, but he didn't build a house to provide much-needed space for his family. Instead, he built a small structure that would become his photography studio, and almost certainly the first photography studio in Custer County.

Photography, still a relatively new technology, was growing in popularity and so were traveling photographers. Butcher leaned into the medium's popularity, and by 1886, he set out to create the first photographic history of Custer County. He spent the next seven years taking photos of farmers in the area, including Shores and Speese. Butcher's odyssey into photography and the Custer County landscape brought him little notoriety during his life and even less money.[19]

As for the Shores and Speese families, their odyssey was just beginning. The brothers prospered in the small community of Westerville, embraced by their neighbors. Jerry and Moses proved up their homesteads, getting their land for free. Other members of their families commuted their homestead claims, meaning they filed for homesteads but found it beneficial to receive title to the land earlier and purchased the claim with cash. Their commutation along with the large weddings of Maggie Shores to Baseman Taylor and Charles Speese to Hannah Rosetta Meehan attested to their growing prosperity.

The Speese and Shores families also gained notoriety for their musical ability. They played the violin, piano, and sang, performing locally and touring under several names including the Speese Jubilee Singers. They encountered limits to their acceptance as they traveled farther from home. On one tour of the western part of the state in 1896, the Speese singers performed their classical show in St. Paul, Nebraska. It flopped as the white audience had expected a slapstick minstrel show. Despite their individual prosperity and the freedoms they gained, the current of American racism still ran through the Great Plains.[20]

Moses Speese died in 1896, and Jerry Shores followed ten years later, passing their wealth to the next generations. Having become so well-liked and prosperous, it is almost surprising that the Speese and Shores families decided to leave Westerville in 1908. They left for a combination of reasons. The families grew concerned about a Nebraska court decision that complicated inheritance claims from marriages between formerly enslaved people. They also became frustrated with Nebraska's lackluster funding for schools. Furthermore, the land around Westerville had been well settled by 1908, and there was little homesteadable land left for successive generations. For myriad reasons, the families saw new opportunities on the horizon. They looked to the open lands in Wyoming with renewed hope. They sold their lands in Nebraska, hoping to turn their fortunes into investments in their children's and grandchildren's futures.[21]

Moses Speese and Jerry Shores took the first steps out of the South and into the West; the next generation would push farther West into Wyoming. Moses's son Charles sold his land for a tidy sum of $16,000, over $500,000 in 2025 money. If the rest of the family holdings sold for as much, they would have realized $56,650, nearly $2 million in 2025. Five of the Speese brothers used some of their money to form the Speese Brothers Land and Cattle Company in the Nebraska Sandhills. The Speese and Shores families eventually left Nebraska altogether and set up a new Black farming enclave in Wyoming. When they finally sold their land in 1908, the *Custer County Chief* reported that "Charles Speese has sold out his first class farm … No one in Westerville holds a better record than Charlie Speese and we are sorry to lose him." Another neighbor later remembered, "Both families were as fine neighbors as any would want." The Shores and Speese families would be missed.[22]

Who Settled the West?

The Shores family's journey from owned to landowner is remarkable. The existence of photographic evidence of that journey is nothing short of extraordinary. Between 1886 and 1912, Solomon Butcher traveled hundreds of miles across four gigantic counties on the central Nebraska plains to document this short period of settlement. He took over 3,000 photographs and his work remains one of the most comprehensive collections of homestead photography in the country. His photographs had little national impact at the time, and Butcher died in 1927 believing he was a failure.[23] But for individual homesteaders, their families, and their descendants, Butcher's photographs are a testament to their grit.

Among Butcher's thousands of glass plate negatives, there are but a handful of photographs of African American homesteaders. This isn't too surprising. Compared to the approximately 1.6 million homesteaders who successfully filed claims under the Homestead Act, there were few Black citizens—approximately 3,500 claimants—who chose to build their futures in the Great Plains. For the Shores family and the generations that followed, Butcher's photo makes a powerful statement that shouts, "We were there!"

Not only was the Shores family in the Great Plains, but they counted themselves as part of a larger movement. Tens of thousands of Black Americans moved into the Great Plains to homestead. Black homesteaders saw their migration West as a grand addition to the American story. The Shores and Speese descendants named their new community in Wyoming, *Empire*. Though it never became a true empire, the name was aspirational.

Communities like Empire popped up across the West. Black homesteaders in Colorado north of Denver called their new settlement *Dearfield* because the land was so dear to them. In New Mexico, Black homesteaders called their colony *Blackdom* as if a great Black kingdom had risen from plains, woven from the prairie grass itself. Charles and Rosetta Speese would leave Empire and move about 100 miles away from Westerville where Jerry Shores and Moses Speese originally homesteaded. Their new community of DeWitty didn't have an aspirational name until the residents renamed it *Audacious*.[24]

The longest-lived and most well-known homesteader colony of Nicodemus, Kansas, might have the most telling name. According to one story, Nicodemus was an African Prince sold into slavery who became the first enslaved man to buy his freedom in America. More likely, the settlement was named for a popular Civil War Era song called *Wake Nicodemus*. The song described an enslaved man named Nicodemus who, as his kin laid him to rest, had one request: "'Wake me up!' was his charge, at the first break of day / Wake me up for the great Jubilee!" Nicodemus had awoken! The great Jubilee, the end of slavery, had arrived, and thousands of Black Americans celebrated by audaciously claiming their own piece of the United States.[25]

Black homesteaders, most of whom had memories of slavery or heard firsthand accounts from their parents, took their new freedoms seriously. Under slavery, they had been deprived of freedom of movement. When denied land ownership and faced with white supremacist violence in the South after the Civil War, they heeded the call of Reverend Robert H. Knox to "seek homes elsewhere ... where there may be enjoyed in peace and happiness by your own fireside the earnings of your daily toil." Black homesteaders affirmed their new freedoms by moving west to exercise their rights and citizenship on free land under the Homestead Act.[26]

The story of the Shores and Speese families as well as all the Black homesteaders who moved to the Great Plains changes the story of who settled the American West and adds depth to our understanding of American history. Their story shows how free land policy created new possibilities for Americans to claim land in the West and fused with the legacy of emancipation to create opportunities for Black Americans outside of the South's unremitting violence under Jim Crow laws.

This story also shows a migration to the rural Great Plains and other points West in a largely agrarian society that preceded the **Great Migration** of millions of Black Americans from the US South to expanding Northern cities. Today, there are approximately 175,000 living Americans who are descendants of Black homesteaders.[27]

The Shores and Speese saga stretched from North Carolina to Indiana, and on to their Nebraska homesteads. The next generation continued their story in Empire, Wyoming; DeWitty, Nebraska; and Sully County, South Dakota. But before the Shores and Speese families had an inkling of just how far their descendants would travel, Jerry Shores sat with his family and a very happy dog so Solomon Butcher could capture an image of their success on a glass plate negative.

Discussion Questions

1   Read the photograph for clues to the Shores and Speese families' success. How do you think Black homesteaders might have defined success differently than their white neighbors?

2   How do the Speese and Shores families change your view of who settled the West? What does their story suggest about the diversity of those who lived in the Great Plains in the nineteenth century?

3   How does the story of Black westward migration expand our understanding of the timing and geography of the Great Migration?

Further Resources

Black Homesteading Project. Center for Great Plains Studies, University of Nebraska. https://plains.unl.edu/projects/black-homesteading-project/.

Carter, John E. *Solomon D. Butcher: Photographing the American Dream.* University of Nebraska Press, 1985.

Edwards, Richard and Jacob K. Friefeld. *The First Migrants: How Black Homesteaders' Quest for Land and Freedom Heralded America's Great Migration.* Bison Books, 2023.

Hager, Kristi. *Evelyn Cameron: Montana's Frontier Photographer.* Far Country Press, 2007.

National Park Service. "Black Homesteaders." Homestead National Historic Park. https://www.nps.gov/home/black-homesteading-in-america.htm.

Nebraska State Historical Society. "Solomon D. Butcher Collection." https://history.nebraska.gov/collection_section/solomon-d-butcher-collection/.

Notes

1   Bureau of Land Management Records, Grand Island Land Office, Township 19N, Range 17W, Section 30 and Township 19N, Range 18W, Section 25, document number 4198. Last accessed May 26, 2024, https://glorecords.blm.gov/details/patent/default.aspx?accession=NE0830__.184&docClass=STA&sid=kt4s4kfo.zrj; and U.S Department of Agriculture, *Yearbook of the United States Department of Agriculture 1919* (Government Printing Office, 1920), 653. The price of horses in 1887 is derived from the Department of Agriculture year book and then compared to 2025 using the OfficialData.org CPI Inflation Calculation; (https://www.officialdata.org/). It is somewhat difficult to determine how much negotiation took place over what appeared in the photograph and how the family posed. According to Butcher's son, the photographer was meticulous about how his subjects posed and would ask them to move or subtract items from the frame. Based on the objects in frame, the family and Butcher agreed to include items and a pose that would signal the importance of family and the wealth they had accrued. See David Bristow, "Look Closely: This Is a Previously Unknown Solomon Butcher Photo," *Nebraska State Historical Society* (blog), April 30, 2020. Last accessed May 25, 2025, https://history.nebraska.gov/look-closely-this-is-a-previously-unknown-solomon-butcher-photo/.

2   Bureau of the Census, *Negro Population: 1790–1915*, 33.

3   Richard Edwards and Jacob K. Friefeld, *The First Migrants: How Black Homesteaders' Quest for Land and Freedom Heralded America's Great Migration* (Bison Books, 2023), 45–8.

4   Edwards and Friefeld, *The First Migrants*, 21–3.

5   Edwards and Friefeld, *The First Migrants*, 185–7. See also Todd Guenther, "The Empire Builders: An African American Odyssey in Nebraska and Wyoming," *Nebraska History* 86 (Winter 2008): 176–200.

6 Benjamin Todd Arrington, "'Free Homes for Free Men': A Political History of the Homestead Act, 1774–1863" (PhD diss., University of Nebraska, 2012), 198–221; Jacob K. Friefeld, "Homesteading and the Making of the Midwest," in *The Making of the Midwest: Essays on the Formation of Midwestern Identity, 1787–1900*, ed. Jon K. Lauck (Hastings College Press, 2020), 184–5.

7 Act of May 20, 1862 (Homestead Act), Public Law 37–64 (12 Stat 392). The requirements changed over the years the Homestead Act was in effect. Notably the residency period was eventually reduced to three years and allowable acreage increased in some regions. For a more comprehensive of the history of homesteading, see Richard Edwards, Jacob K. Friefeld, and Rebecca S. Wingo, *Homesteading the Plains: Toward a New History* (University of Nebraska Press, 2017); and Josh Sides, *Backcountry Ghosts: California Homesteaders and the Making of a Dubious Dream* (University of Nebraska Press, 2021), xi.

8 Jerry Shores, Homestead Records: Grand Island Land Office, Township 17N, Range 18W, Section 32, Fold3.com Digital Archive accessed May 26, 2024, https://www.fold3.com/image/302204032.

9 Roger Welsch, *Sod Walls: The Story of the Nebraska Sod House* (J & L Lee, 1991), 29–42.

10 I.E.M. Smith, "Two City Girls' Experiences in Holding Down a Claim: A Montana Pastoral," *Overland Monthly* 24 (August 1894): 147–9.

11 Rachel Calof, *Rachel Calof's Story: Jewish Homesteader on the Northern Plains*, ed. J. Sanford Rikoon (Indiana University Press, 1995), 26.

12 Welsch, *Sod Walls*, 42–77. See also David B. Danbom, *Sod Busting: How Families Made Farms on the 19th-Century Plains* (Johns Hopkins University Press, 2014); Jerry Shores, Homestead Records, Fold3.com Digital Archive.

13 Jerry Shores, Homestead Records, Fold3.com Digital Archive; Shores took six years from taking residence on the land to prove up. It is unclear why he waited the extra year. Homesteaders typically proved up their claims as soon as possible to leverage their property for bank loans, but the law allowed homesteaders seven years from the date of filing to prove up.

14 Jerry Shores, Homestead Records, Fold3.com Digital Archive; U.S Census, Custer County, Nebraska, 1880 and 1900. For more on homesteading and immigration, see Blake Bell, "America's Invitation to the World: Was the Homestead Act the First Accommodating Immigration Legislation in the United States?," Homestead National Monument of America, National Park Service. Accessed May 26, 2024, http://npshistory.com/publications/home/immigration.pdf.

15 Jerry Shores, Homestead Records, Fold3.com Digital Archive; U.S Census, Custer County, Nebraska, 1880 and 1900.

16 Jerry Shores, Homestead Records, Fold3.com Digital Archive; Edwards, Friefeld, and Wingo, *Homesteading the Plains,* 91–128; Julius Wilm, "'The Indians Must Yield': Antebellum Free Land, the Homestead Act, and the Displacement of Native Peoples," *Bulletin of the German Historical Institute* 67 (Fall 2020): 17–39. Edwards, Friefeld, and Wingo argue that homesteaders were directly responsible for Indian removal in some places particularly in the Dakotas and Indian Territory. In other places like Nebraska and Colorado, Indigenous people experienced dispossession before homesteaders arrived. Julius Wilm challenges their conclusions arguing that in nearly all the Great Plains states, would-be homesteaders sought out land while Native Nations fought to retain their ancestral lands. Wilm argues that the United States, in order to avoid open conflict between settlers and Natives, accelerated the process of dispossession. Similarly, in *Ramp Hollow,* Steven Stoll discusses how the tools of commercial capitalism were used to dispossess the early white settlers of Appalachia. I mention him here because his work shows how "unsettled" land can be rationalized into an instrument of capital as a commodity. See Stoll, *Ramp Hollow: The Ordeal of Appalachia* (Hill and Wang, 2017), 7–29.

17   Moses Speese, Homestead Records: Grand Island Land Office, Township 17N, Range 18W, Section 30, Fold3.com Digital Archive accessed May 26, 2024, https://www.fold3.com/image/302429588.

18   John E. Carter, *Solomon D. Butcher: Photographing the American Dream* (University of Nebraska Press, 1985), 2–3.

19   Carter, *Solomon D. Butcher,* 1–9.

20   Edwards and Friefeld, *The First Migrants,* 192–6; Guenther, "The Empire Builders," 176–200; and *Custer County (Nebraska) Republican,* May 3, 1900.

21   Edwards and Friefeld, *The First Migrants,* 201–6; Guenther, "The Empire Builders," 184–5.

22   Edwards and Friefeld, *The First Migrants,* 197–203; *Custer County Chief,* February 28, 1908.

23   Nebraska State Historical Society, "Solomon D. Butcher Collection." Last accessed May 14, 2025, https://history.nebraska.gov/collection_section/solomon-d-butcher-collection/.

24   Edwards and Friefeld, *The First Migrants*; Catherine Meehan Blount and Joyce Ann Gray, interviews by Mikal Brotnov Eckstrom, May 15, 2016, Black Homesteading Project, Center for Great Plains Studies, University of Nebraska. In her interview, Blount expressed that the story of Black homesteaders shouts "we were there."

25   Henry C. Work, "Wake Nicodemus," 1864, University of Chicago Library Sheet Music Collection; Edwards and Friefeld, *The First Migrants,* 70.

26   Edwards and Friefeld, *The First Migrants,* 21–40; Richard Edwards, "African Americans and the Southern Homestead Act," *Great Plains Quarterly* 39, no. 2 (Spring 2019): 117; US Senate, 46th Congress, 2nd sess., "Report and Testimony of the Select Committee of the United States Senate to Investigate the Causes of the Removal of the Negroes from the Southern States to the Northern States" (Government Printing Office, 1880), 693.

27   Richard Edwards, Jacob K. Friefeld, and Mikal Brotnov Eckstrom, "'Canaan on the Prairie': New Evidence on the Number of African American Homesteaders in the Great Plains," *Great Plains Quarterly* 39, no. 3 (Summer 2019): 235.

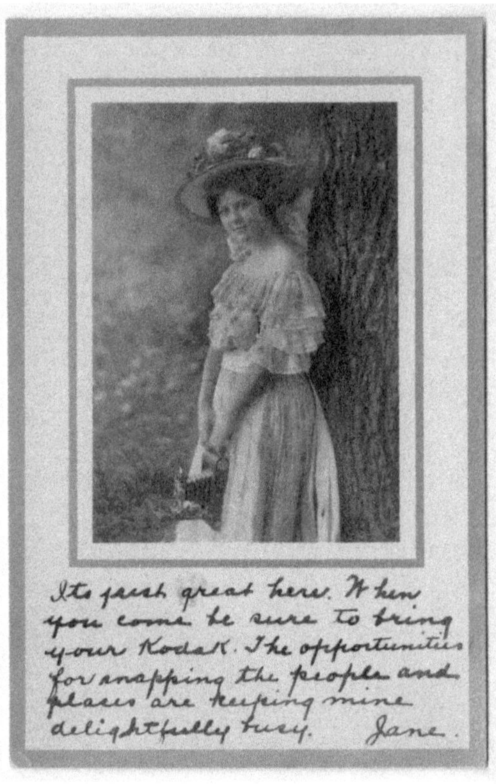

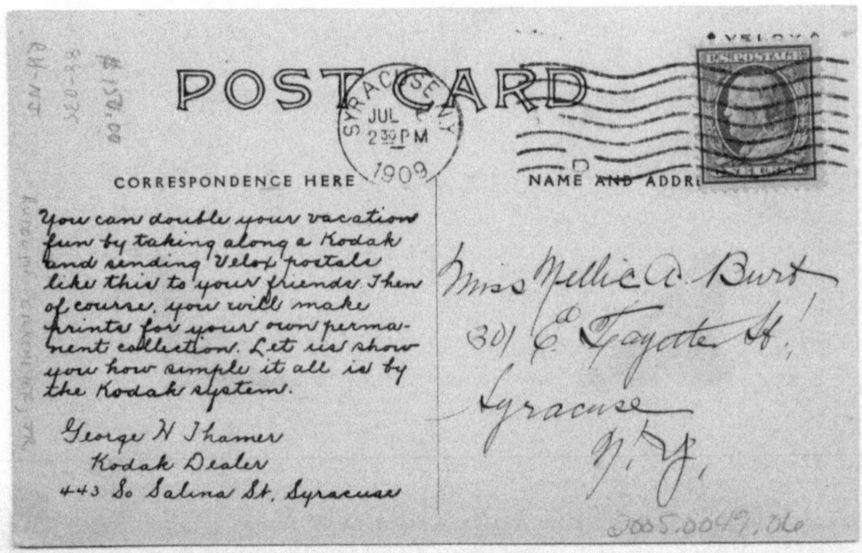

FIGURE 4.1 *A real photo postcard of Kodak Girl, "Jane," 1909. Courtesy of the Photographic History Collection, Smithsonian's National Museum of American History.*

4

Illuminating the Kodak Girl: Style and Marketing in the Gilded Age

By Shannon Perich

Sandwiched between Reconstruction and the Progressive Era, the **Gilded Age** takes its name from Mark Twain's satirical novel *Gilded Age: A Tale of Today* (1873), set against a post-Civil War backdrop of corporate greed and political corruption. From the late 1870s to the late 1890s, the country's rapid industrialization increased demands for skilled labor and lured European immigrants to America's shores. While labor unions championed the eight-hour workday and abolition of child labor, Gilded Age Americans debated a range of social issues including immigration, trust laws, Jim Crow laws, prohibition, and women's suffrage. A laissez-faire capitalism approach advocating for minimal government interference caused economic booms and busts that laid bare a widening wealth gap, particularly in the South.

American consumers benefited from the era's many technological innovations like the light bulb, telephone, and typewriter. Marketing to a growing middle-class, companies like Kodak designed cameras for amateur photographers and new industries emerged for creative photographic printing. This chapter explores the artistic legacy and gender dynamics of Kodak's wildly successful "Kodak Girl" campaign as well as photography's relationship with the environment.

Suggested Topics: Art History, Economic History, Environmental History, Gilded Age, Industrialization, Modern America, Progressive Era, Women and Sexuality

Glossary: Gilded Age, Naturalism, New Woman, Photo-Secessionists, Pictorialism, Progressive Era, Second Industrial Revolution

The photograph of "Jane," leaning against a sun-lit tree and holding a camera against her skirts, offers viewers an alternate lens into contemplating the **Gilded Age**. The casually posed young woman appears on the front of a real photocard, the fastest way to send an image and text in the early 1900s. Much like a social media advertisement today, the image and text are designed to be personal and marketed to a specific demographic. As a model, she is youthful but not excessively beautiful or dressed in overly luxurious clothing for her time period. The natural setting is a lovely yet vague, comfortable space. Her posture is relaxed, and she has stopped her activity to engage the viewer. Appealing to other young women as if she were an old friend, the postcard of "Jane" was part of a wildly successful sales campaign by Kodak that employed a professional photographer named Rudolf Eickemeyer, Jr., to target amateur photographers. The photograph blended Eickemeyer's style of photography with the company's messaging to make photography seem like a safe space for young women to occupy and be themselves.

The **Gilded Age** (1870s–1890s) was a dynamic period in which the manufactured goods mass-produced during the **Second Industrial Revolution** generated new opportunities, new wealth, and new aesthetics. Cheaper access to "luxury" products led to new ways of defining style and opulence. Thanks to labor unions and reformers like the future first woman presidential cabinet appointee, Secretary of Labor Frances Perkins, employers began decreasing working hours (especially on Sundays), which in turn increased leisure time, and with it, the opportunity for workers to spend the money they earned in new types of jobs. Factory-made cameras, mass-produced photography paper, and more stable chemical processes made photography faster and less expensive. As the volume of inexpensive photography materials rapidly expanded, so did the number of people who could make pictures. Amateurs (unskilled, casual hobbyist photographers) placed pressure, competition, and tension upon those who considered themselves professional and artistic photographers. Not only did the number of photographers grow but so did the uses of photography, including using photographs to sell photography.

Kodak's success was predicated on lowering the barrier to photography. In 1888, Kodak introduced a $25 pre-loaded camera with the slogan, "You push the button, we do the rest!" A new type of photographer who didn't want to mess with developing negatives and printing for themselves could now take snapshots. Kodak specifically wanted to tap into one of the most rapidly emerging consumers of the Gilded Age—working- and middle-class white women—who only recently gained a small amount of financial independence. Starting in 1893, Kodak began creating advertisements featuring the "Kodak Girl," a young, fashionable woman teeming with carefree adventure and independence. Further lowering the technical and financial barrier, in 1900, they introduced a simple Brownie camera specifically marketed to women and children for $1. Within five years, Kodak sold 1.2 million Brownies and placed cameras in the hands of one-third of the US population.[1]

"Kodak Girl" was one of the most successful marketing campaigns in history. She evolved throughout the decades alongside shifting definitions of beauty, and the company formally retired the advertisements in the 1970s. "Jane" was manufactured as part of a campaign to appeal to the working women demographic. She was an amalgam of a real woman photographer, Frances Benjamin Johnston, and the "Gibson Girl," a popular illustration of a young woman who personified femininity and social progress. As the postcard suggested, with the right camera, these women could exercise their creativity as amateur photographers. They, too, could be "Jane."

"Jane" offers a lens into how consumerism and advertising shaped the daily lives of millions of Americans. She also offers a lens into Gilded Age gender dynamics and the environmental considerations of photography.

About the Photographers

"Jane" was photographed by Rudolf Eickemeyer, Jr., a former amateur photographer himself.[2] In many ways, Eickemeyer epitomizes the opportunity for economic advancement made possible by the Gilded Age. The son of an immigrant hat-maker, Eickemeyer began as an amateur photographer in Yonkers by documenting his father's inventions and patent submissions. He carefully honed his skills through local camera clubs and eventually became a portrait photographer on Fifth Avenue and highly sought after by New York City's wealthiest residents.

Eickemeyer's particular photographic approach was part of a movement called **Pictorialism**, which is broadly defined as a style and genre of photography in which the image harkens to painting or etching. Frequently, the photographs were soft focused and often had manipulated negatives or additional treatments to indicate the photograph was not a mechanical product, thus conveying the artist's expressive intent.

Pictorialist photographs are meticulous art, unlike the quick, hastily developed snapshots produced by cameras like the Brownie. To distinguish themselves from amateur photography, the subject matter was often associated with ancient Greece and Rome, literary, historical, and biblical references. Pictorialist imagery often also featured costumed models and sentimental tropes associated with family, gender, class, and race in staged settings. Pictorialism began in the late 1900s and was variously championed, ridiculed, and redefined until about the First World War. However, the vestiges of sentimentality and handwork associated with the movement permeated amateur art photography throughout the twentieth century.

Camera clubs and photography associations produced frequent exhibitions, or salons, with prizes and critiques that reinforced ideas about what a "good photograph" might look like. Many of those who participated in photographic salons were not professional photographers. They identified themselves as amateurs, or someone who does not make a living as a photographer yet has artistic skills. They may be independently wealthy or have other jobs. This definition elevates the amateur above the casual photographer, like Jane, whose photographs are unskilled and less serious. As more people entered the photographic image-making world, an art photographer might have distinguished themselves by dismissing and even casting disdain for commercial and utilitarian photography.[3]

Eickemeyer and fellow photographer-artist Alfred Stieglitz formed a duo that championed the early period of the Pictorialist movement. They were the first Americans admitted to the exclusive Brotherhood of the Linked Ring, an elite photographic society based in the United Kingdom. Stieglitz is best known for forging a space in the art world for photography. For a period, they embraced a type of pictorialism espoused by Englishman Peter Henry Emerson called **Naturalism**. Emerson lectured and published art books as well as technical manuals insisting that humans do not see the world with hard edges as cameras do; rather, people see softer shapes and shades running into each other. Prolific and strident in his serious consideration of photography-as-art, he inspired many to challenge themselves and the field to imbue more artistic style in photography.[4]

Eickemeyer and Stieglitz eventually diverged in their approach to Pictorialism. Eickemeyer's style of photography privileged beauty found in nature, people, and landscapes. Like Emerson, he valued knowing the science of photographic chemistry and lenses, in addition to elegant compositions, natural light, and high-quality reproduction (photographic and photomechanical). Stieglitz would come to see this as too ordinary, and believed it resulted in too many people making banal works that lacked artistry. Pulling away from the growing pack of amateurs and commercial photographers, Stieglitz organized and fought for the **Photo-Secessionists**. The small, elite, hand-picked cadre devoted themselves to the art of photography creating unique objects with expressiveness and mastery of materials. They challenged popular photographic conventions and formed a new definition of fine art photography that persists today.[5]

With the ubiquity of photographic sensors embedded in all sorts of handheld devices, it is hard to imagine a world in which the ability for anyone to make a photograph was novel. Kodak was among the most prominent companies seeking to put cameras, film, and photo paper into the hands of the masses. One way to get attention was direct marketing using real photo postcards like the one featuring "Jane." The front of the postcard was a gelatin silver emulsion on regular photo paper cut to the standard 3.5 x 5-inch postcard size with room on the back for a short message, an address, and a stamp. With some mail services running twice a day, it was among the fastest ways to casually send images and text together. Cameras like Jane's Autographic were designed to have negatives the size of postcards for easy printing.

The cursive script on the front of this postcard reads, "It's just great here. When you come be sure to bring your Kodak. The opportunities for snapping the people and places are keeping mine delightfully busy. Jane." Although it looks to be handwritten, the text is part of the photograph. Flipping the postcard over, it becomes clear this is an advertisement that a hopeful camera dealer sent to a woman, Miss Nellie A. Burt. The preprinted message reads, "You can double your vacation fun by taking along a Kodak and sending Velox postals like this to your friends. Then of course, you will make prints for your own permanent collection. Let us show you how simple it all is by the Kodak System. George H. Thamer, Kodak Dealer 443 So Salina St. Syracuse."

Young, white, middle-class women were the target audience for the Kodak Girl campaign because they were an emerging demographic with purchasing power and leisure. The number of colleges and land grant universities increased as did the number of them that admitted women. With education, jobs like teaching and social work gave women opportunities to move away from home. Less expensive products such as readymade fashions available in department stores, urban leisure activities, and a growing definition of youth made leaving rural areas for urban cities with new forms of independence a possibility which included decisions about how to spend money and time.[6] Kodak was eager to be in their line of sight.

Eickemeyer's photograph of Jane is only a small part of the long running, profitable Kodak Girl advertising campaign. Kodak dealers like George Thamer posted Jane and other Kodak Girls as part of a strategy to tap into young women's desire for fashion and adventure, and to drive up their sales. In 1919, two decades into its eighty-year run, Thomas Russell described to a captive audience at the London School of Economics and Political Science the impact of the campaign: "[T]he famous Kodak Girl, in her flying skirts and her stripes … actually influenced fashion at the time: women were everywhere seen in striped frocks." More than influential, Kodak Girl was profitable. A camera was a one-time purchase, but the film and paper could be purchased repeatedly, providing a continuous stream of revenue. Russell continued, "Any competent critic of Advertising could see that Kodak Limited was more desirous of selling roll-films than they were of cameras."[7] As an economic venture, the dealer from the postcard hoped to sell Miss Burt a camera, make recommendations about what paper to buy, and then suggest making multiple prints to share and keep so she keeps buying more paper. The Kodak Girl, with her style, youth, and camera, hints at a lifestyle in which young women were not only the subjects of photographs but also made, collected, and distributed them.

Studying the postcard as both a photograph and an artifact of photography is complicated. At first, it seems like there are two photographers associated with the postcard—Eickemeyer, who made the photograph and the young woman with the camera. However, it might be argued that there are actually four photographers, counting the camera dealer and the person who printed the postcard. Maybe even a fifth, if the receiver of the card purchased a Kodak camera. Each of them has a different relationship to photography and this photograph.

Photographic Materiality and Beauty

In "Sensing Pollution: Picturing 'Bad Air' in Gilded Age New York," art historian Vanessa Meikle Schulman argues that the palpable atmosphere in and around New York City played a significant role in how painters portrayed the landscape. "When it is *not* tainted, air is easily taken for granted; after all, at its most basic, the air around us is ineffable and near impossible to represent."[8] Since pictorialists were highly influenced by painters, it is not hard to make the leap that they shared the same artistic concerns.

Light altered by smoke, clouds, fog, and trees can be seen in a variety of photographs of the era. In their time, these environmental factors wrought by America's ongoing industrialization were just part of daily life. Today, we might find them picturesque and aesthetically pleasing; however, the consequences of these factors shaped not only the lived human experience but also the preservation of the photographs they produced. Sulfuric acid in the air contributed to the rapid decay of photographs, especially tarnishing the silver that makes up the dark areas of photographic paper, as with Jane's hair in the postcard. One solution to manage these detrimental environmental effects was to use platinum. Other solutions would have been to make carbon prints or photomechanical reproductions in ink. Beyond any ego that distinguished pictorialists from amateur and casual photographers, access to these more resilient materials further delineated pictorialists because of the cost, knowledge, and time they required.

Thanks to advances in chemical processing and mass production, there were two common methods for producing platinum photography during the Pictorialist period. Those seeking to create unique images would buy chemicals, mix their own solutions, and hand-coat their papers. Others purchased premade papers. Using prepared papers saved Eickemeyer time and provided consistent print quality to make multiple prints more quickly.

Sufficiently washed platinum prints would not suffer rapid environmental degradation.

Eickemeyer's reputation and financial success was built as an award-winning artist but maintained by his business acumen. He endorsed the Platinotype Company, who periodically placed his photographs in their product catalogs.[9] The Platinotype Company was founded by William Willis, whose experimentation and innovation in the 1870s and 1880s resulted in a dependable and popular platinum printing paper. With operations in London and Philadelphia, Willis would become the premiere supplier of ready-made platinum papers to amateur and fine art photographers alike.[10] Like Kodak, he used the medium to sell the product.

Platinum is a rare noble metal deposited at the edge of meteor impact zones. While found around the world, some 90 percent of the world's supply came from the Ural Mountains in Russia.[11] Willis's business records do not provide a clear path of how platinum moved from Russia to the United Kingdom and the United States, but by about 1906, an ounce of platinum became more costly than gold.[12] Not only does its rarity and cost make it a luxury item but its photographic beauty was considered of the highest quality.

World events can shape economics and by the end of the First World War, platinum from Russia became inaccessible. As platinum became more expensive and rarer, paper manufacturers created silver-based papers that looked similar to platinum prints which photography conservator Sarah Wagner describes as "faux platinum."[13] This is not unlike the difference between the haute couture worn by the robber barons' wives in Eickemeyers's portraits and more affordable department store fashions in which spin-offs of luxury items are produced in mass and worn by Kodak Girls.

Photographers ceased using the metal to make photographs for many decades until supplies became available again. Unlike their historic counterparts, contemporary photographers have a greater understanding of the sources and environmental impacts of photographic material mining.[14] When aesthetic choices and photographic processes are seen with an underpinning layer of global economics, transportation, and labor, interpretations and conceptions of Gilded Age photography become complicated in interesting ways. Extractive mining, shipping, and processing made photography complicit in environmental damage, labor abuse, and other such issues associated with the monopolies of Gilded Age businesses. Today, platinum for photography, jewelry, and industry is mined in South Africa.[15]

Eickemeyer's personal photo album contains two platinum prints of Jane and her camera. At 8 × 10 inches, the luscious paper looks and functions differently than the postcard. Platinum salts adhere to the paper fibers which means that the photographic image is in the paper not on the surface. The result is that the paper is an important part of the image-making process.

Cotton rag papers are of higher quality than wood pulp papers. Each has different fiber qualities that affect the surface, texture, and luminosity of the print. Some photographers wish to maximize exposure to get rich, warm blacks; others use a thinner paper type to increase translucence to create more luminosity in the light areas of the print. Eickemeyer's portraits of society ladies, the wives and daughters of the men who owned department stores, mining businesses, and banks, often emphasized the way light moves across and through high-quality fabrics. In Jane's portrait, the daylight filtered through the leaves is bright, but the process renders it somewhat softer as an aesthetic effect suggesting that being in nature is also pleasing.

Cameras like Jane's were designed to make real photo postcards of Americans' daily life and leisure activities. Factory fumes, the smells of so many humans, stuffy offices, and volumes of horse dung in the streets made getting out of the city on weekends a highly desirable prospect for those with the means to do so. Getting fresh air by going on walks, on hikes, and swimming was often done in small groups and organized social clubs. Photography and cycling clubs in particular were common ways to enjoy unchaperoned mixed gender activities—exactly the kind of activities worthy of printing and sharing. For a relatively low cost, these casual photographers could purchase boxes of sturdy photo paper sized to match the regulations of the US Postal Service. Making a photo postcard was easy—the paper was preprinted with postcard markings on the back and the cameras produced negatives of the same size. Many real photo postcards were sent through the mail and those in museums today still bear the marks of having been handled by the makers, postmen, and friends alike.

The photograph as an object and image changes contexts from rarified platinum print found in the photographer's album within a museum to a vernacular photographic object. As a postcard, it is one of multiple. It was produced, packaged, and shipped by Kodak employees. Camera dealers handled them, hand-wrote addresses, and licked the stamps. Mail clerks marked them with inked postmarks and sorted them for mailmen to deliver. The postcards were advertisements within a direct mail campaign, but when it moved in the recipient's hands, it became personal. Once delivered they were read, pinned to walls, kept in scrapbooks, stuck in drawers, or thrown away. Across time, it is possible a postcard could remain in personal scrapbooks and individual collections. When the postcards fell out of the original recipient's possession, they may be lost to time or find new homes within a range of collectors' interests. Real photo postcards are found in extraordinary numbers in museums, libraries, and archives. They are easily available from online auction sites, antique stores, postcard sellers, and others who sell ephemera.

Pictorialists placed a premium on beauty. Blending the style of the photographer and the depiction of Kodak Girl to represent ideas of beauty in a photograph and a definition of what it means to be a young woman was a clever visual message to the target audience of young women. This postcard is addressed to Miss Nellie A. Burt, 301 E. Fayette St., Syracuse, NY. She appears in the 1909 city directory at her business address where she offers "Chiropody [pedicures] and Manicuring/ Shampooing and Hair Dressing" from 9:00 a.m. to 6:00 p.m., though the days of the week are not listed.[16] Though Miss Burt was about forty-five years old, married, had been in business for at least sixteen years, and was decidedly outside of the Kodak Girl demographic, she may have profited as she helped women negotiate between commercial ideals and their personal style.

Much like industry beauty standards today, a tension exists between the corporate idealized Kodak girl and real women. Beginning as a manicurist 1893, she likely saw many hairstyles and fashions come and go. Perhaps, Miss/Mrs. Burt would have guided young women like the fictitious friend, Jane. Her hair style, braided down her back and tied with a large bow, points to a young teen. Yet, the scoop of the dress's collar line is a more mature style, revealing more skin. The lightly or non-corseted silhouette of the dress prevents offering a sense of the shape of her body, thus rendering her as a youthful young woman not quite moving into a full maturity. Situated between being tethered to rules and conventions and on the cusp of realizing her agency offers the viewer a question about what choices she will make for herself.

The Gibson Girl, the Kodak Girl, the New Woman

Historian Elizabeth Israels Perry coined the phrase "Men are from the Gilded Age, Women are from the **Progressive Era**."[17] Jane is a photographer's model representing a combination of commercial and cultural projections of gender that conflate real and imagined women. The Kodak Girl was born in 1893 under Kodak's advertising manager, Lewis Bunnell Jones, a man who promoted a specific definition of femininity through its marketing campaign.[18] The following year, English author and feminist Sarah Grand used the term **"new woman"** in an 1894 article launching a political movement that radicalized the way women moved in a male-dominated world, advocating for things like bicycling, physical activity, education, and becoming independent career women.[19]

The Gibson Girl emerged the same year, adding complexity to the public debate about how women should look and be perceived. Bringing a character in a story to life in *Century* magazine with pen and ink, satirist Charles Dana Gibson illustrated the "Gibson Girl." With her voluptuous S-shaped curves, she was athletic and adventurous, much like a Kodak Girl, but also fashion conscious with trademark bouffant hairstyles. Although fictitious and hand-drawn, she was among the first to set a national beauty standard.[20] Photographers such as Eickemeyer brought the Gibson Girl to life. In addition to photographing Kodak Girls, Eickemeyer created one of the first equivalents of a "pin up girl" with his photography of Evelyn Nesbit, a real-life manifestation of men's ideas of young women and beauty.

While the Kodak Girl and Gibson Girl were drawn by men, the expanding world of the New Woman empowered girls and women of all ages to take action on their own behalf. Around 1887, Frances Benjamin Johnston received a camera from a family friend, George Eastman, the owner of the Kodak Company.[21] She quickly transitioned from being a young woman who embodied much of the attitude of the Kodak Girl to a progressive woman who spent much of her time advocating for women in photography. Her 1896 self-portrait, *The New Woman*, is both a spoof on a popular stereoview of the same title and an expression of her confidence (Figure 4.2).

The politics, freedoms, and powers claimed by "the New Woman" challenged the definitions of masculinity and femininity. Backlash to New Woman politics produced a widely published comical stereoview in which an overworked and overwrought man is seen doing laundry and caring for children while a relaxed pantalooned woman smokes a cigarette and prepares to go for a bike ride.[22] Referencing that popular photograph, Johnston, with a mustache drawn over her lip, hikes up her skirts, crosses her legs in a manly way, and bares her stockinged legs. She leans forward, holding a beer stein and a cigarette as if in deep conversation in a bar. Hints to whom she might converse with are on the mantle. Among her photographic portraits of men is the Canadian poet Bliss Carman, the largest on the left.[23] He was known for his poem, *Vagabondia*, that begins "Off with the fetters/ That chafe and restrain!/ Off with the chain!/ Here Art and Letters,/ Music and wine,/ And Myrtle and Wanda,/ The winsome witches,/ Blithely combine./ Here are true witches/ … "[24] In Johnston's gender-twisting self-portrait, she asserts comfort with herself and the power she holds as a woman photographer by poking fun of the idea of what the new woman might look like.

Frances Benjamin Johnston embraced the radical idea of the new woman for herself and others. In 1897, she authored, "What a Woman Can Do With a Camera" in *The Ladies Home Journal*.[25] She picks up where Kodak wished women would stay—pursuing photography as a pleasant pastime—and

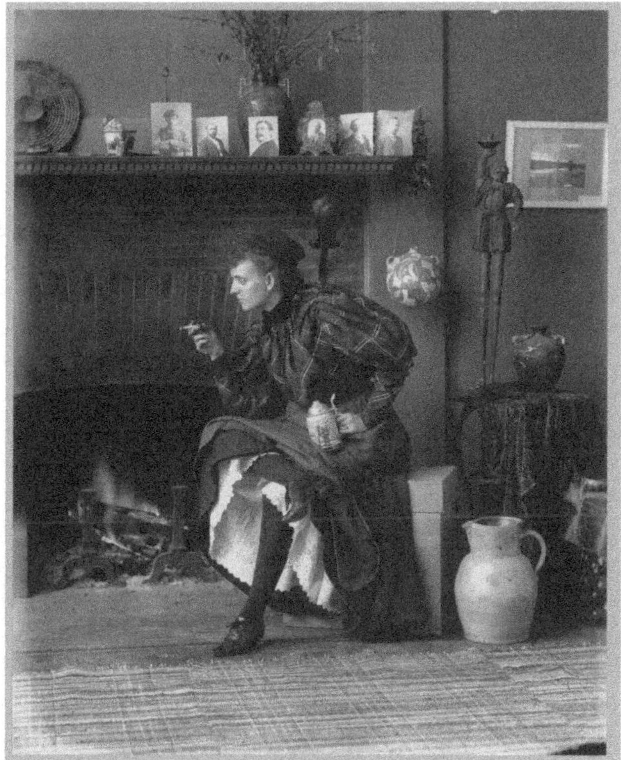

FIGURE 4.2 Self-portrait (A New Woman), *1896. Photo by Frances Benjamin Johnston, in her Washington, DC, studio. Courtesy of the Prints and Photographs Division, Library of Congress.*

offers practical skill building and business advice to become a professional photographer by drawing on their artistic sensibilities.

> … it is wrong to think of photography as purely mechanical. Mechanical it is up to a certain point, but beyond that there is great scope for individual and artistic expression. In portraiture, especially, there are so many possibility for picturesque effects—involving composition, light and shade, the study of pose and arrangement of drapery—that one should go for inspiration to such masters Rembrandt, Van Dyck, Sir Joshua Reynolds, Romney and Gainsboro, rather than the compilers of chemical formulae.[26]

Johnston was friends with George Eastman and knew well where the Kodak Girl figured into American culture. She was not content with relegating women to amateur photography. She not only forged her own career making portraits, architectural photographs, and starting a photo agency, but she also organized the first exhibition of women photographers to uplift their artist value.[27]

The vast majority of American women did not find themselves in a social, financial, or educational status to fully emulate Johnston's bravado. Yet, women across all walks of society pushed boundaries where they could. Advertising and magazines helped spread the look, debates, and ideas of the Kodak Girl, the Gibson Girl, and the New Woman. It is hard to describe just how deeply these marketing and political ideas pervaded in American society. Take for example the 1903 *Allerlei*, a yearbook from Lasell Female Seminary, a pioneering post-secondary school for women founded in 1851 outside of Boston. Highlighting their nonacademic activities on the page after the Canoe Club entry the young women proclaim "This world is full of girls, they say;/ A different type you'll meet each day./ And now I'll tell/ How at Lasell/ You find a few at work or play." The subsequent illustrations and poems tinker with the Kodak Girl archetype. They depict themselves as the Kodak Girl, Gym Girl (with wooden pins), Military Girl (with her fencing epee), Swimming Girl, Golf Girl (with her club over her shoulder), and Society Girl (with her hands demurely in her lap).[28] Class member Edna M. Sawyer, who went on to have a prolific career as an illustrator, drew the accompanying illustrations in the Gibson Girl style.[29] The Kodak Girl's attributes, fun, friendly, outdoorsy, and adventurous, often paired with other attributes to allow women to claim her identity as their own.

The same year the Nineteenth Amendment was passed, giving women the right to vote, in college senior Ruth Ewing's quote that accompanied her name, portrait, and activities in the 1920 DePauw University yearbook, she proclaimed herself, simply, "The Kodak Girl."[30] Decades later, the website creator of *Kodak Girl* also asserted that in the 1950s she identified with and was a Kodak Girl.[31] The long-running campaign provided many women an expressive space to claim as their own.

In *Kodak and the Lens of Nostalgia*, Nancy Martha West argues that the Kodak Girls' persistent youth and state of constant leisure kept women in a place of amateur photography. The text on the back of the postcard affirms that Jane's photography is for fun and to be shared with friends. As encouraged by Johnston and inspired by others, some women found their way into professional photographic circles, though not at the full rate of men. Some women were gaining more economic power and rights to vote, yet a study of women working for Kodak in 1921 reveals that they earned about half of what men made and the highest level of success they might aspire to was office secretary.[32] The extraordinary success and charm of the Kodak and Gibson Girls should be weighed against what was gained by whom. The two advertising campaigns kept "girl" in their names, while the political reformers were working to enable "the new woman."

***

Photography's role during the Gilded Age and Progressive Era is multifaceted as a mass-produced product system that fueled leisure time activities, expanded fine art, and spurred new forms of advertising. As a product of the era, the materials and images visualize values, opportunities, and debates fueled by consumers with varied economic circumstances. Sitting at those intersections, the Kodak Girl postcard provides a way to explore how deeply some women interpreted the commercial campaign as part of their identity, the role men had in describing women, and photographers who helped manifest social, political, and artistic ideas.

Discussion Questions

1   The cost and accessibility of photography changed rapidly throughout the Gilded Age and Progressive Era. How can you use photography as a lens to understand the American economy at the turn of the century?

2   Compare and contrast Jane in the postcard with Frances Benjamin Johnston in her self-portrait. How do clothes, hair, posture, setting, and photographic medium reflect or challenge ideas about class, gender, and/ or femininity?

3   What does the postcard—both the artifact and the medium—indicate about the relationship between marketing and photography?

Further Resources

Library of Congress. "The Gibson Girl's America: Drawings by Charles Dana Gibson." https://www.loc.gov/exhibits/gibson-girls-america/index.html.
Peter Palmquist Collection of Women in Photography. Beinecke Rare Books & Manuscript Library. Yale University. https://beinecke.library.yale.edu/ collections/highlights/peter-palmquist-collection-women-photography.
Turnbow, Diana. "Before Instagram, There Was Kodak." *Smithsonian American Women's History Museum* (blog), November 21, 2023. https://womenshistory. si.edu/blog/instagram-there-was-kodak.
Walker Emma E. "Pretty Paper Girls." *The Ladies Home Journal* 25, no. 10 (September 1906): 25. https://archive.org/details/sim_ladies-home-journal_1906-09_23_10/page/4/mode/2up.

Notes

1 Nancy Martha West, *Kodak and the Lens of Nostalgia* (University Press of Virginia, 2000), 41.

2 Rudolf Eickemeyer, Jr. *Jane*, real photo postcard, catalog number 2005.0049.000, Photographic History Collection, Smithsonian's National Museum of American History. This is not Eickemeyer's only advertisement for Kodak. Another, "Take a Kodak With You," is in the NMAH Eickemeyer Collection. The original photograph is catalog number 76.0.27 and the published advertisement is catalog 76.29.118. Several others can also be found in his collections in Hudson River Valley Museum.

3 Ronald Roon, "Three Factors in American Pictorial Photography," *American Amateur Photographer* 15, no. 8 (August 1904): 346.

4 Ian Jeffery, "Peter Henry Emerson," in *The Golden Age of British Photography*, ed. Mark Haworth-Booth (Aperture, 1984), 154–6.

5 Sarah Greenough, *Modern Art and America: Alfred Stieglitz and His New York Galleries* (National Gallery of Art, 2000), 23–5.

6 Joel Schrock, *The Gilded Age* (Greenwood Press, 2004).

7 Thomas Russell, *Commercial Advertising: Six Lectures at the London School of Economics and Political Science (University of London)* (G.P. Putnam's Sons, 1919), 103–4.

8 Vanessa Meikle Shulman, "Sensing Pollution: Picturing 'Bad Air' in Gilded Age New York," *Panorama* 9, no. 2 (Fall 2023): 3.

9 Rudolf Eickemeyer, Jr., *Records of Films, Photographs, and Negatives.* Catalog number PG.004135.B041, Photographic History Collection, Smithsonian's National Museum of American History.

10 Mike Ware, "The Technical History and Chemistry of Platinum and Palladium Printing," in *Platinum and Palladium Photographs: Technical History, Connoisseurship, and Preservation*, ed. Constance McCabe (American Institute for Conservation of Historic and Artistic Works, 2017), 46–83.

11 Elfric Drew Ingall, *Mineral Resources of Canada: Bulletin No. 1, Platinum* (S.E. Dawson, 1903), 12–8.

12 James W. Wade, *Mining Methods and Costs at Tintic Standard Mine, Tintic District, Utah* (Department of Commerce, United States Bureau of Mines, 1930), 63.

13 Sarah S. Wagner, "Manufactured Platinum and Faux Platinum Papers, 1880s–1920s," in *Platinum and Palladium Photographs: Technical History, Connoisseurship, and Preservation*, ed. Constance McCabe (American Institute for Conservation of Historic and Artistic Works, 2017), 144–83.

14 Siobhan Angus, *Camera Geologica: An Elemental History of Photography* (Duke University Press, 2024).

15 Angus, *Camera Geologica.*

16 *The Syracuse Directory* (Sampson & Murdock, 1909), 1156. Nellie A. Burt first appears in the *Boyd's Syracuse Directory* (Wolcott & West, 1893),

316. The 1920 Census indicates her birth date as 1864, which makes her approximately forty-five years old when she received this postcard. See "Syracuse Ward 19, Onondaga, New York," *1920 United States Federal Census*, Roll T625_1249, 9A E.D. 228. Records of the Bureau of the Census, Record Group 29, National Archives, Washington, DC.

17 Elisabeth Israels Perry, "Men Are from the Gilded Age, Women Are from the Progressive Era," *The Journal of the Gilded Age and Progressive Era* 1, no. 1 (2002): 25–48.

18 West, *Kodak and the Lens of Nostalgia*, 24.

19 Sarah Grand, "The New Woman," *The North American Review* 158, no. 450 (1894): 610–9.

20 Martha H. Patterson, *Beyond the Gibson Girl: Reimagining the American New Woman, 1895–1915* (University of Illinois Press, 2005).

21 Maria Ausherman, "Frances Benjamin Johnston's Legacy in Black and White," *CRM: The Journal of Heritage Stewardship* 4, no. 2 (Summer 2007): 29–49.

22 *The New Woman—Wash Day*, Strohmeyer & Wyman, ca. 1897. Library of Congress Prints and Photographs Division, Washington, DC.

23 Susan Turner-Lowe, "The Pride and Practice of Frances B. Johnston," *Verso* (blog), June 6, 2023. Last accessed February 17, 2025, https://huntington.org/verso/pride-and-practice-frances-b-johnston.

24 Bliss Carman and Richard Hovey, *Songs from Vagabondia* (Small, Maynard, 1894), 1.

25 Frances Benjamin Johnston, "What a Woman Can Do with a Camera," *The Ladies' Home Journal* (September 1897): 6–7.

26 Johnston, "What a Woman Can Do with a Camera," 6.

27 In 1900, Frances Benjamin Johnson organized an exhibition of pictorialist works by American women. It was seen in Paris, France, and St. Petersburg, Russia. The intrepid historian Peter Palmquist spent his life's work bringing women photographers out of history and into the foreground. Griffith Bronwyn, et al., *Ambassadors of Progress: American Women Photographers in Paris, 1900–1901* (Library of Congress, 2001).

28 *Allerlei '03: Volume X* (Lasell Female Seminary, 1902), 62–8. Last accessed February 17, 2025, https://archive.org/details/allerlei1903unse/page/62/mode/2up. For more on the history of Lasell, see "Lasell: Rich Past, Bright Future," Lasell University. Last accessed February 17, 2025, https://www.lasell.edu/discover-lasell/facts-figures-and-faces/lasells-history.html.

29 Edna M. Sawyer later married Richard McGill and became a commercial artist and painter in California, including the May 1915 cover for *Sunset* magazine. Edan Milton Hughes, *Artists in California, 1786–1940: L-Z* (Crocker Art Museum, 2002), 747; "Mrs. McGill, Noted Portrait Painter, Dies in Hospital," *Oakland Tribune*, August 21, 1929; and Edna M. Sawyer, "The War Dance," *Sunset: The Magazine of the Pacific and All of the Far West*, May 1915.

30 B. Ralph Jones, ed., *The Mirage Yearbook* (DePauw University, 1920), 253.

31 Martha Cooper, "Kodak Girls," *KodakGirl.com*. Last accessed February 17, 2025, https://kodakgirl.com/kodakgirlsframe.htm.

32 Kate Fogle, "Women at Work: 'At Kodak Heights' and Female Employment in the 1920s," *Kodak Canada: The Early Years (1899–1939) Exhibition*. Last accessed February 17, 2025, https://kodakcanada.omeka.net/exhibits/show/kodak-canada–the-early-years/women-at-work–the-changing-oc.

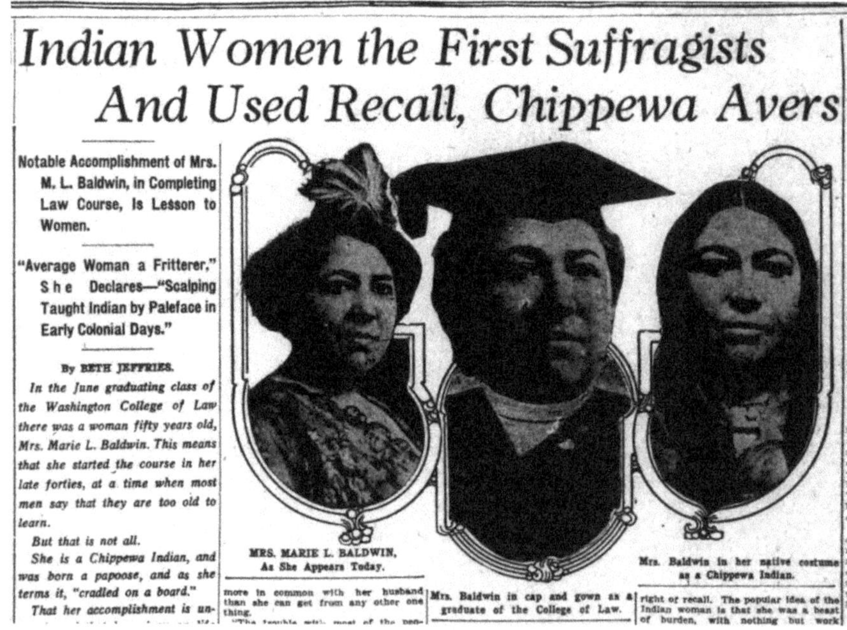

FIGURE 5.1 *Three portraits of Marie Bottineau Baldwin, originally published in* The Washington Times, *August 3, 1914. Digitized by Chronicling America. Courtesy of the Library of Congress.*

5

Native American Women and the Politics of Portraiture at the Turn of the Twentieth Century

By Cathleen D. Cahill

At the turn of the twentieth century Native American cultures, **sovereignty**, and traditions faced sustained attack by federal policies that sought to destroy them. Policymakers drew a contrast between "modern Americans" and "primitive Indians" forming stereotypes that were reflected in clothing, hairstyle, and even perceived intelligence. Imagery of Indians that proliferated in anthropology, art, literature, the built environment, entertainment, and myriad other aspects of American culture reinforced these ideas.

Women's suffrage is one of the most substantial accomplishments from the **Progressive Era** (1890–1920s). While the right to vote largely benefitted white women, African American, Asian American, Native American, and Latina women were vital to sustaining the movement's political momentum. This chapter explores how Marie Bottineau Baldwin (Turtle Mountain Chippewa and French) strategically used self-presentation in her clothing and portraiture to change public opinion about Native communities and their fight for political rights. By engaging with Americans' expected images of Indians, Bottineau Baldwin subverted their stereotypes and instead presented a vision of modern Native peoples and nations with bold plans for the future.

Suggested Topics: Indigenous History, Intersectionality, Interwar Period, Modern America, Progressive Era, Suffrage, Women and Sexuality

Glossary: Allotment Act, Assimilation, Boarding Schools, Respectability Politics, Society of American Indians (SAI), Sovereignty, Suffragists

At the turn of the twentieth century, Marie Louise Bottineau Baldwin, a woman of French and Indigenous heritage of the Turtle Mountain Chippewa (or Ojibwe) Nation, deliberately posed for a series of photos and distributed them to interested parties. In 1914, Bottineau Baldwin gave all three photos to Washington reporter Beth Jefferies. They offered different visions of her: as a fashionable turn-of-the-century woman, a college graduate, and a traditional-looking Native woman with braids over each shoulder. Jefferies used all the photos in her article "Indian Women First Suffragists and Used Recall Chippewa Avers." The headline claimed a modern suffragist identity for Native women even as Bottineau Baldwin appeared in one photo in her regalia. This may have confused her audience who might have wondered if she was a "modern" woman or a "primitive" Indian? Why would Bottineau Baldwin distribute all three photographs? Which one represented her "real" identity?

Federal Assimilation Policy

To understand Bottineau Baldwin's deliberate choices, it is important to know some background about what her audiences expected.[1] At the turn of the twentieth century the broader American public believed that "Indians," as they would have called them, were disappearing.[2] While many Americans would have attributed this to their belief that Native Americans were incapable of surviving the rapid progress of modern society, in fact the federal government's policies were bent on destroying Native cultures.

Native nations are sovereign entities that preexisted European contact and the formation of the United States. After the American Revolution, the federal government continued to acknowledge this **sovereignty** by negotiating treaties—agreements bound by international law.[3] That changed after the Civil War. In 1872, as the US Army was fighting many of those nations and forcing them onto reservations, Congress ended diplomatic relations with Native governments and instead began to treat individual Native people as legal "wards of the government," unfit for full US citizenship. Although the federal government stopped recognizing tribal governments, Native people did not.[4]

To raise up these supposedly "uncivilized" wards, the government created a policy known as **assimilation**. It tasked the Office of Indian Affairs (OIA, later the Bureau of Indian Affairs) with implementing the policy. Designed to destroy Indigenous communities and assimilate them into the body of American citizenry, assimilation relied on three broad policies: breaking up tribally held land, the development of boarding schools, and a series of laws prohibiting cultural practices. Once Native people had been "civilized," policymakers would bestow US citizenship on them.[5]

Congress passed the **Allotment Act** (also known as the Dawes Act) in 1887. Under the law, the government surveyed and divided communally held reservation lands into individually held parcels. They then returned the "excess" land to the public domain and sold it to non-Natives for rock bottom prices. The process used property to encourage heteronormative marriage. Married men received 160 acres; married women received none as under the laws of coverture their property belonged to their husbands. Single women and men each received 80 acres, each with the assumption that upon marriage their family would have 160, under control of the male head of household. The law stipulated that the government would hold the allotments in trust for twenty-five years after which Native people would be granted citizenship and released from government oversight. By the early twentieth century, however, this trust period was extended as policymakers instituted "competency hearings" to determine if people were fit for citizenship.[6]

Simultaneously, the government created a robust system of twenty-seven off-reservation **boarding schools** and numerous other on-reservation boarding schools to remove children from their communities and teach them to behave in a "civilized" manner. The curriculum was gendered. Boys were taught agricultural and trade skills, while girls the domestic skills necessary to run a household. Schools reinforced these assimilative measures through personal comportment and clothing. Upon arrival, students were issued new clothing and hard-soled shoes, and had their hair cut. Female students learned to sew and launder American-style clothing, with the expectation they would raise their children to wear it as well. Clothing, then, was a gauge of their progress toward "civilization," a fact that Bottineau Baldwin played with in her photographic choices.[7]

Finally, Congress used its control of reservations and Native people's status as legal wards to outlaw multiple cultural and religious practices, which included banning polygamy and religious ceremonies such as the Sun Dance. The Indian Office further restricted Native people's ability to travel without permission, and a law in 1902 even stipulated that men had to wear their hair short. Agents of the OIA controlled all aspects of Native life.[8]

Assimilation policies wrought extensive damage as Indigenous nations lost millions of acres of land previously guaranteed through treaties. Moreover, the personal pain and trauma of families and communities torn apart by child removal programs is incalculable. Still, Indigenous people persisted and resisted. They spoke out against assimilation policy, criticized the federal bureaucracy, advocated for tribal sovereignty and self-governance, and defended their cultural traditions.

The Imagery of Assimilation

Photography played a key role in the government's assimilation efforts. Because federal officials perceived cultural markers such as clothing, hair length, and building type as signs of success, they used photographs to demonstrate progress. Captain Richard Henry Pratt founded the federal government's first off-reservation boarding school in Carlisle, Pennsylvania, in 1879. He used before-and-after photos as allegories to demonstrate this transition. Pratt famously described the mission of assimilation as to "kill the Indian in him to save the man."[9] Beyond its documentary function, he saw photography as a persuasive colonial tool by which to measure assimilation and prove the program's success in a bid for continued funding.[10] The Indian Office similarly used photography as an instrument of reform aimed at adults on their reservation allotments. In the 1920s, federal agents photographed houses on reservations across the country for a project known as the US Industrial Surveys, often with a follow-up four years later for comparison. Reservation agents photographically tracked the families' "progress" toward civilization and suggested further changes.[11]

At the same time, many non-Native Americans believed that "real Indians" looked a certain way. Popular culture reinforced this perceived "authenticity" through Wild West Shows, Worlds Fairs, dime novels, and later motion pictures that presented Native people in buckskin, with feathers and blankets—generally mimicking iconography from Great Plains cultures. Those mediums suggested that "real Indians" were disappearing as America modernized through increased industrialization and growing urban populations.[12]

Non-Native audiences thus became accustomed to reading the before photographs as representing the "uncivilized" nature of Native people. "Primitive" images of Indians had captivated non-Native audiences since contact when Theodore de Bry's woodcuts of exotic "New World" scenes spread across Europe in the late 1500s.[13] During the nineteenth century, artists like Karl Bodmer and George Catlin painted thousands of images of the Native peoples of the Great Plains, many of which were purchased by the Smithsonian (founded in 1849) and later the US Bureau of Ethnography (founded in 1879).[14] Catlin, who began painting in the 1850s, believed his work would document "an interesting race of people, who are rapidly passing away from the face of the earth … who have no historians or biographers of their own." His paintings and writings helped publicize the "myth of the vanishing Indian" to a broader American public.[15]

Decades later, although Native people still had not disappeared, white Americans continued to insist that they would. Artists and government officials turned to the new technology of photography to continue these projects, following the familiar script. But the photos were hardly truthful.

Photographer Edward Curtis famously insisted that the people sitting for him have no modern accoutrements. He even brought his own collection of Indigenous clothing and props to make his photographs appear timeless, his sitters stuck in a past that was rapidly being replaced by modernity.

Curtis and others exacerbated the idea of disappearance through their framing and accompanying captions. Curtis unabashedly titled one of his photographs *The Vanishing Race—Navajo* (1904). In this now iconic photograph, a single-file line of Diné (Navajo) people on horseback ride away from the viewer. The light illuminates their blanket-wrapped shoulders and backs, shadows falling to the right of the trail. They ride toward the deep shadow of a dark cliff where they will presumably be swallowed up and disappear. Curtis used this photo as the frontispiece for his multivolume study, *The North American Indian,* adding for his reader: "the Indians as a race, already shorn of their tribal strength and stripped of their primitive dress, are passing into the darkness of an unknown future."[16]

These images and ideas about Indigenous people solidified in American political and cultural thought. Even white **suffragists** mobilized these stereotypes to argue that women were unfairly denied the right to vote. In 1893, Kansas suffragist Henrietta Wall Briggs commissioned a painting called *American Woman and Her Political Peers* for the 1893 World's Fair in Chicago. It depicts a white woman in the center of the canvas surrounded by four male figures representing different stereotypes of "legal wards," or people deemed unable to make their own decisions, including voting. In Briggs' words, they included an Idiot, a Prisoner, a Lunatic, and an Indian in a feathered headdress. White suffragists argued that they did not deserve this company. They were women, not wards.

The woman at the center of the painting was a real person. Frances Willard was the president of the Women's Christian Temperance Union (WCTU), the largest women's organization in the world at the time. Briggs chose Willard because she represented "all the womanhood of this land" with her "sweet, serene, lovely, and intellectual face."[17] Willard embodied mainstream ideas of femininity (which at the time meant white women), effectively countering stereotypes of suffragists as masculine, old, and unattractive. Willard's beauty contrasted with the wards, drawing attention to the difference between the well-known and respected Willard and the men. While the wards' disenfranchisement might seem natural to the audience, the artist used Willard to suggest that white women's exclusion from political rights was unnatural. The painting is representative of a proliferation of pro- and anti-suffrage imagery at the turn of the twentieth century. Women of color were often invisible in these images, though ideas about race and gender were central to their messages.[18]

In this political context, Native women like Marie Bottineau Baldwin, who wanted to engage in political dialogue—especially about citizenship and suffrage, faced the challenge of navigating public conversations murky with preconceptions and misconceptions about their capacity for citizenship. Many Native women wanted to retain and celebrate—not erase—their cultures and art forms. On the one hand, if they looked the part of an authentic "Indian," Native women risked tapping into a visual genre of false binaries, of "civilized" and "uncivilized," created by white Americans to justify Indigenous disenfranchisement. On the other hand, if they didn't look authentic, their white audiences would not necessarily recognize their Indigeneity and reject their message.

As suffrage supporters created images to make pro-suffrage arguments, they centered white women, often erasing the vital work of other women activists. Thus, Marie Bottineau Baldwin and other Native women came up with creative strategies to navigate these dilemmas by controlling their own imagery.

Reframing Her Image

Indigenous activists like Marie Bottineau Baldwin were well-versed in how non-Natives used anti-modern tropes to exclude them from society. By deploying their audiences' anticipated imagery, Bottineau Baldwin and her Indigenous contemporaries subverted those stereotypes and instead presented a vision of modern Native people and nations with bold plans for a future. In sharing multiple photographs—representing her Indigenous culture, as scholar, and as a stylish urban American—Bottineau Baldwin defied a single, static identity.

Bottineau Baldwin was born in 1863 near Pembina in present-day North Dakota. Her family was part of a community of people with mixed Indigenous and French descent in the Red River Valley who had long served as cultural intermediaries in the fur trade. Her immediate family later moved to St. Paul, Minnesota, where she attended Catholic and public schools. She briefly studied at the St. John's Ladies College in Winnipeg, Canada. In 1890 Bottineau Baldwin moved to Washington, DC, to work as a legal clerk for her father, J. N. B. Bottineau, an attorney for the Turtle Mountain Chippewa Nation contesting the legality of a treaty the federal government pressured the tribe into signing. She often helped her father host tribal delegations visiting DC.[19] In 1904 she became a clerk in the OIA, working in the very bureaucracy tasked with assimilating Indian people.

Bottineau Baldwin's experiences in the nation's capital helped her understand the power of self-presentation and photography. Already concerned with sovereignty rights of the Turtle Mountain Chippewa, she thought about political rights intersectionally—both as a Native person and a woman. In 1911 she helped found the **Society of American Indians** (SAI) and served as the organization's treasurer. Similar to the NAACP (founded in 1909), the SAI sought to counteract the stereotypes about Native people and convince the American public that Native people could (and did) exist in the modern world. Like Bottineau Baldwin, many of its members were well-educated and had worked in various capacities for the OIA.

Many of the members of the SAI also practiced what scholars of African American history have called **respectability politics**, encouraging members to present themselves as refined and "civilized." One officer, Arthur Parker (Seneca), wrote, "Proud of the ability of the race to advance, as they were, their clothing was that of citizenship of the great nation. There were no blankets, no feathers, no relics of the past, for these men and women were the Indians of today pleading for the future."[20] While proponents of assimilation like Richard Henry Pratt celebrated the modern in his "after" photos, SAI members had not in fact shed their identities as Native people.

Despite what officials may have thought based on their education and appearance, SAI members had strong critiques of the OIA's assimilation policies. They held annual conferences, published a magazine, and lobbied the government to end legal wardship. Many members believed US citizenship would give Native people a political voice in US governance, which they hoped to use to advocate for tribal sovereignty and treaty rights.[21]

Seemingly paradoxically, members of SAI also fought against the stereotypes of Native people as "uncivilized" by celebrating Native cultures. Bottineau Baldwin focused her advocacy on the appreciation of Native women's art. She also fought against demeaning stereotypes of Native women—especially condemning use of the derogatory word "sq***" with its sexualized overtones.[22] As in the *Washington Times* article, Bottineau Baldwin, along with her SAI colleagues Gertrude Bonnin/Zitkala-Ša (Yankton Sioux) and Laura Cornelius Kellogg (Wisconsin Oneida), made the case that Native women were treated better in their traditional cultures than white women in mainstream US culture. The SAI pointed to matriarchal power and noted that in many Indigenous cultures, women had a say in political decisions, were able to own property, had maternal rights, and could get a divorce—all things white women were unable to do. White suffragists were intrigued.[23]

Shortly after helping to organize the SAI, Bottineau Baldwin enrolled in the Washington College of Law in Washington, DC, and in 1914 became the second Native woman to earn her law degree.[24] Feminists founded the school because most law schools refused to admit women. It was a center for women's activism where Bottineau Baldwin gained the most exposure to the suffrage movement and white suffragists' ideas through the students and staff who encouraged her to join their cause.

In 1913 suffragists planned a parade in the nation's capital the same weekend as President Woodrow Wilson's inauguration. The women of the Washington College of Law were heavily involved. Organizers asked Bottineau Baldwin to create a float celebrating Native women's traditional matriarchal power. They fully expected Bottineau Baldwin to appear as she does in the photograph on the right of Jeffries' article—her hair in braids, wrapped in a blanket, and adorned with Native jewelry. They were so sure that a similar image circulated with announcements about her participation, but she declined to create a float or wear what the newspaper described as her "native costume." Instead, Bottineau Baldwin chose to march with the lawyers who wore caps and gowns, as she does in the middle picture.[25]

Bottineau Baldwin carefully used photography to both engage and undermine the expectations of her audience. She began distributing the third image in Jeffries' series by 1910 when it ran with an article titled "Indian Woman Works for Uncle Sam," a headline designed to raise audiences' curiosity. Again, she also gave the reporter a second photograph of herself with a modern hairstyle, wearing a high-necked blouse and chain necklace. In the interview, Baldwin insisted on her identity as *both* a Native woman, and a modern one. The interviewer reported, "While thoroughly cultured and, as she laughingly expressed it, 'quite civilized' … she is an Indian, all the same, as she proudly declared." She described her childhood, emphasizing its positive aspects: her physical agility, her relationship with her "full blood" grandmother, and Ojibwe children's stories that taught valuable life lessons. She lamented, however, that with few Ojibwe speakers in Washington, her fluency had grown rusty. She described it as "a disgrace" and "humiliating," descriptors that refused the positive narrative of assimilation otherwise advocated by her employer. At no point did she distance herself from her Native identity, instead describing how her clan relationships continued to connect her to other Ojibwe people.[26]

Bottineau Baldwin also directly critiqued American artists' inaccurate portrayal of Native women in headdresses or with feathers in their hair. "I cannot imagine where the illustrators get their idea of female Indian head dresses," she stated. The article seemed to replicate Pratt's before-and-after photos, from Bottineau Baldwin's birth in "the wilderness" through her move to the nation's capital where she worked for the OIA. But she was far from a hapless victim of the OIA's assimilationist agenda. Instead, in this and other articles, she left readers with the image of a proud woman who could simultaneously maintain her culture and enjoy modern experiences, like flying in airplanes.[27]

Bottineau Baldwin used similar rhetoric in her interview with Jefferies, identifying as a modern suffragist and claiming that Native women were ahead of their white sisters in this regard. The three images she chose to give Jefferies challenged the government's narrative of progression toward "civilization." In offering the reporter all three options, she rejected a singular identity; she contained multitudes. Someone, perhaps Jefferies or her editor, laid out the photos so that reading from left to right, as the common American reader would, the transformation was from modern dress to regalia, a reverse before-and-after.

The image of Bottineau Baldwin in regalia published with Jeffries' article is not entirely what it seems. The original photo (Figure 5.2) is a three-quarters length portrait of Bottineau Baldwin sitting with her hands on her thighs looking directly at the photographer. The beaded bracelets at the cuffs on her wrists and the circular floral patterns beaded onto the dark blanket hanging behind her highlight Native women's artistic skill, something she championed. Although she took great care with the setting, it is also clear in the original that her braids are hastily done, not tightly plaited or tied off, suggesting that she took down her hair in the studio and braided it for the portrait. None of this is visible in the printed photograph. The newspaper altered the image before going to press, cropped the beadwork and most of her body, leaving only her face.

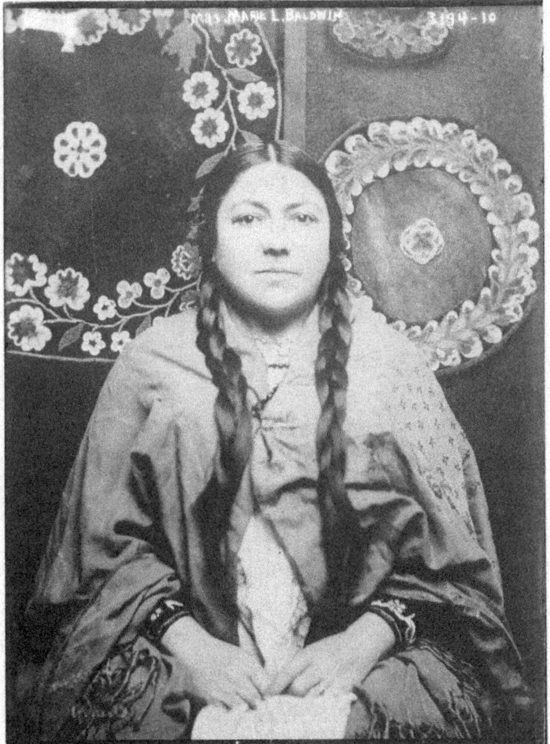

FIGURE 5.2 *Portrait of Marie Bottineau Baldwin seated with loose braids, ca. 1914. Courtesy of the Prints and Photographs Division, Library of Congress.*

In 1914 she sat for another series that even more explicitly engaged with and challenged photographic tropes. The photos are of Bottineau Baldwin and J. N. B. Hewitt, the Bottineaus' good friend at the Bureau of American Ethnology (BAE). Like Bottineau Baldwin, Hewitt was of mixed European and Indigenous descent, being Scottish and Tuscarora. He was a linguist for the BAE writing dictionaries of Native languages. They were both members of the District's Anthropological Society along with Francis LaFlesche (Omaha), who also worked for the OIA. They were all interested in Native history, but at the time it was relegated to the fields of anthropology and ethnology, so that is where they did their work and shared their ideas.[28] As a result, they were quite familiar with contemporary anthropological ideas (and misunderstandings) about Indians.

In 1914, the friends decided to create their own images challenging those ideas. De Lancey W. Gill, a photographer for the BAE and Hewitt's coworker, took the photos. During his four decades at the BAE, Gill took between 2,000 and 3,000 photographs of Native people, more "than all his predecessors combined."[29] Many of those were of Native delegates visiting the capital, like those hosted by the Bottineaus during their time in Washington. Historian Joseph Genetin-Pilawa studied the long history of portraiture of Native delegations, first as paintings and later photographs, displayed in federal buildings and museums. He argues that while these images served one purpose for white Americans, Native peoples often visited the portraits to see their ancestors who fought for their rights in the capital before them.[30]

In one of Bottineau Baldwin's sittings, she poses in an "Indian" outfit. Her hair seems as if it was unpinned from an updo style so that her braids fall over her chest. While she has a plain blanket wrapped around her shoulders her modern dress is still visible underneath. She wears no jewelry except for a wedding ring and a gold band on her left hand. In two of the photos, Bottineau Baldwin sits alone: one shot in profile, one facing the camera. These were standard anthropological poses from the time, which sought to categorize people of the world by their phrenology, or head shape. Bottineau Baldwin certainly knew this convention.

In another, the mysteries of Bottineau Baldwin's motives deepen. She sits in the blanket with her braids, while Hewitt stands next to her in a suit, vest, and bowtie, his watch fob visible. He sports small wire glasses, and his hair is cut short in the western style. An unwitting observer may have assumed that she was Native, and he was white. I have not found this image published anywhere. Perhaps she and Hewitt were merely playing with the genre, leaving this joke winking at us from the federal archives.[31]

All playfulness aside, Bottineau Baldwin deployed her image seriously and deliberately. During President Woodrow Wilson's administration, the Civil Service Commission began requiring employees to submit photographs to more easily eliminate African American applicants.[32] When asked to submit her photograph, Bottineau Baldwin did not choose her Victorian dress or graduation gown, but instead proffered a portrait in celebration of Indigenous art. She appears in close profile, visible from her shoulders up. The side angle emphasizes her braided hair and the long dentalium shell earrings that cascade from her earlobes over her shoulder and down her chest. She wears a buckskin dress with elaborate beading around her shoulders and across her chest.[33] This was a striking choice for her personnel file for the very federal agency responsible for attempting to assimilate Native peoples and destroy their cultures.[34]

Some of her attire may have come from her extensive art collection, which offered a rebuke to the idea that Native cultures had no value. Described as a "remarkable collection of Indian articles, representing a variety of handiwork known to the American aborigines," Bottineau Baldwin built her collection over the course of thirty years. It included many pieces made by her "relatives, friends or ... family." She also purchased a collection of Southwestern art from "a Miami Indian, who at the time was an agent traveling throughout the Indian reservations of the country." While non-Natives often collected Indian art because of the sense that the artists would soon die taking their skills with them, Bottineau Baldwin's collection celebrated their craftsmanship and her relationship to the artists.[35]

She certainly appreciated contemporary fashion too. In a 1928 interview, Bottineau Baldwin appeared in a dropped waist flapper style dress. She described these modern styles as "wonderful and so sensible" and admired the colors.[36] Still, it was her portraits with long braids and vibrant shawls that garnered the most attention and invitations for public speaking and interviews. In her talks, she challenged her audience's expectations about Native women by telling them about her own achievements as well as the many positive aspects of Native cultures. And, when she talked, people listened.

***

Marie Bottineau Baldwin and her Indigenous contemporaries demonstrated incredible savvy through their self-presentation.[37] The photographs that they created remain in our archives in defiance of the thousands of images of "Indians" created by non-Native people.[38] Their carefully deployed imagery opened doors to new and bigger audiences. When they spoke, they defended Native people's cultural traditions and sovereignty. They insisted that federal treaty rights be upheld and demonstrated they could maintain their cultural identities while simultaneously living as modern American citizens.

The Indigenous feminist strategy of using clothing and self-presentation used by Bottineau Baldwin and a number of her contemporaries made powerful political statements about the ongoing present and future of Indigenous cultures. It continues today through Native women like former Secretary of the Interior Deb Haaland (Laguna Pueblo), one of the first of two Native women elected to US Congress in 2018. In 2020, President Joseph R. Biden appointed Representative Haaland as Secretary of the Interior (a role that oversees the Bureau of Indian Affairs), making her the first Native person to serve as a cabinet secretary. During her swearing in, Haaland wore a ribbon skirt created by an Indigenous designer (Aiukli Designs). Haaland often deploys her fashion choices to make statements about Indigenous cultures. Like Bottineau Baldwin, her actions emphasize her connections to the past and the ongoing vibrancy of Indigenous traditions, a powerful message aimed at her non-Native audiences.

But Haaland also had a message for a Native audience. As she asserted regarding her choice to wear a Pueblo dress with a red belt woven over a century ago, "I just felt like I should represent my people. I thought it would just make some folks proud out there."[39]

Discussion Questions

1   How does Marie Bottineau Baldwin's activism complicate our understanding of the suffrage movement in the early twentieth century?

2   In what ways did Bottineau Baldwin use photography to play with and challenge stereotypes about Indigenous peoples? Was she effective?

3   With the ubiquity of digital cameras and social media platforms today, there many ways for people to assert their identities. Do you think they do so with as much intention as Bottineau Baldwin? Why or why not?

Further Resources

Cahill, Cathleen. *Recasting the Vote: How Women of Color Transformed the Suffrage Movement*. University of North Carolina Press, 2020.

Dickinson College. *Carlisle Indian School Digital Resource Center*. https://carlisleindian.dickinson.edu/.

Lange, Allison K. *Picturing Political Power: Images in the Women's Suffrage Movement*. University of Chicago Press, 2020.

Wilbur, Matika. *Project 562: Changing the Way We See Native America*. Ten Speed Press, 2023.

Zotigh, Dennis. "A Lot of Our Traditional Clothing, We Had to Fight to Keep'— Fashion Designer Norma Baker-Flying Horse." *Smithsonian Magazine*, March 29, 2019.

Notes

1 Philip J. Deloria, *Indians in Unexpected Places* (University Press of Kansas, 2004).

2 Like all things, historical terms used to refer to groups of people change over time. Although "Indian" was the term used in the period being studied, I use Indigenous, Native, Native American, or American Indian interchangeably. I only use "Indian" when it appears in a quotation, title, or in reference to cultural ideas. When known, I use individuals' specific tribal affiliation(s).

3 The United States has ratified 374 treaties with Native nations. See the Smithsonian's National Museum of the American Indian's exhibit on treaties, *Nation to Nation: Treaties between the United States and Native Nations.* Last accessed June 11, 2024, https://americanindian.si.edu/nationtonation/.

4 Francis Paul Prucha, *The Great Father: The United States Government and American Indians* (University of Nebraska Press, 1984); and David E. Wilkins and K. Tsianina Lomawaima, *Uneven Ground: American Indian Sovereignty and Federal Law* (University of Oklahoma Press, 2001).

5 David Wallace Adams, *Education for Extinction: American Indians and the Boarding School Experience, 1875–1928* (University Press of Kansas, 1995).

6 Prucha, *The Great Father*, 879–85.

7 Adams, *Education for Extinction*; Brenda J. Child, *Boarding School Seasons: American Indian Families, 1900–1940* (University of Nebraska Press, 1998); and Cahill, *Federal Fathers and Mothers: A Social History the United States Indian Service, 1869–1933* (University of North Carolina Press, 2011).

8 Michael McNally, *Defend the Sacred: Native American Religious Freedom beyond the First Amendment* (Princeton University Press, 2020).

9 Adams, *Education for Extinction*, 52.

10 Brian Dippie, "Photographic Allegories and Indian Destiny," *Montana: The Magazine of Western History* 42, no. 3 (Summer 1992): 40–57.

11 Cody White, "Homes on the Range," *Genealogy Notes* 49, no. 3 (Fall 2017); Rebecca S. Wingo, *Framed: Housing and Photography on the Crow Reservation* [manuscript in progress]; and Thomas Carter, Edward Chappell, and Timothy McCleary, "In the Lodge of the Chickadee: Architecture and Cultural Resistance on the Crow Indian Reservation, 1884–1920," *Perspectives in Vernacular Architecture* 10 (2005): 97–111.

12 Robert F. Berkhofer, *The White Man's Indian: Images of the American Indian from Columbus to the Present* (Vintage Books, 1979); L.G. Moses, *Wild West Shows and the Images of American Indians, 1883–1933* (University of New Mexico Press, 1999); and Deloria, *Indians in Unexpected Places*.

13 Lauren Kilroy-Ewbank, "Inventing 'America': The Engravings of Theodore de Bry," *Smarthistory*, May 18, 2019. Last accessed September 19, 2024, https://smarthistory.org/engravings-theodore-de-bry/.

14 C. Joseph Genetin-Pilawa, "The Indians' Capital City: Diplomatic Visits, Place, and Two-Worlds Discourse in Nineteenth-Century Washington, DC," in *Beyond Two Worlds: Critical Conversations on Language and Power in Native*

North America, ed. James Joseph Buss and C. Joseph Genetin-Pilawa (SUNY Press, 2014), 117–36.

15 George Catlin, *Illustrations of the Manners, Customs, and Condition of the North American Indians, Vol. 1* (H.G. Bohn, 1848), 3.

16 Edward S. Curtis, "The Vanishing Race—Navaho," ca. 1904. Library of Congress Prints and Photographs Divisions, LCCN 2004672871. See also Samuel Redman, *Prophets and Ghosts: The Story of Salvage Anthropology* (Harvard University Press, 2021), 121–54.

17 For more on this painting, see Kansas Historical Society, "American Woman and Her Political Peers Painting," November 1999. Last accessed May 7, 2024, https://www.kshs.org/kansapedia/american-woman-and-her-political-peers-painting/10294. On the WCTU, see Ruth Bordin, *Women and Temperance: The Quest for Power and Liberty* (Temple University Press, 1981).

18 Allison Lange, *Picturing Political Power: Images in the Woman Suffrage Movement* (University of Chicago Press, 2020). For Native women, see Cathleen Cahill, *Recasting the Vote: How Women of Color Transformed the Suffrage Movement* (University of North Carolina Press, 2020), 71–82; and Rabia S. Belt, *Disabling Democracy in America: Mental Incompetence, Citizenship, Voting, and the Law, 1819–1920* (Cambridge University Press, forthcoming).

19 Herman Viola, *Diplomats in Buckskin: A History of Indian Delegations in Washington City* (University of Oklahoma Press, 1995); and Genetin-Pilawa, "The Indians' Capital City," 117–35.

20 Arthur C. Parker, "The Awakened American Indian," *Quarterly Journal of the Society of American Indians* 2, no. 4 (October–December 1914): 274. On respectability, see Evelyn Brooks Higginbotham, *Righteous Discontent: The Women's Movement in Black Baptist Church, 1880–1920* (Harvard University Press, 1994) and Treva Lindsey, *Colored No More: Reinventing Black Womanhood in Washington, DC* (University of Illinois Press, 2017).

21 Hazel W. Hertzberg, *The Search for an American Indian Identity: Modern Pan-Indian Movements* (Syracuse University Press, 1981). See also Chadwick Allen and Beth Piatote, eds., "The Society of American Indians and Its Legacies," *Studies in American Indian Literatures* 25, no. 2 and *American Indian Quarterly* 37, no. 3 (2013).

22 Arthur C. Parker, "The Word 'Squaw' an Out-of-Date Expression," *The Quarterly Journal of the Society of American Indians* 2, no. 4 (October–December 1914): 256–7. This is something Native women have continued to fight against. For example, Secretary of the Interior Deb Haaland (Laguna Pueblo) established a program to rename landmarks on federal land with that slur in their toponym. See Department of the Interior, "Interior Department Completes Removal of "Sq_ _ _" from Federal Use," September 8, 2022. Last accessed October 3, 2024, https://www.doi.gov/pressreleases/interior-department-completes-removal-sq-federal-use.

23 Sally Roesch Wagner, *Sisters in Spirit: Haudenosaunee (Iroquois) Influence on Early American Feminists* (Native Voices, 2001).

24 Kim Dayton, "'Trespassers, Beware!' Lyda Burton Conley and the Battle for Huron Place Cemetery," *Yale Journal of Law and Feminism* 8, no. 1 (1996): 1–30. Although the Washington College of Law admitted Native women,

it refused to admit Black students until later in the century. Virginia G. Drachman, *Sisters in Law: Women Lawyers in Modern American History* (Harvard University Press, 1998), 152–5.

25 See "Equal Suffrage Among Indians," *Los Angeles Times*, January 31, 1913.

26 "Indian Woman Works for Uncle Sam," *Washington Evening Star*, December 4, 1910.

27 "Indian Woman Works for Uncle Sam." A similar story appeared in "Indian Girl's Rise," *The Democrat-Herald*, March 10, 1911; and Gretchen Smith, "Indian Collection Work of 30 Years," *Washington Evening Star*, April 15, 1929.

28 Bottineau Baldwin and Hewitt cowrote her father's obituary when he passed in 1911. See Cahill, *Recasting the Vote*, 102. LaFlesche wrote his childhood autobiography, *The Middle Five* (1900) and worked with white ethnologist, Alice Fletcher, on many publications. See Joan Mark, *A Stranger in Her Native Land: Alice Fletcher and the American Indians* (University of Nebraska Press, 1988).

29 James R. Glenn, "De Lancey W. Gill, Photographer for the Bureau of American Ethnology," *History of Photography* 7, no. 1 (January–March 1983): 7–22.

30 Genetin-Pilawa, "The Indians' Capital City," 117–36.

31 The series of photographs are in the Smithsonian's Anthropological Archives.

32 Erik S. Yellin, *Racism in the Nation's Service: Government Workers and the Color Line in Woodrow Wilson's America* (University of North Carolina Press, 2016), 157–62.

33 In a 1929 interview the reporter described one dress in her collection as "entirely made of tiny shells, or 'wampum,'" that was one of the oldest items in her collection. Smith, "Indian Collection Work of 30 Years."

34 Personnel File of Marie Louise Bottineau Baldwin, National Personnel Records Center, St. Louis, MO.

35 Smith, "Indian Collection Work of 30 Years." On collecting, see Elizabeth Hutchinson, *The Indian Craze: Primitivism, Modernism, and Transculturation in American Art, 1890–1915* (Duke University Press, 2009).

36 "US Workers Have Indian Ancestors: Seven Employes [sic] of Interior Department Trace Lineage to First Americans," *Washington Evening Star*, June 17, 1928.

37 See C. Daniel Redmond, "The Sartorial Indian: Zitkala-Ša, Clothing, and Resistance to Colonization," *Studies in American Indian Literatures* 28, no. 3 (Fall 2016): 52–80.

38 Tom Jones, Michael Schmudlach, Matthew Daniel Mason, Amy Lonetree, and George A. Greendeer, *People of the Big Voice: Photographs of Ho-Chunk Families by Charles Van Schaick, 1879–1942* (Wisconsin Historical Society Press, 2011), 13–22.

39 "Deb Haaland Makes History, and Dresses for It," *The New York Times*, March 19, 2021. Blackfoot actress Lily Gladstone used her outfits during the award season to highlight Indigenous designers. A *Vogue* reporter concluded, "It's a prime example of how fashion can be a powerful call-to-action." Christian Allaire, "Why Lily Gladstone's Red Carpet Style Is Oscar-Worthy," *Vogue World Paris* January, 24, 2024.

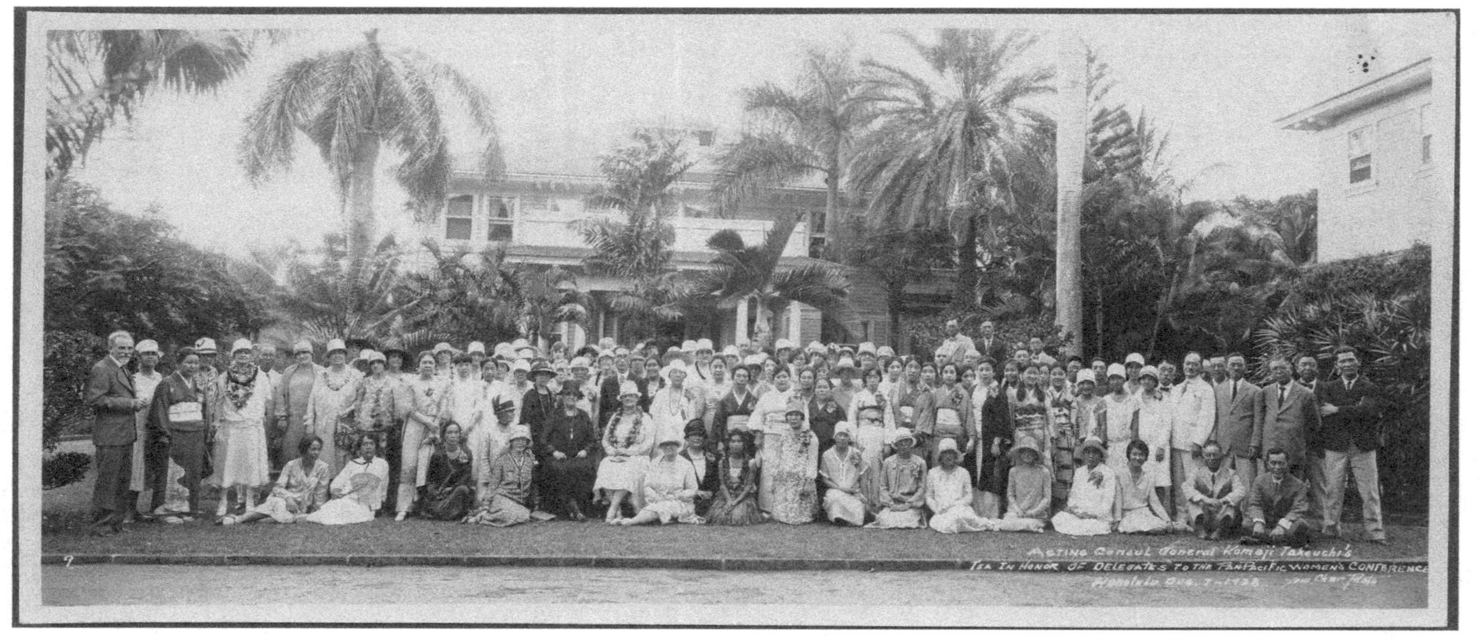

FIGURE 6.1 *Acting Consul General Komaji Takeuchi's tea in honor of the delegates from the Pan-Pacific Women's Conference, August 7, 1928. Photo by Yew Char. Courtesy of the Hocken Collections Uare Taoka o Hākena, University of Otago.*

6

The Interwar Period (1918–39): Internationalism in the Pacific

By Courtney Sato

The **Interwar Period** (1917–41) is often contrasted by the prosperity of the Roaring Twenties and the poverty of the Great Depression, bookends for important cultural moments like the birth of jazz, continued industrial modernization, and women's suffrage. This domestic focus mirrors the groundswell of American **nationalism** and isolationism that would break when Japan's attack on Pearl Harbor forced the country into the Second World War.

Discussion of **internationalism** is most often geographically centered on the Atlantic and the formation of the **League of Nations**, an intergovernmental peace organization that the United States did not join. This chapter shifts the focus to the Pacific, chronicling the development and impact of the Pan-Pacific Women's Association, a philanthropic organization populated by many of the same women who championed suffrage and other Progressive Era social reform movements. This chapter continues conversations about Indigeneity and women's activism from Chapter 5, and introduces a different kind of photographic genre: the group photograph.

Suggested Topics: Asian American History, Internationalism, Interwar Period, First World War, Progressive Era, Roaring Twenties, Women and Sexuality

Glossary: Cartes de Visite, Cultural Internationalism, Interwar Period, League of Nations, Nationalism, Transnationalism, Xenophobia

On August 7, 1928, over 100 delegates from across the Pacific convened at the Japanese Consulate in Honolulu's Nuʻuanu Valley to mark the commencement of the inaugural Pan-Pacific Women's Conference. Despite the sweltering humidity on one of the hottest days of the year, delegates diligently followed photographer Yew Char's instructions to assemble in rows.

Seated at the photograph's center were the conference leaders, including the Honorary Pan-Pacific Women's president and renowned American social reformer Jane Addams. Dressed in all black, Addams contrasted starkly with the sea of delegates dressed in white summer dresses, kimonos, Maria Clara gowns, and cheongsams. Writing in anticipation of the gathering, Conference Chair and Australian internationalist Eleanor M. Hinder noted in *The Brisbane Courier*:

> Never before in the history of this ocean has there been an opportunity for the sharing of experience of women from these countries in such numbers as are now available … Those who are watching the whole scene are convinced that in the very gathering of the national delegations, and in the coming sharing of experience, a land mark [*sic*] is approaching for women in the Pacific.[1]

With delegates from across the Pacific, many who had traveled for a week or more via steamship, this opening reception marked their participation in an experimental, yet highly prestigious, gathering of women leaders from across the region to convene on issues such as women's rights, maternal healthcare, social reform, and education.

What can Yew Char's photograph tell us about the dynamic and vital **interwar period** (1918–39) in the United States? Furthermore, what does this image reveal about the individuals in the photograph—most of whom are unidentified—and the internationalist movement that brought them together from across the Pacific? And what might this photograph allow us to explore about the very genre of the group photograph?

The interwar years—book-ended by the two world wars—are conventionally associated with the affluence and excess of the Roaring Twenties followed by the swift market collapse and the Great Depression.[2] With Char's 1928 Pan-Pacific photograph as the focal point, this chapter highlights the lesser-known history of interwar **internationalism** in the Pacific. In US history textbooks, Hawai'i and the Pacific often receive cursory attention until the December 1941 attack on Pearl Harbor and the US entry into the Second World War. This photograph recalibrates focus to the Pacific to demonstrate how social, political, and racial ideologies were meted out in the name of internationalism and feminism.

Yew's photograph documented what would be the first of many conferences for the Pan-Pacific Women's Association (PPWA). Officially incorporated in 1930, two years after its inaugural conference, the PPWA sought to enact regional reform through "the study and betterment of social conditions" while also fostering "better understanding and friendship" among women from across the Pacific.[3] Jane Addams, pictured in the center of the group, delivered her presidential keynote address at this conference. For Addams, Pacific women's internationalism offered a natural extension for the domestic progressive reform she had undertaken throughout her career to new geographic sites. Addams began her rich legacy of reform in the 1880s through her participation in social work and the women's suffrage movement, often situated as a part of the Progressive Era. Central to her efforts was a commitment to providing education and support services for children, women, immigrants, and the urban poor. In 1889, these reform efforts were most visibly realized when she cofounded Hull House in Chicago, one of the nation's most prominent settlement houses, aimed at fostering solidarity between middle- and working-class women in the pursuit of social betterment. By the 1920s, Hull House had inspired the creation of over 500 settlement houses across the country.[4] By the time Addams cofounded the American Civil Liberties Union in 1920, she was one of the most widely recognized women and social reformers in the United States.

Now at the end of her career, Addams proclaimed in her keynote that Pacific women's internationalism marked a new era of cooperation enacted at the regional level through woman-to-woman relations. Addams drew heavily on the dominant narrative of multiracial Hawai'i as a natural model for "the mutual friendliness of many races," and proof that international peace and progress were possible.[5] The strand of internationalism advanced by the Pan-Pacific Women's Conference highlighted the potential for culture and the interpersonal to rework national relations on a global scale.[6] Pan-Pacific internationalists sought to harness a "praxis of open-minded cosmopolitanism," foster an "international mind," and forge collaborative interpersonal exchange that could counteract what they perceived as the restrictive and overly formal channels of international diplomacy.[7] Furthermore, the PPWA carved out spaces for feminist exchange given that women were most often excluded from the conventionally male-dominated spaces of internationalist organizing.[8]

The Pan-Pacific conference photograph offers a framework for exploring four elements of interwar US social and cultural life. First, this chapter traces the rise of Pacific women's internationalism and the dynamic agendas that drew together social reformers, progressives, commercialists, missionaries, and scientists, demonstrating the motley assemblage of those invested in the internationalist movement. Next, the chapter invites us to reconsider the genre of the group photograph and what it reveals about a **transnational** movement, the conference photograph as a ritualized act, and how such group portraits may reveal internal hierarchies and divisions within the collective. The third section turns to the photographer, Yew Char, as an entry for understanding the broader historical context for interwar Asian American commercial and studio photography. And finally, the chapter concludes by contextualizing the Pan-Pacific Women's Conference photograph against a broader visual and material archive of interwar Pacific internationalism. In addition to the formal conference portraits, Pacific women internationalists also exchanged individual portraits (calling cards) among delegates and compiled organizational scrapbooks. These practices became affective and social conduits for shaping transnational forms of internationalist activism and belonging. They expand how we understand interwar US social and cultural life, revealing how Pacific women internationalists—often overlooked as internationalist agents—wove networks and exchanges that both reinforced and disrupted US global power.

The 1928 Pan-Pacific Women's Conference

The devastation of the First World War and the conflict waged in the name of nationalism drew many to internationalism's promise of cooperation and peace. During the interwar period, the United States vacillated between isolationist impulses and the desire to deepen international engagement. In the war's aftermath, a distinctive isolationist sentiment emerged, manifesting in the US Senate's rejection of the Treaty of Versailles and the refusal to join the **League of Nations**. Yet, this era was also characterized by diplomatic acts such as the Washington Naval Conference, which aimed to limit naval armaments and curb an arms race; the Young Plan, which sought to foster economic interdependence and diminish war incentives; and the Kellogg-Briand Pact, which sought to implement adherence to international law. The interwar years were also some of the most **xenophobic**, instituting the most racially restrictive immigration acts including the 1917 Asiatic Barred Zone Act and the 1924 Johnson-Reed Act, which codified Asian exclusion even further through a unilateral barring of Asian immigration to the United States, thereby delineating a global racial and national hierarchy through national quota systems.[9] In this way, the interwar period was characterized by contradictory impulses—at once an aspiration for pacifism and cooperation and a wariness of binding international alliances.

Most historical studies of interwar internationalism apply a Eurocentric framework through the lens of the League of Nations. By focusing instead on the Pacific as an equally critical site for internationalism, we witness a starkly different form that aligns with what historian Akira Iriye has termed **"cultural internationalism."** Cultural internationalism is rooted in the conviction that international cooperation can be attained through cultural rather than conventional diplomatic, political, or economic means. These cultural channels included international student exchanges, conferences, and the implementation of a universal language, among others. A cultural internationalist approach thus sought to counteract the extreme nationalism and militarism that precipitated the First World War, advocating instead for a stable world order grounded in cultural exchange and intellectual collaboration.[10] Internationalists believed that cultural exchange could cultivate a "world consciousness" or liberal cosmopolitan outlook.[11]

For Pacific internationalists, the US territory of Hawai'i was an ideal base for the new movement. Honolulu was championed as the "new Geneva" of the Pacific—serving as a proxy to Geneva's role as the base for European internationalism and the League of Nations.[12] In 1917, civic booster and former journalist Alexander Hume Ford founded the first Pacific internationalist organization, the Pan-Pacific Union, in Honolulu. Inspired by the formation of the League of Nations in 1920 and calls for self-determination advanced by Woodrow Wilson, Ford described the ambitions of this new organization as a "Pan-Pacific League of Nations created by and for the peoples about the shores of the greatest of oceans [and] races aggregating more than half the population of the globe."[13]

Contrary to the narrative of racial and cultural harmony in the islands which served to justify Honolulu as the base for Pacific internationalism, Hawai'i was the site of longstanding dispossession and violence. Hawai'i had been the site of so-called "civilizing" work by US missionaries for more than seventy years before white American settlers, associated with the islands' plantations, overthrew the Hawaiian monarchy in 1893. In 1898, the United States illegally annexed Hawai'i. That same year, Guam, Puerto Rico, and the Philippines became US possessions at the conclusion of the Spanish-American War. The 1893 overthrow of the Kingdom of Hawai'i and the subsequent annexation in 1898 violated treaties between the United States and the Hawaiian Kingdom. The annexation thus breached international law and the US Constitution, which recognized international treaties as "the supreme law of the land."[14] Acknowledging the historical context from which Pacific internationalism emerged reveals the myriad ways that internationalism and imperialism were entangled and complicit. Indeed, Hawai'i was just one site within a more expansive US empire in the Pacific.[15]

Since the late nineteenth century, the pursuit of international and interracial coalitions between women across the globe was taken up by liberal and Christian social reformists. Unlike organizations such as the YWCA which were overtly Christian, the Pan-Pacific Women's Association (PPWA) offered a more secular transnational women's organization. The assemblage of conference delegates in the photograph speaks to the PPWA's aspiration of transcending diversity through unity. This was certainly not a new phenomenon but part and parcel of a much longer history of feminist political thought.[16] As evinced in visual form, the diverse group of delegates embodied the organization's mission of "friendship pursued on both practical and ideological fronts."[17]

For the PPWA, conference photographs chronicled the possibilities for internationalist organizing and served as a testament to the success of the internationalist movement while also seeking to attract new members. At their series of conferences held from 1928 to 1938, even amid increased hostilities in the Pacific, group photographs enabled participants to envision themselves as part of a collective Pan-Pacific community. For many delegates, the annual conference photograph was a meaningful ritual that fostered an affective kinship with other women in the region. For many of these women, the group photograph served as a visual marker of their own belonging and affinity to the much larger, often geographically disparate, Pan-Pacific women's network. The conference portrait was, in turn, critical to creating a shared visual and affective baseline for understanding not only the nebulous concept of the Pacific but also their belonging as members of a Pan-Pacific women's community.

The History of Group Photography

The history of the group photograph is closely tied to the development of photography itself, reflecting advancements in technology, changes in social customs, and the evolution of collective identity representation. Group photography, which involves capturing multiple subjects in a single image, has been a significant genre since the early days of photography in the mid-nineteenth century. Early group photos required subjects to remain still for several minutes due to long exposure times, resulting in formal and carefully composed images. These early group photos often depicted families, military units, academic classes, and social organizations, reflecting the social hierarchies and collective identities of the time. With advancements in photographic technologies, group photography became quicker, more accessible, and versatile. Shorter exposure times and increased portability of cameras enabled photographers to venture beyond the studio to take group photographs at specific settings or during significant events such as the Pan-Pacific conference.

As a genre, group photographs are often dismissed as formulaic, monotonous, and uninteresting in their form and style. They are often glossed over as difficult to read, or not worth reading, as historical documents. However, the very genre of the group photograph speaks to the central aims of Pacific internationalism. In Alois Riegl's foundational study of painted Dutch group portraits, Riegl defines the group photograph as an ensemble of individuals "in a natural unity or a social corporation bonded by a shared and public-spirited agenda" whereby "the intelligibility of the portrait relies on a composition shaped by the unity's 'inter-group' power dynamics."[18] As a photographic genre, the group photograph's "rigid formula of lining the subjects in rows" can appear as a "weary routine" that often elides any capacity for aesthetic experiment given that "the form is the theme."[19] In an analysis of Late Qing Chinese group photography, Tingting Xu proposes a "ritual approach for exploring the group photograph's constructed intelligibility," arguing that meaning is derived from the ritualized act of assembling and capturing the group photograph.[20] For Xu, group portraits lay bare internal group hierarchies—with delegates expected to abide by unspoken etiquette surrounding group rank and positioning within the collective.

Beneath the otherwise formulaic and routine positioning of individuals in rows, group portraits often reveal internal hierarchies within the gathered assemblage. An early twentieth-century photography handbook made this explicit, instructing photographers to not only compose the group so that each individual face is visible but also position "the important personages" (like in this case, honorary president Jane Addams) at the very front of the group.[21] At international conferences, a session was often set aside for the official conference photograph with proofs made available for pre-order before the event's conclusion. Reproduced in the official conference proceedings and in the prints ordered by delegates, the group photograph served both documentary and social functions, attesting to a degree of collective belonging, while also underscoring internal hierarchies within a group.

In addition to the ritual of the official conference photograph, delegates would often exchange small, signed portrait photographs (**cartes de visite**, or "calling cards"). This practice underscored the personal nature of their diplomacy and gave a visual form to their efforts at forging internationalism at the level of the interpersonal. In one example, a journalist compiled a collage of delegate portraits for her coverage of the 1937 Pan-Pacific Women's Conference in Vancouver, creating a full-page spread in which delegates' portraits were arranged in a collage under the headline of "When East Meets West."[22]

Organized as a collage of women, the PPWA members pictured in Figure 6.2 gestured to the diversity of PPWA delegates. Assembled as a type of "family album," the individual photographs of these women and their accompanying biographical captions signaled that the PPWA was diverse yet committed to shared internationalist ideals.[23] In the collage, the Asian delegates take on a kind of hypervisibility in the focus on their physical appearance and sartorial choices. Certainly, as documented in both the collage and the group photograph, delegates intentionally self-fashioned to convey various cultural traditions, nationalist modernity, and expressions of wealth or status, despite the Orientalist and gendered nature of media commentary.[24] Given that the PPWA sought to carry out international and interracial alliances, the

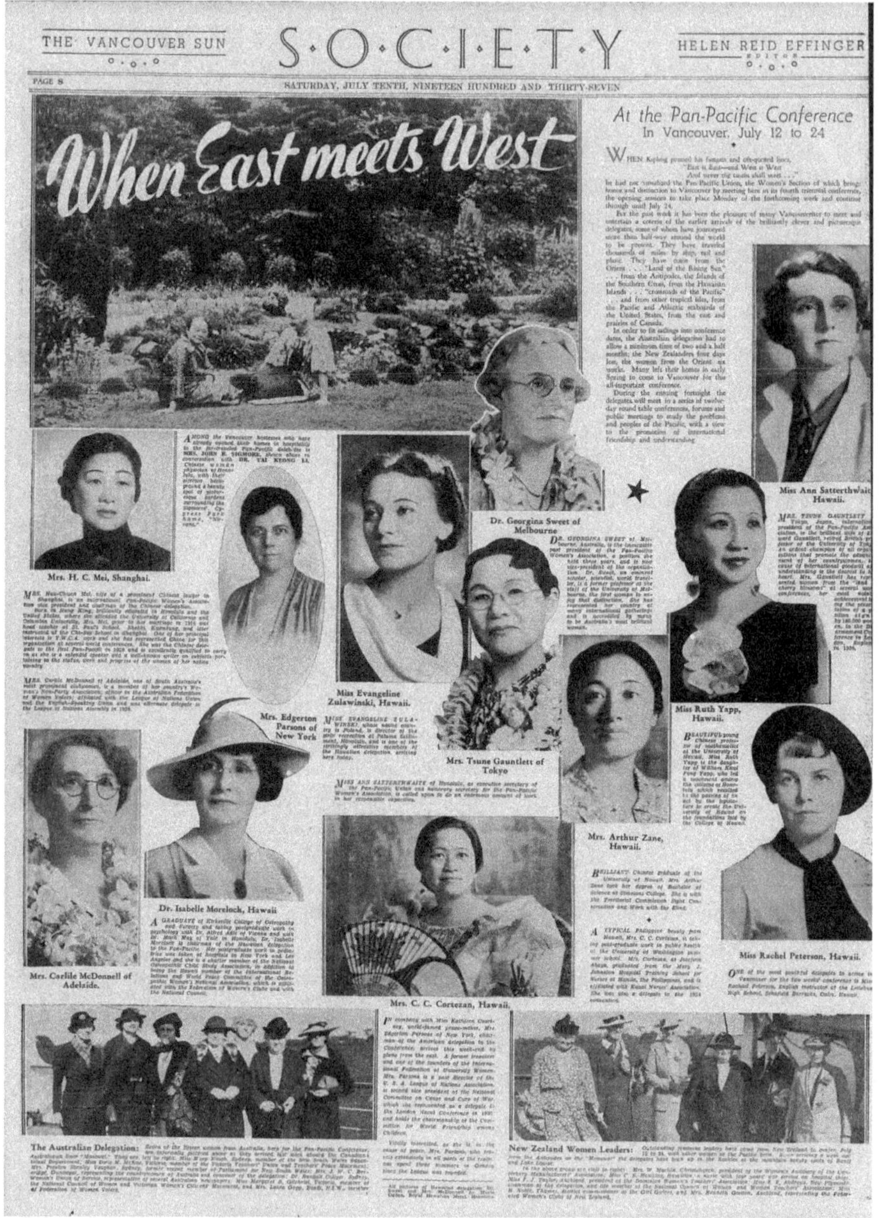

FIGURE 6.2 *A full "Society" page about the Pan-Pacific Women's Association conference in Vancouver, Canada, 1937. The article showcases some of the members' calling cards. "When East Meets West,"* The Vancouver Sun, *July 10, 1937. Material republished with the express permission of* The Vancouver Sun, *a division of Postmedia Network, Inc.*

presence of Asian women at these conferences was both ideologically and practically paramount to the fulfillment of the Pan-Pacific mission. However, their depiction in the media and even the roles that they were assigned to play internally within the PPWA demonstrate the paradoxical position they occupied as both proponents *and* recipients of a Western civilizing mission.

While participation of the "East" (as referenced in the *Vancouver Sun*'s headline) was symbolically critical to the Pan-Pacific's work, "East" primarily referred to Japan and China. Informed by broader imperial impulses, Western international feminist movements had long claimed a mission to uplift Asian and Indigenous women. As early as the 1890s, Asian women became active in local branches of Western women's international organizations, contributing to the spread of Christian internationalism throughout the Pacific. A few had even symbolically taken part in League of Nations-sponsored international conferences in Europe, under the mentorship of Western women who exemplified proper international conference decorum.

Despite their symbolic inclusion, these Asian women were not passive subjects in this narrative. They actively participated in the PPWA and, more importantly, took deliberate control of their representation. By distributing their own portraits and *cartes des visite* during and after conferences, they exercised agency over how they were seen, using these images to assert their identities on their own terms. Their careful curation of their visual presence underscores a complex dynamic, wherein they navigated the intersection of Western philanthropic narratives of uplift and their own self-representation.

Similar to their counterparts from Japan and China, Indigenous women, including delegates from Hawai'i, Fiji, and the Philippines who joined the association, naturally navigated complex internal politics within the organization and movement. They asserted their own agency within a feminist narrative that mostly assumed their premodern status as women of "less advanced" cultures. Ironically, for this very reason, those who did participate were seen as valuable, even prized, delegates at PPWA conferences, where they often took an active and highly visible role in the programming and entertainment.

However, upon closer examination of Yew Char's photograph, there is a palpable absence of Indigenous Pacific Islander and Native Hawaiian delegates despite the conference location. There appears to be a singular Native Hawaiian woman seated in the front row in a traditional hula ensemble of ti leaf skirt and haku lei. Given that the woman is unnamed and no trace of her can be found in the written proceedings of the conference, she may have only been included in both the conference and the group photograph in her capacity as an entertainer. Thinking further about who is and who is not included in the frame reminds us that cultural internationalism still adhered to more entrenched "racial" thinking embedded in notions of nationality and political autonomy. National divisions coexisted (frequently in tension) with internationalist aspirations to a "global family."[25] In both the "East Meets West" *Vancouver Sun* spread and Yew Char's conference portrait, the ideal internationalist "global family" was realized, even if it also reiterated uneven racial dynamics and tokenism, in visual form.

Yew Char and Interwar Commercial Studio Photography

The handwritten inscription in the photograph's bottom-right corner details the image caption and photographer, Yew Char. A renowned local photographer, Yew Char (1893–1982), had already established a thriving commercial photographic business in Hawai'i by the time he was commissioned to photograph the 1928 Pan-Pacific Women's Conference. As the son of Chinese immigrants who worked on the sugar plantations in Kohala, Hawai'i, he later moved with his family to Honolulu where he worked as a newsboy, shoeshiner, and pineapple cannery worker. In 1915, Char utilized his savings to pursue a degree in photography at the Modern School of Photography in Chicago.[26] From roughly 1916 to 1946, Char operated a highly successful commercial photography studio in Honolulu, first as a partner with his brother, On Char, at City Photo Studio, and later through his own business, the Tiffany Photo Studio.[27] Char's photography business afforded him a particular social standing and visibility that later facilitated his foray into local politics. In 1926, Char was elected to the Territorial House of Representatives, one of the first two Chinese Americans to be elected to public office.[28]

During this era, commercial and studio-based photographic practices were largely seen as purely business ventures. And indeed, Char's commercial studio was financially very lucrative. Equally telling is that despite his incredibly large and diverse photographic oeuvre, Char's photographs were never exhibited until the very end of his life. Just one year prior to his passing, the exhibit "Yew Char, Legislator and Photographer" was on view at the Bishop Museum in Honolulu, where his photographs are now archived.[29]

Char's thriving photography business was indicative of the large number of Asian American photographers who operated commercial studios that served the immigrant communities to which they belonged.[30] These studio photographers were critical in the documentation of daily life, traditions, and milestone events for families, and were germane to capturing everyday life for diasporic Asian communities. These communities often turned to these studio photographers out of trust as they were familiar with their customs, language, and were also some of the only studios that would photograph them. These studio photographs, many of which are still preserved in family photo albums, offer a rich archival source of understanding the intimate and quotidian texture of daily life for interwar Asian immigrant and diasporic communities.

From Photographs to Scrapbooks

By the 1930s, the internationalist movement began losing momentum, largely due to the seismic economic shifts of the stock market collapse that soon reached Hawai'i. By 1931, the Great Depression drastically impacted Hawai'i's previously robust plantation economy and labor force. Outside of agriculture and maritime labor, the large numbers of unemployed had few other employment opportunities. By December 1936, an estimated 5,000 people (or 20 percent of the workforce) were unemployed in Honolulu, a number higher than the roughly 17 percent unemployment rate nationwide.[31] Federal legislation such as the Works Progress Administration (WPA) projects, the Federal Emergency Relief Administration (FERA), and the National Industrial Recovery Act (NRA) offered some recourse for the unemployed.

However, the economic instability ushered in by the Depression heightened class and racial tensions. During the interwar years, Filipino and Japanese laborers organized together to lead the longest plantation strike in 1920, which included over 8,300 workers from both communities.[32] During the 1930s, hostilities in the Pacific increased and many Pan-Pacific women activists who had previously advocated for internationalism during the 1920s retreated from the movement or joined nationalist movements back home. In 1937, although unaware of its upcoming hiatus due to the Second World War, the Pan-Pacific Women's Association convened their conference in Vancouver. They wouldn't meet again until 1952 in New Zealand. The conference for the since-renamed Pan-Pacific and Southeast Asian Women's Association still meets annually to this day.

Though Pacific women's internationalism harnessed the power of the photographic image to champion its movement, it also turned to other forms of visual and material documentation to chronicle their labor. This predilection for the visual and material is apparent in the Pan-Pacific women's archives. In contrast to the Pan-Pacific Union records of primarily financial ledgers, newsletters, and membership solicitations, the PPWA archival collection, housed at the University of Hawai'i, mostly contains scrapbooks and correspondence. The disintegrating termite-eaten scrapbooks constitute the core of the PPWA archival records. News clippings, photos, invitations, letters, and postcards were meticulously cut and pasted onto each page by PPWA secretary, Ann Satterthwaite, who collected and preserved.[33] This intimate form of record keeping eschews explanatory or interpretive text.

Similar to Yew Char's 1928 group photograph in which all but the organization's primary leaders are unnamed, these scrapbooks function as "retrospective archives," a carefully curated gallery of life's fragmented "flotsam," loosely connected yet mostly imbued with personal meaning.[34] The mosaic of otherwise seemingly unrelated scraps—both material and visual—retained significance for those who belonged to the collective. Furthermore, scrapbooks gesture to the gendered nature of preservation and labor, with the practice often linked to women's domestic worlds and the implicit responsibility of safeguarding familial memories for posterity.[35] As long acknowledged, institutional archives perpetuate cultural, racial, and colonial logics that privilege certain forms of knowledge while denying the historicity of others.[36] The PPWA archives are no exception. Asian American, Indigenous, and Pacific Islander women are largely absent from records. If included in images, like Yew Char's photograph, these women appear only to remain nameless, unidentified in the caption.

However, one also wonders if there is resonance in the sheer scale and immensity of Pan-Pacific women's internationalism as signaled by the collective rather than at the scale of the individual. When taken in 1928, Char's photograph most likely held little significance to those beyond the conference conveners and delegates. However, in retrospect, the conference photograph reveals how international and interracial friendship was a cardinal tenet of interwar Pacific internationalism—a tenet often articulated in photographic form. Dwelling on the photograph and understanding its form, function, composition, and circulation all gesture to the many ways that internationalist ideology and praxis were collaboratively forged and sustained in the Pan-Pacific Women's Movement. The photograph, in its composition and reach, also complicates the perception of interwar America as insular, inviting us to reconsider how feminist and transnational currents in the Pacific helped forge US internationalist aspirations between the two world wars.

Discussion Questions

1   Take a few moments to carefully consider Yew Char's photograph. Who are the individuals that stand out to you? What does the composition, including the background setting, attire of the delegates, and the prominent positioning of certain leaders like Jane Addams, reveal about the social and cultural dynamics of the interwar period? How might the photograph serve as a tool for both documenting and shaping the narrative of women's internationalism?

2   How did the Pan-Pacific Women's Conference exemplify Akira Iriye's concept of "cultural internationalism"? Discuss the effectiveness

of cultural channels, such as conferences and international student exchanges, in promoting international cooperation compared to traditional diplomatic and political means.

3   Consider the contrasting narratives of Hawai'i as a model for international peace and as a site of historical dispossession and imperialism. How do these dual identities influence our understanding of the importance of Hawai'i as the homebase for Pacific internationalism? What does this tell us about the broader relationship between internationalism and imperialism during the interwar years?

4   Reflect on the long-term impacts of the Pan-Pacific Women's Conference and similar initiatives on women's rights, social reform, and international relations. Can parallels be drawn between early twentieth-century women's internationalism movements and contemporary transnational feminist movements? What are some similar goals? What are shared challenges?

Further Resources

Akami, Tomoko. *Internationalizing the Pacific: The United States, Japan and the Institute of Pacific Relations, 1919–1945*. Routledge, 2002.

Hooper, Paul F. *Elusive Destiny: The Internationalist Movement in Modern Hawai'i*. University of Hawai'i Press, 1980.

Iriye, Akira. *Cultural Internationalism and World Order*. Johns Hopkins University Press, 1997.

Paisley, Fiona. *Glamour in the Pacific: Cultural Internationalism and Race Politics in the Women's Pan-Pacific*. University of Hawai'i Press, 2009.

Woollacott, Angela. *Gender and Empire*. Palgrave Macmillan, 2006.

Yasutake, Rumi. "The Rise of Women's Internationalism in the Countries of the Asia-Pacific Region during the Interwar Years, from a Japanese Perspective." *Women's History Review* 20, no. 4 (2011): 521–32.

Notes

1   Eleanor Hinder, "Pan-Pacific Women's Conference," *The Brisbane Courier*, July 19, 1928.

2   For a comprehensive historiography of the interwar period, see Lisa McGirr, "The Interwar Years," in *American History Now*, ed. Eric Foner and Lisa McGirr (Temple University Press, 2011), 125–50.

3   "Article II. Objects," PPWA Constitution, quoted in the Official Report by Mary Anderson, Director, Women's Bureau, U.S. Department of Labor on the Second Pan-Pacific Women's Conference held in Honolulu, August 9–22, 1930. Box 7, Folder 15, Pan-Pacific Union Collection, Hamilton Library, University of Hawai'i at Mānoa (hereafter, PPUC).

4   For more on Addams, see Victoria Bissell Brown, *The Education of Jane Addams* (University of Pennsylvania Press, 2004); and Louise W. Knight, *Jane Addams: Spirit in Action* (W.W. Norton, 2010).

5   Jane Addams, "The Opening of a Women's Congress," *Mid-Pacific Magazine* 36, no. 4 (1928): 303; See also "Jane Addams to Harriet Cousens Andrews, ca. February 15, 1925 (excerpts)," *Jane Addams Digital Edition.* Last accessed June 22, 2024, https://digital.janeaddams.ramapo.edu/items/show/36146.

6   Akira Iriye, *Cultural Internationalism and World Order* (Johns Hopkins University Press, 1997), 12. On other forms of internationalism, see Daniel Laqua, ed., *Internationalism Reconfigured: Transnational Ideas and Movements between the World Wars* (Taurus, 2011); Daniel Gorman, *The Emergence of International Society in the 1920s* (Cambridge University Press, 2012); and Michael Pugh, *Liberal Internationalism: The Interwar Movement for Peace in Britain* (Palgrave Macmillan, 2012).

7   Fiona Paisley, *Glamour in the Pacific: Cultural Internationalism and Race Politics in the Women's Pan-Pacific* (University of Hawai'i Press, 2009), 3.

8   Rumi Yasutake, *The Feminist Pacific: International Women's Networks in Hawai'i, 1820–1940* (Columbia University Press, 2024).

9   Mae M. Ngai, *Impossible Subjects: Illegal Aliens and the Making of Modern America* (Princeton University Press, 2004).

10   Iriye, *Cultural Internationalism and World Order*, 3–5; 45–7.

11   Glenda Sluga, *Internationalism in the Age of Nationalism* (University of Pennsylvania Press, 2013).

12   "A Switzerland and Its Geneva for the Pacific," Pan-Pacific Union Bulletin New Series 8 (June 1920).

13   Alexander Hume Ford, *Genesis of the Pan-Pacific Union: Being Some Reminiscences of Alexander Hume Ford, First Installment.* Box 1, Folder 2, PPUC. Woodrow Wilson was the Honorary President of the Pan-Pacific Union when founded. For Wilsonian internationalism, see Erez Manela, *The Wilsonian Moment: Self-Determination and the International Origins of Anticolonial Nationalism* (Oxford University Press, 2007).

14   Francis A. Boyle, "Restoration of the Independent Nation State of Hawaii Under International Law," *St. Thomas Law Review* 7, no. 3 (1995): 727–38.

15   Allison L. Sneider, *Suffragists in an Imperial Age: US Expansion and the Woman Question, 1870–1929* (Oxford University Press, 2008), 88–9.

16   Patricia Grimshaw, "Gender, Citizenship and Race in the Women's Christian Temperance Union of Australia, 1890 to the 1930s," *Australian Feminist Studies* 13, no. 28 (1998): 199–214; and Joan Wallach Scott, *The Fantasy of Feminist History* (Duke University Press, 2011).

17   As indicated in the PPWA's mission statement, "friendship" was also one of its central objectives. The larger Pan-Pacific Union also appointed an official "minister of friendship" to carry forth the motto: "There is no friendship in business. Our business is friendship." "PPU Background Materials; A. H. Ford," Box 1, Folder 1, PPUC.

18 Alois Riegl, *The Group Portraiture of Holland* (Getty Research Center for the History of Art and the Humanities, 1999).

19 Tingting Xu, "The Group Photograph as an Imbricated Ritualistic Event: Duanfang and His Altar Bronzes in Late Qing Antiquarian Praxis," *History of Photography* 44, no. 4 (2020): 249–66.

20 Xu, "The Group Photograph as an Imbricated Ritualistic Event," 249–66.

21 J.B. Schriver, *Complete Self-Instructing Library of Practical Photography* (American School of Art and Photography, 1908).

22 Courtney Sato, "'A Picture of Peace': Friendship in Interwar Pacific Women's Internationalism," *Qui Parle* 27, no. 2 (December 2018): 475–510.

23 For more on Asian/American family photography, see LiLi Johnson, "Paper Family Photography: Photography and the State in the Era of Chinese Exclusion (1882-1943)," *Photography & Culture* 10, no. 2 (2017): 105–19; and Thy Phu and Elspeth H. Brown, "The Cultural Politics of Aspiration: Family Photography's Mixed Feelings," *Journal of Visual Culture* 17, no. 2 (2018): 152–65.

24 Paisley, *Glamour in the Pacific*, 51.

25 Matthew Connelly, *Fatal Misconception: The Struggle to Control World Population* (Harvard University Press, 2010); and Paisley, *Glamour in the Pacific*, 4.

26 "Chinese of Honolulu Completes Course in Art of Photography: Yew Char," *Pacific Commercial Advertiser*, June 9, 1916.

27 "On Char Oral History Interview Conducted by Lynda Mair in Honolulu, Hawaii on November 26, 1971." From The Watumull Foundation Oral History Project, 1979. Last accessed May 22, 2024, https://evols.library. manoa.hawaii.edu/server/api/core/bitstreams/299aa221-eaba-4c03-833f-c9f7c22d022c/content. Char also ventured into tourism, see "Yew Char Starts Travel Business," *Honolulu Star-Bulletin*, December 21, 1946.

28 Char went on to serve eight terms in office spanning from 1927 to 1945. See Pei-te Lien and Nicole Filler, *Contesting the Last Frontier: Race, Gender, Ethnicity, and Political Representation of Asian Americans* (Oxford University Press, 2022), 37.

29 "Yew Char, Photographer, Legislator," *The Honolulu Advertiser*, March 31, 1982.

30 For more on Japanese studio photographers, see Lynn Ann Davis, "Japanese Studio Photographers in the Territory of Hawai'i, 1900–1945," *Social Process in Hawai'i* 46 (2020): 36–54.

31 Edward D. Beechert, *Working in Hawaii: A Labor History* (University of Hawai'i Press, 1985), 249.

32 For more on the 1920 Strike, see Franklin Odo, *No Sword to Bury: Japanese Americans in Hawai'i during World War II* (Temple University Press, 2004). See also Ronald Takaki, *Pau Hana: Plantation Life and Labor in Hawaii, 1835–1920* (University of Hawai'i Press, 1983). For the 1936 unemployment rate, see U.S Bureau of Labor Statistics, "Labor Force Statistics from the

Current Population Survey: Unemployment Rate for 1936." Last accessed September 12, 2024, https://data.bls.gov/pdq/SurveyOutputServlet.

33   The Pan-Pacific Record Scrapbook, PPUC.

34   Jason Baird Jackson, *Material Vernaculars: Objects, Images, and Their Social Worlds* (Indiana University Press, 2016), 44.

35   During the early nineteenth century, the popularity of friendship albums among young women further gendered scrapbooking practices. See Katherine Ott and Susan Tucker, "An Introduction to the History of Scrapbooks," in *Scrapbooks in American Life*, ed. Katherine Ott, Susan Tucker, and Patricia Buckler (Temple University Press, 2006).

36   Jacques Derrida, *Archive Fever: A Freudian Impression*, trans. Eric Prenowitz (University of Chicago Press, 1995); Michel Foucault, "The Subject and Power," *Critical Inquiry* 8, no. 4 (1982): 777–95; Anjali Arondekar, *For the Record: On Sexuality and the Colonial Archive in India* (Duke University Press, 2009); Michel-Rolph Trouillot and Hazel V. Carby, *Silencing the Past: Power and the Production of History* (Beacon Press, 2015); and Ann Laura Stoler, *Along the Archival Grain: Epistemic Anxieties and Colonial Common Sense* (Princeton University Press, 2009).

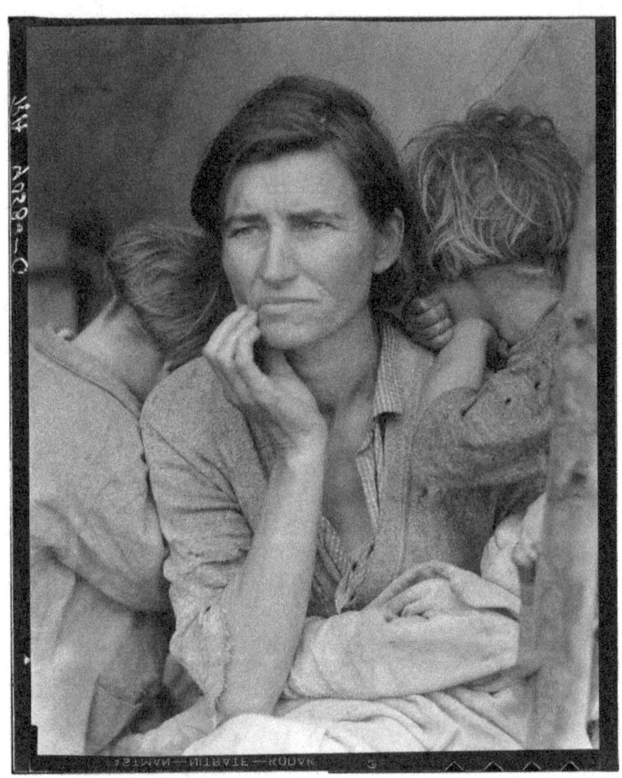

FIGURE 7.1 *Dorothea Lange's most iconic photograph, commonly referred to as* Migrant Mother, *depicting pea pickers in Nipomo, California, March 1936. Photo by Dorothea Lange. Courtesy of the Prints and Photographs Division, Library of Congress.*

7

Complicating the Legacy of Dorothea Lange's Photography

By Linda Gordon

The New York Stock exchange collapse in September 1929 sent the United States into an economic tailspin. The **Great Depression** affected the entire country, but severe regional droughts and the Dust Bowl captured the most attention and seared several iconic images into American memory: billowing clouds of dust choking entire towns; the mass migration of "Okies" in cars precariously stacked with household furniture; "bum blockades" along the California border, preventing an estimated 250,000 domestic refugees from overwhelming the state's social services.

No image is more ubiquitous than Dorothea Lange's *Migrant Mother*, a photograph depicting a woman staring beyond the camera while her children bury their heads in her shoulders. The photograph is so iconic, in fact, that Lange's work—which included thousands of images commissioned by the Resettlement Administration and later Japanese internment camps—is often reduced to this single image. This chapter uses some of Lange's lesser-known photographs to complicate her legacy and reveal a diverse nation struggling to survive.

Suggested Topics: Agriculture, Environmental History, Great Depression, Interwar Period, Labor History, New Deal, Women and Sexuality

Glossary: Farm Security Administration, Environmentalism, New Deal, Misère, Pictorialism, Piece Rate, Sharecropper, Wage Laborer

Dorothea Lange was one of the greatest photographers of the twentieth century. Always an urbanite—born in New Jersey, educated in NYC, then settling in San Francisco, where she joined an arty bohemian crowd—she nevertheless became best known as a photographer of 1930s Depression-era farmworkers.

Though charmed by Franklin Delano Roosevelt and appalled by the plight of homeless men living on the streets of San Francisco, she had never done photography focused on social justice. She was familiar with earlier documentary photography, like that of Jacob Riis and Lewis Hine aimed at bringing attention to the urban poor and child labor, but before the Depression she had done only studio portrait photography. She soon found a way to use that approach in documentary mode.

Like many of the best portrait painters, she saw her work as revealing a subject's personality, even "inner life." That style soon made her the most popular photographer of San Francisco's very rich—such as the Levi Straus clan who made a fortune through their Levi jeans—especially those who considered themselves cultured and sophisticated. This photography came to the attention of Paul Schuster Taylor, a progressive agricultural economist at the University of California, who saw her photographs in a 1935 exhibit and hired her to illustrate a report he was preparing for the US Department of Agriculture's **Farm Security Administration** (FSA) on migrant farmworkers in California. He convinced the FSA to hire photographers whose work could be used to strengthen his campaign to secure federal aid for farmworkers. FSA photographers made over 200,000 photographs, now in the Library of Congress.

Taylor convinced Lange to leave her very successful—and lucrative—studio for a low-paying, arduous job. They worked closely together and married soon after. The FSA wanted photographs of the depression's impact on farms and farmworkers, expecting that they would represent the poor as victims, even unattractive, as was then conventional. But Lange soon took her assignment in an unexpected direction, making portraits of poor farmworkers, notably farmworkers of color, with the same gravitas and respect that had characterized her portraits of the privileged. Doing so changed not only her life but also American politics—and the future of documentary photography.

Lange's most famous photograph, known as "Migrant Mother," illuminates her approach to FSA work. Its backstory was unusual for her: working alone, without Taylor, she was driving north on US-101 on a cold and rainy day in February 1936, returning from a month of working on the road—exhausted, to-the-bone tired, and eager to get home—she faced seven more hours of driving. About two hours north of Santa Barbara, near the town of Nipomo, she noticed a small hand-lettered sign, "Pea-Pickers Camp." At first, she continued driving but something pulled her back. She turned around and found the camp. There she learned that a freak cold snap had killed much of the local crop, so there was no work, and the look of hunger on the faces of the farmworkers was palpable.

She noticed a family group sheltering in a lean-to constructed of torn canvas: a mother with a baby at her breast, two very young children clinging to her, and a sullen teenage girl a few yards away. Since the girl would not cooperate, Lange focused on the woman and kids. She made a series of photos, moving ever closer so she could operate from her strength in portraiture. She saw in that woman, Florence Thompson, an almost classical beauty that many would not have noticed. After a few shots Lange asked the two youngsters leaning on their mother to turn their faces away from the camera. She did so to build the drama and impact of the photograph by leading the viewer to focus on Florence Thompson and her anxiety. In a manner characteristic of her work, Lange made the children's bodies rather than their faces express their dependence on their mother.[1]

Some critics later disparaged this photograph as inauthentic, not really "documentary," because it was "staged" when Lange asked the children to turn away. This criticism reflected a common, naïve understanding of documentary photography. A relatively new concept, many thought that "documentary" and "objectivity" somehow meant that a photographer should not design an image in order to increase its impact, as if "facts" could "speak for themselves," without the maker's interpretation. But all photography reflects the maker's point of view.

Another misconception was almost the inverse—that documentary photography was "biased" because it aimed to promote social reform, as in the work of Riis and Hine, and therefore could not be "art." Moreover, at the time documentary photography was considered naïve, unsophisticated, like personal snapshots. Or worse, it was propaganda, then a pejorative. Lange was perfectly comfortable making photographs in the interest of social justice and did not object to her work being called propaganda. In fact, she once remarked, in answering this criticism, that all photography could be called propaganda because it inevitably expressed the author's values. Her studio portraits could be called propaganda, as they served to announce and enhance the class status of her subjects. Despite the earlier work of **pictorialists** to elevate photography into art (see Chapter 4), few in the 1930s thought photography could be art, including Lange herself. Her work would become instrumental in changing that understanding.

Critics also charged that she beautified her subjects and/or photographed only good-looking people. Lange's studio work had accustomed her to make flattering portraits—if not, she would lose clientele. But she also *believed* in making her subjects look good. She considered portrait photography a collaboration with the subjects, who had a right to want flattering results. She saw her farmworker subjects with equal respect, but as she learned more about the Depression, and the **New Deal**'s attempt to help its victims, she hoped that portraying them with dignity could present them as deserving of help.

Lange's handsome farmworkers could be said to argue a New Deal analysis of the Depression—that their poverty resulted not from individual failure but from structural injustice. True, she probably declined to photograph unpleasant-looking subjects, not just for political reasons but also because she was drawn to beauty and had little interest in photographing what became known as "**misère**."[2] Moreover the beauty of her photographs emerged not only from a design aesthetic but also reflected her ability to see beauty among poor, discriminated-against subjects. That "way of seeing," to use John Berger's concept, explains the popularity of her work: among the dozen FSA photographers, Lange's was the most requested and most published, in large part because it expressed a democratic empathy engendered by the Depression and supported the New Deal's programs of help for those in need.[3] If she had not previously understood how government could and should provide such help, she surely learned it from Paul Taylor.

Empathy also shaped her technique. She worked slowly, for two reasons. She was somewhat disabled by a limp—polio had left her with a wizened foot—which prevented her from moving quickly. But slowness was also central to her method. From years in the studio, she knew that people tended to pose, to stiffen up when facing a camera. She sought in several ways to make her subjects relax. She did not use the new quick 35-mm cameras but rather view cameras with large plate film, and often relied on a tripod, so she took her time setting up her equipment. She never used flashbulbs, even in interior photos, because she disliked their impact on subjects. She conversed with her subjects when she could, asking about their families, work, and travels. She would explain that President Roosevelt—deliberately personalizing the government—wanted photographs that could support the case for aid to depression victims. Conversation was itself part of her method, employed in the studio and in the field, because it helped subjects relax into what she called their "natural body language," which made for more expressive and revealing photographs. When traveling with Taylor, he helped her subjects relax by interviewing them, sometimes in Spanish.

Lange's determination to show her subjects as individuals shows in the captions she wrote to accompany her photographs. Beyond identifying location and date, some constituted capsule narratives of a subject's history. Ever the portrait artist, she did not want her subjects deprived of individuality. Her captions might detail where they had traveled from, which family members accompanied them and which remained behind, how they moved about, the routes they traveled, the crops they worked on. Some of the "captions" were full paragraphs. When finished with a particular shoot, she would hurry back to her car and write down what she learned in a small notebook that she carried everywhere. She listened to their speech, understanding it as an eloquent vernacular. In a book written jointly by Lange and Taylor, the 1939 *American Exodus*, she created end papers that consisted of scores of direct quotations from farmworkers. The characters in the famous 1939 book *Grapes of Wrath* by John Steinbeck, were in many ways a composite of Lange's subjects. Then in 1940 a major Hollywood studio, 20th Century Fox, in a film based on Steinbeck's novel starring Henry Fonda, used images indebted to Lange's.

For some five years, Lange and Taylor were frequently on the road, traveling from the west through the drought-ridden Midwest to the southeast. This transcontinental body of work provides an unparalleled visual record of how environmental change, racism, and exploitation worked synergistically. Among the FSA photographers, Lange did the most to embed what she was photographing in the structures and history of farm labor. Besides, she had Paul Taylor, the country's leading expert on agricultural labor, as a private tutor. Let me add: the influence was mutual, though her influence on his work is not usually noticed. She taught Taylor to *see*; she understood that great documentary photography arose from the ability to see what others might not notice.

Lange was the only FSA photographer to cover three major farm labor systems in the United States: migrant wage labor in the west, tenant farming in the southern plains, and sharecropping in the South. Approximately one-third of her FSA subjects were nonwhite—Filipinos and Mexicans (both immigrants and American-born) in the west, African Americans in the southeast. (During the Second World War her subjects were Japanese Americans imprisoned in camps.)[4] At the time, respectful portraits of people of color were rare in the work of white photographers. Ugly stereotypes dominated, carrying the message that these people were stupid, primitive, and lazy; this was far from the truth, as few occupations required as much labor as farmwork. White people even collected and chuckled over "coon" caricatures and photographs of lynchings. The FSA even refused to distribute images of people of color, afraid that distributing them would alienate conservatives whose animosity could threaten its budget. These photographs are still not published in proportion to their significance in her work and to this day Lange remains identified primarily as a photographer of "Okies," poor white farmers.

As the *Migrant Mother* example shows, Lange's photography is infinitely complex. This one iconic photograph has come to define her work and the era. The following three vignettes are arranged regionally, showing the breadth of her gaze and her compassion, exemplifying Lange's determination to represent and to honor farmworkers usually invisible to most Americans.

The West

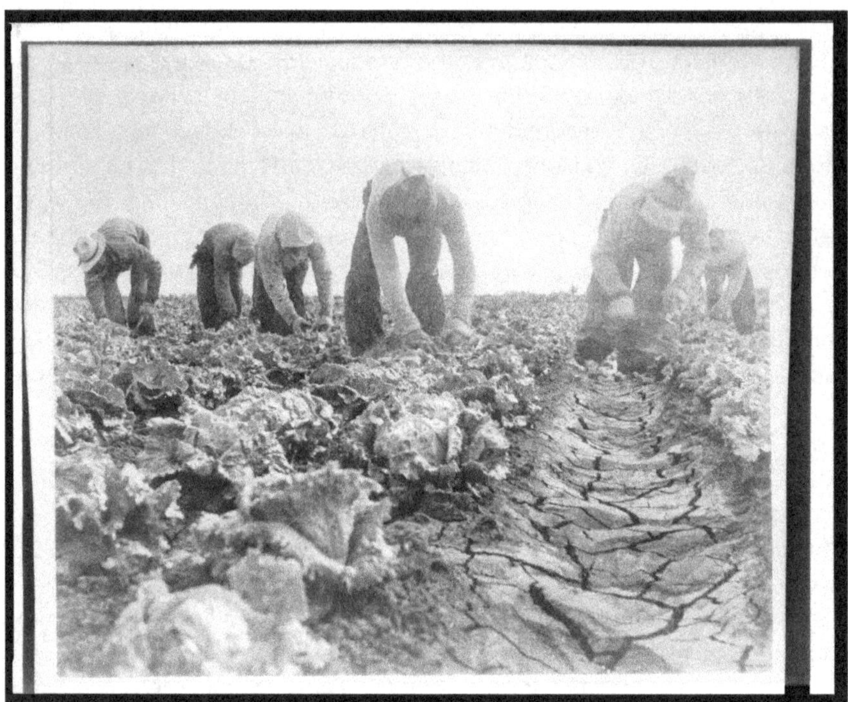

FIGURE 7.2 Filipinos Cutting Lettuce. *Salinas, California, June 1935. Photo by Dorothea Lange. Courtesy of the Prints and Photographs Division, Library of Congress.*

The Lange/Taylor team began their work in California. Here their subjects were not "farmers" in the sense of family farm owners but rather **wage laborers**, working mostly on large plantations. Absentee landlords and big corporations owned most farms. The biggest "farmer" in the region was the Bank of America. This is where her particular interest in people of color developed. Big growers had begun recruiting Filipinos as low-wage labor in the 1920s.[5] Though in alien territory they were by no means docile: they organized unions in the 1930s and were crushed by massive violence deployed by growers' thugs. In the 1960s Filipinos were the vanguard in union organizing, their initiatives jumpstarting Cesar Chavez and the United Farm Workers union. While the majority of Lange's California photographs were of Mexicans, Lange was one of very few who noticed the many Filipino farmworkers.

Photographs like Figure 7.2 do three kinds of work. First, they make visible the human labor that feeds us. Stoop labor like that shown in this photograph rapidly turned a young back into an old back. This bodily damage was created not by the nature of the crops but by growers prioritizing profit: lettuce cutters like these were not allowed by owners and supervisors to sit or kneel, because doing so would slow their productivity. Since the workers were paid **piece rate**, they had to work fast. Showing this grueling labor served also to defetishize food by revealing the circumstances of its production. In an increasingly urban America, lettuce appeared in grocery stores among other taken-for-granted commodities, and shoppers knew nothing of how it was produced or who produced it.[6] Taylor and Lange hoped that visual images might lead consumers—and Department of Agriculture policy makers—to recognize and honor the human labor and human cost involved.

This image is simultaneously, secondly, an abstraction, a layered pattern of inverse U-shaped arcs, echoed in the soft, rounded shapes of the lettuce leaves, contrasting with the sharp cracks in the dry soil. Social justice concerns never overwhelmed Lange's commitment to design. This careful construction of her photographs not only reflected her keen artistic eye but also strengthened their political message.

Third, Lange's unique and radical focus on bodies rather than faces shows throughout her images of farmworkers.[7] Though she intended this focus to bring attention to grueling labor, her own bodily experience certainly contributed to her extraordinary attention to the expressiveness of bodies. Her earlier studio photography often defied conventional portrait head shots by including gestures and bodily positions that could reveal the character of her subjects. After the childhood polio that left her with a crabbed foot, her mother insisted on dressing her in long skirts to hide it, bringing the message that it was an ugly deformity. Today this minor disability might be considered insignificant, but even as Lange rejected this shame, she never entirely shed her self-consciousness about it. Still, the disability was also a gift, underlying her attention to bodies. That consciousness underlay some of her most stunning photography, her ability to make portraits that showed peoples' emotions without faces.

The Plains

Even in this image of a dust storm in New Mexico in 1935, Lange's continued to make photographs that give expressive power to bodies (Figure 7.3). Including the tiny, dark figure of a man intensifies a sensory grasp of what a dust storm is, the damage it creates, and how emotionally terrifying it could be. In this miniature portrait, he is just big enough for his posture to communicate his dejection as his farm is destroyed by dust.[8]

Lange was being educated in **environmentalism** by Taylor. One of the first scholars to analyze the cause of the dust bowl, Taylor explained that it was

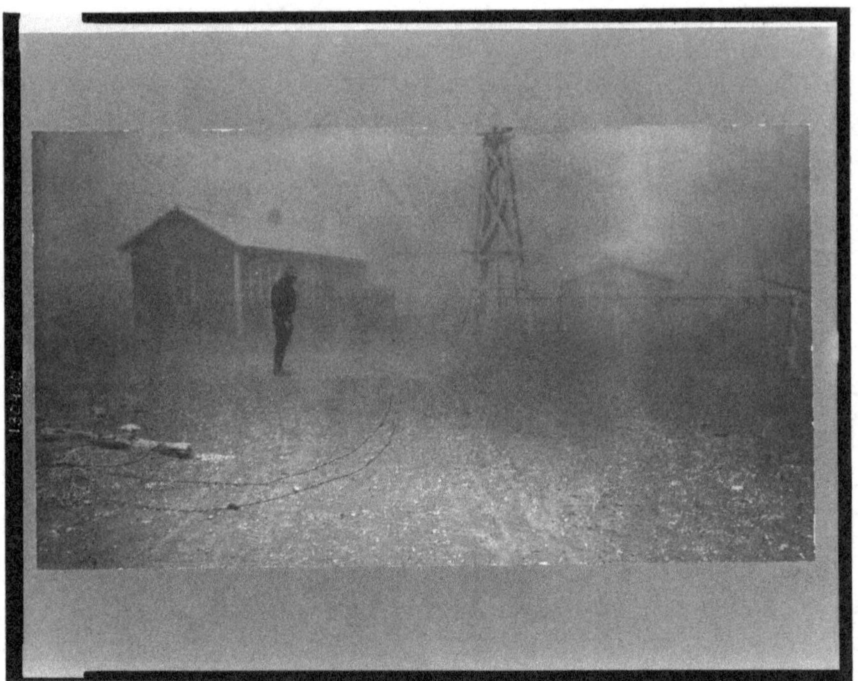

FIGURE 7.3 Dust Storm. It Was Conditions of This Sort Which Forced Many Farmers to Abandon the Area. *New Mexico, April 1935. Photo by Dorothea Lange. Courtesy of the Prints and Photographs Division, Library of Congress.*

not a phenomenon of "nature" but a man-made disaster. In their remarkable small book that featured text and images equally, *An American Exodus*, he recounted how farmers dependent on markets and falling commodity prices coped by plowing up ever more acreage. In doing so they stripped away the natural grasses with deep roots that held down the soil and retained moisture, thus turning a drought into a massive disaster.[9] Lange probably suggested the book's title, associating the forced migration that turned midwestern farmers into landless migrant farmworkers with the Jews' forced exodus from Egypt. Taylor was pushing Department of Agriculture leaders toward more environmentalist policies, and Lange's photographs supported those efforts, showing dried up fields, dying plants—even a close-up of a disc plow which was responsible for making the soil vulnerable to erosion.[10]

American Exodus was not written by Taylor and illustrated by Lange. Rejecting the idea that a photograph can speak for itself, she contributed to the text, especially through her captions, which often provided far more than typical citations of the subject, place, and date. She wrote captions that invited viewers to imagine themselves in this catastrophic situation.

The South

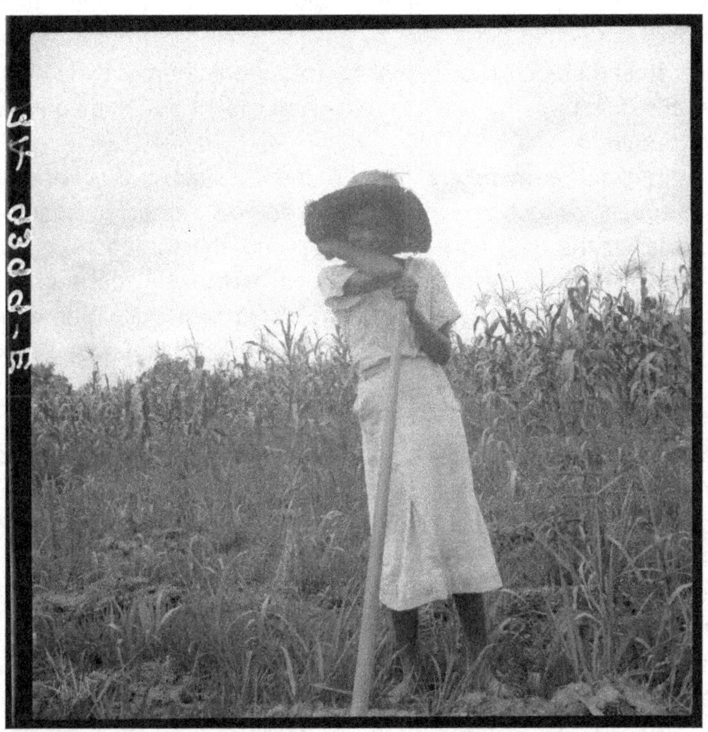

FIGURE 7.4 Negro Girl Working in the Fields. *The Mississippi Delta, July 1936. Photo by Dorothea Lange. Courtesy of the Prints and Photographs Division, Library of Congress.*

In their travels through the southeast—notably North Carolina, Alabama, and Mississippi—their subjects were usually **sharecroppers**, not wage laborers. Sharecroppers did not own the land they worked and could not typically choose the cash crop they grew, though they often grew vegetables for family consumption near their homes. Sharecroppers were harshly exploited and constantly vulnerable to poor harvests which left them without their "share" of the crops, even leading to evictions. Black sharecroppers were also sometimes evicted in retaliation for protests, especially organized protests.[11] Still, in day-to-day work, sharecroppers were their own bosses. They built their houses and barns and fences. Because everyone did a variety of tasks, the work could often be more pleasurable, healthy, and creative than that of workers on the California corporate farms who typically did one task repeatedly.

This was family labor and even the children worked hard—in the fields, barns, house and yard, tending chickens and gathering eggs, cultivating vegetables for themselves as well as for the rent they owed the landlord. The only female FSA photographer, Lange was particularly attentive to children, like the young girl in Figure 7.4. Her work kept her away from her own children and stepchildren, often for months at a time, and she suffered considerable guilt over the fact that her work meant that she could not be a full-time mother.

Among migrant farmworkers, many of her child subjects were endearing, but they appear primarily as victims, often left alone, sometimes dirty, helpless against the heat and the flies. Among sharecroppers, by contrast, her images of children were happier. Boys particularly took pride in their abilities and sometimes bragged to Lange about their skills. She noted, too, that parents might hope for a better life for their children. A Black father working in the sweet potato fields with his thirteen-year-old daughter told Lange that he wanted to send her to high school.[12] A mother, proud that her children were doing well in school, wanted to send them to college.[13] Such observations fit Lange's understanding of her job—demonstrating that these farmworkers were deserving of respect and aid. But it also reflected an optimistic worldview, no doubt strengthened by New Deal policies. She did not produce many of the *misère* images that continued to characterize much of documentary photography both before and after her career.

In her four southern trips, during the summers of 1936 to 1939, Lange focused on three major agricultural products—cotton, tobacco, and turpentine.[14] She aimed to document the cycle of production for each crop, thereby highlighting sharecroppers' multiple skills. This approach was usually impossible among migrant farmworkers, many of whose work was limited to harvesting.

In North Carolina, where the main cash crop was tobacco, Lange was fascinated by the workers' knowledge and skill. These photographs are full of dense activity. Lange was not there for the planting season, so we first see the crop in June, about two feet high. She made close-ups to contrast healthy plants to others with "wilt," for which there was no remedy at this time. The worms were particularly bad one year and she photographed the croppers picking them off, showing her how they hid on the underside of top leaves or deep inside the plant. She pictured a father and small daughter moving through the rows together, he is topping and suckering and she worming; she proudly displays that she had found two worms.[15]

Tobacco growers also "cured" their crop, drying it with techniques that maximized its market value, and Lange's photographs show the skill involved in the process.[16] We see men sawing, hammering, stretching gunny sacks to make the bins for transporting tobacco, and hanging from barn rafters to dry.

She showed women's and children's labor—churning, sewing, hairdressing, pumping water, cooking, feeding and watering animals, gathering eggs, killing chickens, and nursing babies.[17]

As with migrant farmworkers, Lange sought to evoke respect for sharecroppers and to undermine visual cliches through one of her frequent tropes: close-ups not just of faces but of bodies, revealing the grace of skilled labor. Portraits of California farmworkers at work were harder to make because they were often far away, laboring in vast fields; she could rarely trudge through acres of crops to get close to them, or had to avoid overseers who suspected—rightly—her motives. To compensate, she often photographed wage laborers at rest.

By contrast southern sharecroppers worked closer to home and were not surveilled by employers' enforcers, as the portrait of a young girl in the Mississippi Delta illustrates (Figure 7.4). It is vintage Lange, functioning both as portrait and evidence of children's labor. Carefully designed, the image shows the girl's slim body leaning slightly to the left, while her hoe leans right. The background of dry corn plants provides textural contrast. The girl participates in creating the photograph by pausing her work. She doesn't hide but, as if granting only partial access, keeps a bent arm over her mouth. She wears a skirt like most women and girls in this era. For her sharecropper subjects, skirts were also a statement asserting their femininity, combating the southern racism that refused to recognize Black women as "ladies." In her photos we often see girls and women in skirts doing heavy labor—an Alabama woman controlling a plow pulled by a donkey or mule, a North Carolina woman bent over, like the California Lettuce cutters.[18]

Lange's Legacy

No photographer before Lange had photographed farmworkers in this way—honoring their labor while doing portraiture. After her FSA work, she continued to take on some further photographic projects designed to document injustice, such as the internment of Japanese Americans during the Second World War. But much of her photography in the 1940s and 1950s was in Asia and Latin America, where Taylor was working to promote land reform. Her later work is often stunning, and it is a shame that it is not better known. Because she did not know the languages or cultures in these travels, however, these photographs are more purely aesthetic, lacking the social-justice bite of her earlier work.

Still, Lange's Depression-era work had a lasting legacy among others seeking social reform. During the 1960s a group of southern civil rights activists, who had seen her work and understood its anti-racist message, asked her to mentor them. She would have liked to do this, but the request came too late—she was increasingly unwell and died in 1965 from recurring polio symptoms (known as post-polio syndrome). The civil rights movement evoked some powerful photography, and I can imagine how Lange photographs might have contributed to civil rights activism. But her influence remains, almost a century after her FSA work, and extends well beyond the fame of "Migrant Mother," permeating the work of photographers such as Lynsey Addario, Eve Arnold, Bob Fitch, Robert Frank, Meiselas, James Nachtway, Carrie Mae Weems, and hundreds more.

Discussion Questions

1   In what context have you learned about Dorothea Lange or the Great Depression before? How does this broader geographic survey of her photographs change your understanding of Depression-era America?

2   What are some common elements to Dorothea Lange's photographic composition and style? What elements of *Migrant Mother* are present in her other photographs? How do they differ?

3   Although Lange's photography was commissioned by the government, many appeared in newspapers and magazines across the country in the 1930s. What impact do you think they had on the public? What impact do they have on you as a reader today?

4   Imagine these photographs without the human figures. Would they have been as impactful? Or as artful? What does that say about the role human figures play in Lange's photography?

Further Resources

Dorothea Lange Digital Archive, Oakland Museum of California. https:// dorothealange.museumca.org/.

Gordon, Linda. *Dorothea Lange: A Life Beyond Limits*. W.W. Norton, 2009.

Gordon, Linda and Gary Y. Okihiro. *Impounded: Dorothea Lange and the Censored Images of Japanese American Internment*. W.W. Norton, 2008.

Taylor, Dyanna, director. *Dorothea Lange: Grab a Hunk of Lightning*. PBS American Masters, 2014.

Notes

1   Her FSA job required Lange not to name her subjects, an indication of an elite view that the poor had no individuality. The image was reproduced so often that some consider it the most famous photo in the world. Years later Thompson saw the image in newspaper and wrote to Lange asking for a share of the profits. In fact, as Lange had to explain, she earned nothing from the photo; it belonged to the federal government and even today you can buy a print of the photo from the Library of Congress for the small cost of making a print. The correspondence with Thompson, however, yielded something Lange had not known. She had assumed that Thompson was white but now discovered that she was a Cherokee Indian! See Linda Gordon, *Dorothea Lange: A Life beyond Limits* (W.W. Norton, 2009), 235.

2   That term represented the idea, prominent at the time, that showing severe suffering would foster help for the poor. For a discussion of this concept in art, see Linda Nochlin, *Misère: The Visual Representation of Misery in the 19th Century* (Thames & Hudson, 2018).

3   John Berger, *Ways of Seeing* (British Broadcasting Corporation, 1977).

4   Some of Lange's respectful view of people of color may have come from Taylor's own photography, made in support of his research. He was the only agricultural economist to study and write about the exploitation of people of color, even traveling to Mexico to study the situation of migrant farmworkers and of the wives and children they left behind. He was also one of the brave handful who spoke out against the incarceration of Japanese Americans during the Second World War. But Lange also had a history of comfort with people of color—for example, her bohemian community of artists in San Francisco frequented Chinatown, avoided fearfully by most whites. For more on Lange's photography of Japanese internment, see Gordon, *Dorothea Lange*, 314–26; and Gordon and Gary Y. Okihiro, *Impounded: Dorothea Lange and the Censored Images of Japanese American Internment* (W.W. Norton, 2008).

5   Since the Philippines was at the time a US colony and Filipinos could hold US passports, growers found it easy to import their labor.

6   Defetishizing a commodity means reversing the concealment of the labor and social relations through which commodities are produced.

7   The images in the forty-eight photographic plates in my biography of Lange include many examples of making bodies as expressive as faces. The dramatic use of bodies to reveal character and emotion also characterized much of her studio portrait photography. For more, see Gordon, *Dorothea Lange*.

8   A similarly constructed photograph shows a closer view of a single man in the midst of dried out corn stalks, taller than him. Its caption reads, "Corn, drought-stricken and eaten off by grasshoppers. Near Russellville, Arkansas." See Lange, *Corn, drought-stricken and eaten off by grasshoppers*, Russellville, Arkansas, August 1936, US Farm Security Administration, Library of Congress Prints and Photographs Division, LC-USF34- 009654-C. Hereafter, LOC.

9   Dorothea Lange and Paul Schuster Taylor, *An American Exodus: A Record of Human Erosion* (Reynal & Hitchcock, 1939).

10   Lange, *Disc used in corn fields in California. It is drawn by seven horses*, Tulare County, California, May 1937, LOC, LC-USF34- 016564-C. This photo may have been requested by Taylor, but Lange turned these images of earth-moving machines into terrifying monsters in a visceral expression of environmental destruction. See for example Lange, *Laguna Dam. The All American Canal, when completed, will extend desert land to cultivation by irrigation in the southwestern United States*, California Imperial Valley, February 1937, LOC, LC-USF34-016145-C.

11 Lange photographed a collective farm created by evicted sharecroppers, who were interviewed by Taylor—he had a long interest in cooperative farms.

12 Lange field notes, July 4, 1939.

13 Lange field notes, July 4, 1939. Caption from a photo, "On a dirt road off highway 57 near Olive Hill."

14 Turpentine was then an agricultural product, manufactured in small batches out of the oleoresin (balsam) collected from the tree. Distillation of this material produces both turpentine oil and the solid rosin. Steam-distilled (wood) turpentine is derived from finely chopped wood chips and at the time processed by steam distillation.

15 See, for example, Lange, *Tobacco field in early morning where white sharecropper and wage laborer are priming tobacco*, Granville County, North Carolina, July 1939, LOC, LC-USF34-019996-E; and *Children helping father, tobacco sharecropper, at work in tobacco patch*, Person County, North Carolina, July 1939, LOC, LC-USF34-019786-E.

16 See, for example, Lange, *Son of tenant farmer hanging up strung tobacco inside the barn*, Granville County, North Carolina, July 1939. LOC, LC-USF34-019997-E.

17 See, for example, Lange, *Daughter of a Negro tenant churning butter*, Randolph County, North Carolina, July 1939, LOC, LC-USF34-020211-E; and *Negro field hand getting ready to go to town on a Saturday afternoon. His wages seventy-five cents a day and cabin. He has six children*, Georgia, July 1937, LOC, LC-USF34-018013-E.

18 The caption is typical of Lange's insistence on understanding the processes of various agricultural labor. It reads "Thirteen year old daughter of Negro sharecroppers planting sweet potatoes. She walks down the row and places the young plants in the holes her father has dug with a hoe. They will return down the row, water the plants with a bucket of water, then cover roots with earth. Person County, North Carolina." Another image shows the girl's father digging the holes. It is also typical of Lange's focus on bodies: it shows the legs and bent-over body, and in others from this sequence shows only legs. It also represents Lange's almost magnetic attraction to feet. Lange, July 1939, LOC, LC-USF34-019958-E, LC-USF34-019981-E, and LC-USF34-092181-E respectively.

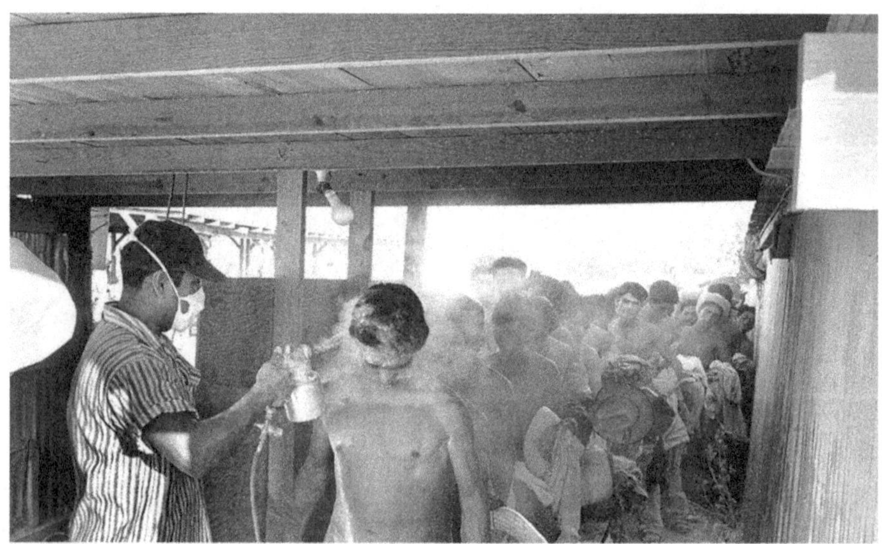

FIGURE 8.1 Braceros Sprayed with DDT at the Hidalgo Texas Processing Center, *1956. Photo by Leonard Nadel. Courtesy of the Archives Center, Smithsonian's National Museum of American History.*

8

Framing a Fractured System: The Bracero Program through Leonard Nadel's Lens

By Mireya Loza

The Second World War permanently shifted America's economic landscape as women began working outside the home, African Americans left the South en masse to cities across the North and Midwest. Farm laborers also flocked to higher paying defense industry jobs, but their absence created a growing fear that the country would not be able to produce enough food to feed its troops or its citizens. Wartime propaganda posters proclaiming "Our Food Is Fighting" spurred American families to plant an estimated 18 million "victory gardens" in order to supplement their dinner plates and keep food prices low.

These small gardens hardly compensated for the labor shortage in "**agribusiness**." In response the American government capitalized on migrant laborers through the **Bracero Program**. From 1942 to 1964, over 4.5 million Mexican citizens received lucrative contracts for legal work in the United States. However, as this chapter demonstrates, the lack of government oversight left the system open to widespread abuse and subjected the "braceros" to dehumanizing and dangerous treatment. The Bracero Program's impact is still visible in our immigration policies and labor laws today.

Suggested Topics: Agriculture, Economic History, Environmental History, Immigration, Labor History, Mexican American History, Second World War

Glossary: Agribusiness, Bracero Program, DDT, Guest Workers, Operation Wetback, Transnationalism, Undocumented Workers

In 1956, photographer Leonard Nadel took this image of state officials spraying Mexican guest workers as they entered the United States through the Bracero Program with the dangerous chemical dichloro-diphenyl-trichloroethane, commonly known as DDT. Years after he shot this image, Nadel noted the importance of this generation of workers. "Not only is this one of the most significant population movements in the Western Hemisphere in the last 25 years," he wrote, "but there is also a dramatic story to be told about which most Americans know extremely little."[1] The men in this photo were leaving everything behind as they were recruited to work in American fields. They left their homes and families enticed by the false promises of high wages, decent living conditions, and fair treatment. This was also the story of the rise of industrial agriculture and how the diet of all Americans was shaped by a legion of international farmworkers.

From 1942 to 1964, the United States entered a series of agreements with Mexico that were collectively known as the **Bracero Program**. The program would facilitate the recruitment and employment of Mexican workers. It was originally designed to address areas that experienced a perceived labor shortage brought on by the Second World War, such as agriculture and railroads. The railroad component was done away with shortly after the war, as returning veterans saw railroad work as desirable, protected, and skilled work with a strong union. Recruitment for agriculture lasted much longer as these jobs were poorly paid, and the living and working conditions were often deplorable.

Prior to the Bracero Program, the labor rights of agricultural workers had been set on a bifurcated path from industrial workers. They were purposely left out of 1930s labor reform laws because southern politicians wanted to make sure to limit the labor protections of Black agricultural and domestic workers, especially to stymie their efforts to organize. This strategic and oppressive move not only shaped the lives of Black agricultural workers in the South but it also produced structural limitations for all agricultural workers including Mexican, Mexican American, and Filipino farmworkers in the West.

During the course of the Bracero Program, over 4.5 million contracts were issued to Mexican males known as "braceros." The word "bracero" comes from the Spanish word *brazos*, meaning arms and was commonly used to refer to field hands. These temporary laborers signed contracts that allowed them to work with a single employer or a grower's association, essentially binding a worker to an employer or an association. These men could not legally sell their labor on the free market. Contracts could be and were often renewed, but the program was originally designed to give complete authority over a worker's labor to the employer, and it also guaranteed that these workers would return to Mexico after their contracts came to an end. In this way, employers from the agricultural industry had unrestricted access to a pool of laborers with few if any rights.

Abuses under the Bracero Program resulted from a power imbalance that ensured the United States would prioritize the demands of the agricultural industry over the humane treatment of the workers. As growers' reliance on these rights-less workers increased throughout the midcentury, many activists and labor organizers began to note the rising human and labor abuses. They witnessed how the program had now morphed from a wartime lifeline for farmers in need of workers into a systematized pool of exploitable and deportable workers, cycling in and out of American farms, to the great benefit of agribusiness.

In Nadel's image, nameless braceros stand in line for a chemical dousing. Only the US state official wears a mask which offers him more protection than the men he is spraying. The central figure drops his pants, bows his head down, and closes his eyes. Many men learned quickly that they had to close their eyes as some described the DDT burning their corneas. The guest workers closer to Nadel's lens are nude and the men in the distance are wearing pants they will quickly drop as they reach the front of the line.

Nadel's photographs conveyed an intentional documentary style, showing the general public some of the inhumane treatment that these workers experienced. However, the framing is far from an unbiased or unconscious choice. While the original image shows the naked bodies more fully, Nadel made the critical decision to present the public a cropped version of this image. The strategic cropping above the genitals of the bracero at the foreground allowed Nadel to publish and circulate this image more widely. His bracero images were printed in notable magazines such as *Pageant*, *Jubilee*, and *Harvester News*, which helped disseminate the visual evidence of the braceros' experiences to broader audiences. He wanted to sensationalize their inhumane treatment, not their nudity, explaining, "The braceros were strained through the seines of immigration, medical and labor department processing, then loaded like cattle in railroad box cars ...."[2] The processing experience was seared in the minds of many braceros. Decades later, former bracero Audmaro G. Zepeda shared in an oral history that he felt that it was "like fumigating some animal."[3] Both Mr. Zepeda and Nadel noted that the treatment during the processing was akin to the treatment of animals, and Americans' casual disregard for the human rights of these braceros would also come to shape their work lives.

Inspired by a Labor Organizer

To be sure this was not the first time growers and industrialists benefitted from the entry of Mexican contracted workers. During the First World War, they successfully lobbied US officials to allow Mexican workers and their families to enter the United States as contracted laborers.[4] The postwar agricultural depression brought the program to a close and was followed by the xenophobic deportation and repatriation of Mexican and Mexican Americans during the Great Depression. The economic crisis fueled anti-Mexican fervor. Throughout this period approximately 2 million Mexican and Mexican Americans were banished from the United States.[5]

Yet, six years after the last large-scale deportations, the United States would once again find itself entering a war and growers and industrialists would once again clamor to ease the entry of temporary Mexican workers. This time around, policy makers would craft a more robust guest worker program specifically targeting Mexican men in order to prohibit the entry of entire families. And more specifically to exclude wives and the possibility of Mexican women giving birth to children on US soil who would undeniably be American citizens.

In an effort to document and call attention to the exploitative experiences braceros faced, Leonard Nadel set out to photograph the bracero journey from Mexico to the border and into the agricultural fields and camps. He followed the footsteps and research of labor organizer Ernesto Galarza, and was committed to capturing the deplorable treatment of braceros. Prior to Nadel's endeavor to photograph the bracero experience, Galarza had spent many years trying to bring awareness to the mistreatment of these workers, often documenting their unlivable housing, inadequate food, health, wage theft, and dangerous work environments. These infractions violated workers' contracts, which guaranteed that growers would provide adequate housing, medical attention, food, etc. But Galarza noted that the contracts were rarely enforced and without any consequences for violations, growers would not abide by the terms of this binational agreement and workers' contracts.

Galarza documented how employers used threats and coercion tactics to prevent braceros from reporting labor abuses. Those braceros who did, risked having their contracts terminated followed by a swift deportation. Essentially growers could get rid of workers who spoke up or organized. In Galarza's view, growers had too much power and made it difficult for braceros to effectively push back against exploitation. Galarza grew convinced that the Bracero Program needed to come to an end.

Galarza received a grant from the Fund for the Republic to create a research report and publication entitled "Strangers in our Fields" chronicling the experiences of braceros. Nadel later described when speaking to other photographers that Galarza's research was "excellent but extremely limited in being able to reach the mass audience it needed to be effective. Within the story were elements of dramatic quality that only a perceptive camera could express and bring to life."[6] To add insult to injury, growers and other proponents of the bracero program argued that Galarza's research was inaccurate. Nadel believed that his camera could capture a reality that no one could refute. To that end Nadel applied for and was also awarded a grant from the Fund for the Republic, a civil liberties fund endowed by the Ford Foundation. His extensive documentation included over 2,000 photographs and provided a visual complement to Galarza's writing. Because Nadel was not fluent in Spanish, he could not gather as much information directly from braceros themselves and instead utilized Galarza's interviews with braceros to guide his photography.

The funding allowed Nadel to document the bracero journey from their homes and through the processing site and into the fields and labor camps. He also managed to document the limited leisure activities of braceros in labor camps and towns in the United States. He began his six-month trip in the summer of 1956 as national discussions around the exploitative plight of agricultural workers gained attention from policymakers and the Department of Labor.[7]

The Bracero Journey

By the time Nadel shot this image of braceros doused with DDT, the program had been in place for fourteen years and men throughout Mexico knew about the program. Some men heard about it through their fathers, uncles, and neighbors who had become braceros. The community networks were invaluable sources of knowledge about what to expect and how to navigate the arduous recruitment process. Securing a contract included an extensive waiting period and an invasive medical inspection with dangerous chemicals and required the men to leave their families behind while they worked and lived in unregulated conditions. Nadel's images provided a visual to key components of the bracero narrative that as one guest worker argued, "we need to go through that to become braceros."[8] This process became a rite of passage that differentiated braceros from undocumented workers who did not experience the baptism by fire required to legally work in the United States.

Most guest workers used their own savings or borrowed money from family members in order to begin the journey. During this first leg, they were commonly known as *aspirantes* because they aspired to garner a much-coveted contract. Many made their way to contracting centers with friends or family from the same town or village. At the contracting center they might also pay a *mordida*, or bribe, to try to get on the list of men who would be called for a potential contract. Many felt compelled to pay the bribe because the wait could be long and there was no infrastructure to host them as they waited. If they had money, they might pay for a meager straw mat and sleep in a private home. They might also buy their own mat and sleep on the street or near the contracting station. There were no public restrooms or facilities designated for these men. And every day they waited for their name to be called was expensive as they also had to buy food from local vendors. Some men went hungry because they had no idea when they would have a chance at a contract. And some men felt that they could not look back and return home because they felt the pressure of paying back the money they borrowed.

It was no secret that officials were in search of the men who could withstand long arduous work. And from the minute men's names were called for a potential contract they experienced a series of inspections that reduced their worth to the value of their bodies, and the work their bodies could produce. Their hands were the first part of their bodies to receive inspection because the processing officials were in search of strong field hands and not bakers, tailors, or college students. People in these professions made their way into the program, nonetheless. They learned to rough up their hands against rocks and tough material in order to develop calluses.

They also endured invasive medical exams conducted in large rooms full of other would-be braceros. They lined up fully naked as doctors looked inside their mouths, checking their private areas for hemorrhoids and sexually transmitted disease. Medical staff would also perform chest x-rays in order to make sure these men had no contagious respiratory diseases such as tuberculosis. The medical exams were carried out in order to make sure that only the healthiest men were issued contracts and to protect American communities that would come in contact with these men from potential illnesses.

In order to ensure this, they would not only experience dehumanizing medical exams en masse but also be exposed to highly toxic chemicals like DDT before being transported to their work sites. Renowned environmentalist Rachel Carson called attention to the dangers of DDT in her 1962 book *Silent Spring*. While DDT was first synthesized in 1874 as an experiment to see how compounds react to each other when mixed, its properties as an insecticide were not discovered until 1939.[9] During the Second World War, it was commonly used on soldiers, refugees, and prisoners to combat lice but after the war it became a popular insecticide in the United States used in agriculture.

Braceros' exposure to DDT was amplified by the toxic pesticides in the fields and by the officials who would douse them with a cloud of the chemical ensuring that it would immediately reach their lungs. As Carson noted in Silent Spring, "once it has entered the body it is stored largely in organs ... such as adrenals, testes, or thyroid."[10] According to the US Centers for Disease Control and Prevention, people exposed to high levels of DDT can experience the immediate effects of tremors, headaches, nausea, and seizures. Long-term effects wreak havoc on their nervous system, liver, and reproductive system, and cause increased cancer rates.[11]

Officials did not give braceros information on what they were being sprayed with, but many guessed it was with a fumigant. In fact, those with prior contracts would come to recognize the equipment, as similar equipment was used in the fields for fumigation. Braceros were never told that this chemical might be hazardous to their health, but many immediately felt its effects. "They didn't tell us what kind of dust [was used]. Many people were poisoned. Many people came out of there with rashes," proclaimed bracero Lucio Nuñez.[12] The effects of the DDT fumigation were felt beyond the physical. Nemecio Meza lamented, "and they would strip us, dust us [with DDT], and well, it was a bit painful. Every time I remember it, I feel a bit bad, but with the need to come work here in the United States, you have to endure it ... They made us suffer a lot."[13] By 1972 the Environmental Protection Agency (EPA) banned DDT because they had enough evidence of its adverse and long-lasting effects on the environment, animals, and humans.

Nadel documented this harmful process and the transformation of these men from *aspirantes* to braceros, and then he followed them across the US-Mexico border. His photography captures their inhumane living and working conditions as well as their humanity through their interrupted family lives and leisure activities. Nadel's work offers an unprecedented and intimate lens into the bracero experience as he accumulated the visual evidence necessary to sway public opinion.

One of Nadel's primary tasks was to document the living conditions and he found growers placing braceros in structures that should have been condemned. He also photographed many makeshift barracks filled with bunk beds. Housing could vary widely, but on large-scale farms it often required braceros to live in tight and subpar conditions. The worst housing often also had the worst bathroom facilities. Nadel explained, "Everywhere I travelled among the braceros, my cameras recorded what I found—filthy living quarters, overcrowded conditions, inadequate and disease-ridden sanitary facilities." He saw "the faces of men which mirrored their problems and their complaints, how they were fed and housed and transported, their paychecks and what they actually earned, the inadequate provisions for their safety and medical care and the conditions under which they worked as stoop laborers."[14]

What the majority of braceros experienced in the United States were long hours as stoop labor, subpar living quarters with very little privacy, few leisure activities, and inadequate food. Employers often short-changed braceros' paychecks because they knew there would be little to no consequence to their wage theft. Nadel photographed braceros holding up their paychecks and also working with a *cortito*, or a short handle hoe, stooped over in large fields. This tool required them to be bent over for hours in the fields and led to many back injuries. The state of California would be the first to abolish the short handle hoe in 1975 as it was deemed unsafe.

The Bracero Program had interpersonal repercussions too as it normalized family separation. Both the US and the Mexican government encouraged men to leave their families behind. Instead of performing their everyday responsibilities as sons, fathers, husbands, and brothers, they were told that it was better to send remittances from the United States than to be physically present for their families. Many men would come to learn about the birth of their children, death of a parent, or an accident that befell a family member, weeks or even months after, through letters. These **transnational** configurations of family stood in stark contrast to the popular ideal of the suburban white nuclear family in which fathers returned home every evening to a wife whose primary work was caring for a husband and children. Braceros would not be encouraged to bring their families nor to marry American citizens and build lives in the United States.

Despite the poor living and working conditions, the men developed a different kind of family through brotherhood and camaraderie. Nadel managed to capture the few leisure activities available in the camps and the occasional visit to the nearest town. After work, braceros played cards and checkers on makeshift boards. They also enjoyed baseball and soccer if the camp provided the balls and bats. One of the most popular recreation activities was listening to the radio. Braceros would save to purchase a radio, and they gathered around it to listen after long days of work. When braceros had the opportunity to visit the nearest town, they might go to a movie or shopping for items unavailable to them in the camps.

However, not all braceros were able to leave for recreation because the worst of the employers kept the men in tightly controlled labor camps. These employers struggled to keep a workforce because, faced with deplorable conditions, braceros sometimes made the tough choice to become "skips." Skips refer to men who would rather skip out on their contract and become **undocumented workers** than live under terrible and exploitative conditions. The most abusive growers would place barbed wire around the camps in order to restrict the men from moving freely and potentially skipping. Galarza argued that skipping "is a mode of protest against conditions that the worker feels cannot be corrected."[15] This could be seen as the ultimate form of protest within the Bracero Program.

During the Second World War, Braceros were not the only **guest workers** setting foot in the United States, and workers in these other programs experienced similar exploitative labor conditions, inadequate housing, and often social isolation. Starting in the spring of 1943, the British West Indies

Labor Program (BWI) allowed laborers from the British West Indies, primarily Jamaica, to enter the United States on temporary work contracts. Many were assigned to cut sugar cane in Florida and to farms on the East Coast.[16] During the wartime years, the American government took on a central role in the administration of both the Bracero Program and the BWI. By the 1950s, growers in the State of California grew concerned with their dependence on the Bracero Program and feared that the Mexican government at some point might suspend the program, leaving them with rotting produce in the field. This fear prompted growers to look for other pools of potential guest workers. And in 1956 they worked with the Department of Labor and the government of Japan to create the Japanese Agricultural Workers' Program (JAWP), which was much smaller than the Bracero Program in scope and scale.[17]

While growers argued that these guest worker programs, and in particular the Bracero Program, would curb the entry of undocumented workers, the number of unsanctioned workers entering the United States climbed during this period. The flow of undocumented migrants grew alongside the Bracero Program as some growers preferred undocumented workers over complying with the program's red tape and costs, some of which included transportation and housing.

By June 1954, the director of the Immigration and Naturalization Service (INS) Joseph M. Swing—in conjunction with President Dwight D. Eisenhower—began **Operation Wetback**, a US law enforcement campaign resulting in over 1 million deportations of mostly Mexicans.[18] The INS had already been deporting numbers of undocumented workers throughout the 1940s and releasing them at the border. Operation Wetback would expand this practice and "deliver Mexican deportees into the custody of Mexican immigration officials who would forcibly relocate the deportee to points south of the border."[19] The goal was to make it more difficult for deportees to return to the United States as undocumented workers. Ironically, in the midst of massive recruitment of Braceros, the US government carried out these large-scale deportation operations.

The Legacy of the Bracero Program

Braceros toiled on American farms during a period which saw significant shifts in our agricultural system. Braceros were key to the growth of agricultural production and these agricultural products became a cornerstone in addressing hunger both domestically and internationally. Growers adopted advances in agricultural sciences and farm technology that propelled the Green Revolution, testing and adopting high-yielding varieties (HYVs), chemical fertilizers, and agrochemicals which in turn produced larger harvests. It also gave rise to the growth of industrial agriculture. This bounty was used by expanding food processors creating regional and national food companies.[20] By 1957, John Davis and Ray Goldberg, Harvard Business School professors, coined the term "**agribusiness**" which at its core acknowledged and lauded corporate-driven models of agriculture.[21] Small farmers were often pushed out as they faced higher input costs and the bias of federal crop subsidies toward larger growers, leading fewer owners to control more acreage.[22]

These shifts within the agricultural system also fueled concerns about agricultural overproduction that shaped international policy. Food became part of a vision for international aid in reconstructing European economies devastated by the Second World War and as a bulwark against Cold War-era communism.[23] The growth of agribusiness, industrial models of agriculture, and food processors would not be possible without farmworkers. In some states such as California, braceros were the key ingredient for the expansion of agribusiness. California was not only the largest employer of braceros, but during the 1950s growers in the state also experienced a 50 percent growth in vegetable production.[24] Whether canned, frozen, or fresh, these vegetables would make their way to homes across the United States.

Nadel's photographs of braceros in the fields would remind Americans of this through features in various mainstream and specialty publications throughout the 1950s. Together with Galarza's writings and interviews, the two men played a significant role in swaying public opinion on abuses within the agricultural industry, immigration policy, and labor practices by portraying the reality of the Bracero Program.

While Galarza, Nadel, and other activists were successful in calling attention to the deep exploitation of braceros and ultimately in helping bring the Bracero Program to an end, guest workers never stopped entering the United States. The H-2 program, originally crafted for workers from the British West Indies, continued after the Bracero Program was terminated. Following the Immigration and Control Act of 1986, the program was split in two categories: H-2A visas for agriculture and H-2B for seasonal non-agriculture. The H-2A program would quietly grow and shift to target Mexicans. In the contemporary moment, Mexicans compose the majority of H-2A visa holders followed by Jamaicans, and growers have also pushed for the recruitment of Central Americans from Honduras and Guatemala.

The H-2A visa is commonly seen as the solution to immigration reform and like its predecessor, promises to protect workers via contracts that lack enforcement. In 2022, the Department of Labor certified 372,000 jobs to be filled by H-2A workers which is approximately the same number of braceros that entered the United States the year before Nadel captured this image of unnamed men coated in clouds of DDT.[25] Along with the growth of the H-2A visa program, there has been a rise in human rights violations and new cases of human trafficking and modern day slavery tied to the program.[26]

While the contracts issued during the Bracero Program failed to protect workers, the program succeeded in bringing to fruition what agri-business desired: a low wage, deportable, expendable workforce with very few labor protections or civil rights. This is the complicated legacy we continue to grapple with as guest workers pick the blueberries and strawberries that make their way into homes across America.

Discussion Questions

1 Examine Nadel's photographs on *The Bracero History Archive* (https:// braceroarchive.org) and analyze the work and living conditions braceros experienced.

2 How did the Bracero Program place power in the hands of the growers, and what kind of risks did this pose to the braceros?

3 What is agribusiness, and how did braceros shape our food system?

4 What is the difference between a guest worker and an undocumented worker?

5 Describe both the recruitment and deportation systems the US government created across the twentieth century.

Further Resources

Galarza, Ernesto. *Strangers in Our Fields*. Joint United States-Mexico Union Committee, 1956. Available via Hathi Trust: https://babel.hathitrust.org/cgi/pt?i d=txu.059172014995126&seq=1&q1=protest.
Hahamovitch, Cindy. *No Man's Land: Jamaican Guestworkers in America and the Global History of Deportable Labor*. Princeton University Press, 2011.
Loza, Mireya. *Defiant Braceros: How Migrant Workers Fought for Racial Sexual and Political Freedom*. University of North Carolina Press, 2016. Available open access: https://uncpress.org/book/9781469629766/defiant-braceros/.

Notes

1 "New Role for the Photographer," undated, Box 10 Folder 13, Leonard Nadel Papers, Archives Center, Smithsonian's National Musuem of American History. Hereafter, Leonard Nadel Papers.

2 "New Role for the Photographer," Leonard Nadel Papers.

3   Audmaro G. Zepeda, interview by Mireya Loza, Salinas, CA, *Bracero Oral History Project*, University of Texas at El Paso, July 28, 2005. Zepeda's original quote is: "Como fumigar a algún animal."

4   For more on the first Mexican guest worker program, see Fernando Saúl Alanis Enciso, *El Primer Programa Bracero Y El Gobierno de México 1917–1918* (Colegio de San Luis, 1999); Mireya Loza, "'Let Them Bring Their Families': The Experiences of the First Mexican Guest Workers, 1917–1922," *Journal of American History* 109, no. 2 (September 2022): 310–23; and Otey M. Scruggs, "The First Mexican Farm Labor Program," *Journal of the Southwest* 2, no. 4 (Winter 1960): 319-26.

5   Francisco E. Balderrama and Raymond Rodríguez, *Decade of Betrayal: Mexican Repatriation in the 1930s* (University of New Mexico Press, 2006), 265; and Marla A. Ramírez, *Banished Citizens: A History of the Mexican American Women Who Endured Repatriation* (Harvard University Press, 2025).

6   "New Role for the Photographer," Leonard Nadel Papers.

7   Richard Steven Street, *Everyone Had Cameras: Photography and Farmworkers in California, 1850–2000* (University of Minnesota Press, 2008), 373.

8   Raúl Canela, informal conversation with Mireya Loza, San Jose, CA, July 27, 2005. Canela's original quote is: "Todos necesitábamos pasar eso para ser braceros."

9   Rachel Carson, *Silent Spring*, 40th Anniversary Edition (Mariner Books, 2002), 20. For more on DDT, see Elena Conis, *How to Sell a Poison: The Rise, Fall and Toxic Return of DDT* (Bold Type Books, 2022).

10   Carson, *Silent Spring*, 21.

11   Agency for Toxic Substances and Disease Registry, "DDT, DDE, and DDD," (US Centers for Disease Control and Prevention, 2022). Last accessed January 2, 2025, https://www.atsdr.cdc.gov/toxfaqs/tfacts35.pdf.

12   Lucio Nuñez, interview by Violeta Mena, Coachella, CA, *Bracero Oral History Project*, University of Texas at El Paso, May 20, 2006. Nuñez's original quote is: "No nos dijeron de … qué clase de polvo. Mucha gente se envenenó. Mucha gente de ahí salió con rochas."

13   Nemecio Meza, interview by Mireya Loza, Los Angeles, CA, *Bracero Oral History Project*, University of Texas at El Paso, May 12, 2006. Meza's original quote is: "Y nos desnudaban, nos polveaban y bueno, pues era un poco algo doloroso. A cada que me acuerdo, pos me siento un poco mal, pero con la necesidad de venir a trabajar aquí en los Estados Unidos tiene que aguantarse … Nos hacían sufrir mucho."

14   "New Role for the Photographer," Leonard Nadel Papers.

15   Ernesto Galarza, *Strangers in Our Fields* (Joint United States-Mexico Union Committee, 1956), 79.

16   For more on the British West Indies (BWI) program, see Cindy Hahamovitch, *No Man's Land: Jamaican Guestworkers in America and the Global History of Deportable Labor* (Princeton University Press, 2011).

17 Mireya Loza, "The Japanese Agricultural Workers' Program: Race, Labor, and Cold War Diplomacy in the Fields, 1956–1965," *Pacific Historical Review* 86, no. 4 (2017): 661–90.

18 Juan Ramon García, *Operation Wetback: The Mass Deportation of Mexican Undocumented Workers in 1954* (Greenwood Press, 1980); and Kelly Lytle Hernández, "The Crime and Consequences of Illegal Immigration: A Cross-Border Examination of Operation Wetback, 1943–1954," *Western Historical Quarterly* 37, no. 4 (Winter 2006): 421–44.

19 Hernández, "The Crime and Consequences of Illegal Immigration," 430.

20 Bryan L. McDonald, *The Rise and Fall of the Postwar American Food System* (Oxford University Press, 2017), 10.

21 John H. Davis and Ray Allan Goldberg, *A Concept of Agribusiness* (Harvard University, 1957).

22 Linda Nash, *Modern Landscapes and Ecological Bodies: A History of Environment, Disease and Knowledge* (University of California Press, 2006), 130.

23 McDonald, *The Rise and Fall of the Postwar American Food System*, 12.

24 Philip Martin, "There Is Nothing More Permanent than Temporary Foreign Workers," Center for Immigration Studies, April 2001, 2.

25 Philip Martin, "H-2A Program Expands in 2023," The Wilson Center (blog), August 25, 2023. Last accessed July 10, 2024, https://www.wilsoncenter.org/article/h-2a-program-expands-2023.

26 One example of this is Operation Blooming Onion, a multi-agency investigation which uncovered more than 100 people from Mexico, Guatemala, and Honduras who were victims of exploitation and modern-day slavery. See US Attorney's Office, Southern District of Georgia, "Human Smuggling, Forced Labor among Allegations in South Georgia Federal Indictment," press release, November 22, 2021. Last accessed June 10, 2024, https://www.justice.gov/usao-sdga/pr/human-smuggling-forced-labor-among-allegations-south-georgia-federal-indictment.

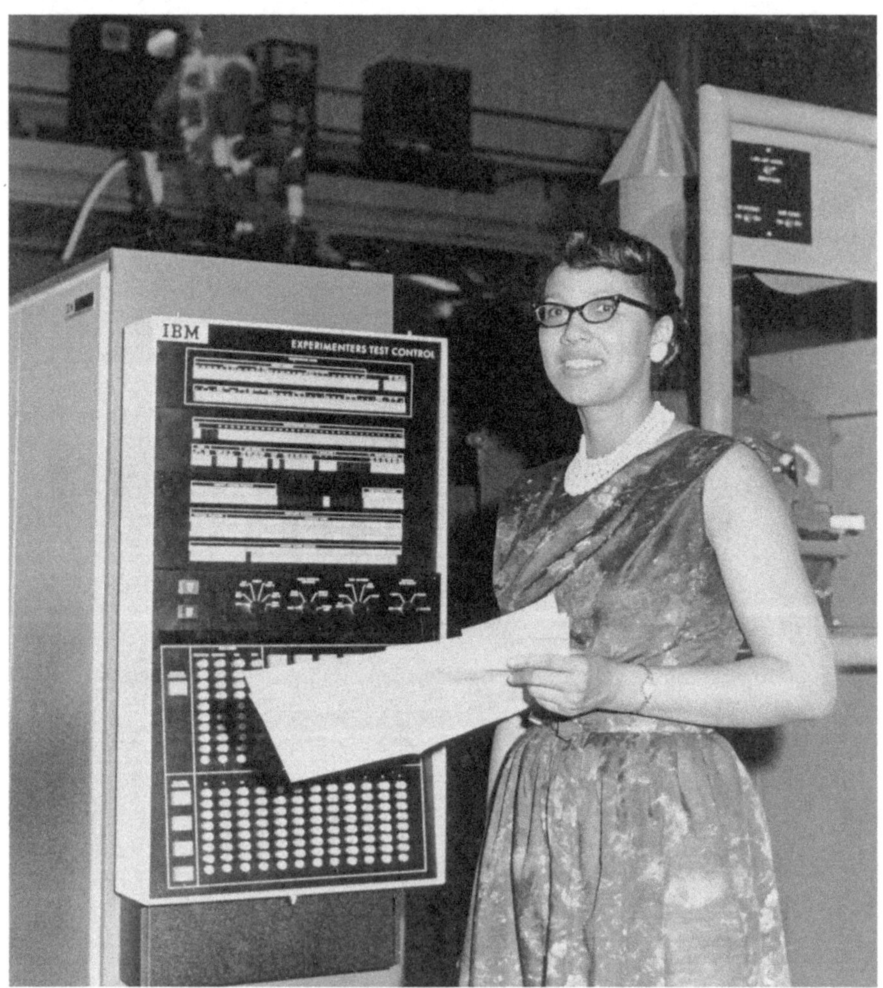

FIGURE 9.1 *Portrait of Melba Roy Mouton, head of a group of "human computers" tracking Echo satellites at NASA, 1964. Courtesy of the National Air & Space Administration, Wikimedia Commons.*

9

Race and the Space Race: Cold War Computing at NASA

By Nabeel Siddiqui and Thomas Haigh

The **Cold War** was a battle over the global influence of communism and democracy. As the United States stood on a pedestal of moral superiority abroad, the Soviet Union criticized its hypocritical treatment of Black and brown citizens at home. In September 1957, the world watched as the governor of Arkansas deployed the National Guard to prevent nine Black children in Little Rock from attending school. A month later, the Soviet Union successfully launched Sputnik, the world's first artificial satellite. The ideological history of Civil Rights and the Space Race are intertwined.

America's rival space program relied on the work of "**human computers**," women who performed complex calculations to determine precise trajectories and launch windows for spacecraft. Following the Second World War, a growing number of these women were African American. Working from the inside, they forced the desegregation of NASA's Langley Research Center, pushed for equal pay, and challenged the promotion structure. They were integral to the transition into electronic computing, becoming some of NASA's foremost computer programmers. This chapter tells the story of Melba Roy Mouton, one of many Black women who made incredible scientific and social advancements in a field dominated by white men.

Suggested Topics: African American History, Atomic Age, Civil Rights, Cold War, History of Science, Labor History, Second World War, Women & Sexuality

Glossary: Cold War, Electronic Computers, Human Computers, Military-Industrial Complex, National Aeronautics and Space Administration

In 1964 a Black woman in her mid-thirties posed before a camera and smiled. Her dress was stylish but professional, exposing her arms which were bare to the shoulder. Large earrings, a pearl necklace, and a slim metal watch completed the ensemble. Her hair was neatly restrained. As historian Margot Lee Shetterly notes in her book *Hidden Figures*, African Americans understand the theorem "of needing to be twice as good to get half as far." They "wore their professional clothes like armor" and "policed their ranks like soldiers against tardiness, sloppy appearance, and the perception of loose morals."[1] This woman's professional photograph—one for which she dressed with particular care—is now preserved in NASA's institutional archive.

Pictures of similarly immaculately dressed women can be found in any issue of *Ebony* magazine from the era. What set *this* image apart, earning it a modicum of internet virality in 2013 after it was shared on Tumblr from the NASA website by the account Vintage Black Glamor, was the background.[2] Melba Roy Mouton stood confidently in front of a large panel of lights, switches, and dials adorned with the IBM logo, instantly recognizable as a space-age mainframe computer. The computer was installed at NASA's Goddard Space Center in the Maryland suburbs of Washington, DC, where Mouton worked as assistant chief of Research Programs at NASA's Trajectory and Geodynamics Division.

The startling juxtaposition of woman, machine, and caption begs for a share button. Bumpy as the ride has been, American society has since the 1960s inched closer to racial equality and moved more rapidly toward gender parity in professional work. We know that today, even as tech companies and their billionaire founders fill ever more outsized roles in American culture and capitalism, relatively few women major in computer science or occupy prominent positions in tech firms. We also know that only a tiny minority of that female minority is Black. Yet somehow this descendent of enslaved peoples subject to the racial violence of the Jim Crow South had stood with that confidence, in those clothes, in that time, and at that place to meet our gaze through the corners of thickly framed glasses, the chic curvy cousins of the heavy black spectacles favored by stereotypical engineers.

History is more complicated than most people want it to be. Figures like Mouton challenge prevailing norms and expand the notion of who contributed to America's technological enterprises. Melba Roy Mouton was not the first woman to make a career out of astronomical calculations, something we trace in this chapter back to the 1870s when women were hired for the first time as "computers" to carry this mathematical labor. Neither was she the first or most famous Black woman to do so at what became NASA, where a small team had been at work since 1943. If you are less startled than the internet users of 2013, it is probably because both Shetterly's book *Hidden Figures* and a rather less historically reliable but hugely successful movie of the same name have reshaped our collective memory of NASA to include Black female mathematicians.[3] The evolution of computing technology during the mid-twentieth century is not merely a story about machines becoming more advanced; it is equally about a society grappling with its prejudices.

From Celestial Calculations to Societal Barriers: Women Computers in Post-Civil War Observatories

Today a "computer" is an electronic device that processes information rapidly and invisibly. In earlier history, though, computers were people. In the early eighteenth century, the burgeoning scientific community needed to carry out intricate mathematical computations. Astronomers required precise calculations to chart the positions of stars and planets and predict celestial events. Many mathematicians relied on **human computers** to turn complex equations into sequences of simple mathematical operations, magnifying their collective output.[4] Women's engagement in mathematics was largely informal and limited to those with strong familial connections, so most early computers were men.

However, the tradition of hiring women to carry out routine but demanding scientific calculations long predated both Mouton's career and the US space program. The template was set back in 1875 when Edward Charles Pickering, director of the Harvard College Observatory, began hiring women.[5] This blending of domestic and professional work started when they hired Anna Winlock, daughter of the observatory's former director who had lived there with her father.[6] In exchange for a modest wage, Winlock committed herself to finalizing the observations her father had started but could not complete. Other women quickly joined her from a variety of educational and familial backgrounds. Their work centered on analyzing a collection of photographic plates that eventually grew to half a million pieces of glass weighing nearly 300 tons. The plates resulted from hours of meticulous work by astronomers who attached cameras to telescopes to capture images of the night sky.

The "Harvard Computers" became a fixture at the observatory. Commentators referred to the women as "Pickering's harem," a winking orientalist innuendo that reflects both the unfamiliarity of a female scientific labor force and the reality of the gendered power dynamic at play.[7] If the women did not serve *for* his pleasure, like the harem of an imagined sultan, they did serve *at* his pleasure. They depended on Pickering for their livelihoods, professional opportunities, and the chance to carry out intellectually rewarding tasks. If they pushed too hard for recognition, autonomy, or pay they could lose everything.

An ideological framework that assumed binary differences between the sexes served as justification for the strong disparities in working conditions. Employers could pay women significantly less than men for the same work because they saw women as inherently suited to handle monotonous tasks and dead-end jobs. Astronomer William Elkin exemplified this attitude. "I am thoroughly in favour of employing women as measurers and computers," noted Elkin in 1901. "Not only are women available at smaller salaries than men, but for routine work they have important advantages. Men are more likely to grow impatient after the novelty of the work has worn off and would be harder to retain for that reason."[8] Their official roles were of the supporting kind, conceptualized as routine computation rather than astronomy. Pickering did not allow most of the Harvard Computers to use the main telescope to carry out observations themselves.[9] In a letter to Harvard President Charles W. Levitt, for instance, Pickering wrote that he felt that "the fatigue and the exposure to the cold in winter are too great for a lady to undergo."[10]

Other observatories followed Harvard's lead, as did other institutions with a need for large-scale computations. Human computing became an increasingly gendered activity. However, the academic community continued to undervalue and overlook women's contributions, and despite their significant achievements, they rarely received the same career advancement opportunities afforded to their male counterparts.

Segregation, Accommodation, and Computation

In 1935, the National Advisory Committee for Aeronautics (NACA), the precursor to the **National Aeronautics and Space Administration** (NASA), started actively recruiting women to work as human computers at the Langley Memorial Aeronautical Laboratory in Hampton, Virginia. Among the four women hired as the first "computing pool" for the facility was a white woman named Virginia Tucker. After earning a mathematics degree from North Carolina College for Women in 1930, Tucker worked as a high school teacher in her hometown. She took the civil servant exam seeking a new career and traveled throughout the South visiting colleges and universities to recruit other women for the computing pool.[11] Tucker alone trained close to 400 (predominantly white) women as human computers for NACA over her career.

The Second World War meant there were fewer men available for computing work even as demand for aircraft performance calculations grew, and by 1945, the facility employed close to 3,200 people, many of them female. Anne Wythe Hall, a dormitory specifically for women, opened in 1943 to provide on-site housing. Residents could utilize a large bathroom and laundry room on the first floor, and a house mother was available to assist with the needs of the women computers. Langley computers also benefited from policies and accommodations unusual for the era that enabled them to maintain their positions even after marriage and motherhood, in an era when many employers banned the employment of married women or fired them when they became pregnant.[12] By blending personal living spaces with the workplace, Langley mingled the private and professional lives of the women, subtly anchoring them to their jobs.[13]

Unlike the early Harvard computers, who had been largely confined to repetitive tasks, the Langley computers participated in significant aircraft research and design projects while earning wages that were, for women, unusually high. This work not only provided an alternative to teaching for women with science degrees but also served as a gateway into the male-dominated field of aeronautical research. These advantages were relative, of course. Langley paid the women less than their male counterparts for similar work and classified them in lower positions. Most women hired at Langley had at least a bachelor's degree, but they were classified as "sub-professionals" with salaries ranging from $1,440 per year for a Junior Computer to $3,200 per year for a Chief Computer. In contrast, the institution hired men with the same qualifications as "Junior Engineers," a "professional" classification with a starting salary of $2,600 per year.[14]

The Langley complex is 75 miles southeast of Richmond, the former capital of the Confederacy. In 1940 zero percent of the female computers at Langley were Black versus a quarter of Virginia's population. That was itself down from almost half in the 1810s before many of Virginia's enslaved residents were resold to face even greater torments in the booming cotton plantations of the deep South. A full human lifespan separated the Second World War from the Civil War, but the legacy of slavery rested heavily on Virginia. Reversing steps toward racial justice made during the Reconstruction era, the state had implemented a full range of "Jim Crow" laws to safeguard white supremacy. Its 1902 constitution enshrined school segregation and mandated poll taxes and literacy tests to keep Black voters off the electoral rolls. Public transport, hospitals, and libraries were segregated by race, and the right of private businesses to discriminate against potential customers was protected by law. Statues of Confederate generals and politicians were mass-produced for public display to reinforce white supremacy visually. More Confederate monuments survive in Virginia than any other state.

Langley was thus an outpost of the United States federal government deep within the former Confederacy. Did the values of the Union still clash with those of the Jim Crow South? Not really. Woodrow Wilson codified the segregation of federal facilities across the country in 1913 to avoid offense and keep Southern support. American armed forces remained segregated throughout the Second World War, just like the New Deal era Civilian Conservation Corps responsible for building trails and cabins on a massive scale.

The first African American computers hired at Langley during the Second World War were segregated in its West Wing, earning them the nickname the "West Area Computers." They had to sit at different tables in the cafeteria and use separate bathroom facilities. Many of the African American women employed engaged in subtle acts of defiance to challenge these policies. Miriam Mann frequently removed the designated seating sign in the cafeteria.[15] Katherine Johnson often ate at her desk and refused to use the segregated bathrooms.[16] Segregation also meant there was little interaction between African American computers and their white counterparts.[17] Their first supervisors were white, but this changed when Dorothy Vaughn began serving as section head in 1949.[18]

Despite these routine humiliations, jobs at Langley were prized by Black women. The federal government, with its growing bureaucracy, employed many women in clerical positions. Public service jobs were among the few avenues available to African Americans for well-paying and prestigious positions. Obtaining higher education was a means to a career in teaching, a secure career with little room for progression. Not only did these roles provide individual economic stability but they also offered a source of communal pride and financial support for local Black businesses and educational institutions.[19]

While the federal government led the way in desegregation, pushed by the growing Civil Rights Movement, the process was painfully slow. Franklin Roosevelt signed Executive Order 8802 in 1941 to prohibit racial discrimination in the national defense industry, but it wasn't until 1948 that his successor, Harry Truman, issued the executive order that remade the US military as the most important desegregated institution in the country. By then, the United States was becoming embroiled in a new kind of conflict that would shape national development over decades: the **Cold War** with the Soviet Union. Internal activism was supplemented by foreign pressure. Soviet propaganda highlighted the contradiction between America's claim to be a beacon of freedom and democracy and the reality of racial oppression within its borders.[20]

Opportunities for West Area Computers gradually improved until the group was merged into a new racially and gender-integrated Analysis and Computing Division in 1958. If you've seen the movie version of *Hidden Figures*, you might be confused right now. To compress the narrative, the film begins in 1961 during the era of manned space flight but still chooses to depict the explicit segregation of the 1950s, severely mangling the actual historical timeline.

That wasn't the only big change in 1958. The NACA Langley Aeronautical Laboratory had become NASA's Langley Research Center, a hub for a new agency intended to unite the struggling US space program under civilian control. The Soviet Union had launched Sputnik, the first artificial satellite, the previous year. Democrats seized on the Sputnik launch to criticize the Eisenhower administration, and the National Aeronautics and Space Act of 1958, which created NASA, was a response to these criticisms.[21] Space became a bloodless battlefield of the Cold War, as the two superpowers showcased their prowess as the rest of the world watched. NASA hired Melba Ray Mouton the following year to join the computing staff at its newly created Goddard Space Center in Beltsville, Maryland. By the time she posed for the photographer in our picture, NASA was receiving five percent of the entire federal budget (ten times its share today).

Electronic Computing at NASA

Mouton was born in 1929 in Fairfax, Virginia. Today both Fairfax and Beltsville where she worked are liberal suburbs on opposite sides of the Washington, DC, beltway. During her childhood, however, Fairfax was firmly under the grip of Jim Crow. For white students, Fairfax had a good school system, but the entire county offered no high school for Black youngsters. Consequently, Mouton commuted to Manassas to continue her education where she thrived academically. In 1950 she earned a degree in mathematics from Howard University, founded in the capital just after the Civil War as a beacon for Black education. She considered beginning her career in teaching but instead went into federal employment with the Army Map Service and the Census Bureau, where she leveraged her education to analyze demographic data and geospatial information about where individuals lived, worked, and migrated.

By the time she arrived at the fast-growing Goddard Center, a modernist suburban campus of blocky buildings and sprawling parking lots, the adoption of electronic computers was transforming scientific practice at NASA. Human computers worked with pencil and paper, adding machines, and, in some cases, complex and expensive mechanical calculators able to multiply and divide as well as add and subtract. In the 1940s and 1950s demand for computation skyrocketed, along with all the actual rockets, supersonic jets, nuclear submarines, and atomic weapons whose behavior had to be modeled with mathematical equations. The technological surge of the early Cold War was underpinned by a new technology: the digital electronic computer.

The first programmable **electronic computer**, ENIAC, was built during the Second World War for the Ordnance Department of the US Army by a team at the University of Pennsylvania. Like Langley, the Army had to compute trajectories, but the objects of interest were shells arcing through the atmosphere rather than celestial bodies moving in a vacuum. Atmospheric drag replaced the clean process of symbolic rearrangement taught in calculus class with a numerical slog requiring computers to simulate the shell's progress from one fraction of a second to the next. Hundreds of women were hired to calculate trajectories for the new artillery pieces introduced during the war, but the backlog of work grew even longer.[22]

In 1943 a small team of scientists and engineers took the opportunity to pitch their plan for an electronic computer. ENIAC wasn't ready for real work until 1946 but it found many applications, simulating nuclear explosions and the flow of air around jets and missiles as well as the flight of shells.[23] ENIAC itself was a quirky one-off machine, but the team behind it proposed a more efficient and flexible successor, EDVAC, which set the template for the widespread adoption of programmable computers in the 1950s.[24] The computer next to Mouton in the photograph was, by 1964, one of several hundred thousand machines indirectly patterned after the EDVAC design.

If you've heard of ENIAC, it is probably as a computer programmed by women. In 1945 six of the women who had proven themselves by carrying out manual trajectory calculations were chosen as the first group of ENIAC operators. They tended to the machine, reconfiguring its switches and wires between calculations, entering parameters, logging results, preparing punched cards full of data, and feeding them into the machine for processing. As the operators knew the machine so well, they collaborated with scientists and engineers to devise new configurations. One of them, Jean Bartik, soon moved on from operations to lead the first group focused entirely on computer programming. Today their contributions are widely celebrated.

Computers didn't so much replace human labor as substitute new kinds of human labor for old ones. Lowering the cost of computation increased demand so that more people were employed carrying out more computations than ever before. The computer took over laborious and repetitive tasks, executing them much faster than any human could. But somebody had to specify the work in minute detail, whether it was production scheduling or nuclear simulation. Somebody had to turn those specifications into coded computer instructions. Somebody had to operate the computer. Given that code rarely worked as expected the first time, all those somebodies had to work together to debug the code and maintain it once it was operational. Software tools like assemblers, compilers, and operating systems appeared to use the computer itself to partially automate some of these tasks. New jobs proliferated: numerical analyst, systems analyst, computer application programmer, computer operator, and systems programmer.[25]

In the photograph, Mouton stood next to the console of a computer. Mainframe computers of the era did not usually have a video display. Instead, the computer's operator used a large panel of switches and lights, known as the console, to start and stop the machine, change its configuration, and inspect data held in its internal registers to figure out what was going on. By 1964, she was already a programming group leader, so it is unlikely that she operated the computer herself. In the picture, she looks not at the console as an operator would but at the camera, holding several sheets of paper on which we might imagine program code or orbital equations to be written. Standing there, rather than at a desk or blackboard, emphasized her authority over the cutting-edge technology of computation. By taking and distributing images featuring novel technologies with a diverse labor force, NASA was emphasizing its progressive employment practices. The federal government was not the only group benefitting.

The Rise of IBM and a Computing Economy

The photo prominently displays the logo of IBM, which dominated the market for computers. IBM's rise to become one of the world's largest and most profitable corporations was driven by its relationship with the US government. Its roots go back to the late 1800s with the invention of punched card machines by Herman Hollerith to more efficiently tabulate data for the US Census Bureau. Its charismatic leader Thomas Watson cultivated connections with presidents and other powerful men.

IBM grew rapidly during the Great Depression of the 1930s thanks to contracts with the new Social Security Administration. During the Second World War, the company used its factories to produce military equipment and special products such as codebreaking machines. IBM's first computer product, the multi-million-dollar IBM 701, was codenamed the Defense Calculator because the market for high-speed computation centered on defense contractors and nuclear labs. Later that decade IBM won huge contracts for special military projects such as the SAGE air defense network, funding its development of advanced technologies with civilian potential. It was a founding partner in what Watson's friend, President Dwight Eisenhower, warningly called a **military-industrial complex** with its own incentives to broaden and deepen the Cold War spending that was transforming America's relationship with its government.[26]

Little wonder, then, that a federal agency hungry for computation relied on IBM equipment. Langley installed its first electronic computers in the mid-1950s. The most powerful was a 704, the initial successor to the 701. IBM built around a hundred of these giant machines using vacuum tubes and hand-woven magnetic core memories. The work of the computer groups began to shift from carrying out computations to writing and running computer programs and checking their results, though the scarcity of computer resources and overhead time involved in writing programs meant that many jobs were still carried out manually.

When computerization shook up the organization of work in unpredictable ways one thing was usually true: with each step up in the occupational hierarchy, there were fewer women. Keypunch workers, who used a keyboard to enter data onto cards, were almost invariably female. Computer operators were sometimes male and sometimes female. Most programmers were men. Systems analysts, who redesigned administrative work processes around computer technology, and business computing managers were overwhelmingly male. Programming and operations were new jobs though, without strongly entrenched gender expectations. Gender patterns varied from organization to organization, guided in part by who had been doing comparable kinds of work previously.

The strong tradition of female labor in applied mathematics, including many women with graduate degrees, gave scientific computing a different gender breakdown from administrative computing. What's more, the patterns of gender and race segregation enforced in the 1950s had an ironic legacy: Black women worked not just as computers but as supervisors who designed and oversaw computations. Some made the transition from manual to electronic calculation. Dorothy Vaughn shifted around 1960, at the age of fifty, from supervising human computers to programming. Others like Annie Wesley and Gladys Mae West also found themselves transitioning into roles as programmers and analysts.

By 1964, the 704 was obsolete. Its replacement as IBM's flagship scientific computer was the far more powerful 7090 series, deployed at NASA installations around the country. President Kennedy's famous challenge to land a man on the moon by the end of the 1960s had dramatically expanded the scope of the US space program; the space race with the Soviet Union was well underway. The Goddard Space Flight Center tracked manned space flights from 1961 onward using two of them. Signals from a worldwide network of tracking stations were transmitted by the computer center, where special software called the Mercury Monitor handled them according to a system of priorities so that the computer could keep up with the flight in real-time rather than, as was normal mainframe practice, wait for large batches of data to accumulate and then processes them as bulk jobs. According to historian Paul Ceruzzi, this "evolved into one of IBM's most ambitious and successful software products and laid the foundations for the company's entry into online systems later adopted for banking, airline reservation systems, and large online data networks."[27]

In 1964, the same year Mouton posed next to the IBM computer at Goddard, Langley interconnected two mainframes to test a new model of computing where users submitted FORTRAN programs directly from remote terminals rather than having to bring paper sheets to the computing center and wait for them to be pushed onto cards and queued for attention by operators. Borrowing from the language of union busters, this was called an "open shop" arrangement because the 400 computer-savvy scientists and scientific programmers at Langley could enter and run programs themselves.[28] The balance of power between mathematical specialists, human computers, specialist programmers, and rocket scientists was still evolving rapidly.

IBM was poised for spectacular growth from its new System/360 product line, introduced in 1964, which gave it a near monopoly in the mainframe computer industry. Today's big tech firms are larger than IBM ever was, but the modern industry offers few opportunities for Black women.

In Search of Melba Roy Mouton

What part did Mouton herself play? Archival clues no doubt wait to be uncovered, but our current picture is fragmentary. The proliferation of the image and a striking portrait photo also released by NASA brought her a minor posthumous celebrity. She's profiled on dozens of websites, each with a few paragraphs recycling the same handful of facts. To populate her rather sparse Wikipedia page, editors were forced to set aside the probation on original research and dive into genealogical records, technical reports, and other primary sources. Much of that material was initially surfaced by a blogger.[29]

Here's what we know. At NASA an early job was to develop orbital element timetables for the Echo 1 satellite launched in 1960. This gigantic balloon-like communication satellite was a passive reflective surface on which signals beamed up from Earth were reflected to bounce back down in different locations. It and a follow-up launched in 1964, transmitted telephone, radio, and television signals across continents. Mouton's success led to her promotion as assistant chief of Research Programs in the Trajectory and Geodynamics Division at Goddard.[30] By 1962 she had already achieved the GS-13 pay grade, reserved for supervisors and high-level specialists.[31]

Delving more deeply, a 1968 technical report credited her as joint leader of the programming of the Goddard General Orbit Determination System while working as head of the Data Systems Division's Advanced Orbital Programming Branch. Satellites were a particular focus of Goddard from its inception, and it retained responsibility for them after work on manned missions shifted to other NASA centers. The program tracked satellites in orbit, not rockets being launched. It had "evolved over about a decade," which implies it was based on mathematical analysis completed not long after Mouton joined NASA.[32] The NASA web exhibit that launched our photograph into the world captioned Mouton as a "human computer" but given this timeline, it seems likely she had shifted quickly to computer work.

Later in her career, she worked with advanced programming languages, leading courses on IBM's APL (A Programming Language), a concise and powerful language well-suited for scientific and engineering applications.[33] As of 1968 Mouton was head of the Mission and Trajectory Analysis Division's Program Systems Branch, which suggests continuing responsibility for satellite tracking software. According to NASA, her final role was as "Assistant Chief of Research Programs for the Trajectory and Geodynamics Division" at Goddard which hints at a shift to broader responsibilities.

These sparse facts sketch a rewarding career, yet she retired in 1973 still in her mid-forties. We don't know why. She died at the age of sixty-one. For that, we do have a cause: a brain tumor. Her brief obituary also reveals that Melba Roy Mouton had three children and two husbands. "Roy" came from the first husband, "Mouton" from the second.[34] Her own name had been Melba Chloe.

Even her picture lies in a strange space between clarity and ignorance. The size and shape of the console shown resemble that of the IBM 7040, a relatively simple and more affordable computer modeled on the ubiquitous 7090. IBM promoted the two as a bundle, known as the Direct Coupled System, which offloaded some work to the smaller machine for increased overall efficiency. Goddard had installed a 7040 by 1964, but the layout of the controls in the picture is completely different from the standard 7040 console. The words "Experimenters Test Control" visible in place of the usual model number suggest that this was custom equipment produced as part of the special relationship between IBM and NASA. We cannot tell you what it did.

In 2022, NASA successfully proposed the naming of a mountain near the South pole of the moon scheduled for a visit by a robotic lander as Mons Mouton, enshrining her in the organization's growing pantheon of Black pioneers. Its press release talked vaguely of Mouton as "one of our pioneering leaders" who "helped NASA take the lead in exploring the unknown" yet her name does not appear in either of the official histories of the Goddard Center. As a symbol of its historical commitment to helping "women and people of color to pursue careers and lead cutting-edge science," NASA gave her a mountain on the moon; as a person, it gave her life and career 158 words.[35]

∗∗∗

We can, with more confidence, situate the photograph within the broad sweep of US history. Since 1948, the official Democratic party platform had included a strong civil rights commitment, but a strong faction of segregationist Southern Democrats had slowed progress to a crawl despite the party holding strong congressional majorities for most of the intervening period. The biggest shift of the 1950s, an effort to desegregate schools, was enforced by the Supreme Court rather than legislators. Not long after taking office in 1961, John F. Kennedy kicked the US space program into high gear with his famous call for a manned moon landing within the decade. His push for civil rights legislation was less successful, though he did issue an executive order mandating "affirmative action" by government agencies to diversify their own workforces. After Kennedy's assassination in 1963, Lyndon Johnson was able to pass the landmark 1964 Civil Rights Act which took direct aim at segregation and discrimination.

In November, Johnson won a full term by a landslide. Virginia backed a Democratic presidential candidate for the first time since 1948 and the last until 2008. In Congress, progressive bipartisan majorities could finally pass legislation without the assent of segregationists. Among the flood of laws that followed was the 1965 Voting Rights Act, which swept away the measures used to keep Black citizens from voting.

You already know what happened next. The tired montage has been assembled by thousands of video editors: the Vietnam War, assassinations, hippies, the burning of cities along with bras and draft cards, Johnson's refusal to seek reelection, and Richard Nixon's victory. After the moon landings won the Space Race, NASA funding was slashed, and since 1972, no human has been more than a few hundred miles from Earth—the moon is 238,900 miles from the Earth. In the 1970s came oil shocks, Watergate, stagflation, and malaise. American society splintered and our never-ending culture wars began. Instead of fading into historical distance, the rival cultures of the late 1960s define an enduring political fault line. Legal regimes that seemed settled for decades are now being aggressively rolled back. Many historians now view the birth of the modern conservative movement as a legacy of the 1960s at least as important as the more immediately visible rise of the New Left.

We chose Mouton's picture, rather than one of Katherine Johnson, to highlight the space between remembering and forgetting. Even before *Hidden Figures* appeared, Barack Obama presented Johnson with the Presidential Medal of Freedom. Two NASA facilities have been named after her, as have several schools, several spacecraft, and a Barbie doll. Johnson lived long enough to tell her own story many times, always compellingly.

Deserved as this recognition is, the elevation of a handful of women involved with the history of computing to superheroine status can crowd out others and obscure the complexity of history. Mouton's photograph sometimes appears online misidentified as one of Johnson, as if history has room for only one Black woman from NASA. Margo Shetterly, who did so much to capture and celebrate this history, noted that as she became iconic,

Johnson was often credited with work done by other Black women who also "participated as protagonists in the epic of America" through their work at NASA.[36] In popular memory, people are either "nameless or renowned, menial or exceptional, passive recipients of the forces of history of superheroes."[37]

Like the rest of us, Melba Roy Mouton made her way through a chaotic and frequently terrifying world toward an uncertain destination. The cultural and political landscape of the Cold War and the electronic technologies introduced by IBM offered opportunities as well as obstacles to those marginalized by race and gender. She stood in 1964 at a pivotal moment in the history of scientific labor where the roles of human computers and machine operators intertwined with technological advancements. She stood also at a pivotal moment in the African American experience, between Martin Luther King's "I Have a Dream Speech" of 1963 and his assassination five years later, by which time the militancy of the Black Panthers already offered a vision of Black pride incommensurate with her quiet rise within the federal bureaucracy of big science. IBM's complicity with the Vietnam War was judged harshly by the protestors who bombed campus computer centers.

What came before was real too. Once upon a time, the federal government was, thanks to the work of generations of activists, primed to aggressively pursue racial justice with policies that achieved tangible social and economic change. Once upon a time, government agencies were places where smart and ambitious people from groups overlooked by other employers could build successful careers in service of national triumphs that resonated around the world. The image of Melba Roy Mouton at an IBM mainframe is much more than a snapshot of a person at work. It captures an intersection of human endeavor and machine capability, a juncture at which the personal and the technological coalesced to push the boundaries of what was possible. In understanding computing through this lens, we affirm that technological development is not just about the machines themselves but also about people.

Discussion Questions

1   This chapter opens with a photograph that became "viral" in 2013. Why do you think this image was so compelling to modern viewers, and what does this tell us about our changing attitudes toward technology, race, and gender?

2   How does Melba Roy Mouton's career at NASA challenge or complicate common assumptions about women's professional opportunities in the 1950s and 1960s? What factors enabled some women to pursue technical careers during this period while others faced significant barriers?

3   Today, we associate advanced computer technologies with big tech firms like Google and Microsoft, whose products are used primarily by individuals and private companies. When government computing makes the news, it is usually for struggling projects or antiquated systems. Why was the federal government, notably NASA, so crucial in the early days of electronic computing?

4   Compare the working conditions of women computers at Harvard Observatory in the 1870s with those at NASA in the 1960s. What changed, and what remained consistent over nearly a century?

5   The chapter notes that many details of Mouton's work remain unknown. What challenges do historians face in reconstructing the careers of women and minorities in computing?

Further Resources

Harris, Duchess. "Human Computers at NASA." Macalester College. https://omeka.macalester.edu/humancomputerproject/.

Key, Keegan-Michael, host. "NASA's Human Computers." Historically Black (podcast). *APM Reports*, September 19, 2016. https://www.apmreports.org/episode/2016/09/19/historically-black-nasa-human-computers.

Thompson, Clive. "The Gendered History of Human Computers." *Smithsonian Magazine*, June 2019. https://www.smithsonianmag.com/science-nature/history-human-computers-180972202/.

Notes

1   Margot Lee Shetterly, *Hidden Figures: The American Dream and the Untold Story of the Black Women Mathematicians Who Helped Win the Space Race* (William Morrow, 2016), 75.

2   vintageblackglamour, "Vintage Black Glamour by Nichelle Gainer," *Tumblr* (blog). Last accessed February 13, 2025, https://ncecire.tumblr.com/post/45081525352/melba-roy-mouton.

3   *Hidden Figures*, directed by Theodore Melfi (20th Century Fox, 2016).

4   David Alan Grier, *When Computers Were Human* (Princeton University Press, 2005), 72–88.

5   Sue Nelson, "The Harvard Computers," *Nature* 455, no. 7209 (September 2008): 36–7.

6   Andrew Fiss, "'For Computing Is Our Duty': Algorithmic Workers, Servants, and Women at the Harvard Observatory," in *Algorithmic Modernity: Mechanizing Thought and Action, 1500–2000*, ed. Morgan G. Ames and Massimo Mazzotti (Oxford University Press, 2023), 127–43.

7   Barbara L. Welther, "'Pickering's Harem'," *Isis* 73, no. 1 (March 1982): 94.

8   Quoted in Nelson, "The Harvard Computers," 36–7.

9   Cristela Guerra, "'Women Computers' Often Couldn't Use Harvard's Telescope. They Changed Astronomy Anyway," *Boston Globe*, August 10, 2017.

10   Quoted in Bessie Zaban Jones and Lyle Gifford Boyd, *The Harvard College Observatory: The First Four Directorships* (Harvard University Press, 1971), 188.

11   Erin Lawrimore, "Virginia Tucker (Class of 1930)," *Encyclopedia of UNCG History*. Last accessed August 3, 2024, https://encyclopedia.uncg.edu/virginia-tucker/.

12   Claudia Dale Goldin, *Understanding the Gender Gap: An Economic History of American Women* (Oxford University Press, 1990).

13   Sarah McLennan and Mary Gainer, "When the Computer Wore a Skirt: Langley's Computers, 1935–1970," *NASA History Program Office News & Notes* 29, no. 1 (2012): 25–32.

14   McLennan and Gainer, "When the Computer Wore a Skirt," 25–32.

15   Shetterly, *Hidden Figures*, 67–71.

16   Katherine G. Johnson, *Reaching for the Moon: The Autobiography of NASA Mathematician Katherine Johnson* (Simon & Schuster, 2019), 158.

17   McLennan and Gainer, "When the Computer Wore a Skirt," 25–32.

18   Johnson, *Reaching for the Moon*, 149.

19   Jennifer D. Keene, "Wilson and Race Relations," in *A Companion to Woodrow Wilson*, ed. Ross A. Kennedy (Wiley-Blackwell, 2013), 133–51.

20   Timothy Borstelmann, *The Cold War and the Color Line: American Race Relations in the Global Arena* (Harvard University Press, 2001).

21   Roger D. Launius, *NACA to NASA to Now: The Frontiers of Air and Space in the American Century* (NASA, 2022), 65–70.

22   Jennifer S. Light, "When Computers Were Women," *Technology and Culture* 40, no. 3 (July 1999): 455–83.

23   Thomas Haigh, Mark Priestley, and Crispin Rope, *ENIAC in Action: Making and Remaking the Modern Computer* (MIT Press, 2016).

24   Thomas Haigh and Paul E. Ceruzzi, *A New History of Modern Computing* (MIT Press, 2021), 14–20.

25   Thomas Haigh, "The Chromium-Plated Tabulator: Institutionalizing an Electronic Revolution, 1954–1958," *IEEE Annals of the History of Computing* 23, no. 4 (October 2001): 75–104; and Mar Hicks, *Programmed Inequality: How Britain Discarded Women Technologists and Lost Its Edge in Computing* (MIT Press, 2017).

26   Thomas Haigh, "Computing the American Way: Contextualizing the Early US Computer Industry," *IEEE Annals of the History of Computing* 32, no. 2 (April 2010): 8–20.

27   Paul E. Ceruzzi, *A History of Modern Computing* (MIT Press, 1998, 2003), 123–4.

28   Roger V. Butler, "The Langley Research Center Remote Computing Terminal System: Implementation and First Year's Operation," in *Proceedings of the*

1966 21st National Conference (Association for Computing Machinery, 1966), 139–48.

29 ncecire, "Melba Roy Mouton," *Tumblr* (blog), Last accessed March 10, 2013, https://ncecire.tumblr.com/post/45081525352/melba-roy-mouton.

30 R. Arvid Nelsen, "Race and Computing: The Problem of Sources, the Potential of Prosopography, and the Lesson of *Ebony* Magazine," *IEEE Annals of the History of Computing* 39, no. 1 (2017): 29–51.

31 Shetterly, *Hidden Figures*, 410.

32 Isabella J. Cole, James P. Murphy, and Joseph W. Siry, "The Goddard General Orbit Determination System," Goddard Space Flight Center, May 1968.

33 Cyrus J. Creveling, "Experimental Use of A Programming Language (APL) at the Goddard Space Flight Center," Goddard Space Flight Center, November 1968.

34 "William Davies, Retired U.S. Geological Official, Dies," *Washington Post*, June 29, 1990.

35 Rachel Hoover, "Moon Mountain Name Honors NASA Mathematician Melba Mouton," *NASA* (blog). Last accessed February 15, 2023, https://www.nasa.gov/people-of-nasa/moon-mountain-name-honors-nasa-mathematician-melba-mouton/.

36 Shetterly, *Hidden Figures*, 397.

37 Shetterly, *Hidden Figures*, 401; More generally, see Thomas Haigh and Mark Priestley, "Innovators Assemble: Ada Lovelace, Walter Isaacson, and the Superheroines of Computing," *Communications of the ACM* 58, no. 9 (August 2015): 20–7.

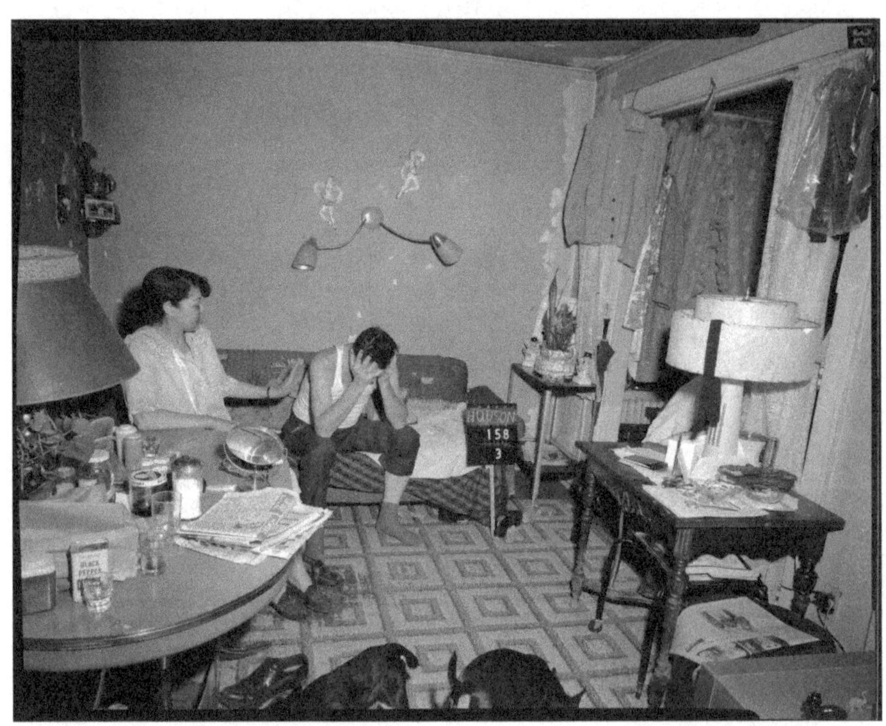

FIGURE 10.1 *Robert and Ethel Mather inside their apartment, Albany, New York, February 28, 1963. Photo by Harold Furlong. Courtesy of the New York State Archives.*[1]

10

Tear Down, Rise Up: Redevelopment and Revolts in American Cities

By Ann Pfau, David Hochfelder, and Stacy Sewell

Following the Second World War, urban decay and outdated infrastructure became a focus of national attention, born out of demographic and financial concerns. Many middle-income white Americans moved out of the city and into the suburbs, a process commonly referred to as "white flight." At the same time, poorer people, including African Americans and other racial and ethnic minorities, moved into urban cores. Residential segregation and **redlining** ensured that the suburbs would remain predominantly, if not exclusively, white.

Federal and state policies pushed redevelopment forward by providing subsidies for **urban renewal** and highway construction. Using these funds, state and municipal government officials hired urban planners with the goal of reinvigorating the nation's cities. In practice, however, building new highways, cultural amenities, and luxury housing meant leveling low-income neighborhoods. Millions of Americans were displaced. By the late 1960s, dislocation combined with overcrowding resulting from exclusionary housing practices would spark waves of protests. This chapter zooms in on how urban renewal and highway construction affected the city and residents of Albany, New York, focusing on the 7,000 people forced from their homes.

Suggested Topics: African American History, Civil Rights, Great Migration, Urban Studies

Glossary: Eminent Domain, Fair Housing Act, Fair Market Value, Gentrification, Redlining, Root Shock, Urban Renewal

Until recently, very few people had seen this photograph. It was one of a collection of hundreds of photographic negatives documenting a place that would soon be destroyed. It shows two people, whom former neighbors have identified as Ethel and Robert Mather. The Mathers sit in their apartment amid their possessions and with their two dogs. Ethel reaches out to Robert, who appears to be upset, leaning forward with his head in his hands. We don't know why, but we do know that the Mathers would soon be forced to move. Via the power of eminent domain, the State of New York had seized the building where they lived.

Seizure of the Mathers' home was part of the South Mall plan, which called for the clearance of 98.5 acres of densely populated land in downtown Albany, New York's capital city. It entailed displacement of roughly 7,000 people and demolition of 1,150 buildings. In 1965, after the South Mall land had been cleared, the State would begin building a new highway interchange (the South Mall Arterial) and a monumental, marble-clad office and cultural complex (the Empire State Plaza). The project was part of a nationwide effort to update urban infrastructure, prioritizing automobility and middle-class amenities over the needs of existing, typically poorer, area residents.

The South Mall plan was the brainchild of Governor Nelson Rockefeller. It was intended, in his words, to turn the "shabby" city of Albany "into one of the most brilliant, beautiful, efficient, and electrifying capitals in all the world."[2] To the governor and his supporters, the South Mall represented progress.

This picture of Robert and Ethel was created as part of the redevelopment process. Government agencies across the nation hired photographers to perform a variety of tasks. Photographs, alongside architectural models and renderings, helped public officials plan for redevelopment by focusing on streets and structures, not the people who walked or inhabited them. The photographs also made a visual argument regarding the need for dramatic change by highlighting disorder, deterioration, and debris. Address signs, like one near Robert's left knee, identified the location to be demolished. These images, though designed to assist or justify redevelopment, provide a glimpse of what was lost in the renewal process.

On February 28, 1963, Harold Furlong was inside the Mathers' apartment as an employee of the State of New York. His job was to photograph construction sites, public events, and seized property. In this case, his assignment was to document the building where the Mathers lived. His photographs of the building's location, condition, and physical attributes were intended as evidence in a legal dispute between the State and the owner. They show a three-story brick building at the corner of a small business district, a liquor store in the storefront. Other photographs document the inside of the Mathers' apartment—a cramped kitchen and bathroom, a bedroom with long strips of paint hanging from the ceiling.

This image of the Mathers is different from the others on the same roll of film.[3] While some of Furlong's photographs captured pedestrians on the street and workers on the job, the photograph of Robert and Ethel Mather experiencing a painful moment is the only one to provide an intimate look inside a private home. By focusing on people rather than property, Furlong turned the cold objectivity of legal evidence into a touching portrait.

There are many things we do not know about the encounter between Furlong and the Mathers. Why did Furlong, a former newspaper photographer, make this portrait? Why did Robert and Ethel cooperate? How spontaneous was their pose? Were they trying to send a message to those in charge? The Mathers had no power to prevent the loss of their home. With Furlong's help, they might have hoped to communicate what it meant to lose not just their admittedly shabby apartment but also the community in which they had made their home for the past fourteen years.

This portrait is one of about fifty we found at the New York State Archives, scattered amongst pictures of kitchens, bathrooms, stairwells, and storefronts. These photographs suggest that, although employed by the State of New York, Furlong and his colleagues empathized with the people whose homes would soon be demolished. Additional evidence of this attitude is one person's decision to write "South Maul," a derisive local nickname for the redevelopment project, on a packet of negatives.[4]

Eminent Domain

This photograph of the Mathers is unusual, but their situation was not. The picture captures a scene that, by 1963, had become increasingly common. The US House of Representatives Committee on Public Works estimated that, between 1961 and 1963, the federal government was instrumental in the seizure of 1.4 million acres of privately owned land per year. Such seizures displaced roughly 73,000 families and 11,000 businesses annually. In future years, the committee predicted that displacements would increase to 111,000 and 18,000 respectively.[5] Cumulatively, between 1950 and 1980, roughly 2.5–3 million Americans were displaced by redevelopment projects—new apartment buildings, highways, shopping centers, sports arenas, and office complexes.[6]

Eminent domain, the government's power to seize private property for public use, predates the 1950s. It is an element of English common law enshrined in state laws and constitutions as well as the Fifth Amendment to the US Constitution. Local, state, and federal governments have long used this power to acquire and clear land for new parks, roads, bridges, dams, and civic buildings. During the New Deal, federal subsidies for public housing expanded use of this power by local housing authorities. After the Second World War, "slum clearance," or **urban renewal**, grants resulted in a similar expansion of eminent domain takings. Using federal renewal funds, municipal governments could afford to seize and demolish private property, not just to build public facilities but also to encourage private development. Finally, the Cold War Era expansion of federal and state highway systems led to additional takings, demolitions, and displacements.

The history of urban renewal is entwined with that of highway and public housing construction. Many urban highways run through renewal areas. Renewal plans typically included some provision for low-income public housing, though not enough to rehouse those displaced. On South Mall land, for example, the State built an elevated spaghetti-bowl interchange designed to bring commuters and visitors into and out of the Empire State Plaza. There were plans for a new housing complex, but that was replaced with a parking garage. In this case, as in countless others, renewal was, as critics charged, more accurately described as "removal."

We lack pictures of most of the people forced out of their homes, but we do know that many looked a lot like the Mathers. Most were renters rather than homeowners. They were disproportionately Black and Brown and lived on limited incomes. Along with African Americans, redevelopment of Manhattan's Upper West Side displaced large numbers of Puerto Rican migrants. Urban renewal in San Francisco, California, threatened the city's Japantown. Rooming houses and single-room occupancy hotels fell victim to redevelopment in New York, San Francisco, Albany, and many other cities.

The people who once lived in these places were among the cities' poorest and most vulnerable. They lived on land city leaders and private developers regarded as valuable—but only after it was cleared. The Puerto Rican activist Aramis Gomez compared renewal area residents to Native Americans in "the Old West, where we, the poor people, are the Indians with valuable land that the [white] settlers want."[7]

At the time of this photograph, Robert, who was white, had recently lost his job as a security guard. Although classified as "white" by the 1950 Census, former neighbors describe Ethel as "Black" or "mixed race." Ethel likely lost her job as well as her home to the South Mall. In the 1950s, she worked as a waitress in some of the neighborhood bars.[8] By 1965, the South Mall plan had forced more than 400 businesses, including those bars, to shut down. Some moved to new locations. Others never reopened.

Three months after Harold Furlong photographed the Mathers, Robert was living in a new apartment, apparently on his own. We do not know where Ethel moved, but as a woman of color (or someone who did not appear to be white), her options were limited by residential segregation.[9] Robert and Ethel probably paid higher rents after displacement than they had before. According to contemporary research, this was a common experience.[10]

Just Compensation

Home- and business-owners shared the Mathers' fate. Although the majority of those displaced were tenants, many South Mall buildings were owner-occupied. Most homeowners rented out rooms or apartments on the upper floors of once-grand townhouses. Most businesses were small—grocery stores, barbershops, laundries, restaurants, taverns, and rooming houses, all catering to a neighborhood clientele. The South Mall project would disperse not only their social network but also their customer base, thereby threatening businesses built up over years.

The Fifth Amendment to the US Constitution requires that private property shall not be "taken for public use without just compensation." Yet those who lost homes, businesses, and property to redevelopment had little voice in determining what was "just." Government agencies offered owners "**fair market value**" for properties seized. Fair market value is a legal construct defined as the price a knowledgeable buyer would pay a willing seller. The problem was that many property owners were unwilling to sell through a process and at a price they regarded as unfair. Appraisers in the employ of government agencies set the amounts offered to property owners. Photographs, like ones Harold Furlong and his colleagues took, were intended to validate the appraisers' judgment. Some owners challenged government offers in court—but doing so was expensive. It required hiring a lawyer and an appraiser.

Lazarus and Sophie Kontis, Greek immigrant entrepreneurs who lived two doors away from the Mathers, were among those who challenged the State's offer. For more than thirty years, the couple had lived, raised their children, and run a shoe repair shop in the same place. They purchased the building for $16,000 in 1930 (about $29,000 in 1963 dollars), but in 1963, the State offered them just $9,200 in compensation. In a letter to the governor, Lazarus and Sophie's daughter, Despina, characterized this offer as inadequate. It failed not just to reimburse the family's investment in real property but also to consider the value of the business Lazarus had built up and, at age seventy-one, would have to close. She insisted that "a fair assessment of the value of this property must include a fair compensation for the loss of my Father's livelihood." The final settlement of $13,850 did not compensate for this loss.[11] The story was the same in other cities, where small businesses closed prematurely as a result of urban renewal and highway construction projects.[12]

Compensation for seized property was often too low to allow homeowners to purchase replacement houses without taking on additional debt. **Redlining**—the refusal of banks to write mortgages—exacerbated this situation in low-income communities of color. The term derives from a series of "residential security" maps initiated by the Home Owners' Loan Corporation (HOLC) in the 1930s. HOLC was a New Deal agency created to help struggling homeowners during the Great Depression. In collaboration with local bankers and realtors, the agency produced a series of maps that rated urban neighborhoods from "best" to "hazardous" based on perceived credit risk. Colored red, hazardous neighborhoods tended to be the places where racial and ethnic minorities lived. These maps reflect prejudices about race, ethnicity, and credit worthiness that would continue to shape bank lending practices into the 1960s. In Albany, bank loans in what would become the South Mall area declined dramatically between the 1940s and 1950s.[13] As in other cities, this disinvestment set the stage for the area's demolition and redevelopment.[14]

Because mortgages were hard to come by, aspiring homeowners in redlined neighborhoods had little choice but to buy on contract. These exploitive contracts were typically rent-to-own deals that left all the power in the hands of the seller, who remained the owner of record. This meant that in the case of property seizures, payment went to the seller rather than the homeowner.[15]

Some owners ended up not just homeless but indebted. This became known as the "Mayme Riley problem." In 1951, Riley, a Black civil servant raising a young daughter and caring for her elderly mother, signed a contract for $9,950 to buy a home in Washington, DC. Three years later, when a government agency seized her house for an urban renewal project, she was offered only $6,250 in compensation, though according to her contract, she owed her creditors $2,000 more.[16] In the mid-1960s, the obvious injustice of the Riley case would motivate federal lawmakers to begin reforming the reimbursement system—but not before tens of thousands of property owners experienced similar financial losses.

Urban Uprisings

In the summer of 1967, the destruction of and disinvestment in inner-city neighborhoods helped spark a wave of urban uprisings. The televised spectacle of civil disorder and cities ablaze prodded white lawmakers to investigate, if not to act.

In Albany, the demolition (without replacement) of 3,300 affordable dwelling units for the South Mall caused housing prices to spiral upward. The overcrowded sections of the city where Black families had little choice but to settle were particularly hard hit. Slum landlords profited from an increase in demand driven by displacement combined with residential segregation. They were able to raise rents and to find tenants for rundown apartments that might otherwise have remained vacant.

An investigative series by reporter William Kennedy, a future Pulitzer Prize-winning novelist, exposed conditions far worse than seen in the Mathers' former apartment:

> The slums of Albany are a horror.
> People are living today in conditions that are unfit for animals. They are
> living in conditions that degrade them as human beings, that degrade
> all the other humans who permit the conditions to exist.
> They are living in rot and stench and filth and dampness.
> They are living with cockroaches that spoil their food, with rats that bite
> sleeping infants.
> They are living in houses that are a constant danger to life—falling
> ceilings, broken stairs, absent banisters …

Kennedy noted that while many "fought" to protect their families and improve living conditions, the odds were stacked against them. "Steady decay, indifferent landlords, and [...] sporadic enforcement of state and city housing laws" stood in their way.[17]

Between 1965 and 1978, construction of the Empire State Plaza and South Mall Arterial added to the discontent, because the building trades unions blocked Black men from securing stable, lucrative jobs. Unresolved complaints about police misconduct combined with lack of access to the levers of power further exacerbated tensions between white city leaders and Black residents. On July 27, 1967, these grievances briefly boiled over into violence between Black teenagers and white police officers, sparked by the rumor that a police car had run down a Black child. The Brothers, a local civil rights organization founded to advocate for Black jobs and empowerment, helped defuse the conflict. The group's leader explained, "the Black man will be the only loser in the event of a racial explosion."[18]

During the "long, hot summer" of 1967, 164 uprisings in 128 American cities revealed similar patterns of abuse and deprivation. Most of the urban uprisings were short-lived. Eight raged on for days, resulting in substantial property damage, significant injuries, and even death. The Detroit, Michigan, uprising was both the most deadly and, in dollar terms, the most costly of these conflicts. At the end of five days, 43 were dead (most of them Black) and 324 injured. Property losses were estimated at $40–45 million.[19]

On July 27, as violence was waning in Detroit and emerging in Albany, President Lyndon Johnson addressed the nation to announce the creation of the National Advisory Commission on Civil Disorders, chaired by Illinois Governor Otto Kerner. The Kerner Commission was charged with investigating the uprisings' origins and recommending ways to avert future conflict.

Rather than demonizing "rioters," the Commission report blamed white racism, including segregation and ghettoization, for causing "the explosive mixture which has been accumulating in our cities." The commissioners took seriously citizens' complaints about job discrimination, police misconduct, substandard housing, and inadequate public services. They found that urban redevelopment contributed to discontent. In many cities, including Albany and Detroit, local governments failed to build new homes to replace those demolished.[20] Furthermore, seizure and clearance of private property meant the reduction of municipal tax revenues and, consequently, city services.

Among the Kerner Commission's recommendations were additional subsidies for construction of low- and moderate-income housing and "a reoriented and expanded urban renewal program" that would prioritize the needs of area residents.[21] Too often in the past, local officials had used federal funds to make space for luxury housing and upscale shopping facilities designed to attract the white middle-class back downtown, thereby rebuilding tax rolls diminished by white flight.

The report further recommended that the federal government take steps to combat residential segregation, both by passing the **Fair Housing Act**, which prohibited discrimination by landlords and home sellers, and by funding the construction of affordable housing "outside of ghetto areas." Without a change in policy, the Commission warned, protests would continue, and polarization would grow worse. On the current path, the nation was headed toward "the permanent establishment of two societies: one predominantly white and located in the suburbs, in smaller cities, and in outlying areas," and one predominantly Black "located in central cities."[22]

Freeway Revolts

In Albany, Detroit, and cities across the nation, highway construction became not just a cause, along with urban renewal, of inner-city uprisings but also the focus of grassroots organizing. Compared with the typical urban renewal plan, which appeared to represent progress and seemed to offer something for everyone, highways promised area residents nothing but displacement and destruction. These roads were designed for suburbanites rather than city dwellers.

As a group, freeway foes encompassed a broad range of perspectives and protest styles. Some acted by lobbying, petitioning, and suing government officials, others by picketing and engaging in civil disobedience. Preservationists focused on preventing the demolition of historic structures. Community groups raised concerns about noise and air pollution. Civil rights activists emphasized the harm to Black residents. "No White Man's Road Through Black Man's Home" became a popular slogan.

In 1968, four Albany civic organizations—two neighborhood associations, a women's club, and the local branch of the NAACP—banded together to oppose construction of a highway connecting the Empire State Plaza to the New York State Thruway. The public response was significantly different from six years earlier, when the State of New York seized Robert and Ethel Mather's home. Back then, there was little grassroots opposition. Now, the protests were impossible for the governor and his allies to ignore. Activists questioned the need for a new highway. They deplored the demolition of hundreds of homes. They charged that the highway would make "conditions intolerable" for those living nearby. The consortium recommended an alternative transportation plan, which the state ultimately adopted.[23]

The leadership of white, well-connected preservationists and neighborhood activists helps explain the success of the Albany protest. Black-led protests— in places like Miami, Florida, Columbia, South Carolina, and Camden, New Jersey—tended to be less successful. Local politicians, business leaders, and real-estate developers regarded urban highway construction as akin to urban renewal, an opportunity to revitalize central business districts by both demolishing "blighted" structures and building roads to bring affluent suburbanites downtown.[24]

The Costs of Redevelopment

Maybe what we are finally experiencing both here and in the nation is a revolt of sorts against the highway program in general. And I think we would be less than candid if we didn't acknowledge that a lot of this feeling has been generated by our past cavalier attitude towards the people on our projects. Historically we have been contract-oriented and not people-oriented. We were so anxious to build highways that we somehow lost sight of the people occupying homes and property along the route. They were a hindrance to our ideas of progress. No matter how much we now try to legislate, or how much we try to "coordinate," we are today faced with this legacy from the past.[25]

P. G. Baldwin, a longtime employee of the New York State Department of Transportation (NYSDoT), shared these thoughts with his colleagues in 1969. This self-reflection was sparked by conflict between NYSDoT officials and local political leaders in the small city of Olean. At issue was the inadequacy of reimbursement payments to property owners. This incident reflected not just local conditions but deep, national wells of discontent. Over time, government seizure of hundreds of thousands of homes and businesses sparked the question: Who was hurt by and who benefited from clearance and redevelopment of our nation's cities?

In Congress, legislators searched for remedies to what many had come to recognize as an unjust situation caused by the housing and transportation laws they had passed. Indeed, Senator Edmund Muskie (D-Maine) proclaimed in 1969 that the mistreatment of displacees "should weigh heavily on the conscience of all who are responsible for the setting of Federal policies." He was introducing the bill that would become the Uniform Relocation Act of 1970. This new law included enhanced compensation payments to property owners and residential and commercial tenants. In the House of Representatives, Representative James Cleveland (R-New Hampshire) explained that the bill was designed to ensure that "no family or individual now owning their own home" be deprived of that status "through any lack of fairness or equity in the acquisition procedures." He continued, "It is also intended to assure that no tenant […] is left in a worsened condition" as a result of redevelopment. However, the Uniform Relocation Act did not provide similar payments to the roughly 2 million people dispossessed and displaced before the bill was passed. Nor, as Representative Frank Annunzio (D-Illinois) pointed out, did the law compensate for the "dislocation of lives" and the loss of "personal ties."[26]

In the long run, community destruction would prove as damaging as the losses of wealth that resulted from urban renewal and highway construction. In 1963, psychologist Marc Fried described "the psychological costs" of involuntary relocation from Boston's white, working-class West End. He found that six months to two years after having moved, more than forty percent of study participants were still "grieving for a lost home" as they might a deceased loved one. They reported feelings of sadness, anger, longing, and helplessness. Fried identified the cause of their suffering as the loss of "spatial and group identity." Those most affected by these losses had known the West End best and had built the strongest social bonds.[27]

More recently, psychiatrist Mindy Fullilove diagnosed the suffering resulting from displacement and demolition as "**root shock**." In her 2005 book by the same name, she describes root shock as "the traumatic stress reaction to the destruction [...] of one's emotional ecosystem." Focusing on predominantly Black neighborhoods, she explores how urban renewal disrupted and damaged individual lives, whole communities, and even the broader culture. The health consequences of this historic injustice, she argues, continue to harm Black communities, affecting not just the people who were displaced but also their descendants.[28]

According to Fullilove, forcible displacement affects not just the mind but also the body.[29] In a 1966 letter to the Mechanicville (New York) Urban Renewal Agency, chiropractor Joseph Desmond described this process. He contended that the seizure of his property had caused the deterioration of his and his wife's health. (Both suffered from arthritis). Desmond wrote, "Any doctor will tell you that emotions have power to change body chemistry, the blood circulation, the output of hormones [...] Our conditions worsened [...] because of the anxieties brought about by Urban Renewal."[30]

We do not know how Robert and Ethel Mather experienced displacement, but Harold Furlong's photograph is suggestive. The couple would soon separate. We do not know what, if any, role their pending eviction had in that outcome. The relationship already may have been on the rocks. Nevertheless, Ethel's tender gesture suggests care and compassion for Robert. His posture indicates grief. After the South Mall, Robert and Ethel's former neighbors lost track of the couple. Robert died in 1991 at age 75 and was buried alone. We do not know where Ethel went after 1963.

Robert and Ethel are only two of the millions of Americans who were forced from their homes as a result of mid-twentieth-century eminent domain property seizures. They fell victim to political decisions about what it meant to renew our nation's cities and upgrade urban infrastructure—which places to bulldoze, what to build, or whose needs to prioritize. Most cities elected to demolish the places where poor people lived and build to attract the more prosperous. Today, as Urban Renewal Era infrastructure decays or becomes obsolete, we must confront the same questions.

Redesign and Removal

Community groups across the nation are now pushing state and local governments to repair some of the damage caused by post–Second World War redevelopment projects. The Albany Riverfront Collaborative, for example, is working with the NYSDoT to redesign a local expressway, I-787, and eliminate the South Mall Arterial. The Arterial is an elevated highway leading to and from the Empire State Plaza. It cuts the city in half and, along with I-787, stands between residents and the Hudson River. The Collaborative hopes to "open downtown to the riverfront" and "reconnect" neighborhoods that bore the brunt of urban renewal and highway construction.[31]

Highway removal projects promise to calm traffic, improve air quality, and enhance access to rivers and green space. It is yet unclear whether these plans will benefit the people who live nearby. Specifically, how will demolition and reconstruction affect air quality and overall quality of life? Will redevelopment of newly cleared land foster market-based displacement in adjacent neighborhoods? Will people like Ethel and Robert be forced to move?

The danger is that **gentrification**, like urban renewal before it, will push lower-income families out of their homes and neighborhoods. The actions of public office holders, residents, and activists will help determine that outcome, because local plans and permits require public input and, in some cases, votes. In the coming years, American citizens have the opportunity to make choices different from the one that in 1962 forced the Mathers and their neighbors from their homes and community.

Discussion Questions

1   Looking at Harold Furlong's photo of Robert and Ethel Mather, what do you think he was trying to convey? What do you think the Mathers were trying to communicate to the viewer?

2   Do you think government seizure of homes and property for public use (eminent domain) is fair? For private use? Under what circumstances?

3   Why did city officials and urban planners believe urban renewal was necessary for progress and the long-term economic health of cities? Do you think history has proved them right or wrong?

4   Is it the responsibility of the government—local, state, or national—to provide replacement housing for people displaced by redevelopment projects? Did the government owe more to these people? Does it owe anything to their descendants?

5   What is gentrification? How is it similar to and different from urban renewal?

Further Resources

The Atlas of Drowned Towns. https://www.drownedtowns.com.
Cebul, Brent. "Tearing Down Black America." *Boston Review*, July 22, 2020. https://www.bostonreview.net/articles/brent-cebul-tearing-down-black-america/.

Crockett, Karilyn. *People before Highways: Boston Activists, Urban Planners, and a New Movement for City Making*. University of Massachusetts Press, 2018.
PBS American Experience. *The Riot Report: A Presidential Commission Defied Expectations by Telling the Truth*, 2024. https://www.pbs.org/wgbh/americanexperience/films/riot-report/#film_description.
Sugrue, Thomas. *The Origins of the Urban Crisis: Race and Inequality in Postwar Detroit*. University of Princeton Press, 2005.

Notes

1   Our thanks to Mike Wren for scanning this and other photo negatives in the collections of the New York State Archives.

2   Nelson Rockefeller speech, June 21, 1965, New York State Temporary Commission on the Capital City, New York State Archives.

3   Envelope 8475, February 28, 1963, Empire State Plaza Construction Progress Photographs (15727-89), New York State Archives.

4   Envelope 8580B, March 7, 1963, Empire State Plaza Construction Progress Photographs (15727-89), New York State Archives.

5   House Committee on Public Works, *Study of Compensation and Assistance for Persons Affected by Real Property Acquisition in Federal and Federally Assisted Programs* (Government Printing Office, 1965), 10–2, and 15–18.

6   This estimate is based on data from the Department of Housing and Urban Development, *Statistical Yearbook* (Government Printing Office, 1972); and Aaron Jette, "Accounting for Federal Highway Displacement from 1956 to 1976" (unpublished manuscript, US Department of Transportation Volpe Center, 2021).

7   New York Department of City Planning, "Transcript of Public Hearing before the City Planning Commission in the Matter of the Lincoln Square Urban Renewal Plan and Project," September 11, 1957, 102.

8   City directories, the 1950 Census, and local news articles partially document the Mathers' employment during this period.

9   Because the Mathers' marriage appears to have been common-law rather official, we do not know Ethel's surname and have not been able to learn where she moved.

10 See Chester Hartman, "The Housing of Relocated Families," *Journal of the American Institute of Planners* 30, no. 4 (1964): 266–86.

11 Despina Kontis to Gov. Nelson Rockefeller, April 12, 1963, courtesy of Angelo Kontis; "Our Name Means Shoemaker," *98 Acres in Albany* blog, November 30, 2015. Last accessed May 12, 2024, https://98acresinalbany.wordpress.com/2015/11/30/our-name-means-shoemaker/.

12 Ann Pfau, Kathleen Lawlor, David Hochfelder, and Stacy Kinlock Sewell, "Using Urban Renewal Records to Advance Reparative Justice," *RSF: The Russell Sage Foundation Journal of the Social Sciences* 10, no. 2 (June 2024): 120, https://www.rsfjournal.org/content/10/2/113.

13 Ann Pfau, David Hochfelder, and Stacy Sewell, "How the Albany Residential Security Map Was Created," in Robert K. Nelson, LaDale Winling, et al., "Mapping Inequality: Redlining in New Deal America." *American Panorama: An Atlas of United States History*, ed. Robert K. Nelson and Edward L. Ayers, 2023. Last accessed November 8, 2024, https://dsl.richmond.edu/panorama/redlining/map/NY/Albany/context.

14 The *Renewing Inequality* website allows users to compare renewal areas against redlined maps. However, because the South Mall project was state rather than federally funded, it is not included on the map. Last accessed November 8, 2024, https://dsl.richmond.edu/panorama/renewal/.

15 Senate Committee on Public Works, *Urban Highways: Hearings before the Subcommittee on Roads of the Committee on Public Works* (Government Printing Office, 1968), 309. For more about buying on contract, see "The Plunder of Black Wealth in Chicago: New Findings on the Toll of Predatory Housing Contracts," The Sam Dubois Cook Center on Social Equity, Duke University, 2019.

16 House Committee on Public Works, *Study of Compensation and Assistance*, 86–7.

17 Bill Kennedy, "Shameful Slums of Albany—A Study in Human Misery," *Albany Times Union*, August 1, 1965.

18 Mike Wales, "Van Dyke Says Brothers Dedicated to Peace," *Albany Times Union*, July 28, 1967.

19 National Advisory Commission on Civil Disorders, *Report of the National Advisory Commission on Civil Disorders* (Government Printing Office, 1968), 47–61, 65–7, 202, and 325–6. This commission is more commonly referred to as the Kerner Commission for its chairman, Governor Otto Kerner of Illinois. Hereafter, Kerner Commission, *Report*.

20 Kerner Commission, *Report*, 80–3.

21 Kerner Commission, *Report*, 262.

22 Kerner Commission, *Report*, 218–20 and 260–3.

23 Chuck Malley, "Washington Park Urges Arterial Elimination," March 6, 1968; "Mid-Crosstown Arterial Hit by Residents," March 9, 1968; and "Group Seeks Crosstown Arterial Veto," June 21, 1968. All from the *Albany Times Union*. David Eno, "Washington Park Area Fights to Retain 'Fashionable' Quality," *Albany Times Union*, June 22, 1968.

24 Mark H. Rose and Raymond A. Mohl, *Interstate: Highway Politics and Policy since 1939* (University of Tennessee Press, 2012), 97, 100–11.

25 P. G. Baldwin to J. Burch McMorran, June 16, 1969, Department of Transportation Commissioner's Correspondence and Subject Files (10487-99A), New York State Archives.

26 *Legislative History, Public Law 91–646, S.1*, 1971. Last accessed November 12, 2024, https://archive.org/details/PL91646/page/n1/mode/2up.

27 Marc Fried, "Grieving for a Lost Home: Psychological Costs of Relocation," in *Urban Renewal: The Record and Controversy*, ed. James Q. Wilson (MIT Press, 1966).

28 Mindy Fullilove, *Root Shock: How Tearing Up City Neighborhoods Hurts America, and What We Can Do about It* (One World, 2004), Chapter 1.

29 Fullilove, *Root Shock*, 14.

30 Joseph and Mary Desmond, "To Whom It May Concern," August 4, 1966, Mechanicville Urban Renewal Agency Records, City of Mechanicville, NY.

31 Albany Riverfront Collaborative, "Together We Can—I-787 Study Opens New Paths to Reconnection." Last accessed November 12, 2024, https://www.albanyriverfrontcollaborative.com/together-we-can.

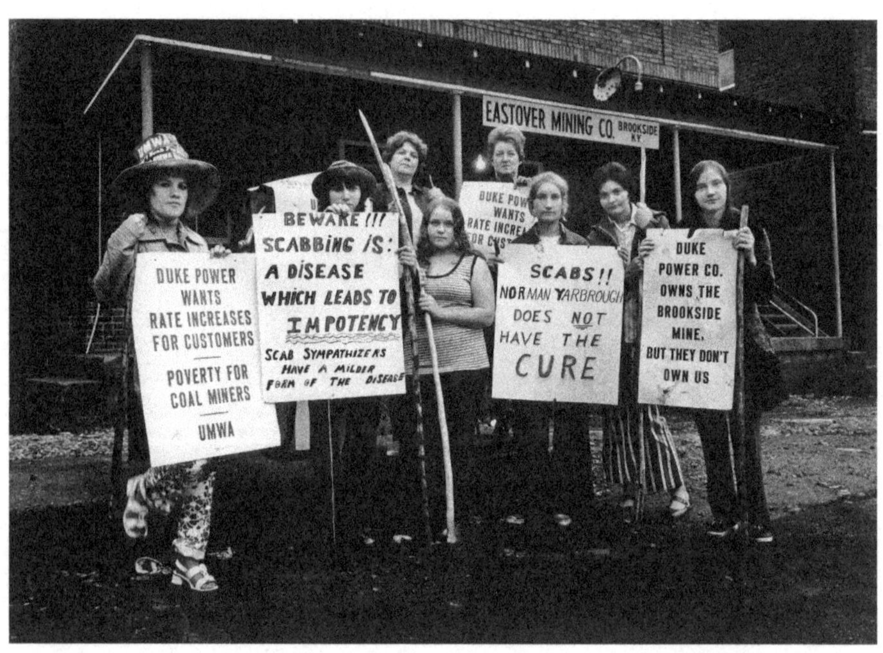

FIGURE 11.1 Brookside Women's Club Picket, *1973. Photo by Earl Dotter. Courtesy of Earl Dotter.*

11

They Don't Own Us: Harlan County, the Brookside Coal Strike, and the Forgotten History of the Working Class

By Grace Elizabeth Hale

Despite the unfavorable opinion of President Johnson's escalated involvement in the Vietnam War, his sweeping "Great Society" domestic reforms designed to improve education, protect the environment, and remove obstacles to voting have a more favorable legacy. Johnson declared his **War on Poverty** in 1964, which included an increase in the minimum wage and job placement programs. The results are still visible today through programs like food stamps, Head Start, Medicare, and Medicaid.

In a tiny corner of eastern Kentucky, far outside of Washington, DC, a groundswell of activism around labor unions came to a head as coal miners in Brookside went on strike against the Eastover Mining Company and its parent company, Duke Power. The thirteen-month strike would have failed without the publicity and monetary support of **United Mine Workers of America** (UMWA), and embroiled in its own political turmoil, the UMWA would have failed without Brookside. Notably, it was the women of Brookside and the surrounding communities in Harlan County who proved to be the backbone of the strike. This chapter challenges us to reconsider what we think we know about the labor movement, and when and where women's activism occurred.

Suggested Topics: Economic History, Environmental History, Labor History, Women and Sexuality, Vietnam War

Glossary: American Labor Movement, Black Lung, Miners for Democracy, Neoliberalism, United Mine Workers of America, War on Poverty

For historians, photographs can be powerful forms of evidence. They make historical actors and places come alive. They conjure lost worlds. And they assert the existence of people, movements, events, and stories left out of the dominant historical narratives. No other medium is quite so good at reminding us of the material reality of the past. No other type of source makes more concrete the paradox at the heart of any historical investigation, that no matter how much we share with people in photographs, we know something they cannot: their future.

In the face of all these strengths, it is easy to forget the medium's limitations. But like other kinds of historical evidence, photographs establish certain kinds of facts while obscuring others. Images made with cameras offer proof that at some point in the past, light bounced off something in the world and registered its surface on light sensitive material. That something might be anything physically present: people, animals, buildings, landscapes, or objects, including photographic prints themselves. Photographs tell us that the particular things they depict existed. Beyond that, they do not provide much certainty. They do not explain anything about the intentions of either the photographer or any human subjects. They do not reveal what exists outside the frame. And they do not offer much insight into what a given image might mean at the time it was made or today. To answer these questions, historians must bring in other kinds of sources.

Earl Dotter's 1973 photograph *Brookside Women's Club Picket* shows that half a century ago, a group of eight women in eastern Kentucky coal country armed themselves with sharpened sticks and signs and took on one of America's largest power companies. Yet this photograph alone is not enough to understand the importance of these women's actions and the larger meaning of their protest. Standard narratives of American history mostly leave out the story of workers and their fight for unions, especially after the Great Depression and the Second World War. Unless their own family members were involved, most people know little about the last eighty years of labor history, much less the pivotal decade of the 1970s. At best, high school and college survey curricula skip from New York's hard hat riots in 1970, when hundreds of construction workers and other men attacked students protesting the Kent State massacre and the Vietnam War, to Reagan's firing of unionized air traffic controllers in order to break their 1981 strike. Many don't mention the labor movement at all in this crucial period in American history.

The women in this photograph did not know that the movement they were a part of and the egalitarian America they envisioned would not be realized in most of their lifetimes. Remembering the activism of these eastern Kentucky women and their vital role in a coal strike they helped win in a longer battle that was ultimately lost offers a window to a mostly forgotten history of the late 1960s and 1970s. In these years, working-class Americans mobilized to realize the radical promise of both the New Deal and civil rights movements, and secure the benefits of American prosperity for all. On the ground, this work sometimes took the form of union organizing but it also extended beyond the labor movement and encompassed many other kinds of activism and organizations. Central Appalachia—a region encompassing the coalfields of eastern Kentucky, southwest Virginia, and West Virginia—was one of the key sites of this fight.

Dotter's image takes us into a world that once was and its dreams of a future that did not, at least in the next half century, come to be. It resurrects a moment from a broad movement too grassroots and fractured to have a name, though the writer and broadcaster Studs Terkel called it at the time "the new, new left."[1] Today, when this outpouring of activism from the late 1960s through the early 1980s is remembered at all, particular strands have been understood as part of labor or civil rights movements or environmental, anti-poverty, or women's rights organizing. None of these labels are wrong. But the cumulative effect is to distract attention from the common characteristic at work across all of them—the class consciousness of these organizing efforts and the struggles of Americans to achieve and to hold onto security, democracy, and dignity in all aspects of life, including the workplace.

Because we live in these Brookside women's future, we know what happened next. What they could not entirely grasp then is for us clear. *Brookside Women's Club Picket* was one small but important moment in one piece of the massive battle against the formation of the American present, the political and economic structures that scholars today call **neoliberalism**.

Brookside: A Mine and a Town

Today, Brookside is a ruin. To get there, I drive east of Harlan on Kentucky State Road 38 for about six miles and look for the baseball field on the right before an unincorporated town called Ages. Just past the field, I pull into a soggy parking lot, empty except for a portable toilet and a couple of tractor trailer trucks. On the other side of the Clover Fork, a branch of the Cumberland River, the rusting remains of the coal tipple and pieces of old conveyor belts are visible on the hillside. The road has been rerouted since 1973 and the banks of the Clover Fork are completely covered in vegetation, but there, beneath the thin gravel and mud near the parked trucks, I find faint traces of the foundations of houses and an edge of a road. This is all that remains of the coal camp where mining families once lived in about seventy-five wood frame houses along the river.

Trying to get a closer look at the mine, I get back in my car and head toward Ages a few hundred yards. There, on the left, only a short, dead-end spur of what had been the main road past Eastover Mining Company's headquarters and the company store survives. Narrow paved tracks branch off here. One leads to a now closed post office built after the strike. The other heads uphill to one of the mine entrances and the tipple. I follow this road up the hill until it too is eventually blocked. From here, I can look down on the fenced off area—Brookside's "downtown" in its heyday—and just make out through the overgrowth the red brick Eastover building in Dotter's photograph, now painted a faded and moldy green.

Someone mows the baseball field, but beyond it, along both banks of the Clover Fork, the flat land along the water, and up the ridge, kudzu is rapidly covering the rest. In a year or two, there won't be anything left of Brookside to see.

By eastern Kentucky standards, Brookside was a fairly small place, nothing like the big mines and surrounding coal towns that International Harvester built at Benham and US Steel at Lynch at the eastern end of Harlan County. For more than half a century, Benham and Lynch were run by the corporations that owned them but in the early 1960s, they became independent towns controlled by elected officials. Brookside, in contrast, was always controlled by the owner of the mine. When the Brookside strike began, the settlement had a tiny post office and a company store, a common feature of coal camps and mill towns across the United States, where workers could buy on credit but paid higher prices and interest for the privilege. For school or church or anything else, Brookside residents had to go to Ages or Harlan. But the biggest problem was the quality of the housing. Most camp houses lacked indoor plumbing. Residents got their water from outdoor spigots and used outhouses, many of which dumped their waste right into the river.

What the Brookside coal camp did have was a strong sense of community. In the early 1970s, there were residents who had been born and raised there by the Clover Fork and then as adults buried their babies and their parents in the Brookside cemetery. For them, Brookside was much more than a mine. It was also home.

Working-Class Activism in Appalachia

As global energy markets, working-class Appalachian activism, and the US labor movement all intersected in this out-of-the-way place, tiny Brookside became an essential site in an unfolding struggle over the economic and political future. Soaring demand for electricity, much of it generated in coal-fired plants, had finally halted a postwar decline in the coal mining industry. Oil and gas companies noticed and bought up many of the largest coal companies. Power companies began to purchase the rest, hoping to secure a steady supply at a set cost. In 1970, Duke Power, which generated electricity for consumers and industries across North and South Carolina, created a subsidiary called Eastover Mining Company to acquire Brookside and several other eastern Kentucky and Virginia mines.

In these same years, coal miners, still almost all men, and their family members participated in a massive outpouring of direct action and grassroots organizing across Appalachia at a level equal to the simultaneous and much better-known wave of civil rights activism. In hundreds of unauthorized wildcat strikes beginning with the roving picket movement in 1963, miners protested against both their bosses, the coal operators, and their union, the **United Mine Workers of America** (UMWA). Upset about safety practices, healthcare, pensions, and other benefits as well as wages, they targeted nonunion mines and union mines with what they called "sweetheart contracts," deals with coal operators that resulted in lower pay and smaller contributions to the union's health and welfare fund. Some miners turned their anger against the union itself for cutting off the benefits of some disabled and retired miners.

Other miners and their family members formed new organizations including the Black Lung Association and Disabled Miners and Widows of West Virginia to push for stronger safety and health regulations and for disability payments. Mechanization had created conditions in which more miners suffered at younger ages from **black lung**, a form of pneumoconiosis that occurs when inhaled coal dust scars the lungs and makes breathing increasingly difficult. In 1969, over 40,000 West Virginia coal miners, the vast majority of workers in the industry in that state, went out on strike. They succeeded in winning a state black lung bill that compensated sufferers and served as a model for the Federal Coal Mine Health and Safety Act of 1969 passed that same year. At the same time, residents of coal country also organized environmental and anti-poverty organizations to fight strip mining and mine-related water pollution and to oppose state and local tax structures that favored coal operators and timber companies.

Appalachians also played an essential role in creating a union reform movement still active today. That effort began after an insurgent candidate for the presidency of the UMWA, Joseph "Jock" Yablonski, was murdered in his home along with his wife and daughter in late 1969. His supporters suspected the involvement of union officials, and at his funeral, they formed **Miners for Democracy** (MFD) to continue the fight against union corruption. In time, leaders of UMWA District 19 (which included Harlan County) as well as UMWA President Tony Boyle were convicted and sent to prison for crimes related to these murders. In 1972, a federal court ordered a new election of national UMWA officers, and the reform organization put forward a slate of candidates led by Arnold Miller, a disabled miner from West Virginia who had been a leader in the Black Lung Association. In July, the MFD candidates kicked off their campaign to take over the union with a rally in Harlan County, a place they called "the belly of the beast" because of Boyle's past strength there. Six months later, they won. For the first time in American history, rank-and-file members had gained control of a powerful labor union.

That summer a MFD rally had taken place just down State Road 38 from the Brookside coal camp in Evarts, a place locals called a "free town," because it had never been a coal camp. Brookside miners in the audience heard Miller speak and they took to heart his promise to commit a reformed UMWA to organizing the unorganized, the work that had made the union so powerful in the past and enabled it to lead the Congress of Industrial Organizations and the federation of industrial unions, and to help launch the United Auto Workers and the United Steelworkers.

Brookside had been a UMWA mine until 1964, when the former owners of the mine refused to sign the union contract and then broke the resulting strike. After the rally, a core group of miners began working to bring the union back. In June 1973, Brookside miners voted to join the UMWA, but Eastover refused to sign the union contract. A month later, without any communication with the UMWA leadership, Brookside miners, all men at the time, put down their tools and went out on strike.

Back at UMWA headquarters, union officials had spent that spring and summer developing a strategic plan for organizing nonunion mines. Brookside was not on their list. No rational person would choose to start this difficult work in Harlan County with its history of violent labor conflict and notoriously anti-union coal operators. But the Brookside miners forced the issue. By August, union leaders decided the reformed union's credibility was on the line. Vice President Mike Trbovich traveled to Harlan County to give the Brookside strikers the news in person. The UMWA would provide a level of support unprecedented among major unions—weekly strike benefits of $100 a week and full healthcare coverage—for as long as it took to win. In this way, Brookside became the cornerstone of the reformed UMWA's new organizing drive and the broader fight to revive the **American labor movement** which the miners had done so much to build.

Brookside men, in other words, got the UMWA into this strike. But they alone, even with all the resources of the national union, could not win it. That took the efforts of many other local residents as well as union officials. No single group contributed more to the eventual victory than the Brookside women, the wives, daughters, and other relatives and friends of the striking miners.

"The Women Did It"

Earl Dotter made the photograph he calls *Brookside Women's Club Picket* while working as a photojournalist for the *United Mine Workers Journal*. As he recalled when I interviewed him, he moved to the Appalachian region in the late 1960s to work for VISTA, or Volunteers in Service to America, the domestic version of the Peace Corps founded in 1964.[2] VISTA was a part of President Lyndon Johnson's **War on Poverty**, a series of federal government initiatives designed to help the almost 20 percent of Americans living without the most basic resources. Many of those poor people lived in Central Appalachia, where poverty rates had begun soaring in the 1950s as a rural version of deindustrialization expanded across the Appalachian coalfields.

In 1972, Dotter began taking photographs for Miners for Democracy. After the MFD slate of officers won, the new editor of the *United Mine Workers Journal (UMWJ)* transformed what had been a boring PR publication dedicated to glorifying the union leadership into a real magazine serving the interests of rank-and-file miners. The editor hired Dotter to be the journal's photographer.

At the *UMWJ*, Dotter developed a particular way of working. Whenever he went to a new place, he would first talk to community members. He would ask them what they thought was important for him to look for and document, and he would listen hard to their answers. This kind of collaboration, he believed, resulted in photographs that, in his words, "meant something," that opened a window on the experiences of the people he photographed.[3]

Dotter's first trip to Harlan County to document the strike just happened to occur in the days when the wives, daughters, and mothers of Brookside miners and other women were taking on a more visible role in the strike. It all started spontaneously, according to multiple oral history interviews recorded with participants in the late 1980s.[4] Betty Eldridge, one of the women in Dotter's photograph, did not live at Brookside, but her husband worked there. On September 27, Eldridge went to a UMWA support rally in the town of Harlan. There, she caught up with other miners' wives and learned that some of the women who lived in the Brookside coal camp were gathering at the mine to try to talk the strikebreakers—the women called them "scabs"— out of crossing the picket line. The women at the rally decided to drive to Brookside to help. By chance, they arrived at a shift change.

Eldridge described what happened next: "Here come these cars off the mountain. Car after car after car. Instead of them stopping, they done their best to run over us. If I hadn't flattened against that building, they would have killed me." Outraged, she "swore to God that I would do everything in my power to stop them from working. And I did."[5] Even on that day, some of the women managed to fight back. Mary Widner, a woman who lived in a coal camp house very close to the Eastover offices, jumped on a strikebreaker and began hitting him with a soda bottle.[6]

A court injunction limited the union to three striking men at each of the Brookside mine's two main entrances. But on that day, the women stopped enough strikebreakers to shut down the mine. It was the first time anyone could ever remember women forming their own picket line. Dotter had no way of knowing it then, but he was witnessing a revolution in coal country.

Buoyed by their own success, many of the women showed up the next few mornings with new women they had recruited. One of these new participants was Lois Scott, another woman in Dotter's photograph and a union supporter whose husband worked under a UMWA contract at another mine. Scott and some of the women brought weapons, sticks with sharpened ends that they called "switches."

It's not clear exactly which day Dotter made this photograph, but it must be after September 28. From that day on, women showed up every day on the road that passed the company store and the Eastover offices, the structure in the background of Dotter's image, before continuing on to one of the mine's entrances. Eldridge was almost always there along with Scott, who was often accompanied by one of her grown daughters. Many days, the women succeeded in shutting down the mine. After only a week, they forced Eastover to close its company store. Disabled and retired miners not covered by the court injunction against the union often turned out to help them. But the women were the backbone of the effort that eventually forced Eastover to give up trying to mine coal at Brookside.

The *UMWJ* published Dotter's photograph in its October 12–31, 1973, issue as an illustration for an article titled "Women, Children Jailed in Harlan County." The label he gives it now, *Brookside Women's Club Picket*, does not appear in the caption, and it is likely that the Brookside Women's Club was not officially formed until after this photograph was taken. I have only been able to identify three of the women here. Scott and Eldridge stand together in the back. Wilma Osborne holds the sign that says DUKE POWER OWNS THE BROOKSIDE MINE, BUT THEY DON'T OWN US. It is likely that one of the other young women is Scott's daughter, Melba Strong, though I have not been able to confirm this as both Scott and Eldridge are dead. I have been unable to locate Osborne, born in 1954 and possibly still alive.

But Dotter recalls it all quite clearly. Bernie Aronson, his former roommate and another former VISTA volunteer who went to work for MFD and ended up as a UMWA advisor, designed the printed signs. In other Dotter photographs taken by the Eastover buildings on that same rainy day, the three official UMWA pickets, including the only Black man working at Brookside during the strike, hold these signs. One of them—DUKE POWER WANTS RATE INCREASES FOR CUSTOMERS—POVERTY FOR COAL MINERS—also appears in the picture of the women's picket line. Aronson created these messages to appeal not just to people in eastern Kentucky but also to Americans who lived far beyond the mountains who would see them in photographs that appeared alongside newspaper articles about the strike.

Surviving oral history interviews with Eldridge and Scott and other sources make it clear that the handwritten signs in *Brookside Women's Club Picket* are the women's own creations. In the *UMWJ* article that accompanied Dotter's photograph, Nannie Rainey, a resident of the Brookside coal camp and a UMWA supporter, made the kind of comment that would become increasingly common during the strike. "The president of Duke Power must not be much of a man to let the people suffer like this," she said after she and her husband Jerry, a Brookside miner, were both arrested and had to bring a few of their seven children with them to jail.[7]

Much like the women's actions that shut down the mine, the rhetoric they used on their signs shows a similar scrappiness. They took jabs at the scabs' manhood, suggesting that SCABBING IS A DISEASE WHICH LEADS TO IMPOTENCY, and that scab sympathizers would contract a milder form of the disease. Brookside women also criticized the masculinity of the leaders of Eastover and Duke Power and anyone who worked for them as a strikebreaker or an armed guard. Using salty humor, homemade signs, and homegrown wit, they turned their region's traditional ideas about gender into weapons in the strike.

In this way, they drew on what they knew of their own history—generations of Appalachian women in coal mining communities supporting past strikes— and adapted it to the changing times. As a member of the Brookside Women's Club later told the *New York Times*, "We seen all those women libbers picketing on tv and we didn't see why we couldn't do it too." But they also understood what their activism would mean in their Appalachian world. In a mine war, almost everyone is armed. Lois Scott often tucked a pistol in her bra. In this context, the women understood that their gender could work as a weapon and a shield. Armed strikebreakers—Appalachian men themselves—would be very unlikely to shoot a woman, even one beating them with a stick.

★★★

Dotter's photograph presents eight women very consciously posing. Some of the young women have even dressed up for the protest. One wears floral pants, white sandals, a funky jacket, and a broad brimmed hat covered with UMWA bumper stickers. Another has on striped pants and Mary Janes. All are damp from the drizzle. Four carry "switches." They stand close with their shoulders, arms, and hands often touching and lift their chins in defiance as they look directly at Dotter. Their expressions are mostly serious, though at least one seems to be suppressing a smile.

In all their particular glory, these eight working-class women pose for the future not yet knowing the outcome of the strike. In that moment, all the accolades lay ahead of them, including Scott's starring turn in Barbara Kopple's Academy Award-winning documentary *Harlan County USA* (1976). But a little less than a year later when Duke Power finally signed the UMWA contract, Darrell Deaton, the vice president of the new UMWA Brookside local, put it this way: "None of us really knew these women. We didn't know they would be violent. They was our wives. But there's some nervy women in that bunch. There's some women that's just as tough as any man I ever met. There isn't any doubt about it, but that the women did it."[8] More than any other single factor, the Brookside women won this strike.

Their actions not only helped save their husbands, sons, and neighbors jobs but they also kept the strike going on the ground at Brookside long enough that the UMWA had time to create an effective nationwide offensive against Duke Power. The UMWA attacked Duke's corporate image, its stock and bond prices, and its requests for electricity rate increases, a major advance in labor organizing tactics beyond product boycotts that would come to be called a corporate campaign.

The women also helped preserve the credibility of the reformed UMWA as the union began negotiations for the new 1974 national coal contract. And the effects of the union reform movement that began with coal miners still echo today in the reform organization Unite All Workers for Democracy that transformed the United Auto Workers and achieved a massive victory in their 2023 strike against Ford, GM, and Stellantis. Dotter's photograph asks viewers to reckon with these women's achievements and their vision as well as the forgotten era of working-class activism of which they were a part.

Discussion Questions

1   What role does photography as a medium play in social movements like labor rights?

2   How do the Brookside women use their gender and ideas about gender to advance their movement? How do their actions fit within the history of the women's movement in the 1960s and 1970s?

3   How does centering the rural working-class change how we understand US history in the 1960s and 1970s?

4   Where do you encounter protest photographs today? How are they similar to or different from Dotter's photograph of the Brookside Women's Club?

Further Resources

Appalshop. *Coal Camp: Life below the Tipple*. An unreleased 22-minute film about Brookside shot before the strike began. https://appalshoparchive.org/Detail/objects/8719.

Cobble, Dorothy Sue. *The Other Women's Movement: Workplace Justice and Social Rights in Modern America*. Princeton University Press, 2004.

Dotter, Earl. Photographer. https://earldotter.com/.

Kopple, Barbara, director. *Harlan County USA*. 1976. Cabin Creek Films.

Kopple, Barbara, director. *American Dream*. 1990. Cabin Creek Films.

Lichtenstein, Nelson. *State of the Union: A Century of American Labor*. Princeton University Press, 2002.

Smith, Barbara Ellen, with photographs by Earl Dotter. *Digging Our Own Graves: Coal Miners and the Struggle over Black Lung Disease*, updated edition. Haymarket Books, 2020.

Wilkerson, Jessica. *To Live Here You Have to Fight: How Appalachian Women Led Movements for Social Justice*. University of Illinois Press, 2018.

Notes

1 Studs Terkel, "The New Left: A Trucker Speaks Out," *New York Times*, December 28, 1973.

2 Earl Dotter, interview (unpublished) by Grace Elizabeth Hale, March 2, 2023.

3 While photographers have their own unique styles and approaches, photojournalists like Dotter who use their cameras to affect social change carry forward the legacy of social reformers like Jacob Riis, Lewis Hine, Dorothea Lange, and Gordon Parks. For more, refer back to "The Camera Never Lies" in the introduction.

4 See Sally Maggard's interviews with women who participated in the Brookside strike, archived as "Women and Collective Protest Oral History Project," Louie B. Nunn Center for Oral History, University of Kentucky Libraries. Last accessed January 3, 2025, https://kentuckyoralhistory.org/ark:/16417/xt7rv11vhp7d. Hereafter, "Nunn Center for Oral History."

5 Betty Eldridge, interview by Sally Ward Maggard, July 23, 1986, Nunn Center for Oral History.

6 Mary Widner, interview by Sally Ward Maggard, October 9, 1986, Nunn Center for Oral History.

7 Nannie Rainey, interview by Sally Ward Maggard, September 23, 1986, Nunn Center for Oral History.

8 Irene Nolan, "The Brookside Women," *Louisville Courier-Journal and Times*, September 1, 1974.

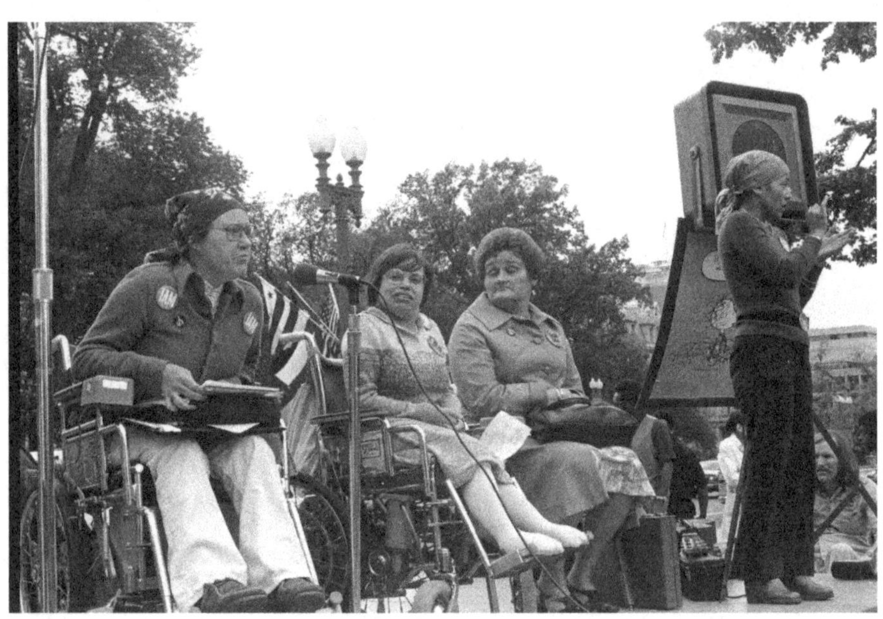

FIGURE 12.1 *Disability rights advocates Kitty Cone, Judy Heumann, Eunice Fiorito, and American Sign Language interpreter Jadine Murello on stage at a Section 504 protest rally in Lafayette Square. Washington, DC, April 26, 1977. Photo by HolLynn D'Lil. Courtesy of Getty Images.*

12

"Very Strong Women You Don't Mess With": The Section 504 Disability Rights Protest

By Scot Danforth

The 1960s and 1970s were a time of great upheaval as marginalized groups pushed for social, political, and economic liberties. Liberal counterculture movements offered a new vision of American society as beatniks, hippies, and anti-establishmentarians challenged everything from fashion and sexuality to corporations and war. California was fertile ground for many of these protest movements, and the Bay Area in particular sustains the legacy of a progressive political ethos to this day.

One civil rights movement that receives marginal attention is the **disability rights movement** whose activists cut their teeth and forged future alliances in Berkeley's Free Speech and anti-war protests. Disability affects people of all races, ethnicities, and genders, making the disability rights movement that catalyzed in the 1970s inherently **intersectional**. This chapter chronicles the work of disability activists who stood up to power by coordinating simultaneous takeovers of federal buildings in ten different cities across the country, and the women who forced the Carter administration to implement measures outlined in the **Rehabilitation Act of 1973**.

Suggested Topics: African American History, Civil Rights, Counterculture, Disability Rights, Intersectionality, Women and Sexuality

Glossary: American Coalition for Citizens with Disabilities, Center for Independent Living, Disability Rights Movement, Free Speech Movement, Intersectionality, Rehabilitation Act (1973), Second Wave Feminism, Section 504

This is a photograph of three disability rights activists—left to right, Kitty Cone, Judy Heumann, and Eunice Fiorito—the architects and managers of the victorious Section 504 disability rights sit-in protest in April 1977.

Section 504 was a single sentence in the 1973 revision of the federal Rehabilitation Act that, for the first time ever, guaranteed anti-discrimination protections for disabled people in government-funded programs and facilities, but it wasn't enforced. Cone and Heumann led an intensive, four-week political campaign featuring simultaneous demonstrations in ten cities across the country, eventually landing on the steps of the nation's capital. There, they were joined by Fiorito's Washington-based **American Coalition for Citizens with Disabilities** (ACCD). In a true-life Judith beheads Holofernes story, these women successfully compelled Carter to enact Section 504, the first national disability discrimination law in the United States.

From Civil Rights to the Vietnam War, the 1960s and 1970s were decades unlike any Americans had ever experienced. The Bay Area was an intellectual and political greenhouse for many liberation movements, including disability rights. Most histories of this movement start and end either with the passing and enacting of federal legislation or with the story of disabled men in Berkeley who successfully sued the school and created the Center for Independent Living, the place where Cone and Huemann first met.

Instead, this story focuses on how strong, thoughtful women leaders arose in the context of the male-dominated disability rights movement to defy the Department of Health, Education, and Welfare, and bring President Jimmy Carter's administration to its knees. Coordinating with Fiorito's ACCD, Cone and Heumann led over 100 people with a variety of disabilities in a dramatic twenty-five-day occupation of a San Francisco federal building. Uniting a broad coalition of supporters that included the International Association of Machinists, the Black Panthers, church leaders, and gay rights groups, Cone and Heumann successfully arm-twisted HEW Secretary Joseph A. Califano into approving regulations enacting Section 504.

It's hard to describe the scene unfolding around this photograph taken in late April 1977. In Lafayette Square with a prime view from the White House, Cone, Heumann, and Fiorito led a massive demonstration to insist on their rights under Section 504. At the right edge of the photo is Jadine Murello, an American Sign Language interpreter who translated their words, cluing the modern viewer to the presence of a Deaf audience. Beyond the frame, hundreds of protestors with disabilities of all kinds, many using wheelchairs, shouted and sang to the White House across the street. This was one of the first cross-disability protests in the country.

The photograph was taken by photojournalist and disability rights advocate HolLynn D'Lil. The Library of Congress houses her collection of over 300 photos of Cone and Heumann's occupation of the San Francisco federal building.

D'Lil's photographic record is one of a kind, depicting both the powerful and intimate moments of an occupation otherwise written off as a human-interest piece by the national press.

But what pushed these women, and those who joined them, to this breaking point?

Section 504

The 1977 **Section 504** sit-ins were the result of a long legacy of activism and an even longer legacy of the government's indifferent attitude toward disability rights—or in the case of Califano, blatant foot-dragging to appease anti-504 lobbyists. Passed almost four years earlier, the **Rehabilitation Act**'s Section 504 prohibited discrimination on the basis of disability in any organization or activity receiving federal dollars. The broad statute covered public schools, all levels of national, state, and local government, as well as hospitals, public transportation systems, and universities. But 504 could only be enacted when the Department of Health, Education, and Welfare (HEW) approved the official implementation regulations. President Gerald Ford's HEW Secretary F. David Mathews wrote a comprehensive set of 504 regulations that were widely accepted by the disability community. Caving to pressure from hospitals and universities who did not want to make the physical changes to their buildings necessary for compliance, Mathews didn't even sign his own rules.

When President Jimmy Carter took office in January 1977, his HEW director Joseph Califano delayed 504 yet again, ordering yet another round of policy reviews. Administration insiders leaked information to disability rights leaders that Califano's task force was compiling a long list of what activist and ACCD co-chair Frank Bowe called "loopholes, waivers, and exemptions."[1]

Eunice Fiorito, a blind woman with experience advising the New York City mayor on disability issues and president of the ACCD, arranged to have a cup of tea with Secretary Califano at his office. She was a statuesque woman who spoke with the fullness and authority of a Roman orator. Califano professed in pleasant government-speak that the administration supported the principles of Section 504. Califano assured her that the task force was just dotting I's and crossing T's. Unimpressed, Fiorito demanded a definitive promise that Califano would not diminish the scope of legal protections. He refused.

Fiorito held her ground. "Mr. Secretary, I won't be able to leave until you give me some kind of assurance that you're going to sign the regulations." After a prolonged period of handwringing, Califano's staff finally escorted her out of the office. In response, Fiorito and Bowe issued a warning to President Carter: sign the Mathews 504 regulations without modification by April 4, 1977, or protests will break out across the country. Carter and Califano didn't take this seriously. After all, what could a bunch of people in wheelchairs really do?[2]

On April 5th, demonstrations erupted at federal sites in ten cities across the nation. Activists took over the buildings with HEW offices in cities like Denver, Washington, and Los Angeles. Califano swiftly retaliated, cutting off food, medication, and water. Starved out, occupations ended as quickly as they started except for one. Heumann and Cone's team of over one hundred militants persevered in holding the fourth-floor San Francisco HEW offices. The protesters, largely people with significant physical disabilities, didn't even bring a change of clothes. Sleeping on floors and bathing in bathroom sinks, they occupied the offices for twenty-five days.

Against the Odds

Two noteworthy facts from this photograph point to the long odds faced by these political activists: they had disabilities, and they were women. How Cone and Heumann became the influential leaders who dropped President Carter to his knees is a story of how disability rights and second wave feminism emerged in a politically radical Berkeley. Residents of the Bay Area didn't just embrace justice movements. They insisted on it.

The early origins of the disability rights movement developed within the university village's fierce, multi-cause protest culture. UC Berkeley's most famous protest movement, the **Free Speech Movement** (FSM), started in October 1964, when the university arrested a former graduate student named Jack Weinberg for distributing information for the Congress of Racial Equality (CORE), a Black civil rights group. The police loaded Weinberg into their cruiser where he sat for over thirty hours. Hundreds of students spontaneously surrounded the vehicle in protest. The sock-footed Mario Savio, recently returned from Student Nonviolent Coordinating Committee (SNCC) activities in Mississippi, and others made impromptu speeches from the roof of the cop car, denouncing the university's actions. In January 1965, the university backed down, allowing political speech on campus.[3]

The FSM was the first spark in an anti-establishment and anti-war fire that came to define Berkeley's counterculture movements that raged throughout the 1960s and 1970s. The Vietnam War was one of these constant targets of militant fury. As President Lyndon Johnson increased bombing raids and troop deployments, he also threatened to end draft deferrals for many college students. Thousands at UC Berkeley and university campuses across the country turned out to oppose the increasingly unpopular war. The 1967 Stop the Draft Week marches from Berkeley's campus to the Army induction center in nearby Oakland exploded into street fights between 2,000 protesters and what the *Los Angeles Times* called a "flying wedge of police, swinging nightsticks and squirting eye irritant." The violent multi-day melee resulted in dozens of serious injuries and hundreds of arrests.[4]

Around the same time, students of color launched campus demonstrations to seek a greater presence in historically white colleges. Beginning at San Francisco State College and quickly spreading to UC Berkeley in January 1969, the Third World Liberation Front unified Black, Asian American, and Mexican American students to demand the admission of more students of color and the creation of ethnic studies programs.

A few months later, widespread demonstrations over a weedy vacant lot called the People's Park deteriorated into a daylong battle between rock-throwing militants and police firing buckshot. A sheriff shot and killed a man watching from a rooftop. A second police shotgun round blinded a man. Army helicopters dumped tear gas from the sky on the crowds below. Then governor of California, Ronald Reagan, sent in military troops to lock down Berkeley.[5]

While racial injustice and an unpopular war were the motivators for many of these movements, the FSM sparked another movement too. In September 1969, from this activist hothouse, the American **disability rights movement** took off. The movement's leader, Ed Roberts, cut his activist chops by helping the Graduate Coordinating Council organize FSM's student strike five years earlier when over 800 protesters were arrested during a sit-in at Sproul Hall. So, when the California Department of Rehabilitation, the state agency that provided specialized housing and support services for students with disabilities, pulled funding from two disabled students by citing poor academic performance, Roberts was once again called to action. Roberts, a graduate student paralyzed by polio, led a group of eleven disabled university students in a fight against the Department.[6]

Dubbing themselves the Rolling Quads, the disabled students united under the idea that people with disabilities had civil rights. The problem, they said, wasn't how their bodies worked. It was how society responded to their bodies, devaluing them and holding them out. Roberts smartly persuaded the *San Francisco Chronicle* and the *Berkeley Daily Gazette* to depict the disabled students as victims of a cold, unresponsive state agency. The Rolling Quads won the reinstatement of their friends' good academic standing, one of the first victories of the Disability Rights Movement.[7]

Over the next three years, the Rolling Quads founded two pioneering organizations that put disabled people in the driver's seat. The Physically Disabled Students Program (PDSP) was the first university-based disabled student support program founded and operated by disabled people. Also run by disabled people, and directed by Roberts, the Berkeley **Center for Independent Living** (CIL) offered one-stop shopping for everything a disabled person might need to live independently in the community. With the right kinds of support, people with a variety of disabilities could escape nursing homes and institutions to live on their own. A CIL client could hire personal care attendants, apply for government benefits, find a job, rent an accessible apartment, learn adaptive technologies, receive peer counseling, locate accessible recreation opportunities, catch a ride to anywhere in the East Bay, earn a master's degree, or get their wheelchair repaired.

Kitty Cone moved to Oakland in 1972 and began working at the CIL. There, she met Judy Heumann, and the duo forged a friendship that would soon lead them from the HEW occupation in San Francisco to the White House. Although the CIL proved to be an ideal launching pad for the San Francisco sit-in, it also struggled with persistent gender inequities. Mary Lester, a nondisabled woman who started as CIL receptionist and later became a successful grant writer, observed, "I know a lot of women felt that there was a lot of sexism at CIL in the power structure."[8] Beginning in Rolling Quad days, men like Ed Roberts, John Hessler, and Hale Zukas ran the show.

The CIL wasn't unique in this power dynamic, as the default to male leadership extended to almost every sector of American society. Women rarely held leadership positions in corporations, universities, or government. In 1977, only 2 of the 100 Senators and 18 of the 435 Congressional representatives were women. The list of women executives leading Fortune 500 companies was limited to *Washington Post* publisher Katherine Graham and financier Marion O. Sandler.[9] Even New Left progressive organizations such as the Students for a Democratic Society (SDS) and the Student Nonviolent Coordinating Committee (SNCC) were male dominated. As carefully documented by SNCC activist Mary King and SDS member Mary Hayden, the men ran the show and the oft-silent women organized the meetings, ran mimeograph machines, and swept the office floors.[10]

Though women's long-standing activism is etched across American history, the 1970s was a particularly turbulent decade. Many women contested post-Second World War cultural gender roles and historians today commonly call this period "**second wave feminism**." Betty Friedan's *The Feminine Mystique* (1963), often cited as the catalyst for this movement, directly critiqued the limited domestic role of woman as homemaker, a mother and wife serving as the caring keystone of the nuclear family unit. Women across the country started gathering in "rap sessions," or unstructured group conversations, sharing their deepest emotions and experiences, creating bonds and insights that raised their consciousness.

The national modern women's movement gained traction when President John F. Kennedy formed the President's Commission on the Status of Women in 1963. The diverse commission included leading women representatives from the National Association for the Advancement of Colored People, the

American Association of University Women, the International Brotherhood of Teamsters, and numerous Christian and Jewish faith groups. Their first legislative victory was the Equal Pay Act, outlawing wage and salary discrimination against women. The President's Commission, led by none other than Eleanor Roosevelt, issued a final report which, to these activists' dismay, confirmed the traditional necessity of women homemakers to care for husbands and children. But for the first time, it also collected an enormous amount of data about the lives of women.

Armed with new information, all fifty states created similar commissions tracking the status of women. At the national conference of the state commissions in June 1966, Friedan famously scribbled the acronym NOW on a napkin and passed it around the dinner table. The National Organization for Women was founded, with Friedan serving as its first leader. NOW grew in the 1970s to become the largest and most influential national organization pursuing equality for women.[11]

Unsurprisingly, Berkeley—the city and the university—embraced the groundswell of feminism. Cone and Heumann operated in this rich hub of activity. They were resourced by a Berkeley-based librarian, Laura X, who followed the example of Malcom X and the Nation of Islam in shedding her patriarchal surname. She published *SPAZM*, a newsletter tracking women's liberation work around the United States and later founded and directed the Women's History Research Center, the first archive of the women's liberation movement. A second stalwart of Berkeley feminism was Pat Cody of Cody's Books, a mainstay of the downtown business community. A three-decade regular in a local women's discussion group, she led an effort to expose the negative health effects of diethylstilbestrol, a medication widely prescribed to prevent miscarriages.[12]

Berkeley women's movement groups often took forceful action. In 1969, Cal students held a campus rally to demand that the university launch a women's studies program. Graduate students and faculty threw their university degrees into a burning fire, symbolizing the worthlessness of an education lacking women's experiences and knowledge. Seventy-five Berkeley activists occupied the *San Francisco Examiner* offices, demanding an increase in female hiring and a freeze on exploitative advertising. The Radio Free Women Five sneaked into the KPFA radio studio one summer night in 1970 to confront the on-air announcers, resulting in new programming on women's issues, news, and events.

Despite living in the fiery center of women's activism, disabled women felt stymied by the reluctance of Bay Area women's groups to discuss the social obstacles confronted by disabled women. They were likewise frustrated by the male-dominated leadership in the disability rights movement and at the CIL. You see, they had disabilities, *and* they were women. Many years later, legal scholar Kimberle Crenshaw coined the term "**intersectionality**" to describe how persons with multiple marginalized identities often experience interactive legal and political effects of disadvantage.[13] Crenshaw generated an important ideological shift in social movements that continues to frame justice movements to this day.

Most assuredly Cone, Heumann, and their other collaborators like Corbett O'Toole would have benefitted from Crenshaw's framework. Both Cone and O'Toole spoke of their disappointment with feminist friends who only wanted to discuss one side of the equation. But these women were used to working against the odds. In 1974, they founded the Disabled Women's Rap Group, unpacking the twin oppressions of gender and disability.[14] They created their own spaces of belonging, and in that space, they found their power.

While undoubtedly patriarchal, the CIL was also wide open. The hippy founders were deeply skeptical of button-up organizations like corporations and universities they viewed as corrupt. They built the CIL as an anti-organization, organic and freewheeling, without the usual stiff structures and stuffy systems. Heumann described it as "a very grass rootsy kind of place." O'Toole called it "a very free-flowing environment (that) allowed a lot of things to happen."[15] An assertive person with a big idea could rally together a few hard-working friends to launch a new initiative. That's exactly what Cone and Heumann did, creating a CIL committee to plan and direct the San Francisco protest.

The 504 Sit-Ins

The twenty-somethings Heumann and Cone were already seasoned disability rights activists by the time Frank Bowe and Eunice Fiorito sent up a red flare from the ACCD in the spring of 1977. When Heumann graduated from Long Island University, the New York Board of Education denied her application for a teaching credential because she used a wheelchair. After she won a court case against the board, she formed Disabled in Action. Her protest group blocked traffic in Times Square when President Richard Nixon initially vetoed the 1973 Rehabilitation Act. Cone previously worked with other CIL staffers (Hale Zukas and Greg Sanders) to build curb cuts on the sidewalks of Oakland. Cone united the Easterseals, a nonprofit health organization, and United Cerebral Palsy to create the Committee for Accessible Oakland. She was elected to the Oakland development commission that funded the downtown curb cuts program.[16]

Cone and Heumann were both working for the CIL in the spring of 1977, when the ACCD demanded that President Carter and HEW Secretary Califano immediately sign the 504 regulations. Doubtful of their willingness to do so, activists in ten cities—Washington, Atlanta, Boston, New York, Los Angeles, San Francisco, Philadelphia, Dallas, Chicago, and Denver—readied to occupy federal buildings.[17]

The Berkeley CIL team prepped for action under Heumann and Cone's leadership. The duo spent weeks planning to invade the San Francisco federal building. They created a sit-in team widely representing a variety of disabilities—mobility impairments, blind, D/deaf,[18] developmental disabilities—and multiple racial and ethnic groups.

A sit-in of this scale requires support, and the Bay Area's vast number of activist groups, including Black civil rights workers and LGBT advocacy groups, were ready to serve. They recruited and organized nurses to provide on-site medical care to participants with complex health needs. McDonald's restaurants, Safeway markets, and the Delancey Street drug rehabilitation program supplied food. Every evening, the Black Panthers turned those donations into delicious, fully cooked dinners. Congregants of the Glide Memorial Church, longtime social justice advocates, handled food deliveries. In the plaza outside the building, Reverends Cecil Williams and Norman Leach of the Council of Churches led a constant support vigil.[19]

Heumann also directed a strong media strategy in the belief that favorable national press accounts would win over the public and convince top Democrats to pressure the White House into action. The savvy Bay Area media provided full coverage, including daily video reports from San Francisco Channel 7 television reporter Evan White. Heumann and Cone held regular press conferences with complete instruction on disability issues and preferred terminology. But the national media largely viewed the sit-in as a mere human-interest story.

Except for one. Photojournalist and disability rights activist HolLynn D'Lil working for *Ms. Magazine*, a feminist news magazine founded by Gloria Steinem, snapped over 300 candid photographs narrating the entire protest. Inside the San Francisco federal building, her poignant depictions captured demonstrators debating issues in late night strategy meetings and collapsing weary on staircases for a rough night's sleep. Her photographs of the continuous rally outside the San Francisco occupation, and later the variety of protest actions in Washington, captured the humanity and intensity of the lengthy political operation.[20]

Although Cone and Heumann built a well-oiled, multi-faceted, dedicated protest machine, they operated from a weak political position. Disabled people had little power or money. They were widely viewed as "cripples" lacking the competence and strength to be political agents speaking and acting on their own behalf. The common understanding was that disabled people were diseased unfortunates who could not work or go to school, objects of pity who needed medical care in isolated settings. Prominent disability-focused organizations were either charities like the Muscular Dystrophy Association or professional groups like Rehabilitation International. When it came to disability issues, the loudest speakers were not the people who had disabilities.

By the late 1970s, other minoritized groups such as LGBT, African American, and women's rights organizations had taken substantial steps to gain electoral power, making inroads primarily with the Democratic Party. Disability rights leaders like Roberts and Heumann followed suit, developing close working relationships with a host of liberal California Democrats like Congressmen Phil Burton and George Miller and Senators Tom Harkin and Alan Cranston. While sympathetic to the cause, neither major political party viewed the disability community as a vital constituency that would raise campaign funds and deliver votes. Disabled people were politically and socially invisible.

D'Lil's photographs show us something very different. Her day-by-day photographic chronicle of the occupation shows 150 people with the grit to persevere for nearly a month, living in an office building without showers or beds. The undeniable dignity and resolve captured by D'Lil's skilled camera was ignored by Carter and Califano. The president and HEW director played a waiting game, assuming the disabled people—a group stereotyped as sick and weak—would soon tire and give up.

But the occupants and supporters were anything but weak.

The protest leadership team made two chess moves to raise the stakes. First, Ed Roberts, the quadriplegic man widely lauded as the hero of the Disability Rights Movement, leaned on his political allies and arranged for Congressmen Burton and Miller to hold a congressional hearing with a HEW representative inside the occupied building. The tense five-hour session on the Section 504 regulations pitted a roomful of angry disabled people against Secretary Califano's representative, the overmatched and underinformed bureaucrat Gene Eidenberg. Still the White House didn't seem to notice.

The second tactic was riskier. Leaving a hundred weary but determined activists to continue the San Francisco occupation, Cone and Heumann led a small sortie to Washington, DC. Like any good reporter, D'Lil followed the story. Combining forces with Fiorito's Washington-based ACCD team, they directly confronted the national leaders. Carted around in the back of a closed truck provided by the International Machinists Union and sleeping at night in the pews of Luther Place Memorial Church, the activists dogged Califano at every turn. They held round-the-clock candlelight vigils outside his house, slammed their wheelchairs into the glass doors of his government office, and trolled him at public speaking engagements. The president wasn't immune from their ire either. They picketed outside the First Baptist Church on 16th Street as President Carter and his wife Rosalynn attended Sunday services.

Carter snuck out the back door, leaving the First Lady to exit the front church steps alone.[21]

These actions resulted in democratic leaders pressuring their own president. Congressman George Miller led a group of twenty-nine congressional representatives demanding that Carter approve the 504 regulations "without change, immediately." Senate Whip Alan Cranston publicly urged Carter to immediately issue "tough, effective regulations." After almost four weeks, the longest occupation of a federal building in history, Carter cried uncle. Califano signed the regulations. The San Francisco demonstrators won.[22]

"Beyond Your Wildest Imagination"

On April 30, 1977, twenty-six days after Heumann first rolled them into the building, the exhausted, smiling occupiers exited the glass doors of the San Francisco federal building into the cheering arms of the celebrating crowd. In a raspy, brittle voice, Kitty Cone shouted: "Did the disabled people in the HEW building show strength beyond your wildest imagination?"

"Yes!" the raucous throng howled back.
Cone continued, "And did we show courage?"
"Yeah!"
"And did we show commitment?"
"Yeah!"
"And did we show power?"
"Yeah!"

Cone thundered on, "We showed strength and courage and power and commitment [...] that we the shut-ins or the shut-outs, we the hidden, supposedly the frail and the weak, that we can wage a struggle at the highest level of government, and win!"[23]

The historic 504 sit-in initiated the first national disability discrimination law. For many of the activists, the experience was the transformational high-water mark of their lives.

"I believe the 504 sit-in was probably a watershed for every participant," said Ally Karen Parker. "I think it was life changing."[24]
Ray Uzeta called the 504 sit-in "one of the most exhilarating experiences of my life."[25]

Bruce Oka felt, "There wasn't a minute that I was there that I didn't feel inspired by my colleagues inside. It was amazing."[26]

Ron Washington, a member of the team that traveled to Washington, felt a new comfort in his identity as a disabled man. "It helped me to accept myself more."[27]

Many disabled Americans, both those involved in the protests and those who cheered in front of their television sets, held their heads a little higher. Kitty Cone observed, "We brought new confidence and pride, not only to ourselves, but to the thousands and thousands of disabled people who were with us in spirit."[28]

D'Lil's photographs are a unique testament to the resolve of the 504 activists, but her photographs are more than a record of movement. They are a record of her compassion and dedication to the cause, and the people who led it. Taken from below, even the angle of her photograph reflects the empowerment Heumman, Cone, and Fiorito must have felt when they stood up to America's highest office and emerged victorious.

The Washington Post's tone harmonized with D'Lil's, celebrating what they called the "newly militant disabled." Rising up from the margins of society, Cone, Heumann, and Fiorito were pioneers, creating a new form of American radicalism. No longer willing to be seen as pitiful, ill, and isolated, captained by leaders that journalist Evan White described as "very strong women you don't mess with," the women in this photo proved to be skilled political actors who secured their civil rights—and those of generations to come—by defeating the most powerful men in the country.[29]

Discussion Questions

1   Why might activists keenly focused on inequities in the lives of persons with disabilities not have a similar consciousness around inequities in women's lives?

2   In what ways can organizations and government entities that are loosely or even poorly organized offer greater opportunities for persons from oppressed groups to take leadership roles?

3   What is the most recent photograph or video of disabled persons that you have seen? What was the context? Do you believe that disabled persons continue to be an underrepresented minority group in American society?

4   Experience the Virtual Tour of the "Patient No More" museum exhibit that tells the story of the 504 sit-in from the perspective of the participants. Name three things that surprised you about that protest. https://longmoreinstitute.sfsu.edu/patient-no-more/virtual-tour.

Further Resources

Cone, Kitty. "Patient No More: Kitty Cone's Victory Speech." Paul K. Longmore Institute on Disability YouTube Channel. https://youtu.be/HQ3kcSgAX-w?si=7–1iL61ZSUBsvAS.

D'Lil, HolLynn. *Becoming Real in 24 Days: One Participant's Story of the 1977 Section 504 Demonstration for Disability Rights.* Hallevaland Productions, 2015.

Disability Rights and Independent Living Movement Oral History Series, Bancroft Library, University of California, Berkeley. https://www.lib.berkeley.edu/visit/bancroft/oral-history-center/projects/disability-rights.

Heumann, Judith, with Kristen Joiner. *Being Heumann: An Unrepentant Memoir of a Disability Rights Activist.* Beacon Press, 2020.

Paul K. Longmore Institute on Disability Collection, San Francisco State University. https://diva.sfsu.edu/collections/longmoreinstitute/#browse-collections.

Notes

1   Kitty Cone, interview by David Landes, 1998, Disability Rights Independent Living Movement Oral History Series, Bancroft Library, University of California, Berkeley; and Jon Margolis, "Protest for Guaranteed Rights Isn't Handicapped by Disabilities," *Chicago Tribune*, April 10, 1977.

2   Kitty Cone, Disability Rights Independent Living Movement Oral History Series; and Kitty Cone, Paul K. Longmore Institute on Disability Collection, San Francisco State University.

3   See Hal Draper, *Berkeley: The New Student Revolt* (Grove Press, 1965; Robert Cohen, *Freedom's Orator: Mario Savio and the Radical Legacy of the 1960s* (Oxford University Press, 2009); and W.J. Rorabaugh, *Berkeley at War: The 1960s* (Oxford University Press, 1990).

4   Jim Newton, *Man of Tomorrow: The Relentless Life of Jerry Brown* (Little, Brown, 2020); Darle E. Lembke, "Oakland War Protest Quelled," *Los Angeles Times*, October 18, 1967; Darle E. Lembke, "Third Day of Oakland Antiwar Protests Results in 91 Arrests," *Los Angeles Times*, October 19, 1967; and *Los Angeles Times*, "Newsmen Groups Protest Oakland Police Tactics," October 18, 1967.

5   *Berkeley Barb*, "Herrick Injury Reports" and "Medic Amidst Madness," May 23–9, 1969; Robert Sommer and Robert L. Thayer, "The Radicalization of Common Ground People's Park, Berkeley: An Unnatural History," *Landscape Architecture Magazine* 67, no. 5 (November 1977): 510–4; Jon David Cash, "People's Park: Birth and Survival," *California History* 88, no. 1 (2010): 8–29, 53–5; Newton, *Man of Tomorrow*; Lembke, "Oakland War Protest Quelled"; Lembke, "Third Day of Oakland Antiwar Protests Results in 91 Arrests"; and "Newsmen Groups Protest Oakland Police Tactics."

6   Timothy Pfaff, "A Conversation with Ed Roberts: California Q & A," *California Monthly*, February 1985; and James Donald, interview by Cathy Cowan,

1998, Disability Rights and Independent Living Movement Oral History Series.

7   "Students Accuse State Worker" and "UC Cripples Score Cut of Monies," *Berkeley Daily Gazette*, September 20, 1969; "They Fought Disabilities and Won," *Daily Ledger*, May 2, 1982; and Scot Danforth, "Becoming the Rolling Quads: Disability Politics at the University of California, Berkeley, in the 1960s," *History of Education Quarterly* 58, no. 4 (2018): 506–36.

8   Mary Lester, interview by Susan O'Hara, 1998, Disability Rights and Independent Living Movement Oral History Series.

9   "History of Women in the US Congress," Center for American Women and Politics. Last accessed December 22, 2024, https://cawp.rutgers.edu/facts/levels-office/congress/history-women-us-congress; and Catalyst, *Historical List of Women CEOs of the Fortune Lists: 1972-2023*, June 22, 2023. Last accessed August 7, 2025, https://www.catalyst.org/insights/2023/historical-list-of-women-ceos-of-the-fortune-lists-1972-2023/.

10   Ruth Rosen, *The World Split Open: How the Modern Women's Movement Changed America* (Penguin, 2000); and Anonymous, "SNCC Position Paper, November, 1964," *Civil Rights Movement Archive*, Duke University Archives. Last accessed December 22, 2024, https://www.crmvet.org/docs/snccfem.htm.

11   Flora Davis, *Moving the Mountain: The Women's Movement in America Since 1960* (Simon and Schuster, 1991); Rosen, *The World Split Open*; and Barbara Ryan, *Feminism and the Women's Movement: Dynamics of Change in Social Movement Ideology and Activism* (Routledge, 1992).

12   Rosen, *The World Split Open*.

13   Kimberle Crenshaw, "Demarginalizing the Intersection of Race and Sex: A Black Feminist Critique of Antidiscrimination Doctrine, Feminist Theory and Antiracist Policies," *University of Chicago Legal Forum* 1, no. 8 (1989): 139–67.

14   Corbett O'Toole, interview by Denise Jacobsen, 1998, Disability Rights and Independent Living Movement Oral History Series. Corbett O'Toole, interview by author, May 15, 2019.

15   Corbett O'Toole, interview by Denise Jacobsen, 1998, Disability Rights and Independent Living Movement Oral History Project.

16   Cone, Disability Rights and Independent Living Movement Oral History Series.

17   Cone, Disability Rights and Independent Living Movement Oral History Series; and Margolis, "Protest for Guaranteed Rights."

18   "Deaf" is often used to signify those who identify with the language and culture of the Deaf community, whereas "deaf" frequently refers to a person with a functional hearing loss or impairment.

19   Ron Washington, interview, 2014, Paul K. Longmore Institute on Disability Collection. See also Lillian Faderman, *The Gay Revolution: The Story of Struggle* (Simon and Schuster, 2015).

20   HolLynn D'Lil, *Becoming Real in 24 Days: One Participant's Story of the 1977 Section 504 Demonstration for Disability Rights* (Hallevaland Productions, 2015).

21 Evan White, interview, Paul K. Longmore Institute on Disability Collection; Judith Heumann with Kristen Joiner, *Being Heumann: An Unrepentant Memoir of a Disability Rights Activist* (Beacon Press, 2020); Kitty Cone, Disability Rights and Independent Living Movement Oral History Series; and D'Lil, *Becoming Real in 24 Days*.

22 Joseph D. Whitaker, "Handicapped Protest Turned Away at HEW," *Washington Post*, April 23, 1977; Evan White interview, Paul K. Longmore Institute on Disability Collection; and letter by George Miller and others to President Carter, April 20, 1977, as cited in Hollynn D'Lil, *Becoming Real in 24 Days*, 158–9.

23 Kitty Cone, "Patient No More: Kitty Cone's Victory Speech," Paul K. Longmore Institute on Disability YouTube Channel. Last accessed December 22, 2024, https://youtu.be/HQ3kcSgAX-w?si=7–1iL61ZSUBsvAS.

24 Ally Karen Parker, interview, Paul K. Longmore Institute on Disability Collection.

25 Ray Uzeta and Connie (Soucy) Uzeta, interview, Paul K. Longmore Institute on Disability Collection.

26 Bruce Oka, interview, Paul K. Longmore Institute on Disability Collection.

27 Cone, "Patient No More"; and Ron Washington, interview, Paul K. Longmore Institute on Disability Collection.

28 Kitty Cone, interview, Paul K. Longmore Institute on Disability Collection.

29 Myra MacPherson, "Newly Militant Disabled Waging War on Discrimination," *Washington Post*, May 9, 1977; and Evan White, interview, Paul K. Longmore Institute on Disability Collection.

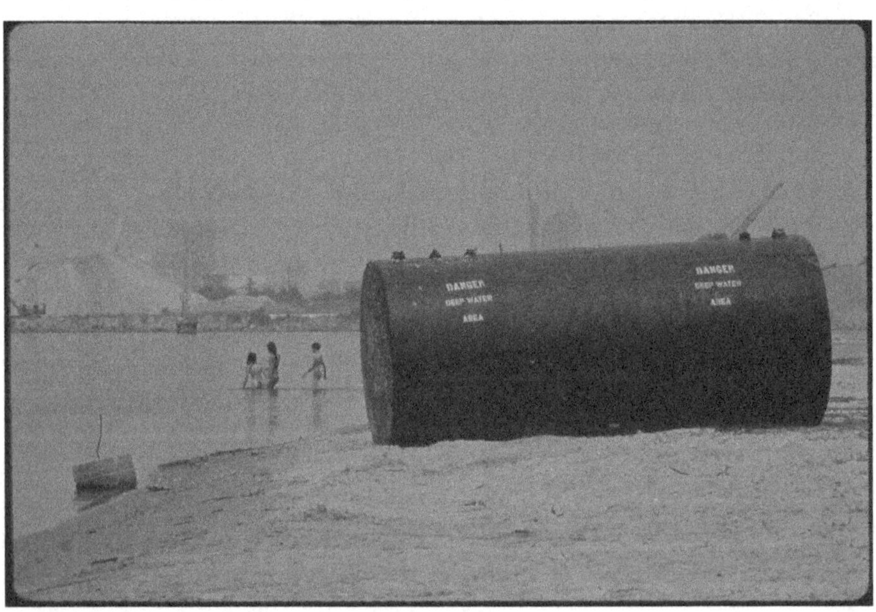

FIGURE 13.1 Chemical Plants on Shore Are Considered Prime Source of Pollution. *Lake Charles, Louisiana, June 1972. Photo by Marc St. Gil for Documerica. Courtesy of the National Archives & Records Administration.*

13

Documerica: Picturing Pollution in the 1970s

By Lauren Tilton and Mia Lazar

Environmentalism emerged in the late nineteenth century as an important byproduct of America's rapid industrialization. Concerns continued into the twentieth century as raw sewage filled the waterways and smokestacks clouded the air. Post–Second World War research revealed the harmful effects of common chemicals, and the pollution that followed white middle-class Americans into the suburbs mobilized a new wave of environmentalists. As unregulated waste across the Rust Belt literally caused the rivers to burn, Congress passed legislative landmarks like the **Clean Water Act** (1972).

Environmental risks disproportionately affect low-income and communities of color, and African American activists worried about lead poisoning in inner cities, for example, received far less attention. The environmental justice movement emerged from the intersection of social justice and environmentalism after the **Environmental Protection Agency** (EPA) approved a toxic landfill in a predominantly Black North Carolina community in 1982. This essay focuses on **Documerica**, an EPA project photographing pollution sites throughout the United States. Using a photograph of children swimming against a backdrop of industrial waste in Lake Charles, Louisiana, the authors address what is in the frame—and the Black community just outside it.

Suggested Topics: African American History, Economic History, Environmental History, Industrialization, Urban Studies, Second World War

Glossary: Clean Air Act (1970), Clean Water Act (1972), Documerica, Environmental Protection Agency, Eutrophication, Organization of Petroleum Exporting Countries

On June 8, 1972, photographer Marc St. Gil strolled along the beach in Lake Charles, Louisiana. Holding a camera loaded with 35-mm Kodachrome, he snapped photos of the oil refineries and chemical plants lining the city's major waterway while trash and dead fish lined the shore. St. Gil did not comment on the smell, but he described his shots of the day in writing, remarking on the "general debris and sadness in the area."[1] The families around him enjoyed an entirely different experience on that sunny summer day, splashing around in the water in their bathing suits with their inflatable toys and picnicking on the beach. St. Gil captured the sharp contrast between recreation and the polluted Calcasieu River in his photograph *Chemical Plants on Shore Are Considered Prime Source of Pollution*, which depicts three children playing in the lake as factories belch out smoke in the background.

St. Gil's photograph demonstrates a key shift in thinking about the environment that came in the 1970s. Americans grew concerned about how human actions harmed the environment and called on the federal government to act. The national pressure led to the formation of the Environmental Protection Agency, known as the EPA, in 1970. Congress passed a flurry of laws to clean the nation's air, land, and water. To document and evaluate their work, the EPA launched Documerica, an internal photography agency led by Gifford Hampshire and modeled on the famed Farm Security Administration's photo unit of the 1930s. Dozens of photographers across the country produced over 20,000 images. Choosing just one cannot convey the scope or extent of the environmental issues plaguing America in the 1970s.[2] St. Gil's photograph shows the interconnectedness of air, water, and waste pollution amid Americans' efforts to enjoy the leisure of postwar prosperity. The picture asks: what have industrialization and capitalism cost us?

Building the Environmental Movement

In the 1960s, calls to address the state of the environment were amplified. Media coverage of natural disasters garnered millions of people's attention through TV screens. Science research about pollution began to name and quantify the toxins spewing into the air and waste tossed into waterways. In her 1962 book *Silent Spring*, marine biologist Rachel Carson brought attention to DDT, a chemical that kills agricultural pests and devastates bird populations by making their eggshells too thin to hatch. *Silent Spring* quickly became an international bestseller. Along with making scientific facts about the environment accessible to the public, the book's success provided evidence of a shifting cultural and political landscape now deeply concerned about environmental issues, which would change local, regional, and national politics.

The year after *Silent Spring*'s call to action, Louisianans began to find fish acting erratically and floating dead in the Mississippi River. By March 1964, biologists estimated that more than 5 million fish had died. In a state that prided itself as a sportsman's paradise, this alarmed many residents.[3] Louisiana officials asked the federal government to help figure out what happened. A US Public Health Service investigation determined that Endrin, an agricultural chemical used in sugarcane fields to fight the cane borer beetle, had poisoned the fish. As national newspapers brought attention to the issue, pressure mounted for the government to take action.[4] Louisiana was not alone in the headlines. In 1969, the Cuyahoga River, which flows through Cleveland, Ohio, to Lake Erie, was so polluted by runoff from nearby farms and waste from factories that the river caught fire—for the thirteenth time.[5]

The public's concern over water pollution increased as disaster after disaster hit front pages and news hours throughout the 1960s. The country beneath Americans' feet was in crisis, and something had to be done. Thousands of local and national environmental groups formed amid all the negative environmental news. On April 22, 1970, Americans across the nation gathered in their cities and towns for the first Earth Day.[6] They planted trees, marched, hosted "teach-ins," and wrote their congressional representatives. In his national Earth Day special on CBS, famed reporter Walter Cronkite summarized the message with a simple and effective statement: "act or die." Local environmental problems, network TV news coverage, and federal policy converged into a full-fledged environmental movement.

The federal government took steps to address the public's environmental concerns with one of the most significant consolidations and expansions of the federal government of the era. In December of 1970, President Nixon created the **Environmental Protection Agency** (EPA). The EPA absorbed pre-existing federal government programs, including the Federal Water Quality Administration, several federal pesticide research programs, and the Bureau of Radiological Health. Nixon chose former Indiana Attorney General William D. Ruckelshaus as the agency's first administrator. The federal government provided the money and the people to power the new agency, leaving Ruckelshaus to decide how to allocate resources and implement new policies like the Clean Air Act of 1970. As Frank Corrado, a former EPA official who worked in the agency's early days, put it, "When the government puts together a new agency, things are basically very loose and free. There's not a lot of rules, people are just getting organized."[7]

The existence of St. Gil's photograph itself is evidence of the EPA's flexibility at its inception. In 1971, an EPA public information officer, Gifford Hampshire, approached Ruckelshaus with an idea that the EPA create a federally sponsored documentary photography program.[8] Hampshire later recalled, "In those early EPA days the small group around Bill Ruckelshaus was always floating new ideas. We'd have informal meetings and try these ideas on each other. When one of them took hold, we all felt a part of it."[9] He named the project **DOCUMERICA**, basing the idea on a previous program known as "the FSA" from the 1930s and 1940s. Farm Security Administration (FSA) photographers documented American life during the Great Depression and the Second World War and produced several of the most iconic images of the United States, including Dorothea Lange's famed *Migrant Mother*.[10] These photographs circulated widely, and many photojournalism aficionados, including Hampshire who spent years editing for photo magazines, were inspired by their work.[11] Hampshire believed that Documerica could bring awareness to environmental issues and spur change in the same way the FSA changed the American public's perception of rural poverty. Ruckelshaus approved the project and set aside $68,000 for the rest of the 1971 fiscal year.[12]

Hampshire invited Arthur Rothstein, one of the FSA's most famous photographers, to help lead Documerica. They hired prominent photojournalists, including several from the former FSA, magazines like *National Geographic* and *Time*, well-known newspapers, and even photojournalism professors. St. Gil was one of the first of more than 100 photographers the agency hired. Documerica deployed photographers to all fifty states on short assignments, usually around a week or two, and tasked them to create a "visual baseline" of their assigned location. The EPA planned to rehire the photographers to return after a few years to document and assess the efficacy of the EPA's regulations. Documerica set out to provide visual evidence of the gains, setbacks, and new policies needed to clean up the nation.[13]

Unlike written mediums, photographs show more than they tell. Through careful framing and wide distribution, they work from multiple angles by galvanizing citizens into grassroots action, pressuring legislators to enact new laws, and leaving visual evidence for future generations. For the EPA's mandate in particular, photography offered a way to communicate the scope of environmental issues to people who were not environmental experts. Although tables of data, pages of statistics, and paragraphs of rigid prose made for powerful scientific evidence and policy documents, they lacked the rhetorical flourishes and approachable storytelling of a skilled writer like Rachel Carson.

St. Gil started his career as a writer in the 1950s in Amsterdam before he moved to the United States. He explained, "I didn't have enough command of any language to write even a decent obituary other than in Dutch, and it will be instantly clear why I had to try my luck in photography."[14] From his experience as an immigrant, he knew that photography could tell stories in a more universal language and connect people from various backgrounds to complex scientific arguments. EPA officials agreed with his passion for photojournalism.[15]

On Assignment in Lake Charles

St. Gil's image of children wading into the water amid the refuse of industry was a common sight along the nation's coastlines. He spent his three-week Documerica assignment driving around the Gulf Coast, assessing industrial impact on water and air quality. Water and air regulations were two of the EPA's first goals following the passage of the **Clean Air Act** (1970) and the **Clean Water Act** (1972). The EPA wanted to document how their new regulations would improve life in the region.

St. Gil photographed a region that underwent significant environmental change over the prior decades. At the beginning of the twentieth century, Lake Charles was a small farming town. Located next to the slow, shallow, difficult-to-navigate Calcasieu River, the city was largely isolated from the rest of the country. In 1926, the construction of the Calcasieu Ship Canal linked Lake Charles to the Gulf of Mexico (a distance of 34 miles), allowing fossil fuels to be shipped out of the region more efficiently. In 1934, a chemical company called Olin became the first industrial plant built in the area. One magazine nicknamed the plant "the Grandfather of Lake Charles' chemical industry."[16] Eager for more industrial development, the city expanded the Port of Lake Charles by dredging a new channel in 1938.

The industrialization of Lake Charles happened fast. The channel attracted industries like Continental Oil and Firestone that flourished on its riverbanks, and the port soon became a vital national asset following the outbreak of the Second World War. The federal government helped fund the production of new plants to create supplies to aid the war effort, including a Mathieson-run ammonia plant. The military used Mathieson's chlorine in high-octane jet and tank fuel, plastics and fabrics, insulation, and explosives. While all this investment boosted the region's economy, it also contributed to the erosion of Louisiana marshes, the natural barrier between the city and the ocean during hurricanes, boasting a vibrant animal ecosystem that has been fundamental to the state's economy.

After the Second World War, America's relationship to controlling its environment changed. Trees in national forests were cut down at a higher rate to build houses amid an emerging consumer economy the Second World War marked by segregation.[17] Around the same time, the United States doubled its fertilizer use. Federally funded chemical plants constructed during the war, like the ones at Lake Charles, were purchased by private companies who refocused the ammonia production from wartime needs to chemical fertilizers, exponentially expanding the American agriculture industry's chemical consumption. Before the World Wars, many USDA officials discouraged farmers from buying chemical fertilizers because they were expensive and often imported overseas. But after the war, their message changed. In 1945, the United States Secretary of Agriculture encouraged farmers to take advantage of the availability of domestic fertilizers.[18] Farmers listened. So did the rest of America. Suburbia sprawled out from cities, making room for the returning soldiers and their families, with pesticide-guzzling grassy lawns and grocery store produce.

The booming pesticide business fueled changes in the Lake Charles landscape. After the Second World War, Continental Oil expanded its Lake Charles facilities dramatically in less than twenty years, enabling it to produce nine times the capacity of petrochemicals. Mathieson also enlarged their Alkali Works facility and shifted to fertilizer and pesticide production. With their factories densely packed into the Port of Lake Charles, these companies created their economic ecosystem by buying and selling their products to each other to support their operations. For instance, Mathieson used local oyster shells in its ammonia production and sold the shells it couldn't use to the Lone Star Cement company.[19] Similarly, Cities Service Oil Co. Refinery operated a butadiene synthetic rubber plant and used products from Lake Charles refineries to make it.[20] Industrial operations quickly lined the river, comprising the backdrop in which the children swim in St. Gil's photograph.

In the 1940s, Lake Charles' city government encouraged more industries to move in by creating a one-year tax exemption for new companies in the area. Soon, life in Lake Charles revolved around the chemical industry, employing 15,000 people by the 1950s, but the booming economy would not last.[21] New technological developments increased automation, and the factories required fewer and fewer people to operate their equipment. For example, in the early 1960s, Mathieson built a $19-million ammonia plant, the largest in the world at the time, in Lake Charles. The plant increased the company's ammonia capacity by 1,400 tons a day. A 1965 article explained that the new plant would only have thirty-two employees because so much labor was automated. The article explained, "This contrasts with the 71 persons currently on the payroll to operate a plant with one-quarter of the output, built on the old high-pressure synthesis principle."[22]

The growing employment crisis in Lake Charles was a microcosm of a more significant shift in the US economy that would speed up by the 1980s and be compounded by global outsourcing. In 1970, the city ran an advertisement in *Fortune Magazine* encouraging businesses to "Move Your Plant to Port ... Instead of your Cargo! Then, when your ship comes in, it'll come right to you!"[23] A similar story played out across the region in the 1960s, with chemical plants dictating the economic growth or decline in places like Geismar and Donaldson (Louisiana), Pascagoula (Mississippi), and Blytheville (Arkansas).[24]

Along with advertising itself to future industries, Lake Charles also vied for attention from tourists. In August 1971, *Travel Magazine* published an article called "Good-Time Charlie's Lake," encouraging travelers to explore Lake Charles' fishing and boating. The article boasted, "Lake Charles is the nation's only city with a natural lake and a magnificent beachfront adjacent to the highway."[25] Yet, visitors to Lake Charles' beachfront waded in the waters amid automobile and industrial discharge and waste, swimming in the wake of a surging chemical industry. St. Gil's photograph offers a more complicated view than travel writers and city boosters. To what degree could industrial growth that left the river a wasteland and a thriving tourism industry built around the city's natural features coexist?

A Closer Look: Zooming in on the Shore

During his assignment, St. Gil tried to photograph the visible effects of the invisible pollution.[26] He relied on captions, camera techniques, and composition to show the American public Lake Charles's environmental issues. St Gil's *Chemical Plants on the Shore* uses framing and scale to communicate the toxic impact of chemical industries on America's present and future. The children are small and dwarfed by the production and waste of chemicals. In the background, the factories rise into the air and are slightly out of focus. They are becoming one with the sky, signaling the factory's output as becoming the air that the children breathe.

The factories' dimness among the haze appears almost ghost-like, a haunting presence next to the dominance of the oil tank. The large rusting cylinder rests on the sand in the foreground, dominating the image through color and scale. The stark contrast draws the eye to the oil tank's warning: "DANGER: Deep Water Area." Yet the children face an invisible danger, too, from the pollutants mixed in the water. St. Gil noted in the caption of another photo he took of the lake that "mercury content in this water is too high but warnings inadequate." The water also contained sulfur oxides, which can cause damage to the lungs and contribute to acid rain.[27]

The oil tank in St. Gil's image reflects the tangled connection between the Gulf Coast region and the oil industry. At the beginning of the twentieth century, an oil company started drilling for oil in Jefferson County, Texas. On January 10, 1901, they found it—a 100-foot oil geyser erupted from the ground. Oil rig workers struggled to cap it off for more than a week.[28] News of the discovery spread quickly. Investors rushed to invest in oil fields, transforming the Texas landscape into a maze of new oil fields, refineries, and pipelines, which spread into neighboring Louisiana parishes. Companies like Cities Service Oil in Lake Charles took advantage, building refineries to accommodate the influx of Texas petroleum. Dozens of oil and gas wells popped up in the Lake Charles area, which boasted seventy-eight wells by 1949. By the time St. Gil visited Lake Charles in 1972, the petrochemical industry had made up 45 percent of Louisiana's GDP.[29] Louisiana had few environmental regulations, and the sector pumped pollutants into the water and air with impunity.

The nation's postwar affluence depended on the region's oil, resulting in a precarious reliance on an environmentally harmful resource. This outsized dependence is mirrored in the photograph as the leaching tank and the Olin Mathieson chemical plant loom over the children, making it appear that the waste of industrial America may consume them. Leisure activities like the beach vacation children enjoy are another byproduct of affluence. By the 1970s, the hard-won gains of labor organizers and workers since the late nineteenth century to secure an eight-hour workday and free weekends meant leisure had become a right. Amid a consumer republic, the biggest concern was supposed to be *how* to enjoy free time, not *if* one could. The children's toxic swimming pool brings into question what kind of relaxation and fun was possible and what the environmental cost of all those physical consumer goods meant for leisure made by chemicals that often caused more harm than benefit. In other words, what have industrialization and affluence cost us?

Everything Is Connected

When St. Gil started working for Documerica, the EPA gave him a green and white lapel pin and a fact sheet that explained at the very top: Documerica is "based on EPA's acceptance of Dr. Barry Commoner's First Law of Ecology: 'Everything is connected to everything else.'" By referencing Commoner's bestselling work, Documerica aimed to add visuals to popular environmental conversations at the time.

Commoner's law is evident in St. Gil's photograph. Olin Mathieson's pollution of the water in Lake Charles was not isolated. It was connected to pollution elsewhere in the United States as their fertilizer shipped to growers across the Midwest farm belt. In the 1970s, environmental scientists explored the role of fertilizer runoff in **eutrophication**. The excess nutrients from the fertilizer runoff enabled too much algae to bloom, which lowered the available dissolved oxygen in the water and, in turn, caused more fish die-offs elsewhere. The oil refineries in Lake Charles polluted the Calcasieu River and the tons of oil shipped from the port fostered the burning of gasoline elsewhere. The factories in the photo's background directly impacted the people in the photograph—whether they knew it or not. The fertilizer helped grow the crops that fed them, and the spandex in their swimsuits was created from petroleum products such as the ones refined in Lake Charles.

Even as the children played on the beach, the EPA was busy addressing some of the problems St. Gil documented in his work. Four months after St. Gil photographed Lake Charles, the EPA enacted the Clean Water Act (1972). The act regulated pollutants in water and aimed to make water "fishable" and "swimmable." Factories nationwide needed to retrofit their facilities with new filters to abide by the act. This caused massive shifts in how companies disposed of water, which also often tightened their profit margins.[30] The United States participated in conversations about these environmental issues with other countries. The same week that St. Gil explored Lake Charles in 1972, representatives of 113 nations met in Stockholm to discuss the environment on a global scale and propose environmental policies focusing on water and air pollution.

But instead of ushering in massive reform, the United States experienced a significant setback in environmental policies in 1973 when the **Organization of Petroleum Exporting Countries** (OPEC) issued an oil embargo. The United States relied on OPEC for a third of its oil, but when the United States continued to supply Israel during the Arab-Israeli War, the Arab member countries cut off their supply lines. The embargo hit Americans' pockets as gasoline prices skyrocketed and compounded already severe inflation. As a result, the American public became increasingly more skeptical about the economic impacts of environmental regulations. The EPA's fuel economy standards took effect the following year which required, among other things, car manufacturers to begin producing energy-efficient cars. Jimmy Carter inherited a poor economy and high unemployment when he became president during a recession. In 1977, President Carter created the Department of Energy, which intended to help tackle the oil crisis by regulating America's energy use.[31]

The fight for clean water in Louisiana lasted long after the 1970s. In 1982, Lake Charles activists created the Calcasieu League for Environmental Awareness Now (CLEAN), which gained significant local support over the next decade. Still, Louisiana ranked first in the nation for emitting the most toxic pollution in 1990.[32] Despite federal law and local activism, the massive chemical companies that line Louisiana's Gulf Coast continued to cause immense environmental infractions. In 2006, Citgo Petroleum's Lake Charles Manufacturing Complex leaked millions of slop oil and 18.5 million gallons of wastewater into the Calcasieu River. Exposure to these chemicals (hydrogen sulfide, benzene, toluene, xylene, ethylbenzene) is known to cause respiratory and neurological problems. Unlike in the 1970s, these violations did not go without punishment.[33] Citgo was required to pay more than $19 million for natural resource damages on top of an $81-million Federal Clean Water Act civil penalty. According to the *US News and World Report*, as of 2024, Louisiana still emits 3,134 pounds of industrial waste per square mile, compared with the national average of 937 pounds per square mile.[34] The state's inhabitants and ecology have been asked to pay a significant price to fuel the nation.

Beyond the Frame

Environmental movement history tends to focus on the efforts of white, wealthy Americans. St. Gil did not photograph Mossville, the small Black town where the factories in the photo's background are located. Mossville bore the brunt of the environmental pollution from industry in the Lake Charles area. By 1950, several oil refineries, pipelines, and a chemical plant were located half a mile from Mossville. This came at a time when residential racial segregation in the United States was increasing.

In 1997, a law firm in Lake Charles showed high dioxin levels in blood samples from Mossville residents. They sent their report to the EPA, which directed the Agency for Toxic Substances and Disease Registry (ASTDR) to investigate. ASTDR found that the concentration of polychlorinated biphenyls (PCBs) was 2.8 times higher in Mossville residents than in the rest of the parish. Despite this, ASTDR did not blame local industries.[35] In 2012, the chemical company Sasol began to buy up residential property in Mossville to build their facility, displacing residents. As of the early 2000s, 80 percent of Black Louisianians live within three miles of a toxic waste-emitting facility despite comprising roughly a third of the state's population.[36] In 2021, the first Black EPA administrator, Michael Regan, visited Mossville to speak with community members about the impact of pollution. Since the 1980s, calls to center environmental justice have asked us to think critically about who is included and not included in the photograph and the more significant environmental movement.

St. Gil's message still rings true. As it does in his photograph, America's industrial infrastructure looms hauntingly in the background. Almost out of view, one must squint or take a magnifying glass to make out the large factories rising into the sky. Without regulation and enforcement, their waste flows. The abundant life promised by postwar affluence becomes mauled in pollution, as dead fish and toxic waste line areas of natural beauty. In the foreground, St. Gil shares his message of caution with a large, rusting oil cauldron marked in bright yellow, "Danger." As we look toward the future, will we heed his call?

Discussion Questions

1   What role is photography playing in government policy and the environmental movement?

2   A motto of the EPA and Documerica was "Everything Is Connected." What did they mean by this? How does the photograph visualize this motto?

3   Select one or two photographs from Digital Documerica (www. digitaldocumerica.org). Situate and analyze the photograph(s) in the history of the era. What kind of visual rhetoric do the photographs use? What do they tell us about 1970s America and the environment?

4   How do these photographs about the environmental movement and policy change your understanding of the 1970s? How do they change your understanding of the environment today?

Further Resources

Arnold, Taylor and Lauren Tilton. "Digital Documerica: Exploring Environmental Photography from the 1970s." 2025. www.digitaldocumerica.org.

Barnes, A. James, John D. Graham, and David M. Konisky, eds. *Fifty Years at the US Environmental Protection Agency: Progress, Retrenchment, and Opportunities*. Rowman & Littlefield, 2021.

François, Pierre, director. *Documerica: Forgotten Pictures of America*. 2023. https://www.arte.tv/en/videos/108941-000-A/documerica/.

National Archives and Records Administration. Documerica, by Topic. https://www.archives.gov/research/environment/documerica-topics.

Notes

1   Marc St. Gil Shot Notes, June 8, 1972, RG 412-P, Box 16, Folder 0018, Records of the United States Environmental Protection Agency, Documerica: Photographers' Correspondence and Assignment Folders, National Archives and Records Administration, College Park, Maryland. Hereafter, "Documerica, NARA II."

2   To explore the wide range of images, visit DigitalDocumerica.org.

3   Jonathan Zachary DeLaune, "Unwelcome Neighbors? Industrial Growth and Water Pollution in Lake Charles, Louisiana, 1940–1960" (MA thesis, Louisiana State University, 2007), 111.

4   Craig E. Colten, "Mississippi River," in *History in Dispute, Volume 7: Water and the Environment since 1945*, ed. Char Mille, Mark Cioc, and Kate Showers (St. James Press, 2001), 160–5.

5   A. James Barnes, John D. Graham, and David M. Konisky, eds., *Fifty Years at the US Environmental Protection Agency: Progress, Retrenchment, and Opportunities* (Rowman & Littlefield, 2021), 1.

6   Barnes, Graham, and Konisky, *Fifty Years at the US Environmental Protection Agency*, 2.

7   Frank Corrado, interview (unpublished) by Mia Lazar, May 2023.

8   Gifford Dean Hampshire, *My American Heritage: A Genealogy* (Fairfax, 1997), 139.

9   Hampshire, *My American Heritage*, 139.

10   For more on Dorothea Lange's expansive work and complicated legacy, see Linda Gordon's essay in Chapter 7.

11   Hampshire, *My American Heritage*, 139.

12   Frank E. Stanfield, "Project Documerica in the Southeast: The Use of Documentary Photography by the Environmental Protection Agency to Publicize Environmental Problems in the 1970's," (MA thesis, University of Georgia, 1980), 40.

13   For more on the formation of Documerica, see Caleb Wellum, "The Ambivalent Aesthetics of Oil: Project Documerica and the Energy Crisis in 1970s America," *Environmental History* 22, no. 4 (October 2017): 723–32.

14   Diary Entry by Marc St. Gil, May 9, 1972, 14, Documerica, NARA II.

15   The EPA was only one in a variety of governmental and non-profit agencies to engage in visual mediums to garner support for environmental activism. For more, see Finis Dunway, *Seeing Green: The Use and Abuse of Environmental Images* (University of Chicago Press, 2015).

16   "Lake Charles' Deep-Water Port … Keeps Warbuilt Plants Humming," *BusinessWeek*, June 12, 1948.

17   For more on racial inequalities embedded in the postwar Federal Housing Authority, see Richard Rothstein, *The Color of Law: A Forgotten History of How Our Government Segregated America* (Liveright, 2017).

18   Timothy Johnson, "Nitrogen Nation: The Legacy of World War I and the Politics of Chemical Agriculture in the United States 1916–1933," *Agricultural History* 90, no. 2 (Spring 2016): 226.

19   DeLaune, "Unwelcome Neighbors?" 98.

20   "Lake Charles' Deep-Water Port," 72.

21   Rebecca O. Johnson, "A Lot Like War: Petrocapitalism, 'Slow Violence,' and the Struggle for Environmental Justice," *Social Justice* 46, no. 1 (2020): 110.

22   "Ammonia's New World: More Plant, Less Crew," *Business Week*, November 13, 1965, 134.

23   "Port of Lake Charles," *Fortune*, August 1, 1970, 26.

24   "Ammonia's New World" 134.

25   "Good-Time Charlie's Lake," *Travel Magazine*, August 1, 1971, 27.

26 Diary Entry by Marc St. Gil, June 26, 1972, 65, Documerica, NARA II.

27 St. Gil, Marc, Captions for Selects, 1972–1973, Documerica, NARA II.

28 James S. Olson, with Shannon L. Kenny, *The Industrial Revolution: Key Themes and Documents* (Bloomsbury Press, 2015), 196–7.

29 Thomas Estabrook, *Labor-Environmental Coalitions: Lessons from a Louisiana Petrochemical Region* (Baywood Publishing, 2007), 92.

30 Kendra Smith-Howard, "Absorbing Waste, Displacing Labor: Family, Environment, and the Disposable Diaper in the 1970s," *Environmental History* 26, no. 2 (April 2021): 222.

31 Benjamin Kline, *First along the River: A Brief History of the U.S. Environmental Movement*, 2nd Edition (Acada Books, 2000), 108.

32 Peggy Frankland, with Susan Tucker, *Women Pioneers of the Louisiana Environmental Movement* (University Press of Mississippi, 2013), xiv.

33 US Department of Justice, "CITGO Petroleum Corp. Will Pay over $19 Million for Injuries to Natural Resources Resulting from Its Oil Spill at Its Refinery in Lake Charles, Louisiana," Press Release, June 17, 2021.

34 "Louisiana Rankings," *U.S. News and World Report*, 2024. Last accessed March 12, 2025, https://www.usnews.com/news/best-states/louisiana.

35 Clare Kelsey, "Life in Mossville, Louisiana: Policy Implications of Toxic Waste Exposure and Environmental Racism" (MS thesis, Rochester Institution of Technology, 2022), 23.

36 Jeannine Cahill-Jackson, "Mossville Environmental Action Now v. United States: Is a Solution to Environmental Injustice Unfolding?," *3 Pace Int'l L. Rev. Online Companion* 173 (2012).

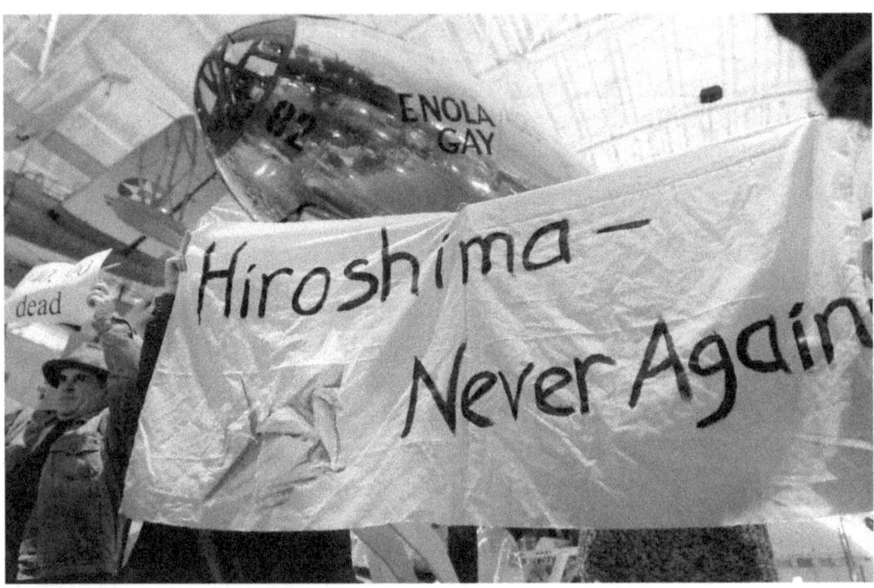

FIGURE 14.1 *Demonstrators protesting the Smithsonian National Air and Space Museum's* Enola Gay *exhibit at the Steven F. Udvar-Hazy Center. Chantilly, Virginia, December 15, 2003. Photo by Joyce Naltchayan Boghosian. Courtesy of Getty Images.*

14

The *Enola Gay* and the Culture Wars

By Rebecca S. Wingo

The Atomic Age began with the end of the Second World War and the bombing of Hiroshima and Nagasaki in 1945. With weapons of "mutually assured destruction" at the ready, the United States and Soviet Union entered into a tense Cold War. Over the next fifty years, the political pendulum swung widely. The conservatism that defined McCarthyism in the 1950s clashed with the social liberalism of civil rights, counterculture, and antiwar movements of the 1960s and 1970s. The Christian right gained a stronger foothold during the **Reagan Era** in the 1980s as they took aim at gay rights, feminism, and affirmative action. Bipartisan divisions between conservatives and liberals hardened into what became known as the "**Culture Wars**."

In 1995, when the Smithsonian Institution planned an anniversary exhibit reflecting on the end of the Second World War and the decision to drop nuclear weapons, they were unprepared for the backlash from conservative lawmakers, veterans, and the American public. Displaying the *Enola Gay*, the plane that dropped the bomb on Hiroshima thrust the Smithsonian directly into the political crossfire of the Culture Wars. This chapter chronicles the *Enola Gay*'s final battle in a culture war waged over how Americans choose to remember (or forget) the past.

Suggested Topics: Atomic Age, Cold War, Commemoration and Memorialization, Contemporary America, Culture Wars, Environmental History, History of Science, Second World War

Glossary: Atomic Diplomacy, Culture Wars, Hibakusha, Reagan Era, Revisionist History, Social History

On August 6, 1945, the *Enola Gay*, a US Air Force B-29 bomber, dropped an atomic bomb on Hiroshima. Three days later, *Bockscar* dropped another on Nagasaki. Within days Japan surrendered, bringing an end to the Second World War. Although it's unknown exactly how many people died, the current consensus is approximately 200,000 civilians.[1] There is also no clear estimate of how many American lives were saved through an aerial assault versus a ground invasion. At the heart of this question is a complex moral calculus used to condemn or justify US military actions to end the Second World War.

The deployment of the bombs in Japan ushered in a Cold War that would last until the collapse of the Soviet Union in 1991. As Soviet scientists rushed to develop nuclear weapons of their own, the USSR and United States engaged in a tense holding pattern, each with the capacity to unleash "weapons of mutually assured destruction," but neither willing to do it.

A nuclear bomb vaporizes within microseconds upon detonation, transforming into a gas hotter than the sun's core that funnels a massive fireball into the atmosphere. For bombs the size of the ones dropped in Japan, the thermal flash that follows causes severe burns to anyone in a 20-mile radius. The blast wave creates a powerful shift in air pressure that punches outward from the epicenter at thousands of miles per hour, collapsing nearly every structure in its wake.[2] Over 65 percent of Hiroshima's buildings were destroyed in 1945, including homes, hospitals, and schools.[3] Effects of radiation exposure linger, resulting in infertility, blood disorders, and increased rates of cancer.

There have been no nuclear attacks since the Second World War, but countries across the globe have continued to develop even more destructive nuclear weapons. Scientists hypothesize that the environmental effects of a large-scale nuclear war would persist for decades, forcing enough radioactive particles into the stratosphere to produce a global fallout. These particles would consume the ozone layer and the soot from the nuclear firestorms would block sunlight, triggering a "nuclear winter" characterized by rapid global cooling. Some estimates warn of mass extinction, including of the human species.[4]

In this context, the photograph of antinuclear protestors standing beneath the *Enola Gay* with a sign that says "Hiroshima—Never Again" hardly seems like a controversial sentiment. But in the 1990s, the history of atomic warfare and the politics of memory collided as the Smithsonian Institution's *Enola Gay* exhibit became a battleground for a gamut of polarizing political issues in America's Culture Wars. Recovering the story of this image requires looking within and beyond the frame of this photograph, to a time before and a time after it was taken, to what we can see and what we cannot see, to what we remember and what we choose *not* to remember.

The Smithsonian was caught in a political crossfire when the National Air and Space Museum (NASM) put the *Enola Gay* on display for an exhibition commemorating the fiftieth anniversary of the end of the Second World War.

Despite its size, the *Enola Gay* was not the exhibit's intended focal point. Instead, the curators encouraged visitors to reflect on the decision to bomb Japan. Arguing that the exhibit was too sympathetic to the Japanese and did not do enough to recognize the valor and sacrifice of American soldiers, military and veteran lobbyists allied with conservative politicians and took aim at the Smithsonian, NASM curators, and historians.

The *Enola Gay*'s last battle would be fought in news headlines and debated on the Senate floor. The battle was not over the facts of its mission or even over the morality of dropping the bomb. Rather, it was a rhetorical clash fought on the vitriolic battlefields of anti-intellectualism, memory, and political correctness in a war waged over the very tone of history.

The Bomb

President Truman learned of the top-secret Manhattan Project in April 1945, after the death of President Roosevelt. Though the USSR and United States fought as allies during the Second World War, the ideological tensions between communism and democracy simmered below the surface. When it became clear that the Soviet Union intended to violate the Soviet-Japanese Neutrality Pact and enter the war on the Pacific front, American officials worried the USSR would wield too much power in the region. At the Potsdam Conference between allied leaders in July 1945, Truman attempted to gain the upper hand by telling Joseph Stalin about the bombs. Historian Gar Alperovitz later termed this tactical move "**atomic diplomacy**."[5]

When Truman and his advisors decided to force Japan's surrender by deploying their new weapons, they spent little time debating the human or environmental cost. Instead, they discussed how the bombs would debut America's formidable military might to the USSR. Bombing Japan may have expedited the end of the war, but scholars agree that Japan's military power was already on the decline and that Truman exaggerated the estimates of American casualties in the event of a ground invasion to justify an aerial assault.[6] Bombing Japan was an excuse—a proxy for the anti-communism that would define Cold War America.

The gravity of any country possessing nuclear weaponry slowly settled into the American conscience over the following decades. The bomb disturbed many of the people involved. Scientists for the Manhattan Project struggled over the ethics of using their creation. Popularized in the film *Oppenheimer* (2023), physicist and project director Robert Oppenheimer famously paraphrased the *Bhagavad Gita*: "Now I am become death, the destroyer of worlds."[7] Admiral William Leahy, chairman of the Joint Chiefs of Staff under both Roosevelt and Truman, wrote that when they dropped the bombs, America officially "adopted an ethical standard common to the barbarians of the Dark Ages."[8] Even General Dwight D. Eisenhower, who supervised the invasion of Normandy in the Second World War and later succeeded Truman as president, referred to the bomb as "that awful thing."[9]

Throughout the 1940s and 1950s, the loudest opposition to nuclear warfare came from the political right. Within weeks, Felix Morley, the former *Washington Post* editor and founder of the conservative journal *Human Events*, reflected on the moral toll. "Perhaps the cost of [Hiroshima] is even heavier for us than the Japanese," he wrote, "for its measure is the loss of an ideal which, far more than our moral strength, has made America great and distinctive in the long human history."[10] A decade later, conservative historian Harry Elmer Barnes condemned the decision, too. "Well-informed persons have known for years that the bombing of these Japanese cities was not needed to bring the war to a speedy end," he wrote. "The tens of thousands of Japanese who were roasted at Hiroshima and Nagasaki were sacrificed not to end the war or save American and Japanese lives but to strengthen American diplomacy *vis-à-vis* Russia."[11]

Meanwhile, Americans grew accustomed to living in the shadow of the decision to bomb Japan. America in the 1950s was submersed in a virulent strain of patriotism and an intense backlash against foreign influences, exacerbated by a deeply entrenched fear of nuclear fallout. Although America's Atomic Age is commonly synonymous with McCarthyism and his politically fueled witch hunts for communist spies, a moral panic permeated American society too. Schoolchildren performed "duck and cover" drills and learned to cower under their desks in the event of a nuclear attack. Federal employees had to sign loyalty agreements. Even the Cincinnati Reds—the oldest Major League Baseball team in the country—briefly changed their name to the Redlegs to avoid any insinuation that they were communists. Anti-communist propaganda papered America and consumed its airwaves telling people that they could trust no one—not even their neighbors.[12]

By the time progressive counterculture took hold in the 1960s and 1970s, the loudest opposition to nuclear warfare came from the political left. Between liberation movements, a growing antiwar sentiment, and environmental concerns over nuclear power and weapons, American society was in tumult. In academia, scholars started studying "**social history**," a method that examines the lives of ordinary people and their social worlds. "New Left" historians like Alperovitz who focused on "the machinations of the powerful and the resistance of the powerless" emerged in the 1960s.[13] But when these historians repeated the arguments conservatives made just a few decades before, they were labeled "left-wing revisionists."[14]

The truth is that Allied victory in the Second World War was never guaranteed, yet Americans believed that because they fought with morality on their side, the defeat of Germany, Japan, and other Axis powers was predestined.[15] By the time the fiftieth anniversary of the Second World War began in 1991, the schism between popular memory of American victory and historical analysis of the methods of that victory was insurmountable. Americans—the global defenders of democracy—struggled to reconcile the defeat of Hitler's Third Reich with the devastation of Japan.

These two truths are part of the same war, but as the Smithsonian discovered, the mere suggestion that America's moral victory was predicated on an amoral decision to bomb civilians was framed by conservatives as unpatriotic.

The Plane

After the war, the Smithsonian Institution acquired the *Enola Gay*. The plane was eventually parked outdoors at Andrews Air Force Base in Maryland where weather and vandalism took their toll. In the 1960s, curators disassembled the plane and moved it to a nearby restoration facility where it sat until Martin Harwit, an astrophysicist from Cornell University, assumed directorship of the NASM in 1987. Harwit expressed his commitment to display the *Enola Gay*. It was an opportunity to transform the NASM from a shrine of American aeronautic ingenuity into a place where visitors could critically engage in nuanced conversations about America's technological past.

As a Second World War survivor whisked out of Czechoslovakia by the Allies as a young boy, Harwit respected the American military. Before becoming a professor at Cornell, he served in the US Army supervising nuclear weapons tests in the Marshall Islands. These tests contributed to more than half of the nuclear radiation in the atmosphere today, severely degraded several coral atolls, and forced the relocation of the Marshallese who still experience high rates of cancer and birth defects.[16] Radiation levels on some of the islands are still nearly double "safe" exposure levels.[17] Harwit was no stranger to war or the catastrophic effects of atomic weapons. If anyone could oversee the plane's interpretation, it was Harwit.

The controversy over whether to display the *Enola Gay* predated Harwit's appointment. During congressional appropriations hearings in 1970, Barry Goldwater, a republican senator from Arizona and Air Force veteran in the Second World War, voiced his opposition to its installation. Others agreed, adding that it would be offensive to see the *Enola Gay* in the NASM alongside American aeronautical advancements that otherwise conjured immense national pride.[18]

Veterans disagreed. Some suggested that the plane might be better suited in a different museum entirely and lobbied to move it to the Wright-Patterson Air Force Base in Dayton, Ohio.[19] Others felt that if the Smithsonian wasn't going to let someplace else have the plane, then they should at least restore it. Prodding the Smithsonian into action, veterans formed the "Committee for the Restoration and Proud Display of the *Enola Gay*" and gathered over 8,000 signatures for their petition. The Smithsonian relented. They began restoring the plane in 1984, but NASM staff remained internally conflicted about its display.[20]

Harwit formed a Research Advisory Committee (RAC) comprised of curators, veterans, and scholars to make recommendations on how and where to install the *Enola Gay*. Some RAC members resisted any installation citing concerns that visitors would take away the wrong message. Admiral Noel Gayler was one of these opposing voices. Before retiring, Gayler was a flying ace in the Second World War, the former director of the National Security Agency, and the commander of the Pacific Command. While he fervently defended the bravery of Air Force bomber crews, he believed that dropping atomic bombs on Japan was nothing short of genocide. The RAC ultimately recommended developing an off-site traveling exhibition that would allow them to establish a more somber tone and convey the message that nuclear bombs have no place in civil society.[21]

By 1993, a different exhibit took shape, one that incorporated the *Enola Gay* in the main museum and contextualized the end of the Second World War as the beginning of the Atomic Age. Given the museum's physical constraints, only the front fuselage would go on display. The curators figured they could transform the mood of the exhibit hall from celebratory to solemn through lighting, photographs, and a careful selection of artifacts.[22]

None of these plans came to fruition. In January 1995, the Smithsonian cancelled the exhibit. Instead, the forward fuselage would go on display without any interpretation at all.

The First Exhibit

Shortly after midnight on a cold, moonless night in late November 1994, a flatbed under police escort rolled down Independence Avenue toward the National Mall in Washington, DC. The route would normally be deserted at that hour, but protestors huddled in clusters, shouting and waving banners that read "DISARM." NPR's *Morning Edition* recorded one man as he sang a song of peace. He was a **hibakusha**, a survivor of the bombs dropped on Hiroshima and Nagasaki.[23] Ghoulishly shrouded in white plastic on the back of the truck was the gleaming aluminum hull of the *Enola Gay*, a lightning rod for America's political and social unrest.

The original exhibit, "The Crossroads: The End of World War II, the Atomic Bomb, and the Origins of the Cold War," examined the decision to use nuclear weapons and its complicated legacy. It envisioned five chronological sections: "Fight to the Finish," "Decision to Drop the Bomb," "Delivering the Bomb," "Ground Zero," and "Legacy of Hiroshima and Nagasaki." A planning document from July 1993 summarized the exhibit's central argument: "that nuclear weapons never be used in anger again."[24]

Through careful diplomacy with the City of Hiroshima and the Hiroshima Peace Memorial Museum, Harwit negotiated loans of several powerful artifacts: a wristwatch frozen in time, a rosary fused by the heat, a child's lunchbox with carbonized rice and peas. They would appear in the "Ground Zero" section, the exhibit's "emotional center."[25] Harwit and the curators knew the exhibit would be provocative, but they were woefully unprepared for the vitriol they received from veterans, lawmakers, and the American public.

The term "**Culture Wars**" gained popularity in 1991 through a groundbreaking sociological study about the rapid polarization of American politics.[26] Throughout the 1980s, American politicians moved away from the liberal New Deal and Great Society programs that lifted the nation from the Great Depression and carried through the Cold War. **Reagan Era** policies such as the War on Drugs and the growing AIDS epidemic emboldened conservative Christian lobbyists and lawmakers. They blurred the lines between church and state, channeling their energies into "hot button" issues like abortion rights, censorship, gun control, homosexuality, and political correctness.[27] Media outlets leaned in too, giving rise to conservative figureheads like talk show host Rush Limbaugh. Other self-proclaimed "culture warriors" like *Fox News*' Bill O'Reilly followed. The anniversary of the Second World War coincided with an extreme political upheaval that hardened party lines and sowed division between seemingly irreconcilable worldviews.

In the years preceding the exhibit's development, Harwit and his team hosted countless public lectures and invited hard conversations with the foremost military and academic experts on strategic bombing.[28] In late 1993, Harwit attempted to proactively diffuse any critiques by inviting the American Legion and the Air Force Association (AFA) to review the exhibit script. The veterans requested more balance—a little more about American sacrifice and a little less about American sacrifice of Japanese civilians. The NASM strengthened language around Japan's "naked aggression and extreme brutality" and added that the bomb "played a crucial role in ending the Pacific War quickly"—an uncritical assertion they knew to be false.[29]

With these changes in place, the NASM formally released the script in January 1994. The AFA and American Legion were waiting. They responded immediately, calling the exhibit a "slap in the face." They cast public accusations that the museum was "politically biased" and not respectful enough of veterans' heroics. With headings like "Politically Correct Curating," John Correll, the editor of *Air Force Magazine*, released an AFA Special Report condemning the Smithsonian for insinuating a moral equivalency between Japan and the United States. The exhibit was "**revisionist history**" full of "gratuitous social commentary"—a perversion of the museum's core mission.[30]

The AFA hired a PR firm to keep the controversy in the spotlight. They took advantage of the 1994 midterm elections that repopulated the legislature with conservative politicians desperate to regain control over America's cultural institutions. Legislators new and old embraced the AFA's challenge to the NASM. The Senate and the House both passed resolutions "regarding the appropriate portrayal of men and women of the Armed Forces." Citing the Smithsonian's founding documents, they condemned the script as "revisionist and offensive" and resolved that any exhibit featuring the *Enola Gay* "should avoid impugning the memory of those who gave their lives for freedom."[31]

Back at the NASM, Harwit assembled a team of six reviewers, including two high-ranking veterans, two curators, a docent, and Harwit's assistant.[32] They mined the script for any common ground in the chasm between how the public remembered the war and the historical analyses that evolved since 1945. In May 1994, the NASM released a new script called "The Last Act: The Atomic Bomb and the End of World War II." It was not good enough. They released three more versions in the months that followed, writing a new introduction about the Pacific front and dramatically reducing the "Ground Zero" and "Legacy of Hiroshima and Nagasaki" sections.

Of particular concern to the AFA was the lunchbox loaned from the Hiroshima Museum. Although the curators never planned to prominently display graphic images of bomb victims, artifacts—like photographs—are often more evocative than words. The lunchbox alluded to death. There was no question as to the fate of the child who carried it. Harwit's team grudgingly eliminated all the artifacts from the Hiroshima Museum and replaced them with expanded text about Japanese aggression.

Harwit tried to mount a defense, but the Smithsonian was no match for the AFA's rank-and-file members and their media chokehold. He maintained that his engagement with Japanese museums was designed to "include the point of view of the vanquished as well as the point of view of the victors." In a confrontational interview with Correll, Harwit stated emphatically, "We will never apologize for this country, nor are we tempted to, nor do we take moral stances."[33]

Congress threatened to withdraw the Smithsonian's congressional appropriation if they did not cater to the AFA and American Legion's demands.

At the time, the Smithsonian received 85 percent of its funding from the federal government. They couldn't risk it. To appease their critics, the NASM compromised on every potentially controversial aspect of their exhibition, but it didn't matter. Dismissing any historical evidence to the contrary from the left or the right, the AFA would not be satisfied until the NASM declared in no uncertain terms that the bomb ended the war, that it saved American lives, and that there was no alternative.[34] After five drafts, the executive director of the AFA declared that the "fix-up plan was *too little, too late.*" It was "time *to shut down this exhibit and start over with different curators.*"[35]

Amidst a firestorm of critique, media-fueled public hysteria, and death threats, the Smithsonian conceded defeat. On January 30, 1995, Smithsonian Secretary Michael Heyman canceled the exhibit and issued a formal statement acknowledging that they should not have tried to couple a deeper conversation about the decision to drop the bombs with the commemoration of the Second World War. The Greatest Generation "[was] not looking for analysis," he said. "Veterans and their families were expecting, and rightly so, that the nation would honor and commemorate their valor and sacrifice."[36] Harwit resigned as director of the NASM saying, "I believe that nothing less than my stepping down from the directorship will satisfy the Museum's critics and allow the Museum to move forward."[37]

On June 28, 1995, the NASM unveiled the *Enola Gay.* Heyman personally oversaw its display. Devoid of any interpretation, the label instead recounted the plane's restoration. Nearby, a short video played, narrated by snippets from interviews with the *Enola Gay's* pilot, Paul Tibbets, and his crew. A Smithsonian spokesman said the new exhibit "allows the airplane and the crew to speak for themselves."[38] The casualties in Hiroshima and Nagasaki were enumerated only as "many tens of thousands." Nestled beneath the forward fuselage was "Little Boy," a disarmed L-11 bomb like the one dropped on Hiroshima.[39]

Over 800 visitors flocked to the NASM to see the *Enola Gay* in the first two hours alone.[40] Museumgoers were greeted by antinuclear demonstrators who knelt in front of the exhibit chanting, "Acting in genuine justice, we commit our lives!" and "We repent!" A second wave of protestors unfurled long banners from the balcony above the lobby and shouted "Never again! Never again!" The banners conveyed what the label did not: the number of dead at Hiroshima and Nagasaki. When US Park Police arrested twenty demonstrators for creating a public nuisance, the lines of people waiting to see the exhibit applauded.[41] A few days later, three others were arrested and charged with a federal crime for throwing human blood and ashes on the plane.[42]

Japanese newspaper and television reporters described the scene surrounding America's "holy relic" to their publics back home. "The *Enola Gay* is presented here not as a warning against the great horror of nuclear war," Hideaki Saito reported, "but as a national hero that brought World War II to an end."[43] Their criticism that the exhibit legitimized American military actions echoed an old exchange between Truman and the Hiroshima City Council in 1958. "The need for such a fateful decision, of course, would never have arisen had we not been shot in the back by Japan at Pearl Harbor in December 1941," Truman wrote. The Hiroshima City Council responded, "had your decision been based on [Pearl Harbor], why could you not choose a military base for the target? You committed the outrage of massacring 200,000 noncombatants as revenge, and you are still trying to justify it."[44]

Historians protested too through teaching sit-ins and countless articles and books. They established guidelines for exhibiting controversial subjects and argued that museums were vital to making accurate historical analysis accessible to the public. The newly formed "Historians' Committee for Open Debate on Hiroshima" sent a letter accusing the Smithsonian's leadership of "surrender[ing] to political censorship" that perpetuated an American mythology through "historical cleansing." But if the public's historical amnesia showed us anything, it's that scholarship from the so-called "liberal elite" is ineffective against "partisan campaigns aimed at victory by any means."[45]

In September 1995, Correll published the names of historians and journalists who opposed the AFA in his magazine and defended his position that the exhibit was "incredibly propagandistic and intellectually shabby."[46] As culture warriors slapped revisionist labels on academic and public historians in an attempt to undermine their scholarship and training, scholars called out the irony that their repetition of Truman's version of events "represents the *original* attempt at 'revisionist' history."[47]

The *Enola Gay* attracted over a million visitors in the first year and remains one of the most popular exhibits the NASM has ever put on display. Visitors did not seem to mind the plane's partial display—fragmented in form and dislodged from its historical context. The plane's last battle was fought in a lose-lose war, one in which the American public lost the most.[48]

The Second Exhibit

In 1998, NASM relocated the *Enola Gay* to the Stephen F. Udvar-Hazy Center, a new annex facility near Dulles airport that houses everything from the prototype for the Boeing 707 to the space shuttle *Discovery*. There, the *Enola Gay* was reunited with its wings and body for the first time since 1960.

The photograph of protestors underneath the nose of the *Enola Gay* was taken at the Udvar-Hazy Center's grand opening in 2003.[49] As in 1995, anti-nuclear activists protested its display and issued calls for nuclear disarmament.[50] Joyce Naltchayan Boghosian, the staff photographer for *Agence France-Press* who made the photo in 2003, also photographed the 1995 protest. She didn't plan it that way. Both exhibit openings were just her beats on those days.

Boghosian's memory isn't as clear as it was several decades ago. Photojournalists tend to move quickly from one assignment to the next. In addition to her freelance work, her career spans five presidential administrations as a staff photographer (and later, director) for the White House Photo Office. Born in the late 1960s, Boghosian came of age during the Cold War. In 1990, when President George H.W. Bush hosted Soviet President Mikhail Gorbachev at the Washington Summit, she was in the press riser above the White House lawn. She focused her 600-mm lens on the two leaders and thought to herself, "My gosh, I've grown up my whole life afraid of nuclear war and now I'm photographing my president and Russia's president standing next to each other." The following year, Bush and Gorbachev signed a pact to reduce their nuclear arsenals. It was a surreal moment for Boghosian. "It gives you hope, you know?"[51]

All of which is to say, the *Enola Gay* protests are a blip in Boghosian's otherwise storied career, but she does remember them. She remembers that the protests in 1995 took everyone by surprise, and that the protest in 2003 seemed more planned. She remembers that the Udvar-Hazy Center's opening ceremony was a private event with big-wigs like Vice President Dick Cheney and space legends like Neil Armstrong and John Glenn. She remembers that as she descended a set of stairs, she looked over to find that she was walking next to actor (and pilot) John Travolta. She also remembers that seeing the *Enola Gay* was emotional and moving. "Whether you like it or not, it is history."[52]

After the ceremony was over, the museum welcomed the general public into the halls for the first time. Boghosian was near the *Enola Gay* when protestors blocked the exhibit with posters depicting its victims. She was in the fray when a man threw red paint at the plane and dented its hull. She looked around and saw a lot of people, and a lot of kids. "It gets a little scary because you don't know what the next move is going to be, or if someone has something that could hurt the people around them."[53]

Boghosian's composition is tight, and the protestors fill the frame. Her close vantage magnifies the high-stress situation, which she described as "unsettling." It also makes the crowds appear denser than she remembers. The demonstrators were certainly disruptive, but the Udvar-Hazy Center is a massive, seventeen-acre complex housing entire air and spacecraft. They were fifty people in a space roughly equivalent to twenty-three football fields. Had Boghosian been on the other side of the complex, she may not have heard them or gotten there before they were escorted out by police. "I guess I was just in the right place at the right time," she said upon learning that her photos are among the few public photographic records of either protest.[54]

Although the protestors' bodies and signs obscure the exhibit in this photo, there are gallery images showing the full display.[55] The *Enola Gay* is imposing, elevated above the heads of onlookers and protestors alike, and surrounded by other aircraft from the Second World War. Although the bomber was only deployed on the Pacific front, small Nazi fighter jets are placed alongside kamikaze aircraft in the shadow of its wings. There is no accompanying interpretation, nothing to interrupt the misleading, ahistorical visual triumph of the *Enola Gay* over both the Japanese *and* Nazis.

A handful of survivors also attended the protest. The hibakusha are an aging population, but they still remember—the black rain, the inescapable smell of burning, the maggots they picked from each other's skin at school for months after the bombing. They are "the backbone of atomic memory."[56] Seeing the polished plane hoisted above his head must have been haunting for Minoru Nishino. "This is the second time I have seen the *Enola Gay*," he told a reporter. "The first time was on August 6, 1945, when I saw it flying high in the sky. When I saw the *Enola Gay* today, I was overcome by anger."[57]

Terumi Tanaka was at the protest, too. Tanaka devoted his life to ending nuclear warfare as secretary general for Nihon Hidankyo, a peace organization founded by hibakusha. In 2024, Nihon Hidankyo received the Nobel Peace Prize and at the age of ninety-two, Tanaka delivered the acceptance speech. He recalled his childhood experiences in Nagasaki and noted that, ever since, nuclear weapons have continued to proliferate around the globe. There are nine countries—China, France, India, Israel, North Korea, Pakistan, Russia, the United Kingdom, and the United States—with approximately 12,000 nuclear warheads. While many pay lip service to disarmament, global expenditures on nuclear weapons development increased by $10.7 billion between 2022 and 2023. "The world," Tanaka told the audience, "is not meant to be a prison in which we await collective annihilation."[58]

Like the debate over the *Enola Gay*, the Culture Wars of the 1990s seemed to have two sides—conservatives and liberals, or traditionalists and progressives—but this view is too simplistic. In 1995, cultural historian Louis Menand argued that the term "Culture Wars" is a catchall metaphor into which Americans crammed everything from abortion to porn, from curriculum to school prayer.[59] By meaning everything, it effectively means nothing. "Culture Wars" became a blank slate onto which people *applied* meaning, pitting rhetoric around concepts like the "moral majority" against "freedom of expression," and revealing the tenuous threads holding together an America fractured by severe political and social divisions.

Modern Culture Wars

One of the NASM curators called the *Enola Gay* controversy "an ominous warning of the battles to come."[60] Indeed, the Modern Culture Wars of the 2020s are waged over the same issues, amplified on the familiar battlefields of anti-diversity, climate change, education, sexuality, and history.

Even the rhetoric has stayed the same. During Pat Buchanan's famous "Culture War" speech at the 1992 Republican National Convention, he endorsed future President George H.W. Bush by announcing a "struggle for the soul of America." Almost thirty years later following the Electoral College certification in 2020, President-elect Joe Biden echoed, "in this battle for the soul of America, democracy prevailed."[61] In the same election, incumbent Donald Trump ran campaign ads with video footage of police clashing with Black Lives Matter protestors spliced with an S.O.S. to "Save America's Soul."[62]

But some things have changed, like the speed with which Americans can consume, produce, or delete information. The *Enola Gay* once again became a lightning rod of controversy in March 2025 after President Donald Trump passed an executive order for all federal agencies to purge any content related to diversity, equity, and inclusion. The Pentagon flagged over 26,000 images for deletion across all military branches, specifically targeting women and minorities. Among the images were Tuskegee Airmen, the first Black military pilots who served in the Second World War; a team of women Air Force pilots from the Second World War; and, of course, images of the *Enola Gay*. Originally named for the pilot's mother, the *Enola Gay* was removed through an ahistorical, homophobic blanket search for anything with the word "gay."[63]

Two weeks later, Trump issued another executive order to "Restore Truth and Sanity to American History." The order accuses American cultural institutions of revisionism, noting "the widespread effort to rewrite history deepens societal divides and fosters a sense of national shame, disregarding the progress America has made." Just as both chambers of Congress did in 1995, the order took direct aim at the Smithsonian claiming that it has "come under the influence of a divisive, race-centered ideology."[64]

The claims of revisionism in the 1990s almost seem quaint in comparison to the large-scale digital disinformation campaigns that use falsehoods and half-truths to erode Americans' trust in education, government, media, and cultural institutions like the Smithsonian.[65] Museums remain highly contested spaces, bellwethers in a war over memory that shapes our culture and reflects minute shifts in our political winds.

In 1995, conservatives and liberals alike warred over a single historical truth—that the *Enola Gay* was either an instrument of peace or a weapon of destruction—when, in fact, the *Enola Gay* was an instrument of peace *and* a weapon of destruction. If there's any one truth about the *Enola Gay* at all, it's that there is no such thing as historical consensus.

Discussion Questions

1   What role do museums and other cultural institutions play in American society? How should they balance the tensions between politics, public memory, and scholarship?

2   Practice writing for a public audience by drafting a fifty-word label for the *Enola Gay*. What will you include or exclude, and why?

3   If you could pick a photo of a "hot button" issue to interpret in a museum, what would it be and why?

Further Resources

American Historical Association. "Standards for Museum Exhibits Dealing with Historical Subjects." January 31, 2017. https://www.historians.org/resource/standards-for-museum-exhibits-dealing-with-historical-subjects/.

AP Archive. "USA: Washington: Enola Gay Exhibition Causes Protests." June 28, 1995. https://www.youtube.com/watch?v=Is1NC6qKQQY&t=2s.

Kingsbury, Kathleen, W.J. Hennigan, and Spencer Cohen. "The Last Survivors Speak. It's Time to Listen." *New York Times,* August 6, 2024.

Linenthal, Edward T. and Tom Engelhardt, eds. *History Wars: The* Enola Gay *and Other Battles for the American Past.* Henry Holt, 1996.

Notes

1   Alex Wellerstein, "Counting the Dead at Hiroshima and Nagasaki," *The Bulletin of the Atomic Scientists*, August 4, 2020.

2   Richard Wolfson and Ferenc Dalnoki-Veress, *Nuclear Choices for the Twenty-First Century: A Citizen's Guide* (MIT Press, 2021).

3   Kathleen Kingsbury, W.J. Hennigan, and Spencer Cohen, "The Last Survivors Speak. It's Time to Listen," *New York Times*, August 6, 2024. Last accessed January 28, 2025, https://www.nytimes.com/interactive/2024/08/06/opinion/hiroshima-nagasaki-atomic-bombing.html.

4   Wolfson and Dalnoki-Veress, *Nuclear Choices*.

5   Gar Alperovitz, *Atomic Diplomacy: Hiroshima and Potsdam. The Use of the Atomic Bomb and the American Confrontation with Soviet Power* (Simon & Schuster, 1965).

6   J. Samuel Walker, "The Decision to Use the Bomb: A Historiographical Update," *Diplomatic History* 14, no. 1 (Winter 1990): 97–114.

7 Vasudha Narayanan, "Oppenheimer Often Used Sanskrit Verses," *The Conversation,* August 16, 2023. Last accessed February 4, 2025, https://theconversation.com/oppenheimer-often-used-sanskrit-verses-and-the-bhagavad-gita-was-special-for-him-but-not-in-the-way-christopher-nolans-film-depicts-it-211253.

8 William D. Leahy, *I Was There: The Personal Story of the Chief of Staff to Presidents Roosevelt and Truman, Based on His Notes and Diaries Made at the Time* (Whittlesey House, 1950), 441–2.

9 "Ike on Ike," *Newsweek,* November 11, 1963.

10 Felix Muskett Morley, "The Return to Nothingness," *Human Events,* August 29, 1945.

11 Harry Elmer Barnes, "Hiroshima: Assault on a Beaten Foe," *National Review* (May 1958): 441–3.

12 Landon R.Y. Storrs, *The Second Red Scare and the Unmaking of the New Deal Left* (Princeton University Press, 2013); and Michael Barson and Steven Heller, *Red Scared! The Commie Menace in Propaganda and Popular Culture* (Chronicle Books, 2001).

13 Rich Yelson, "What New Left History Gave Us," *Democracy* 35 (Winter 2015): 24–40.

14 Uday Mohan and Sanho Tree, "Hiroshima, the American Media, and the Construction of Conventional Wisdom," *The Journal of American-East Asian Relations* 4, no. 2 (1995): 159.

15 Richard Overy, *Why the Allies Won* (W.W. Norton, 1995).

16 Charles E. Land, et al., "Projected Lifetime Cancer Risks from Exposure to Regional Radioactive Fallout in the Marshall Islands," *Health Physics* 99, no. 2 (August 2010): 201–15.

17 Autumn S. Bordner, et al., "Measurement of Background Gamma Radiation in the Northern Marshall Islands," *Proceedings of the National Academy of Sciences* 113, no. 25 (June 2016): 6833–8.

18 Edward T. Linenthal, "Anatomy of a Controversy," in *History Wars: The Enola Gay and Other Battles for the American Past*, ed. Edward T. Linenthal and Tom Engelhardt (Henry Holt, 1996), 13.

19 Wright-Patterson is now the repository for *Bockscar*, the B-29 that bombed Nagasaki.

20 Linenthal, "Anatomy," 13–5.

21 Linenthal, "Anatomy," 16.

22 Linenthal, "Anatomy," 18–9.

23 Edward T. Linenthal and Tom Engelhardt, eds., *History Wars: The Enola Gay and Other Battles for the American Past* (Henry Holt, 1996), 1–2.

24 Exhibition Planning Document, "The Crossroads: The End of World War II, the Atomic Bomb, and the Origins of the Cold War," 15. Quoted in Linenthal, "Anatomy," 28.

25 John T. Correll, "Air Force Association Special Report: The Smithsonian and the *Enola Gay*," *Air Force Magazine,* March 15, 1994.

26   James Davidson Hunter, *Culture Wars: The Struggle to Define America* (Basic Books, 1991).

27   Hunter, *Culture Wars;* and Kristin Kobes Du Mez, *Jesus and John Wayne: How White Evangelicals Corrupted a Faith and Fractured a Nation* (Liveright, 2020).

28   Linenthal, "Anatomy," 16–9.

29   Correll, "The Smithsonian and the *Enola Gay.*"

30   Correll, "The Smithsonian and the *Enola Gay.*"

31   S.Res. 257–103rd Congress (1993–1994), "A Resolution to Express the Sense of the Senate Regarding the Appropriate Portrayal of Men and Women of the Armed Forces in the Upcoming National Air and Space Museum's Exhibit on the *Enola Gay,*" September 23, 1994.

32   Gregg Herken, "The Smithsonian's Decision to Exhibit the 'Enola Gay'," *Public History Weekly* 10, no. 7 (2022).

33   Correll, "The Smithsonian and the *Enola Gay.*"

34   Herken, "The Smithsonian's Decision," 7.

35   Martin Harwit, *An Exhibit Denied: Lobbying the History of the* Enola Gay (Copernicus, 1996), 283.

36   Karen de Witt, "Smithsonian Scales Back Exhibit of B-29 in Atomic Bomb Attack," *New York Times*, January 31, 1995.

37   Harwit, *An Exhibit Denied*, 424.

38   Lonnae O'Neal Parker, "*Enola Gay* Exhibit Opens to Protest," *Washington Post*, June 28, 1995.

39   Jennifer Wright, "Exhibiting the *Enola Gay,*" Smithsonian Institution Archives, June 25, 2020. Last accessed January 30, 2025, https://siarchives.si.edu/blog/exhibiting-enola-gay.

40   Les Blumenthal, "20 Arrests at Smithsonian Protest," *The Press Democrat,* June 29, 1995.

41   Parker, "*Enola Gay* Exhibit"; and AP Archive, "USA: Washington: *Enola Gay* Exhibition Causes Protests," June 28, 1995. Last accessed January 29, 2025, https://www.youtube.com/watch?v=ls1NC6qKQQY&t=2s.

42   "Trio Douses 'Enola Gay' with Blood, Ashes," *Tampa Bay Times*, July 3, 1995.

43   T.R. Reid, "*Enola Gay* Exhibit Angers Japan," *The Press Democrat*, June 29, 1995.

44   Quoted in Barnes, "Hiroshima: Assault on a Beaten Foe," 443. A copy of Truman's response is located in the Harry S. Truman Library, Independence, Missouri.

45   Harwit, *An Exhibit Denied*, vii.

46   John T. Correll, "The Activists and the *Enola Gay,*" *Air Force Magazine*, September 1995.

47   Mohan and Tree, "Hiroshima," 160.

48   Harwit, *An Exhibit Denied*, vii.

49 Newspapers only printed a handful of grainy pictures of the original protest in 1995, mostly of American and Japanese reporters at an advanced press event.

50 Herken, "The Smithsonian's Decision," 7.

51 Joyce Naltchayan Boghosian, interview (unpublished) by Rebecca S. Wingo, May 21, 2025.

52 Boghosian, interview, 2025.

53 Boghosian, interview, 2025.

54 Boghosian, interview, 2025.

55 For a full view of the gallery, see "Boeing B-29 Superfortress *Enola Gay*," National Air and Space Museum, Smithsonian Institution. Last accessed June 9, 2025, https://airandspace.si.edu/collection-objects/boeing-b-29-superfortress-enola-gay/nasm_A19500100000.

56 Kingsbury, et al., "The Last Survivors Speak."

57 "*Enola Gay* Display Angers Victims," *BBC News*, December 16, 2003.

58 Seyed Ismail Nafeesa,"Japanese Atomic Bomb Survivor Warns Nuclear Taboo Is at Risk in Nobel Peace Prize Speech," *NBC News,* December 11, 2024.

59 Louis Menand, "Mixed Paint," *Mother Jones*, March/April 1995.

60 Herken, "The Smithsonian's Decision," 7.

61 Patrick J. Buchanan, "Address to the Republican National Convention," August 17, 1992, Houston, TX; and Joseph R. Biden, Jr., "Remarks by President-Elect Joe Biden on the Electoral College Vote Certification," December 14, 2020, Wilmington, DE.

62 Elizabeth Dias, "Biden and Trump Say They're Fighting for America's 'Soul.' What Does That Mean?" *New York Times*, October 17, 2020.

63 Tara Copp, Lolita C. Baldor, and Kevin Vineys, "War Heroes and Military Firsts Are among 26,000 Images Flagged for Removal in Pentagon's DEI Purge," *AP News*, March 6, 2025. Last accessed March 13, 2025, https://apnews.com/article/dei-purge-images-pentagon-diversity-women-black-8efcfaec909954f4a24bad0d49c78074.

64 The White House, Executive Order, "Restoring Truth and Sanity to American History," March 27, 2025.

65 Steven Livingston and W. Lance Bennett, eds., *The Disinformation Age: Politics, Technology, and Disruptive Communication in the United States* (Cambridge University Press, 2021).

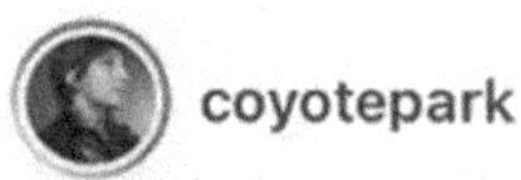

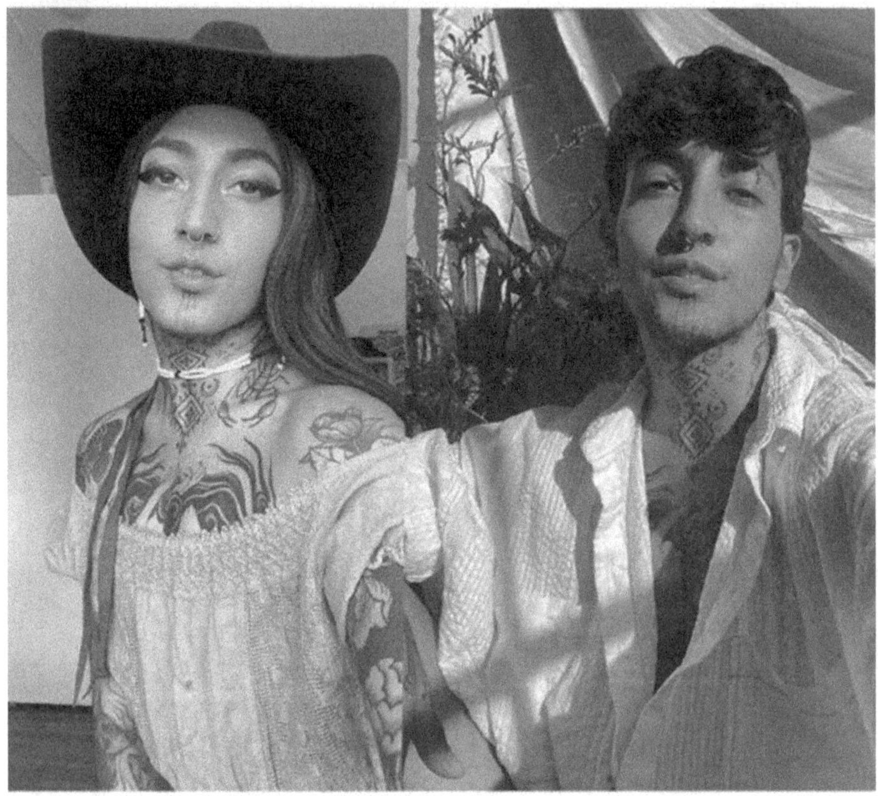

coyotepark Happy Indigenous Peoples day to my relatives, my Yurok & Karuk kin that share my blood & my heart, my other Cali natives, my native kin to Turtle Island, my Pasifika siblings, my Kānaka Maoli cousins, my extended Indigenous fam outside of these lands that I named that are all celebrated today. Sending love from this 2Spirit girl boy boy girl to every other Indigenous trans & queer person that needs a reminder that you have always been medicine to our people.

FIGURE 15.1 *Instagram post by Coyote Park on October 10, 2022. Photos by Coyote Park. Courtesy of author, with permission from Coyote Park.*

15

Selfie as Self-Love: Coyote Park's Decolonizing of Photography

By Ace Lehner

Photographic technologies inherited the artistic legacies of previous generations, including everything from stylized portraiture to lighting. Photography and camera work also inherited the beliefs of their inventors, from colonialism to the privileging of whiteness. Originally a tool of men with means, early photographers would have struggled to imagine the ubiquity of photography today. With the rapid conveyance of information through cables and satellites, an exchange of ideas, beliefs, and values can happen in the matter of milliseconds, a speed that far outpaces historic forms of communication.

The modern selfie is a popular form of self-representation and identity formation. This chapter examines selfie culture as a tool for creating more inclusive, affirming spaces for trans community-building. It showcases the work of artist Coyote Park, an Indigenous (Yurok) and Korean-American trans artist who responds to the dominance of Western art canon by playing with its structures. They leverage social media platforms to create important representational interventions in the art world. This chapter directly engages with photography's colonial legacy and positions the selfie as a mechanism for affirmation, reinvention, and freedom.

Suggested Topics: Art History, Asian American History, Contemporary America, Indigenous History, Intersectionality, Women and Sexuality

Glossary: Daguerreotype, Decolonialism, Diptych, Pseudologic, Stereotype, Triptych

Coyote Park (he/she/they) is a 2Spirit, Indigenous (Yurok) Korean-American transgender artist. Currently based in Los Angeles, the photographer, filmmaker, writer, and actor was born in Spain in 1999 and raised on the island of Oahu. In their multi-disciplinary practice, Park often investigates themes of self-portraiture, queer intimacy, polyamory, and non-monogamous queer love. Their art has been exhibited at the Leslie-Lohman Museum in NYC, the Koppel Project in London, the Chapter House in Los Angeles, SOMArts, San Francisco, the University of Southern California, and beyond.[1]

Park moves comfortably between museums, galleries, and Instagram. Park is well aware of the power dynamics embedded in representation. Their work intervenes in the aesthetics of art history. Park inserts themself/herself/himself and those close to them/her/him as creators and subjects of art rather than those depicted only as stereotypes or otherwise excluded from the canon of Western art tradition. Using the global connectivity of Instagram to quickly reach massive audiences, Park's selfies are an integral part of their/her/his creative practice.

Trans self-representations in photography over the past decades have begun to demonstrate that gender is far more complex than ideologies derived from colonialism would have us believe. Much like gender itself, this genre is yet to be understood in all its complexities. Trans selfies are particularly well-situated to provide an opportunity for methodological intervention in gender, portraiture, and photography.

The selfie offers a nuanced and timely **decolonial** intervention into discourses of gender, photography, and representation in a digital world. The endless stream of selfies on platforms like Instagram presents perpetually transforming versions of our collective selves. When such representations are made by folks whose constituencies are otherwise marginalized or stereotyped, they have the potential to create powerful photographic interruptions and disruptions, inserting otherwise unseen and sometimes unimaginable identities into contemporary visual culture.

The interventions trans figures make in our visual culture are particularly important when one considers the tumultuous and often violent struggle for trans rights in the United States (and globally) today. Against this backdrop, Park's insertion of their likeness as a trans, genderqueer, or gender-expansive 2spirit person is a significant intervention into a culture that would prefer to create stereotypes of trans people in the service of their disenfranchisement and demise.

The Stakes of Representation

Not only does Park identify under an umbrella of LGBTQ+ and trans but Park is also 2Spirit Indigenous (Yurok) and Korean-American. Park is undoubtedly one of many people who identify this way. However, there is no precedent for someone with these intersectional identifications being included in the canon of Western art history. In fact, one is hard-pressed to find artists who fall under just one of Park's intersectional identities throughout American art history.

Artists like Park confront a long legacy of exclusion and/or marginalization to succeed in the art world. Recently, both trans and Indigenous artists have made incredible strides toward mainstream acceptance. Their work has featured at some of the nation's largest art venues and won some of the most prestigious honors, including the Guggenheim and MacArthur "Genius" Fellowships. Still, artists at the intersections of Indigenous and trans identities remain underrepresented in the art world—save for Toronto-based, Cree artist Kent Monkman and his work with his alter ego Miss Chief Eagle Testickle. Korean-American artists of any identities face similar struggles to break into the art world.

While this might feel like an exercise in futility for someone like Park who intersects with all these identities, it is also an opportunity. Selfies like Park's reach massive audiences immediately without going through the exclusionary channels of the art world establishment. Being careful not to equate Park as exemplar, Park's selfie can be viewed as filling a vacancy in the representation and visibility of 2Spirit, Indigenous (Yurok) Korean-American transgender folks.

Park's intervention can yet be more fully appreciated when one considers the impact of representation more broadly. The intersection of visual culture and societal rights is an ongoing and pressing issue in the United States. This is particularly true for individuals from socially oppressed and representationally marginalized groups, where visibility is often the only way a given culture gets introduced to their identities. For instance, Frederick Douglas and Sojourner Truth used early prototypes of selfies, *cartes de visites*, in similar ways in order to combat racist representations of African Americans during the 1800s by controlling their own portrayals. Social media has afforded people like Park an analogous platform from which to assert and control their representations, and propel the momentum of trans visual culture by insisting on a seat at the art world table.

While increased representation has worked to galvanize aspects of the trans movement, visibility without political and social support often is met with hostility, violence, and political aggression. This backlash is not confined to social media spaces. At the time of this writing, the American Civil Liberties Union is tracking 616 anti-LGBTQIA+ bills in the United States alone, many of which explicitly attack the rights of trans people.[2] Within this sociopolitical climate, selfies like Park's are more than calls to action for the art world to become inclusive. They are necessary challenges to a dominant culture that attempts to erase and oppress trans representations and trans lives.

Selfie Self-Love

On October 10, 2022, Coyote Park posted two side-by-side images of them/her/himself on Instagram, both taken with their right arm outstretched, camera phone in hand. Park's post reflects their deep understanding of art history as well as the ethos of their artistic intervention. This post exemplifies the power of selfies, and it is a diptych.

A **diptych** is a form of art comprised of two pieces that, when combined, create a third fully realized work of art. Diptychs rely on a sense of balance to imply a narrative or message arising from the interaction between the two images. A successful diptych requires great attention to aesthetic detail, layout, and content. Diptychs are believed to have emerged as a form of religious art often related to Christian stories popular in Western Europe in the 1300s. Two painted panels were typically connected by hinges and often used as altarpieces, and are most certainly considered part of the Western art canon.

In the image on the left, Park appears softly and evenly lit. The low-contrast light prevents any harsh shadows, softening their features. Park wears long dark hair cascading over their/her/his shoulder, head tilted slightly to the side, eyes adorned with thick dark makeup accentuating their rich brown eyes beneath. Park wears an off-white lacey top that falls off their/her/his shoulders, revealing numerous black and gray tattoos that emphasize the subtle curves of their/her/his body. The black outline of a scorpion curves around their neck beneath a beaded necklace, diamond filigree, and squares traced down the front of their neck. A·rose, peeking from the top of their sleeve, flows across their shoulder and extends down their arm, cut off by the frame in the lower right corner where Park held the camera to snap the picture. Park looks slightly down at us through the picture plane, lips pursed and parted; the look feels somewhat self-aware and flirtatious.

On the right, Park appears in a nearly identical pose, wearing the same septum ring and nose ring, head tilted slightly back and to the side, peering at us across the picture plane with a look that one might describe as *bedroom eyes*, flirtatious and relaxed, inviting and self-assured. The picture is shot in harsh daylight, creating high contrast and deep shadows that cast a more angular look on Park's face. In this image, Park has short dark hair and thick wavy bangs, and they/she/he also sport facial stubble absent in the left image. Here, Park again wears a creamy white top. This time, however, the style is more associated with masculinity. The collar is open in the front with two front chest pockets adorned by dark stitching.

In keeping with the diptych style, the two images are aesthetically balanced, cropped to fit side by side into the standard Instagram square. The left image is slightly thinner and cropped tightly around Park's large, dark hat.

In comparison, the picture on the right, also vertical, is a bit wider, allowing the viewer to see their casual pose, their arm propped on their knee. Long green stems and leaves of the deep red flowers fill the negative space behind.

While the conventions of Western binary gender assumptions and expectations may encourage viewers to ascribe femininity and female pronouns to the left figure and masculinity and masculine pronouns to the right figure, both are Coyote Park. Park is simultaneously feminine and masculine. Neither image is more accurate to whom Park is. As a trans 2Spirit person living in the United States, Park is well aware of how the aesthetics they deploy via hair, clothing, accessories, dress, pose, lighting, gesture, and more play with the gender stereotypes viewers see.

The diptych exemplifies the complexity of Park's gender identity and Park's ability to embrace the selfie as a creative means of photographic intervention. Park is self-imaging in a fashion in which they appear comfortable, self-assured, sexy, and desirable across gender presentations. But this act of self-representation is a defiant and assertive intervention into identity, representation, and photography. Deploying different aesthetics of gender simultaneously, Park complicates the discourses of identity and photography, while visually challenging binary gender. Park makes plain that gender identity exceeds what a binary gender framework can visualize, articulate, or fully comprehend, while highlighting the limited capacity of a photograph to capture the fullness or complexity of any given person in a single frame.

The Colonial Origins of Portraiture

To understand Park's nuanced intervention, it is necessary to discuss the ideologies undergirding portraiture and photography in Europe and the United States. The camera was developed in the early decades of the nineteenth century by white European amateur scientists, men of means vying for the glory of making the first photograph. Scientists and artists of this period were steeped in traditions of Western art history, which in turn framed how they approached making photographs of people. In other words, photography emerged from traditions of Western art history and photographic portraiture—and like its creators—was deeply informed by the dominant ideologies of the day, reinforcing colonial ideas about gender, race, and power.

As I wrote in *Self-Representation in an Expanded Field*:

Self-portraiture has a long-standing art-historical tradition. Although not always explicitly stated, in the Western European and North American art-historical context, self-portraiture has been associated with the work of canonized artists made within specific media-based, aesthetic, and conceptual frameworks, and visual traditions. In Western art, this translates into the canonization of self-portraits by recognized artists produced using traditional and established materials.[3]

The portrait in Western European and North American contexts has been historically and ideologically entwined with the belief that visual representations of a person can transmit information about them. In his book titled *Portraiture*, Richard Brilliant insightfully points out, "There is a great difficulty in thinking about pictures, even portraits by great artists, as art and not thinking about them primarily as something else, the person represented."[4]

Photography's origins in science—a seemingly objective field—created the falsehood that photography must also be objective. As Abigail Solomon-Godeau writes, "Photography, a medium which by virtue of its supposed transparency, truth and naturalism has been an especially potent purveyor of cultural ideology—particularly the ideology of gender."[5] Amelia Jones observes that our cultural tendency—especially when it comes to portraiture—is to conflate the image, the portrait, the representation, and the person it represents.[6] Due to the above presumptions, it is easy to follow Mieke Bal's argument that the power-holding classes in Western European and North American contexts repeatedly assert dominant value systems in visual culture and tend to set themselves up as heroes via the "cult of portraiture."[7]

In 1839, American amateur scientist and early adopter of photography Robert Cornelius made what is often dubbed the first-ever selfie. The photograph is known as **daguerreotype**, a type of photographic process published by Louis J. M. Daguerre earlier that year. Creating the image required Cornelius to hold still for at least ten minutes, and the image has stood the test of time. The image shows Cornelius from the chest up surrounded by negative space. His expressionless face is positioned between frontal and three-quarter view. While Cornelius's self-image was technologically novel, it was otherwise quite conventional in subject matter. His subject matter and aesthetic choices drew from (and upheld) the artistic legacies of his predecessors, and are thus rooted in and supporting American (and European) society's celebration of wealthy, white, cis, and able-bodied hetereo-patriachy.

One of the earliest European photo theorists and a contemporary of the advent of photography, Charles Sanders Peirce was influential in formulating the discourse around the study of photography. The dominant modernist ideologies of the time included a strong belief in binary and essentialized oppositions, and a belief that science was objective, free of ideologies or predetermined biases. With science's emphasis on observation, sight became the most important of all senses. Peirce believed that non-photographic images were creative outputs and photographs provided a new type of representation derived from the "effects of the radiations from the object."[8] In other words the camera captures light reflected from an object, and thus cannot be influenced by subjectivity; the process was purely mechanical.[9]

Pierce's unexamined argument that photography is purely observational persists today, and photographs are still commonly viewed as "windows into a world." But the production of photography is not a neutral act. Photographs are two-dimensional renderings on a specific surface, perhaps paper, digital screen, or otherwise. They are ideological and thematic constructions, edited, produced, and created by the image-maker to a specific end. In other words, while a photograph may *look like* a window into a world, this conception is inaccurate and intellectually lackluster. It is also highly problematic considering the ideological framing inherited from its inventors.

Photography historian Shawn Michelle Smith has rightly noted that since its earliest days, white supremacist ideologies have informed photography. For example, in *The Pencil of Nature* (1844), early photographer and author William Henry Fox Talbot wrote that as science developed, photographs intentionally privileged light-colored subjects, ostensibly because their high reflectivity worked better with the technology of the time. However, as Smith observes, this encouraged the development of photographic film and lighting practices that privileged light skin, creating an implicit bias toward Caucasian subjects.[10]

This historical precedent continues to inform lens-based imaging technologies to this day. In the contemporary period, favorable and even beautiful cinematographic depictions of African American skin tones have been outliers, not the standard. Best Picture at the Academy Awards in 2017 *Moonlight* (Dir. Barry Jenkins) made headlines for how the film aesthetically depicted African American actors. Similarly, Issa Rae's wildly popular television series *Insecure* (first aired in 2016) was also lauded for its beautiful depiction of African American skin tones on screen. Relatedly, the recent emergence of #OscarsSoWhite called attention to the ongoing privileging of white subjects. The fact that these issues remain today is part of photography's historical and colonial legacy.[11]

Postcolonial theorists have forged intellectual inroads to deconstruct **pseudologics** (a seemingly logical argument that is designed to produce a false outcome) around stereotypes and how they perpetuate within societies. As Homi K. Bhabha argues, **stereotypes** produce representations of subjects as "a fixed reality which is at once an 'other' and yet entirely knowable and visible."[12] The stereotype is "not a simplification because it is a false representation of a given reality"; rather, the stereotype is "a simplification because it is an arrested, fixated form of representation."[13] Stereotypes work by prolifically circulating reductive representations with problematic ideas affixed. Although they are false, when repeated over time, people begin to accept them as accurate. Stereotypes, in turn, solidify ideas and expectations about groups of people based on pseudologics that uphold systems of hierarchical oppressions.

Portrait photography developed out of colonialism and in some lineages continues to replicate the value systems of its inventors rather than creatively advancing the genre of portraiture. However, artists like Park are slowly transforming photography from a tool that perpetuates stereotypes into a tool that disrupts them, while simultaneously expanding ideas about identity, representation, and art.

Selfie Disruptions

Trans self-images open opportunities for intentional, methodological interventions in gender, portraiture, and photography. While trans portraits by and for trans people have always existed, technological advancements like camera phones have begun to demonstrate the power of trans self-representation. Trans selfie culture often builds coalitions that exchange information and fight for collective rights, and also proves, celebrates, and expands trans existence. Trans selfies demonstrate that gender is far more complex than dominant ideologies would have one believe while simultaneously showing that photography is yet to be fully understood.

Defined as a self-image made with a hand-held mobile device capable of being shared instantaneously over social media, selfies have become an integral component of contemporary life throughout the last decade. The proliferation of image-makers creating, posting, and sharing selfies on platforms like Facebook, Instagram, Snapchat, and Tumblr prompted Oxford Dictionaries to proclaim "selfie" the 2013 word of the year. Selfies have garnered much derision and scorn, but there is also a growing acknowledgment of their potential upside.[14] The debates over selfies have facilitated an outpouring of intellectual consideration and research across fields from sciences and mental health to visual studies and beyond.

From an art-historical perspective, studying selfie interventions is critical to understanding photography now. Amelia G. Jones argues that the very idea of the artist is a social and political creation dating back to the European Enlightenment. Jones elaborates,

[...] beliefs about and perceptions of identity haunt our relationship to art as we define it today, understood as a fundamentally European concept forged in the early modern period, not coincidentally at the same moment as the first encounters with colonized others [...] Art became one of the key means through which Europeans claimed their superiority to those they colonized who, in the framework of European aesthetics, could only make fetishes that could never compare in value to the transcendent qualities of European "art." [15]

Jones describes not only the aesthetics and representation of "Art" [with a capital "A"] but also the materials used to create it, which emerged from a Western framework of thought. [16]

A eurocentric conception of "Art" dates back to the earliest contact between colonizers and the colonized in the fifteenth century. Europeans reinforced their self-appointed superiority by depicting people from other cultures as lesser humans, less than human, and even nonhuman. Europeans used stereotypes—the visual representation and the ideas they connoted—to justify the domination, oppression, and horror they inflicted on others. [17] This false hierarchy extended into materiality as well, which delegitimized the work and perspectives of artists without access to (or interest in) using the mediums canonized by Western high art. While numerous artists and scholars—primarily of feminist, queer, critical race, decolonial perspectives—have incessantly critiqued this, the hierarchy endures. [18]

The troubled legacy of exclusion is one reason why selfies are such a divisive genre. Not only are selfies a radical divergence from accepted forms of portraiture, but they are also a medium of the masses. If anyone with a digital camera or cell phone can produce a self-portrait, what even is "Art"? And who counts as an "Artist"?

The selfie debate revolves around the question of authority, legitimacy, and the control over the aesthetics and methods required to constitute a self-portrait. *Merriam-Webster Dictionary*, for example, defines a self-portrait as "a portrait of oneself done by oneself." [19] In contrast, *Oxford Dictionary* defines a self-portrait as "a portrait that an artist produces of themselves." [20] Selfies permit anyone with access to a mobile device with a camera to instantly create a self-image and exhibit it to a potentially massive audience. This shift circumnavigates the need to pass through art historical and art world channels to garner legitimacy as a self-image maker. Selfies are a necessary and significant part of contemporary global art and visual culture.

Historically, materials and media have divided the boundary between high art and pop culture. This has changed significantly since the advent of photography—a media which in and of itself inherently challenges such boundaries due to its promiscuity and ubiquity, i.e., photographs appear in fine—advertising, in journalism, in medicine—defying any "proper place." Still, photographs tend to confound easy attribution to one particular area and thus defy the bounds of high art and pop culture.[21] Even more so than photos from the analog era, however, selfies move in ever more free directions, which challenges preconceived notions about the bounds of art and who may be dubbed an artist.

Due to their instantaneous global connectivity and investment in photographic communication, platforms like Instagram are uniquely well suited to facilitate the use of self-images to announce oneself, perform, and explore one's likeness globally. One can receive reaction and build community without living the embodied dangers of being trans while walking the world. At the same time, the endless post-ability and scrollability of platforms like Instagram defy the fixity and essentialism needed for stereotypes to function. When image-makers like Park repeatedly image them/her/himself on Instagram, there is room to be constantly evolving and transforming. Social media aesthetics challenge the ideological construction of a single, iconic image being collapsible with an identity. When studied seriously, selfies make it clear that pictures are performative iterations captured in a fraction of time, highly specific (temporally and geographically), and always constructed.

Coyote Park's diptych selfie serves as a poignant example of the limitations of a singular, isolated photograph in representing a person's identity. It reminds us that people are multifaceted, and a single picture can only capture a fraction of one's complexity or identity. A single instant in Park's life cannot demonstrate who they are in their entirety. Their gender alone cannot be imaged in the frame of one photo; their gender is beyond the essentializing practice of a single picture.

The images together in a diptych begin to suggest the complexity of Park's gender identity and Park's ability to embrace the selfie as a creative means of photographic intervention. Self-imaging in a fashion in which they appear comfortable, self-assured, sexy, and desirable across gender presentations creates an intervention into identity, representation, and photography. Deploying different aesthetics of gender simultaneously, Park's images challenge the enduring colonial gaze of photography that otherwise collapses the image and sitter into a reductive binary.

Beneath the two side-by-side selfies, Park has posted the following text:

Happy Indigenous Peoples day to my relatives,
my Yurok & Karuk kin that share by blood & my heart, my
other Cali natives, my native kin to Turtle Island, my

> Pasifika siblings, my Kānaka Maoli cousins, my extended
> indigenous fam outside of these lands that I named that
> are all celebrated today. Sending love from this 2Spirit girl
> boy boy girl to every other Indigenous trans & queer
> person that needs a reminder that you have always been
> medicine to our people.

Park's text turns their powerful diptych into a **triptych**, offering an even more complex picture of Park. They reach beyond the frame to connect and send love and recognition to their kin across the globe. Their selfies *visually* declare their gender complexity, and their caption *textually* directs their viewers on how to read their selfies by naming their gender position as "2Spirit girl boy boy girl." Park then embraces those who also identify as "Indigenous trans & queer" by issuing a validation, not just in solidarity and recognition but as a reminder that "you have always been medicine to our people." Park's triptych extends self-love, solidarity, care, and recognition, reminding kin that while Western cultures may have historically imposed gender binaries, they have historically been (and often still are) regarded as sacred by others. It is only via the gaze of colonialist ideologies about gender that binary gender has been held up as the norm.

Collective Futurity

In the United States today, there are 574 federally recognized Native American nations, and more than 100 other nations recognized by individual states. Although many Americans commonly conceive of Native Americans as a racial group, according to the US Constitution, Native nations are in fact distinct, sovereign political entities. As Park indicated in their triptych, Indigenous epistemologies reject not just the gender binary imposed by colonization but colonialism itself. Turtle Island, as Park refers to North America, is partitioned by boundaries between Canada, the United States, and Mexico. For Native nations, these borders are arbitrary divisions established in the 1700s and 1800s by invading colonial powers. By speaking directly to "my extended indigenous fam outside of these lands," Park is nodding to a groundswell of solidarity that reimagines relatedness through a global Indigeneity.

Relatedness and kinship are inclusive principles that embrace Indigenous histories as a means of reimagining collective futures. In *Becoming Kin: An Indigenous Call to Unforgetting the Past and Reimagining Our Future*, Patty Krawec writes,

From our earliest creation stories, the Anishinaabeg (plural of *Anisinaabe*) understood themselves to be related not only to each other but to all of creation. Our language does not divide into male and female the way European languages do. It divides into animate and inanimate. The world is alive with beings that are other than human, and we are all related, with responsibilities to each other.

This concept of relatedness is by no means unique to the Anishinaabeg. After the Standing Rock pipeline protests, the Lakota phrase mitakuye oyasin became well known outside of Lakota communities. But it came to mean something less than what it means to the Lakota. Many people think it means "all my relations," and it does, but it also means much more than that. It is specific to the Lakota people and their thinking in a way that can't be fully translated.[22]

As Krawec explains, colonial languages are extraordinarily limited. Here, they fail to adequately translate the complex concept of connectivity. Elsewhere, they fail to translate the complexity of gender identity, defaulting instead to a binary wrought by colonialism. And yet, these complexities exist, regardless of whether we choose to recognize them or have the words to call them.

Park's diptych selfie made triptych is just a small component of their oeuvre. In studying even this one work, it is evident that the language and concepts inherited to explain photography and identity not only need reworking, they need a collaborative reimaging that exceeds the language and discourses presently at play. Park's work calls upon Indigenous pasts and creative practices to challenge accepted discourses on photography, gender, identity, collectivity, and futurity. In the process, they show glimpses of ways to resist colonial pseudologics through alternative, more expansive futures.

Park's work lays bare the fallacy that a photograph is in any way a stand-in for the sitter. Photography must be viewed as inherently subjective, performative, and highly situated. Park's Instagram post challenges not only the problematic and reductive structure of binary gender but also gestures toward its interconnection with colonialism. Rather than didactically calling out these gruesome legacies, Park calls in those who continue to be medicine to all people and invites all to think more expansively and lovingly about portraiture, identity, representation, and photography.

Discussion Questions

1   When you first looked at Coyote Park's selfie, what did you see? What assumptions did you make about Park or their gender? How have your views changed?

2   Pick up your phone and scroll through your camera roll. How recent was your last selfie? What were you doing? Why did you make it? What were the performative choices you deployed? What were you wearing? How did you pose? Who was your audience?

3   You have at your command something capable of capturing high-resolution digital images and transmitting them instantaneously around the globe. Not only are selfies ubiquitous, but they can also be used as interventions into visual culture. How are you going to wield this power? What contributions will your self-imaging make to the ongoing, collaborative visual discourse on American identity?

Further Resources

Davidson, Jane Chin and Amelia Jones, eds. *A Companion to Contemporary Art in a Global Framework.* Wiley Blackwell, 2024.

Lehner, Ace, ed. *Self-Representation in an Expanded Field: From Self-Portraiture to Selfie, Contemporary Art in the Social Media Age.* MDPI, 2021.

Masters, Jeffrey, host. "Alok Vaid-Menon: Trans People Have Always Existed." *LGBTQ&A* (podcast), May 4, 2021. https://podcasts.apple.com/us/podcast/alok-vaid-menon-trans-people-have-always-existed/id1151561226?i=1000520023077.

Wilbur, Matika and Temryss Lane, hosts. "Indigiqueer." *All My Relations* (podcast), April 3, 2019. https://www.allmyrelationspodcast.com/podcast/episode/47547617/indigiqueer.

Notes

1   Coyote Park, "About," https://coyotepark.format.com/about; and "Coyote Park—TRNK." Last accessed May 15, 2024, https://trnk-nyc.com/collections/coyote-park.

2   ACLU, "Mapping Attacks on LGBTQ Rights in U.S. State Legislatures in 2024." Last accessed October 13, 2025, https://www.aclu.org/legislative-attacks-on-lgbtq-rights-2024.

3   Ace Lehner, ed., *Self-Representation in an Expanded Field: From Self-Portraiture to Selfie, Contemporary Art in the Social Media Age* (MDPI, 2021), 4.

4   Richard Brilliant, *Portraiture* (Reaktion Books, 1991), 23.

5   Abigail Solomon-Godeau, *Photography at the Dock: Essay on Photographic History, Institution, and Practices* (University of Minnesota Press, 1991), 257.

6   Western art-historical and social conceptions of representation originating in the Renaissance. During this time, the belief in the ability of the artist to render truth and insight into a subject through representational likeness was established. For more on discussing the conception of representations as a subject originating in the Renaissance, see Amelia Jones, *Self Image:*

Technology, Representation, and the Contemporary Subject (Routledge, 2006), 2–5 and 13–4.

7 Mieke Bal, "Visual Essentialism and the Object of Visual Culture," *Journal of Visual Culture* 2, no. 1 (2003): 5–32.

8 Allan Sekula, "The Body and the Archive," *October* 39 (Winter 1986): 55. Charles Saunders Pierce (1839–1914) was an American philosopher, theorist, mathematician, and scientist who was influential in developing philosophies about photography.

9 Marita Sturken and Lisa Cartwright, *Practices of Looking: An Introduction to Visual Culture* (Oxford University Press, 2001), 16.

10 Shawn Michelle Smith, *At the Edge of Sight: Photography and the Unseen* (Duke University Press, 2013), 14–5.

11 Nadia Latif, "It's Lit! How Film Finally Learned to Light Black Skin," *The Guardian*, September 21, 2017, https://www.theguardian.com/film/2017/sep/21/its-lit-how-film-finally-learned-how-to-light-black-skin; *Inquire Publication* (blog), "'Black Boys Look Blue under Moonlight': The Importance of Humanizing Dark Skins in Cinema," March 30, 2017, https://inquirepublication.com/black-boys-look-blue-under-moonlight-the-importance-of-humanizing-dark-skins-in-cinema/; Katie Kasperson, "Illuminating Diversity," *Definition Magazine*, November 3, 2023, https://definitionmagazine.com/features/illuminating-diversity/; Chris O'Falt, "Moonlight Cinematography: Bold Color, Rich Skin Tone, High Contrast," *IndieWire*, October 26, 2026, https://www.indiewire.com/awards/industry/moonlight-cinematography-color-barry-jenkins-james-laxton-alex-bickel-1201740402/; Xavier Harding, "Keeping 'Insecure' Lit: HBO Cinematographer Ava Berkofsky on Properly Lighting Black Faces," *Mic*, September 6, 2017, https://www.mic.com/articles/184244/keeping-insecure-lit-hbo-cinematographer-ava-berkofsky-on-properly-lighting-black-faces; "BBC World Service—World Update, Lighting Dark Skin for Screen," *BBC*, November 30, 2017, https://www.bbc.co.uk/programmes/p05pmwjn; and "Here's How the Woman behind the Camera on Insecure Properly Lights Its Black Actors," *FASHION Magazine* (blog), June 16, 2020, https://fashionmagazine.com/flare/insecure-lighting/. All last accessed December 23, 2024.

12 Homi K. Bhabha, *The Location of Culture* (Routledge, 1991), 23.

13 Bhabha, *The Location of Culture*, 27.

14 For more on selfie debates, see Lehner, *Self-Representation in an Expanded Field*; Will Storr, *Selfie: How We Became so Self-Obsessed and What It's Doing to Us* (Abrams Press, 2019); Katrin Tiidenberg, *Selfies: Why We Love (and Hate) Them* (Emerald Publishing, 2018); Sorelle Amore, *Take Your Selfie Seriously: The Advanced Selfie and Self-Portrait Handbook* (Laurence King Publishing, 2021); Adam J. MacLeod, *The Age of Selfies: Reasoning about Rights When the Stakes Are Personal* (Rowman & Littlefield, 2020); Alicia Eler, *The Selfie Generation: Exploring Our Notions of Privacy, Sex, Consent, and Culture* (Skyhorse Publishing, 2019); and Derek Conrad Murray, ed., *Visual Culture Approaches to the Selfie* (Routledge, 2022).

15 Amelia Jones, "Who Is an Artist? Identity, Individualism, and the Neoliberalism of the Art Complex," *Arts* 12, no. 6 (2023): 234. For more, see Jones, *Seeing Differently: A History and Theory of Identity and the Visual Arts* (Routledge, 2012) and "Ethnic Envy and Other Aggressions in the Contemporary 'Global' Art Complex," *Journal of Contemporary African Art* 48 (2023): 96–110.

16 Carolyn Dean, "The Trouble with (the Term) Art," *Art Journal* 65, no. 2 (June 2006): 24–33.

17 See Alexander G. Weheliye, *Habeas Viscus: Racializing Assemblages, Biopolitics, and Black Feminist Theories of the Human* (Duke University Press, 2014).

18 Jones, "Who Is an Artist?," 234.

19 *Merriam-Webster Dictionary, Merriam-Webster.com Dictionary* (Originating with the Eleventh Edition of Merriam-Webster Collegiate Dictionary, the online dictionary continues to be updated and expanded. They claim it is "specifically designed for the digital user.") See "self-portrait": https://www.merriam-webster.com/about-us/faq and https://www.merriam-webster.com/dictionary/self-portrait#h1 Last accessed September 19, 2019.

20 *Oxford Online Dictionaries.* Accessed through Lexico, https://www.lexico.com/en/definition/self-portrait, https://www.lexico.com/en/about. Last accessed September, 15, 2019.

21 For more on the complexity of photography, see David Campany, ed., *Art and Photography* (Phaidon Press, 2012); Susan Bright, *Art Photography Now* (Thames & Hudson, 2011); Roland Barthes, *Camera Lucida: Reflections on Photography* (Hill and Wang, 2010); Mark Sealy, *Decolonising the Camera: Photography in Racial Time* (Lawrence & Wishart, 2019). Susan Sontag, *On Photography* (Picador, 2001); and Charlotte Cotton, *The Photograph as Contemporary Art* (Thames & Hudson, 2020).

22 Patty Krawec and Nick Estes, *Becoming Kin: An Indigenous Call to Unforgetting the Past and Reimagining Our Future* (Broadleaf Books, 2022), 1.

Works Cited

There's More to It Than Meets the Eye

Alinder, Mary Street. *Group F.64: Edward Weston, Ansel Adams, Imogen Cunningham, and the Community of Artists Who Revolutionized American Photography*. Bloomsbury, 2014.

Barasch, Alixandra, Gal Zauberman, and Kristin Diehl. "How the Intention to Share Can Undermine Enjoyment: Photo-Taking Goals and Evaluation of Experiences." *Journal of Consumer Research* 44, no. 6 (April 2018): 1220–37.

Barr, Nathaniel, Gordon Pennycook, Jennifer A. Stolz, and Jonathan A. Fugelsang. "The Brain in Your Pocket: Evidence That Smartphones Are Used to Supplant Thinking." *Computers in Human Behavior* 48 (July 2015): 473–80.

Barthes, Roland. *Camera Lucida: Reflections on Photography*. Hill and Wang, 1981.

Benjamin, Walter. "Work of Art in the Age of Mechanical Reproduction." In *Illuminations: Essays and Reflections*, edited by Hannah Arendt. Translated by Harry Zohn. Schocken Books, 1968.

Boyd, Sophia Alvarez. "Smithsonian Acquires Rare Antique Portraits by First Black Photographers." *NPR's Weekend Edition Sunday*, August 29, 2021. Last accessed March 20, 2025, https://www.npr.org/sections/pictureshow/2021/08/29/1031703142/smithsonian-acquires-rare-antique-portraits-from-first-black-photographers.

Buk-Swienty, Tom. *The Other Half: The Life of Jacob Riis and the World of Immigrant America*. W.W. Norton, 2008.

Campt, Tina M. *Listening to Images*. Duke University Press, 2017.

Cole, Teju. "When the Camera Was a Weapon of Imperialism (And When It Still Is.)" *New York Times*, February 6, 2019. Last accessed March 17, 2025, https://www.nytimes.com/2019/02/06/magazine/when-the-camera-was-a-weapon-of-imperialism-and-when-it-still-is.html.

Czarnecki, Jessica. "Decolonizing the Language of Photography." *Photographers without Borders*, June 29, 2021. Last accessed March 17, 2025, https://www.photographerswithoutborders.org/online-magazine/decolonizing-the-language-of-photography.

Del Barco, Mandalit. "How Kodak's Shirley Cards Set Photography's Skin-Tone Standard." *NPR Morning Edition*, November 13, 2014. Last accessed March 19, 2025, https://www.npr.org/2014/11/13/363517842/for-decades-kodak-s-shirley-cards-set-photography-s-skin-tone-standard.

Del Barco, Mandalit. "The 'Napalm Girl' Photo Shocked the World. Now, There Are Questions about Who Took It." *NPR Morning Edition*, June 6, 2025. Last accessed June 8, 2025, https://www.npr.org/2025/06/05/nx-s1-5400606/napalm-girl-photo.

Freedman, Russell. *Kids at Work: Lewis Hine and the Crusade against Child Labor*. Clarion Books, 1994.

Hall, Stuart, ed. *Representation: Cultural Representation and Signifying Practices*. SAGE Publications, 1997.

Harris, Geoff. "Love the Skin You're In: How TECNO Is Beating Skin-Tone Bias in Phone Cameras." *Amateur Photographer*, November 15, 2024. Last accessed March 20, 2025, https://amateurphotographer.com/latest/photo-news/how-tecno-is-beating-skin-tone-bias-in-phone-cameras.

Henkel, Linda A. "Point-and-Shoot Memories: The Influence of Taking Photos on Memory for a Museum Tour." *Psychological Science* 25, no. 2 (2013): 398–402.

Hine, Lewis W. "Social Photography." In *Classic Essays on Photography*, edited by Alan Trachtenburg. Leete's Island Books, 1980.

Houck, Davis W. and Amos Kiewe. *FDR's Body Politics: The Rhetoric of Disability*. Texas A&M University Press, 2003.

Hutton, Belle. "'The Camera Could Be a Weapon': Gordon Parks on the Power of Photography." *AnOther*, July 1, 2020. Last accessed March 20, 2025, https://www.anothermag.com/art-photography/12638/gordon-parks-quotes-of-note-exhibition-alison-jacques-gallery-life-magazine.

Jurovics, Toby. *Framing the West: The Survey Photographs of Timothy H. O'Sullivan*. Smithsonian American Art Museum, 2010.

Katz, James E., Michael Barris, and Anshul Jain. *The Social Media President: Barack Obama and the Politics of Digital Engagement*. Palgrave Macmillan, 2013.

Kindy, David. "New Collection of Portraits Presents the Diversity of 19th-Century American Photography." *Smithsonian Magazine*, August 17, 2021. Last accessed March 20, 2025, https://www.smithsonianmag.com/smithsonian-institution/trove-new-portrait-photographs-presents-rarely-seen-diversity-19th-century-america-180978456/.

Link, Alessandra. "Editing for Expansion: Railroad Photography, Native Americans, and the American West, 1860–1880." *Western Historical Quarterly* 50, no. 3 (Autumn 2019): 281–313.

Klich, Lynda and Benjamin Weiss. *Real Photo Postcards: Pictures of a Changing Nation*. MFA Publications, 2022.

McGregor, Nesta. "Beyonce and Other Stars Struggle to Control Their Image." *BBC News*, February 7, 2013. Last accessed March 17, 2025, https://www.bbc.com/news/newsbeat-21373659.

Meta. "Meta Platform Terms: 2. Intellectual Property Rights." Last accessed March 18, 2025, https://developers.facebook.com/terms#intellectualpropertyrights.

Mitchell, W.J.T. *What Do Pictures Want?: The Lives and Loves of Images*. University of Chicago Press, 2005.

Murphy, Samantha. "Meet the Man behind the Very First Camera Phone." *Mashable*, March 6, 2012. Last accessed March 20, 2025, https://mashable.com/archive/philippe-kahn-camera-phone.

Nemerov, Alexander. *Soulmaker: The Times of Lewis Hine*. Princeton University Press, 2016.

Parks, Bob. "The Big Picture." *Wired* 8, no. 10 (October 2000). Last accessed March 20, 2025, https://web.archive.org/web/20060326205210/http://www.wired.com/wired/archive/8.10/kahn.html.

PBS Digital Studios. "Did This Photo Make Lincoln President?" *The Bigger Picture with Vincent Brown*, August 9, 2022. Last accessed March 15, 2025, https://www.pbs.org/video/did-this-photo-make-lincoln-president-perejr/.

Pew Research Center. "Americans' Social Media Use." January 31, 2024.

Pew Research Center. "Mobile Fact Sheet." November 13, 2024.

Resnick, Brian. "What Smartphone Photography Is Doing to Our Memories." *Vox*, March 28, 2018. Last accessed March 12, 2025, https://www.vox.com/science-and-health/2018/3/28/17054848/smartphones-photos-memory-research-psychology-attention.

Riis, Jacob. *How the Other Half Lives: Studies among the Tenements of New York*. Charles Scribner's Sons, 1890.

Smithsonian American Art Museum. "Photography." Last accessed March 20, 2025, https://americanart.si.edu/art/highlights/photography.

Sontag, Susan. *On Photography*. Farrar, Straus and Giroux, 1977.

Steinbach, Daniel and Robert S.G. Fletcher. "Photography, Colonialism, and War: Five Exposures." *War & Society* (February 2025): 1–8.

Stone, Deborah. "How Images Can Help Dementia Sufferers Engage with Life." *Psychology Today*, May 13, 2021.

Strathman, Nicole Dawn. *Through a Native Lens: American Indian Photography*. University of Oklahoma Press, 2020.

Trachtenburg, Alan. *Reading American Photographs: Images as History, Mathew Brady to Walker Evans*. Hill & Wang, 1989.

Wexler, Laura. *Tender Violence: Domestic Visions in an Age of U.S. Imperialism*. University of North Carolina Press, 2000.

Yochelson, Bonnie and Daniel Czitrom. *Rediscovering Jacob Riis: Exposure Journalism and Photography in Turn-of-the-Century New York*. University of Chicago Press, 2007.

Reading Photographs Like a Historian

Bain, David Haward. *Empire Express: Building the First Transcontinental Railroad*. Penguin Publishing Group, 2000.

Caldera, Mary A. "Guide to the Andrew J. Russell Photographs Taken during Construction of the Union Pacific Railroad." Beinecke Rare Book & Manuscript Library, Yale University, April 2025, 3–4. Last accessed June 5, 2025, https://ead-pdfs.library.yale.edu/13771.pdf.

Chang, Gordon H. *Ghosts of Gold Mountain: The Epic Story of the Chinese Who Built the Transcontinental Railroad*. Houghton Mifflin Harcourt, 2019.

Garcilazo, Jeffrey Marcos. *Traqueros: Mexican Railroad Workers in the United States, 1870 to 1930*. University of North Texas Press, 2012.

Golden Spike National Historic Park Utah. "Andrew J. Russell." National Park Service, April 29, 2025. Last accessed June 9, 2025, https://www.nps.gov/gosp/learn/historyculture/a-moment-in-time.htm.

Karuka, Manu. *Empire's Tracks: Indigenous Nations, Chinese Workers, and the Transcontinental Railroad*. University of California Press, 2019.

Pattison, William D. "The Pacific Railroad Rediscovered." *Geographical Review* 52, no. 1 (January 1962): 25–36.

Russell, Andrew J. *The Great West Illustrated in a Series of Photographic Views across the Continent Taken along the Line of the Union Pacific Railroad West from Omaha, Nebraska*. Union Pacific Railroad, 1869.

"The East and West." *Crofutts Trans-Continental Tourist's Guide*. The American News Company, 1873. Made available by the Beinecke Rare Book and Manuscript Library, Yale University. Last accessed June 8, 2025, https://collections.library.yale.edu/catalog/2032119/.

Thomas, William G. *The Iron Way: Railroads, the Civil War, and the Making of Modern America*. Yale University Press, 2011.

White, Richard. *Railroaded: The Transcontinentals and the Making of Modern America*. W.W. Norton, 2012.

"Yale Collection of Western Americana." Beinecke Rare Book & Manuscript Library, Yale University Libraries, 2025. Last accessed June 9, 2025, https://beinecke.library.yale.edu/collections/curatorial-areas/yale-collection-western-americana.

Chapter 1: Veiled History

Alexander, Ann Field. *Race Man: The Rise and Fall of the "Fighting Editor," John Mitchell, Jr*. University of Virginia Press, 2002.

American Civil War Museum. *On Monument Avenue*. Last accessed March 28, 2025, https://onmonumentave.com/onlineexhibits.

Andrews, Gordon. *Undoing Plessy: Charles Hamilton Houston, Race, Labor, and the Law, 1895–1950*. Cambridge Scholars Publishing, 2014.

Ayers, Edward L. "How the Enemies of Reconstruction Created Reconstruction." In *Reconstruction and the Arc of Racial (in)Justice*, edited by Julian M. Hayter and George R. Goethals. Edward Elgar Publishing, 2018.

Ayers, Edward L. *What Caused the Civil War?: Reflections on the South and Southern History*. W.W. Norton, 2006.

Boehm, Lisa Krissoff and Steven H. Corey. *America's Urban History*. Routledge, 2023.

Brooks, Richard R.W. and Carol M. Rose. *Saving the Neighborhood: Racially Restrictive Covenants, Law, and Social Norms*. Harvard University Press, 2013.

Brumfield, Dave. "A Monument Avenue Mystery." *Richmond Magazine*, December 3, 2017. Last accessed March 30, 2025, https://richmondmagazine.com/news/sunday-story/a-monument-avenue-mystery/.

Case, Sarah H. "The Historical Ideology of Mildred Lewis Rutherford: A Confederate Historians New South Creed." *The Journal of Southern History* 68, no. 3 (August 2002): 599–628.

Cox, Karen L. *Dixie's Daughters: The United Daughters of the Confederacy and the Preservation of Confederate Culture*. University Press of Florida, 2019.

Desjardins, Lisa. "Robert E. Lee Opposed Confederate Monuments." *PBS News*, August 15, 2017. Last accessed April 2, 2025, https://www.pbs.org/newshour/nation/robert-e-lee-opposed-confederate-monuments.

Domby, Adam H. *The False Cause: Fraud, Fabrication, and White Supremacy in Confederate Memory*. University of Virginia Press, 2020.

Driggs, Sarah Shields, Richard Guy Wilson, and Robert P. Winthrop. *Richmond's Monument Avenue*. University of North Carolina Press, 2001.

Du Bois, W.E.B. *Black Reconstruction in America, 1860–1880*. Free Press, 1998.

Earle, Laura Byrd. "Richmond's Monument Avenue: Memorializing the Lost Cause." *The Valentine*, October 6, 2023. Last accessed March 31, 2025, https://thevalentine.org/explore/richmond-stories/featured-stories/richmonds-monument-avenue-memorializing-the-lost-cause-myth/.

Fitt, Rob Alex. "Conservative Activists in Texas Have Shaped the History All American Children Learn." *Washington Post*, October 19, 2020. Last accessed April 2, 2025, https://www.washingtonpost.com/outlook/2020/10/19/conservative-activists-texas-have-shaped-history-all-american-children-learn/.

Foner, Eric. *Reconstruction Updated Edition: America's Unfinished Journey, 1863–1877*. Harper Perennial Modern Classics, 2014.

Foner, Eric. "Rooted in Reconstruction: The First Wave of Black Congressmen." *The Nation*, October 15, 2008. Last accessed March 30, 2025, https://www.thenation.com/article/archive/rooted-reconstruction-first-wave-black-congressmen/.

Franklin, John Hope and Loren Schweninger. *Runaway Slaves: Rebels on the Plantation*. Oxford University Press, 2000.

Gallagher, Gary W. and Alan T. Nolan. *The Myth of the Lost Cause and Civil War History*. Indiana University Press, 2000.

Gillette, Jr., Howard. *Between Justice and Beauty: Race, Planning, and the Failure of Urban Policy in Washington, D.C.* University of Pennsylvania Press, 2011.

Goldstein, Dana. "Two States. Eight Textbooks. Two American Stories." *New York Times*, January 12, 2020. Last accessed April 2, 2025, https://www.nytimes.com/interactive/2020/01/12/us/texas-vs-california-history-textbooks.html.

Hayter, Julian Maxwell. "Confederate Monuments Are about Maintaining White Supremacy." *Washington Post*, July 27, 2017. Last accessed March 28, 2025, https://www.washingtonpost.com/news/made-by-history/wp/2017/07/27/confederate-monuments-are-about-maintaining-white-supremacy/.

Hayter, Julian Maxwell. "Redlining Is Only Part of the Story." *Bunk History*, October 5, 2022. Last accessed March 30, 2025, https://www.bunkhistory.org/resources/redlining.

Holt, Thomas C. *The Movement: The African American Struggle for Civil Rights*. Oxford University Press, 2021.

Janney, Caroline. *Burying the Dead but Not the Past: Ladies' Memorial Associations and the Lost Cause*. University of North Carolina Press, 2008.

Janney, Caroline. "The Lost Cause." *Encyclopedia Virginia*, Virginia Humanities, December 2020. Last accessed March 30, 2025, https://encyclopediavirginia.org/entries/lost-cause-the/.

Lancaster, Robert A. *Historic Virginia Homes and Churches*. Lippincott, 1915.

Levin, Kevin M. "Richmond's Confederate Monuments Were Used to Sell a Segregated Neighborhood." *The Atlantic*, June 11, 2020. Last accessed March

30, 2025, https://www.theatlantic.com/ideas/archive/2020/06/its-not-just-the-monuments/612940/.

McElya, Micki. *Clinging to Mammy: The Faithful Slave in Twentieth Century American*. Harvard University Press, 2007.

Mount, Guy Emerson. "When Slaves Go on Strike: DuBois's Black Reconstruction 80 Years Later." *African American Intellectual History Society*, December 28, 2015. Last accessed March 31, 2025, https://www.aaihs.org/when-slaves-go-on-strike/.

Mumford, Eric. *Designing the Modern City: Urbanism since 1850*. Yale University Press, 2018.

Nolan, Alan T. *Lee Considered: General Robert E. Lee and Civil War History*. University of North Carolina Press, 1996.

Pew Research Center. *Civil War at 150: Still Relevant, Still Divisive*. April 8, 2011. Last accessed March 28, 2025, https://www.pewresearch.org/politics/2011/04/08/civil-war-at-150-still-relevant-still-divisive/.

Richardson, Heather Cox. *How the South Won the Civil War: Oligarchy, Democracy, and the Continuing Fight for the Soul of America*. Oxford University Press, 2022.

Richmond Planet. "John Mitchell, Jr." June 7, 1890.

Richmond Times-Dispatch. "Mr. Lancaster, Historical Club, Dies." August 27, 1940.

Robert E. Lee Papers, University of Virginia Archives.

Rutherford, Mildred Lewis. *A Measuring Rod to Test Textbooks, and Reference Books in Schools, Colleges, and Libraries*. United Confederate Veterans, 1920.

Silver, Christopher. "The Racial Origins of Zoning." In *Urban Planning and the African American Community: In the Shadows*, edited by June Manning Thomas and Marsha Ritzdorf. Sage Publications, 1997.

Southern Poverty Law Center. "Whose Heritage? Public Symbols of the Confederacy." February 1, 2019. Last accessed March 30, 2025, https://www.splcenter.org/resources/reports/whose-heritage-public-symbols-confederacy/#findings.

Springston, Rex. "Happy Slaves? The Peculiar Story of Three Virginia School Textbooks." *Richmond Times-Dispatch*, April 15, 2018. Last accessed March 29, 2025, https://richmond.com/news/local/happy-slaves-the-peculiar-story-of-three-virginia-school-textbooks/article_47e79d49-eac8-575d-ac9d-1c6fce52328f.html.

Stevens, Matt. "For a Black Man Hired to Undo a Confederate Legacy, It Has Not Been Easy." *New York Times*, April 17, 2022.

Williamson, Thad, Julian M. Hayter, and Amy L. Howard. *The Making of Twentieth Century Richmond: Politics, Policy, and Governance 1988–2016*. University of North Carolina Press, 2024.

Chapter 2: Regarding Sovereign History as Incomplete

Allen, Lee. "Smudging the Colonizer's Lens: Artists Challenge Old Imagery with 'Regarding Curtis.'" *Indian Country Today*, November 29, 2014. Last accessed

March 11, 2025, https://ictnews.org/archive/smudging-the-colonizers-lens-artists-challenge-old-imagery-with-regarding-curtis.

Azoulay, Ariella Aïsha, Wendy Ewald, Susan Meiselas, Leigh Raiford, and Laura Wexler. *Collaboration: A Potential History of Photography*. Thames & Hudson, 2023.

Calof, Rachel with J. Sanford Rikoon, ed. *Rachel Calof's Story: Jewish Homesteader on the Northern Plains*. Indiana University Press, 1995.

Deloria, Phil. *Indians in Unexpected Places*. University of Kansas Press, 2004.

Hoskin, Jr., Chuck. "Teach Kids about the Oklahoma Land Run, but Don't Glorify It." *Native News Online*, April 28, 2024. Last accessed March 11, 2025, https://nativenewsonline.net/opinion/teach-kids-about-the-oklahoma-land-run-but-don-t-glorify-it.

Kohl, Edith Eudora. *Land of the Burnt Thigh*. Minnesota Historical Society Press, 2008.

Lovett, John R. "Prettyman, William S. (1858-1933)." *The Encyclopedia of Oklahoma*. Oklahoma Historical Society. Last accessed March 11, 2025, https://www.okhistory.org/publications/enc/entry?entry=PR010.

Phipps, Laura and Neal Ambrose-Smith. *Jaune Quick-to-See Smith*. Whitney Museum of American Art, 2023.

Saunt, Claudio. *Unworthy Republic: The Dispossession of Native Americans and the Road to Indian Territory*. W.W. Norton, 2020.

Schmucker, Kristine. "Picture Man: William S. Prettyman." *Harvey County Historical Museum* (blog), September 15, 2017. Last accessed March 11, 2025, https://hchm.org/picture-man-william-s-prettyman/.

Shupe, Andrew G. "William Sheldon Prettyman: Mayor of Blackwell—Indian Photographer." *Rootsweb*, archived by the Internet Archive. Last accessed March 11, 2025, https://web.archive.org/web/20001007032119/http://www.rootsweb.com/~okkay/prettyman.htm.

Stewart, Elinore Pruitt. *Letters of a Woman Homesteader*. Open Road Media, 2020.

Strathman, Nicole Dawn. *Through a Native Lens: American Indian Photography*. University of Oklahoma Press, 2020.

Willert, Tim. "Oklahoma City Public Schools Seeks 'Respectful' Alternative to Land Run Reenactments." *The Oklahoman*, December 23, 2014. Last accessed March 11, 2025, https://www.oklahoman.com/story/news/local/oklahoma-city/2014/12/23/oklahoma-city-public-schools-seeks-respectful-alternative-to-land-run-re-enactments/60776375007/.

Chapter 3: Owned to Landowner

Act of May 20, 1862 (Homestead Act), Public Law 37–64 (12 Stat 392).

Arrington, Benjamin Todd. "'Free Homes for Free Men': A Political History of the Homestead Act, 1774–1863." PhD diss., University of Nebraska, 2012.

Bell, Blake. "America's Invitation to the World: Was the Homestead Act the First Accommodating Immigration Legislation in the United States?" Homestead National Monument of America, National Park Service.

Blount, Catherine Meehan. Interview. By Mikal Brotnov Eckstrom. May 15, 2016. Black Homesteading Project, Center for Great Plains Studies, University of Nebraska.

Bristow, David. "Look Closely: This Is a Previously Unknown Solomon Butcher Photo." *Nebraska State Historical Society* (blog), April 30, 2020, https://history. nebraska.gov/look-closely-this-is-a-previously-unknown-solomon-butcher-photo/.

Bureau of Land Management Records. Grand Island Land Office.

Bureau of the Census. *Negro Population: 1790–1915.*

Calof, Rachel with J. Sanford Rikoon, ed. *Rachel Calof's Story: Jewish Homesteader on the Northern Plains.* Indiana University Press, 1995.

Carter, John E. *Solomon D. Butcher: Photographing the American Dream.* University of Nebraska Press, 1985.

Custer County Chief, February 28, 1908.

Custer County (Nebraska) Republican, May 3, 1900.

Danbom, David B. *Sod Busting: How Families Made Farms on the 19th-Century Plains.* Johns Hopkins University Press, 2014.

Edwards, Richard. "African Americans and the Southern Homestead Act." *Great Plains Quarterly* 39, no. 2 (Spring 2019): 103–30.

Edwards, Richard and Jacob K. Friefeld. *The First Migrants: How Black Homesteaders' Quest for Land and Freedom Heralded America's Great Migration.* Bison Books, 2023.

Edwards, Richard, Jacob K. Friefeld, and Mikal Brotnov Eckstrom. "'Canaan on the Prairie': New Evidence on the Number of African American Homesteaders in the Great Plains." *Great Plains Quarterly* 39, no. 3 (Summer 2019): 223–41.

Edwards, Richard, Jacob K. Friefeld, and Rebecca S. Wingo. *Homesteading the Plains: Toward a New History.* University of Nebraska Press, 2017.

Friefeld, Jacob K. "Homesteading and the Making of the Midwest." In *The Making of the Midwest: Essays on the Formation of Midwestern Identity, 1787–1900*, edited by Jon K. Lauck. Hastings College Press, 2020.

Gray, Joyce Ann. Interview. By Mikal Brotnov Eckstrom. May 15, 2016. Black Homesteading Project, Center for Great Plains Studies, University of Nebraska.

Guenther, Todd. "The Empire Builders: An African American Odyssey in Nebraska and Wyoming." *Nebraska History* 86 (Winter 2008): 176–200.

Nebraska State Historical Society. "Solomon D. Butcher Collection." Last accessed May 14, 2025, https://history.nebraska.gov/collection_section/solomon-d-butcher-collection/.

Sides, Josh. *Backcountry Ghosts: California Homesteaders and the Making of a Dubious Dream.* University of Nebraska Press, 2021.

Smith, I.E.M. "Two City Girls' Experiences in Holding Down a Claim: A Montana Pastoral." *Overland Monthly* 24 (August 1894): 147–9.

Stoll, Steven. *Ramp Hollow: The Ordeal of Appalachia.* Hill and Wang, 2017.

US Census. Custer County, Nebraska, 1880 and 1900.

US Department of Agriculture. *Yearbook of the United States Department of Agriculture 1919.* Government Printing Office, 1920.

US Senate, 46th Congress, 2nd sess. "Report and Testimony of the Select Committee of the United States Senate to Investigate the Causes of the

Removal of the Negroes from the Southern States to the Northern States." Government Printing Office, 1880.

Welsch, Roger. *Sod Walls: The Story of the Nebraska Sod House*. J & L Lee Co., 1991.

Wilm, Julius. "'The Indians Must Yield': Antebellum Free Land, the Homestead Act, and the Displacement of Native Peoples." *Bulletin of the German Historical Institute* 67 (Fall 2020): 17–39.

Work, Henry C. "Wake Nicodemus." 1864. University of Chicago Library Sheet Music Collection.

Chapter 4: Illuminating the Kodak Girl

1920 United States Federal Census. Records of the Bureau of the Census. National Archives, Washington, DC.

Allerlei '03: Volume X. Lasell Female Seminary, 1902.

Angus, Siobhan. *Camera Geologica: An Elemental History of Photography*. Duke University Press, 2024.

Ausherman, Maria. "Frances Benjamin Johnston's Legacy in Black and White." *CRM: The Journal of Heritage Stewardship* 4, no. 2 (Summer 2007): 29–49.

Boyd's Syracuse Directory. Wolcott & West, 1893.

Bronwyn, Griffith, and Verna Posener Curtis. *Ambassadors of Progress: American Women Photographers in Paris, 1900–1901*. Library of Congress, 2001.

Carman, Bliss and Richard Hovey. *Songs from Vagabondia*. Small, Maynard, 1894.

Cooper, Martha. "Kodak Girls." *KodakGirls.com*. Last accessed February 17, 2025, https://kodakgirl.com/kodakgirlsframe.htm.

Eickemeyer, Jr., Rudolf. *Records of Films, Photographs, and Negatives*. Catalog number PG.004135.B041, Photographic History Collection, Smithsonian's National Museum of American History.

Fogle, Kate. "Women at Work: 'At Kodak Heights' and Female Employment in the 1920s." *Kodak Canada: The Early Years (1899-1939) Exhibition*. Last accessed February 17, 2025, https://kodakcanada.omeka.net/exhibits/show/kodak-canada–the-early-years/women-at-work–the-changing-oc.

Grand, Sarah. "The New Woman." *The North American Review* 158, no. 450 (1894): 610–9.

Greenough, Sarah. *Modern Art and America: Alfred Stieglitz and His New York Galleries*. National Gallery of Art, 2000.

Hughes, Edan Milton. *Artists in California, 1786–1940: L-Z*. Crocker Art Museum, 2002.

Ingall, Elfric Drew. *Mineral Resources of Canada: Bulletin No. 1, Platinum*. S.E. Dawson, 1903.

Jeffery, Ian. "Peter Henry Emerson." In *The Golden Age of British* Photography, edited by Mark Haworth-Booth. Aperture, 1984.

Johnston, Frances Benjamin. "What a Woman Can Do with a Camera." *The Ladies' Home Journal* (September 1897): 6–7.

Jones, B. Ralph, ed. *The Mirage Yearbook*. DePauw University, 1920.

Oakland Tribune. "Mrs. McGill, Noted Portrait Painter, Dies in Hospital." August 21, 1929.

Patterson, Martha H. *Beyond the Gibson Girl: Reimagining the American New Woman, 1895–1915*. University of Illinois Press, 2005.

Perry, Elisabeth Israels. "Men Are from the Gilded Age, Women Are from the Progressive Era." *The Journal of the Gilded Age and Progressive Era* 1, no. 1 (2002): 25–48.

Roon, Ronald. "Three Factors in American Pictorial Photography." *American Amateur Photographer* 15, no. 8 (August 1904): 346–9.

Russell, Thomas. *Commercial Advertising: Six Lectures at the London School of Economics and Political Science (University of London)*. G.P. Putnam's Sons, 1919.

Sawyer, Edna M. "The War Dance." *Sunset: The Magazine of the Pacific and All of the Far West*, May 1915.

Schrock, Joel. *The Gilded Age*. Greenwood Press, 2004.

Shulman, Vanessa Meikle. "Sensing Pollution: Picturing 'Bad Air' in Gilded Age New York." *Panorama* 9, no. 2 (Fall 2023): 1–27.

Syracuse, New York, City Directory. 1909.

The New Woman—Wash Day. Strohmeyer & Wyman, ca. 1897. Library of Congress Prints and Photographs Division, Washington, DC.

Turner-Lowe, Susan. "The Pride and Practice of Frances B. Johnston." *Verso* (blog), June 6, 2023. Last accessed February 17, 2025, https://huntington.org/verso/pride-and-practice-frances-b-johnston.

Wade, James W. *Mining Methods and Costs at Tintic Standard Mine, Tintic District, Utah*. Department of Commerce, United States Bureau of Mines, 1930.

Wagner, Sarah S. "Manufactured Platinum and Faux Platinum Papers, 1880s–1920s." In *Platinum and Palladium Photographs: Technical History, Connoisseurship, and Preservation*, edited by Constance McCabe. American Institute for Conservation of Historic and Artistic Works, 2017.

Ware, Mike. "The Technical History and Chemistry of Platinum and Palladium Printing." In *Platinum and Palladium Photographs: Technical History, Connoisseurship, and Preservation*, edited by Constance McCabe. American Institute for Conservation of Historic and Artistic Works, 2017.

West, Nancy Martha. *Kodak and the Lens of Nostalgia*. University Press of Virginia, 2000.

Chapter 5: Native American Women and the Politics of Portraiture

Adams, David Wallace. *Education for Extinction: American Indians and the Boarding School Experience, 1875–1928*. University Press of Kansas, 1995.

Allaire, Christian. "Why Lily Gladstone's Red Carpet Style Is Oscar-Worthy." *Vogue World Paris*, January 24, 2024.

Allen, Chadwick, and Beth Piatote, eds. "The Society of American Indians and Its Legacies." *Studies in American Indian Literatures* 25, no. 2 and *American Indian Quarterly* 37, no. 3 (2013).

Belt, Rabia S. *Disabling Democracy in America: Mental Incompetence, Citizenship, Voting, and the Law, 1819–1920*. Cambridge University Press, forthcoming.

Berkhofer, Robert F. *The White Man's Indian: Images of the American Indian from Columbus to the Present*. Vintage Books, 1979.

Bordin, Ruth. *Women and Temperance: The Quest for Power and Liberty*. Temple University Press, 1981.

Cahill, Cathleen. *Federal Fathers and Mothers: A Social History the United States Indian Service, 1869–1933*. University of North Carolina Press, 2011.

Cahill, Cathleen. *Recasting the Vote: How Women of Color Transformed the Suffrage Movement*. University of North Carolina Press, 2020.

Carter, Thomas, Edward Chappell, and Timothy McCleary. "In the Lodge of the Chickadee: Architecture and Cultural Resistance on the Crow Indian Reservation, 1884–1920." *Perspectives in Vernacular Architecture* 10 (2005): 97–111.

Catlin, George. *Illustrations of the Manners, Customs, and Condition of the North American Indians, Vol. 1*. H.G. Bohn, 1848.

Child, Brenda J. *Boarding School Seasons: American Indian Families, 1900–1940*. University of Nebraska Press, 1998.

Dayton, Kim. "'Trespassers, Beware!' Lyda Burton Conley and the Battle for Huron Place Cemetery." *Yale Journal of Law and Feminism* 8, no. 1 (1996): 1–30.

Deloria, Philip J. *Indians in Unexpected Places*. University Press of Kansas, 2004.

Department of the Interior. "Interior Department Completes Removal of 'Sq_ _ _' from Federal Use." September 8, 2022. Last accessed October 3, 2024, https://www.doi.gov/pressreleases/interior-department-completes-removal-sq-federal-use.

Dippie, Brian. "Photographic Allegories and Indian Destiny." *Montana: The Magazine of Western History* 42, no. 3 (Summer 1992): 40–57.

Drachman, Virginia G. *Sisters in Law: Women Lawyers in Modern American History*. Harvard University Press, 1998.

Genetin-Pilawa, C. Joseph. "The Indians' Capital City: Diplomatic Visits, Place, and Two-Worlds Discourse in Nineteenth-Century Washington, DC." In *Beyond Two Worlds: Critical Conversations on Language and Power in Native North America*, edited by James Joseph Buss and C. Joseph Genetin-Pilawa. SUNY Press, 2014.

Glenn, James R. "De Lancey W. Gill, Photographer for the Bureau of American Ethnology." *History of Photography* 7, no. 1 (January–March 1983): 7–22.

Hertzberg, Hazel W. *The Search for an American Indian Identity: Modern Pan-Indian Movements*. Syracuse University Press, 1981.

Higginbotham, Evelyn Brooks. *Righteous Discontent: The Women's Movement in Black Baptist Church, 1880–1920*. Harvard University Press, 1994.

Hutchinson, Elizabeth. *The Indian Craze: Primitivism, Modernism, and Transculturation in American Art, 1890–1915*. Duke University Press, 2009.

Jones, Tom, Michael Schmudlach, Matthew Daniel Mason, Amy Lonetree, and George A. Greendeer. *People of the Big Voice: Photographs of Ho-Chunk Families by Charles Van Schaick, 1879–1942*. Wisconsin Historical Society Press, 2011.

Kansas Historical Society. "American Woman and Her Political Peers Painting." November 1999. Last accessed May 7, 2024, https://www.kshs.org/kansapedia/american-woman-and-her-political-peers-painting/10294.

Kilroy-Ewbank, Lauren. "Inventing 'America': The Engravings of Theodore de Bry." *Smarthistory*, May 18, 2019. Last accessed September 19, 2024, https://smarthistory.org/engravings-theodore-de-bry/.

Lange, Allison. *Picturing Political Power: Images in the Woman Suffrage Movement*. University of Chicago Press, 2020.

Lindsey, Treva. *Colored No More: Reinventing Black Womanhood in Washington, DC*. University of Illinois Press, 2017.

Los Angeles Times. "Equal Suffrage among Indians." January 31, 1913.

Mark, Joan. *A Stranger in Her Native Land: Alice Fletcher and the American Indians*. University of Nebraska Press, 1988.

McNally, Michael. *Defend the Sacred: Native American Religious Freedom beyond the First Amendment*. Princeton University Press, 2020.

Moses, L.G. *Wild West Shows and the Images of American Indians, 1883–1933*. University of New Mexico Press, 1999.

National Museum of the American Indian. "Nation to Nation: Treaties between the United States and Native Nations." Last accessed June 11, 2024, https://americanindian.si.edu/nationtonation/.

Parker, Arthur C. "The Awakened American Indian." *The Quarterly Journal of the Society of American Indians* 2, no. 4 (October–December, 1914): 269–74.

Parker, Arthur C. "The Word 'Squaw' an Out-of-Date Expression." *The Quarterly Journal of the Society of American Indians* 2, no. 4 (October–December 1914): 256–7.

Personnel File of Marie Louise Bottineau Baldwin. National Personnel Records Center, St. Louis, MO.

Prucha, Francis Paul. *The Great Father: The United States Government and American Indians*. University of Nebraska Press, 1984.

Redman, Samuel. *Prophets and Ghosts: The Story of Salvage Anthropology*. Harvard University Press, 2021.

Redmond, C. Daniel. "The Sartorial Indian: Zitkala-Ša, Clothing, and Resistance to Colonization." *Studies in American Indian Literatures* 28, no. 3 (Fall 2016): 52–80.

Smith, Gretchen. "Indian Collection Work of 30 Years." *Washington Evening Star*, April 15, 1929.

The Democrat-Herald. "Indian Girl's Rise." March 10, 1911.

The New York Times. "Deb Haaland Makes History, and Dresses for It." March 19, 2021.

Viola, Herman. *Diplomats in Buckskin: A History of Indian Delegations in Washington City*. University of Oklahoma Press, 1995.

Wagner, Sally Roesch. *Sisters in Spirit: Haudenosaunee (Iroquois) Influence on Early American Feminists*. Native Voices, 2001.

Washington Evening Star. "Indian Woman Works for Uncle Sam." December 4, 1910.

Washington Evening Star. "US Workers Have Indian Ancestors: Seven Employes [sic] of Interior Department Trace Lineage to First Americans." June 17, 1928.

White, Cody. "Homes on the Range." *Genealogy Notes* 49 no. 3 (Fall 2017).

Wilkins, David E. and K. Tsianina Lomawaima. *Uneven Ground: American Indian Sovereignty and Federal Law*. University of Oklahoma Press, 2001.

Wingo, Rebecca S. *Framed: Housing and Photography on the Crow Reservation* [manuscript in progress]

Yellin, Erik S. *Racism in the Nation's Service: Government Workers and the Color Line in Woodrow Wilson's America.* University of North Carolina Press, 2016.

Chapter 6: The Interwar Period (1918–39)

Addams, Jane. "Jane Addams to Harriet Cousens Andrews, ca. February 15, 1925 (excerpts)." *Jane Addams Digital Edition.* Last accessed June 22, 2024, https://digital.janeaddams.ramapo.edu/items/show/36146.

Addams, Jane. "The Opening of a Women's Congress." *Mid-Pacific Magazine* 36, no. 4 (1928): 303–6.

Arondekar, Anjali. *For the Record: On Sexuality and the Colonial Archive in India.* Duke University Press, 2009.

Beechert, Edward D. *Working in Hawaii: A Labor History.* University of Hawai'i Press, 1985.

Boniface, James, ed. *Complete Self-Instructing Library of Practical Photography.* American School of Art and Photography, 1908.

Boyle, Francis A. "Restoration of the Independent Nation State of Hawaii under International Law." *St. Thomas Law Review* 7, no. 3 (1995): 723–56.

Brown, Victoria Bissell. *The Education of Jane Addams.* University of Pennsylvania Press, 2004.

Char, On. "On Char Oral History Interview Conducted by Lynda Mair in Honolulu, Hawaii on November 26, 1971." The Watumull Foundation Oral History Project, 1979. Last accessed May 22, 2024, https://evols.library.manoa.hawaii.edu/server/api/core/bitstreams/299aa221-eaba-4c03-833f-c9f7c22d022c/content.

Connelly, Matthew. *Fatal Misconception: The Struggle to Control World Population.* Harvard University Press, 2010.

Davis, Lynn Ann. "Japanese Studio Photographers in the Territory of Hawai'i, 1900–1945." In *Social Process in Hawai'i: Celebrating 100 Years of Local Studies,* edited by Lori Pierce and John P. Rosa. University of Hawai'i Press, 2020.

Derrida, Jacques. *Archive Fever: A Freudian Impression.* Translated by Eric Prenowitz. University of Chicago Press, 1995.

Ford, Alexander Hume. *Genesis of the Pan-Pacific Union: Being Some Reminiscences of Alexander Hume Ford, First Installment.* Box 1, Folder 2. Pan-Pacific Union Collection. Hamilton Library, University of Hawai'i at Mānoa.

Foucault, Michel. "The Subject and Power." *Critical Inquiry* 8, no. 4 (1982): 777–95.

Gorman, Daniel. *The Emergence of International Society in the 1920s.* Cambridge University Press, 2012.

Grimshaw, Patricia. "Gender, Citizenship and Race in the Women's Christian Temperance Union of Australia, 1890 to the 1930s." *Australian Feminist Studies* 13, no. 28 (1998): 199–214.

Hinder, Eleanor. "Pan-Pacific Women's Conference." *The Brisbane Courier,* July 19, 1928.

Honolulu Star-Bulletin. "Yew Char Starts Travel Business," December 21, 1946.

Iriye, Akira. *Cultural Internationalism and World Order*. Johns Hopkins University Press, 1997.

Jackson, Jason Baird. *Material Vernaculars: Objects, Images, and Their Social Worlds*. Indiana University Press, 2016.

Johnson, LiLi. "Paper Family Photography: Photography and the State in the Era of Chinese Exclusion (1882-1943)." *Photography & Culture* 10, no. 2 (2017): 105–19.

Knight, Louise W. *Jane Addams: Spirit in Action*. W.W. Norton, 2010.

Laqua, Daniel, ed. *Internationalism Reconfigured: Transnational Ideas and Movements between the World Wars*. Taurus, 2011.

Lien, Pei-te and Nicole Filler. *Contesting the Last Frontier: Race, Gender, Ethnicity, and Political Representation of Asian Americans*. Oxford University Press, 2022.

Manela, Erez. *The Wilsonian Moment: Self-Determination and the International Origins of Anticolonial Nationalism*. Oxford University Press, 2007.

McGirr, Lisa. "The Interwar Years." In *American History Now*, edited by Eric Foner and Lisa McGirr. Temple University Press, 2011.

Ngai, Mae M. *Impossible Subjects: Illegal Aliens and the Making of Modern America*. Princeton University Press, 2004.

Odo, Franklin. *No Sword to Bury: Japanese Americans in Hawai'i during World War II*. Temple University Press, 2004.

Ott, Katherine and Susan Tucker. "An Introduction to the History of Scrapbooks." In *Scrapbooks in American Life*, edited by Katherine Ott, Susan Tucker, and Patricia Buckler. Temple University Press, 2006.

Pacific Commercial Advertiser. "Chinese of Honolulu Completes Course in Art of Photography: Yew Char." June 9, 1916.

Paisley, Fiona. *Glamour in the Pacific: Cultural Internationalism and Race Politics in the Women's Pan-Pacific*. University of Hawai'i Press, 2009.

Pan-Pacific Union. "A Switzerland and Its Geneva for the Pacific." *Pan-Pacific Union Bulletin*, New Series, 1920.

Pan-Pacific Union Collection. Hamilton Library, University of Hawai'i at Mānoa.

Phu, Thy and Elspeth H. Brown. "The Cultural Politics of Aspiration: Family Photography's Mixed Feelings." *Journal of Visual Culture* 17, no. 2 (2018): 152–65.

Pugh, Michael. *Liberal Internationalism: The Interwar Movement for Peace in Britain*. Palgrave Macmillan, 2012.

Riegl, Alois. *The Group Portraiture of Holland*. Getty Research Center for the History of Art and the Humanities, 1999.

Sato, Courtney. 'A Picture of Peace': Friendship in Interwar Pacific Women's Internationalism." *Qui Parle* 27, no. 2 (December 2018): 475–510.

Scott, Joan Wallach. *The Fantasy of Feminist History*. Duke University Press, 2011.

Sluga, Glenda. *Internationalism in the Age of Nationalism*. University of Pennsylvania Press, 2013.

Sneider, Allison L. *Suffragists in an Imperial Age: US Expansion and the Woman Question, 1870–1929*. Oxford University Press, 2008.

Stoler, Ann Laura. *Along the Archival Grain: Epistemic Anxieties and Colonial Common Sense*. Princeton University Press, 2009.

Takaki, Ronald T. *Pau Hana: Plantation Life and Labor in Hawaii, 1835–1920*. University of Hawai'i Press, 1983.

The Honolulu Advertiser. "Yew Char, Photographer, Legislator," March 31, 1982.

Trouillot, Michel-Rolf and Hazel V. Carby. *Silencing the Past: Power and the Production of History.* Beacon Press, 2015.

US Bureau of Labor. "Labor Force Statistics from the Current Population Survey: Unemployment Rate." Last accessed September 12, 2024, https://data.bls.gov/timeseries/LFU21000100&series_id=LFU22000100&from_year=1929&to_year=1939&periods_option=specific_periods&periods=Annual±Data.

Xu, Tingting. "The Group Photograph as an Imbricated Ritualistic Event: Duanfang and His Altar Bronzes in Late Qing Antiquarian Praxis." *History of Photography* 44, no. 4 (2020): 249–66.

Yasutake, Rumi. *The Feminist Pacific: International Women's Networks in Hawai'i, 1820–1940.* Columbia University Press, 2024.

Chapter 7: Legacy of Dorothea Lange's Photography

Berger, John. *Ways of Seeing.* British Broadcasting Corporation, 1977.

Gordon, Linda. *Dorothea Lange: A Life beyond Limits.* W.W. Norton, 2009.

Gordon, Linda and Gary Y. Okihiro. *Impounded: Dorothea Lange and the Censored Images of Japanese American Internment.* W.W. Norton, 2008.

Lange, Dorothea. US Farm Security Administration, Library of Congress Prints and Photographs Division.

Lange, Dorothea and Paul Schuster Taylor. *An American Exodus: A Record of Human Erosion.* Reynal & Hitchcock, 1939.

Nochlin, Linda. *Misère: The Visual Representation of Misery in the 19th Century.* Thames & Hudson, 2018.

Chapter 8: Framing a Fractured System

Agency for Toxic Substances and Disease Registry. "DDT, DDE, and DDD." U.S. Centers for Disease Control and Prevention, 2022. Last accessed January 2, 2025, https://www.atsdr.cdc.gov/toxfaqs/tfacts35.pdf.

Alanis Enciso, Fernando Saúl. *El Primer Programa Bracero Y El Gobierno de México 1917–1918.* Colegio de San Luis, 1999.

Balderrama, Francisco E. and Raymond Rodríguez. *Decade of Betrayal: Mexican Repatriation in the 1930s.* University of New Mexico Press, 2006.

Canela, Raúl. Informal Conversation. With Mireya Loza. San Jose, CA. July 27, 2005.

Carson, Rachel. *Silent Spring.* 40th Anniversary Edition. Mariner Books, 2002.

Conis, Elena. *How to Sell a Poison: The Rise, Fall and Toxic Return of DDT.* Bold Type Books, 2022.

Davis, John H. and Ray Allan Goldberg. *A Concept of Agribusiness.* Harvard University, 1957.

Galarza, Ernesto. *Strangers in Our Fields*. Joint United States-Mexico Union Committee, 1956.

García, Juan Ramon. *Operation Wetback: The Mass Deportation of Mexican Undocumented Workers in 1954*. Greenwood Press, 1980.

Hahamovitch, Cindy. *No Man's Land: Jamaican Guestworkers in America and the Global History of Deportable Labor*. Princeton University Press, 2011.

Hernández, Kelly Lytle. "The Crime and Consequences of Illegal Immigration: A Cross-Border Examination of Operation Wetback, 1943–1954." *Western Historical Quarterly* 37, no. 4 (Winter 2006): 421–44.

Loza, Mireya. "'Let Them Bring Their Families': The Experiences of the First Mexican Guest Workers, 1917–1922." *Journal of American History* 109, no. 2 (September 2022): 310–23.

Loza, Mireya. "The Japanese Agricultural Workers' Program: Race, Labor, and Cold War Diplomacy in the Fields, 1956–1965." *Pacific Historical Review* 86, no. 4 (2017): 661–90.

Martin, Philip. "H-2A Program Expands in 2023." The Wilson Center (blog), August 25, 2023. Last accessed July 10, 2024, https://www.wilsoncenter.org/article/h-2a-program-expands-2023.

Martin, Philip. "There Is Nothing More Permanent than Temporary Foreign Workers." Center for Immigration Studies, April 2001.

McDonald, Bryan L. *The Rise and Fall of the Postwar American Food System*. Oxford University Press, 2017.

Meza, Nemecio. Interview. By Mireya Loza. Los Angeles, CA. *Bracero Oral History Project*, University of Texas at El Paso. May 12, 2006.

Nadel, Leonard. "New Role for the Photographer." Undated. Box 10 Folder 13. Leonard Nadel Papers, Archives Center, Smithsonian's National Museum of American History.

Nash, Linda. *Modern Landscapes and Ecological Bodies: A History of Environment, Disease and Knowledge*. University of California Press, 2006.

Nuñez, Lucio. Interview. By Violeta Mena. Coachella, CA. *Bracero Oral History Project*, University of Texas at El Paso. May 20, 2006.

Ramírez, Marla A. Banished Citizens: A History of the Mexican American Women Who Endured Repatriation. Harvard University Press, 2025.

Scruggs, Otey M. "The First Mexican Farm Labor Program." *Journal of the Southwest* 2, no. 4 (Winter 1960): 319–26.

Street, Richard Steven. *Everyone Had Cameras: Photography and Farmworkers in California, 1850–2000*. University of Minnesota Press, 2008.

US Attorney's Office, Southern District of Georgia. "Human Smuggling, Forced Labor among Allegations in South Georgia Federal Indictment." Press Release. November 22, 2021. Last accessed June 10, 2024, https://www.justice.gov/usao-sdga/pr/human-smuggling-forced-labor-among-allegations-south-georgia-federal-indictment.

Zepeda, Audmaro G. Interview. By Mireya Loza. Salinas, CA. *Bracero Oral History Project*, University of Texas at El Paso. July 28, 2005.

Chapter 9: Race and the Space Race

Borstelmann, Timothy. *The Cold War and the Color Line: American Race Relations in the Global Arena*. Harvard University Press, 2001.

Butler, Roger V. "The Langley Research Center Remote Computing Terminal System: Implementation and First Year's Operation." In *Proceedings of the 1966 21st National Conference*. Association for Computing Machinery, 1966.

Ceruzzi, Paul E. *A History of Modern Computing*. MIT Press, 1998, 2003.

Cole, Isabella J., James P. Murphy, and Joseph W. Siry. "The Goddard General Orbit Determination System." Goddard Space Flight Center, May 1, 1968.

Creveling, Cyrus J. "Experimental Use of a Programming Language (APL) at the Goddard Space Flight Center." Goddard Space Flight Center, November 1968.

Fiss, Andrew. "'For Computing Is Our Duty': Algorithmic Workers, Servants, and Women at the Harvard Observatory." In *Algorithmic Modernity: Mechanizing Thought and Action, 1500–2000*, edited by Morgan G. Ames and Massimo Mazzotti. Oxford University Press, 2023.

Goldin, Claudia Dale. *Understanding the Gender Gap: An Economic History of American Women*. Oxford University Press, 1990.

Grier, David Alan. *When Computers Were Human*. Princeton University Press, 2005.

Guerra, Cristela. "'Women Computers' Often Couldn't Use Harvard's Telescope. They Changed Astronomy Anyway." *Boston Globe*, August 10, 2017.

Haigh, Thomas. "Computing the American Way: Contextualizing the Early Us Computer Industry." *IEEE Annals of the History of Computing* 32, no. 2 (April 2010): 8–20.

Haigh, Thomas. "The Chromium-Plated Tabulator: Institutionalizing an Electronic Revolution, 1954–1958." *IEEE Annals of the History of Computing* 23, no. 4 (October 2001): 75–104.

Haigh, Thomas and Mark Priestley. "Innovators Assemble: Ada Lovelace, Walter Isaacson, and the Superheroines of Computing." *Communications of the ACM* 58, no. 9 (August 24, 2015): 20–7.

Haigh, Thomas and Paul E. Ceruzzi. *A New History of Modern Computing*. MIT Press, 2021.

Haigh, Thomas, Mark Priestley, and Crispin Rope. *ENIAC in Action: Making and Remaking the Modern Computer*. MIT Press, 2016.

Hicks, Mar. *Programmed Inequality: How Britain Discarded Women Technologists and Lost Its Edge in Computing*. MIT Press, 2017.

Hoover, Rachel. "Moon Mountain Name Honors NASA Mathematician Melba Mouton." *NASA* (blog), Last accessed February 15, 2023. https://www.nasa.gov/people-of-nasa/moon-mountain-name-honors-nasa-mathematician-melba-mouton/.

Johnson, Katherine G. *Reaching for the Moon: The Autobiography of NASA Mathematician Katherine Johnson*. Simon & Schuster, 2019.

Jones, Bessie Zaban and Lyle Gifford Boyd. *The Harvard College Observatory: The First Four Directorships, 1839–1919*. Harvard University Press, 1971.

Keene, Jennifer D. "Wilson and Race Relations." In *A Companion to Woodrow Wilson*, edited by Ross A. Kennedy. Wiley-Blackwell, 2013.

Launius, Roger D. *NACA to NASA to Now: The Frontiers of Air and Space in the American Century*. NASA, 2022.

Lawrimore, Erin. "Virginia Tucker (Class of 1930)." *Encyclopedia of UNCG History*. Last accessed August 3, 2024. https://encyclopedia.uncg.edu/virginia-tucker/.

McLennan, Sarah and Mary Gainer. "When the Computer Wore a Skirt: Langley's Computers, 1935–1970." *NASA History Program Office News & Notes* 29, no. 1 (2012): 25–32.

Melfi, Theodore, director. *Hidden Figures*. 20th Century Fox, 2016.

NASA on the Commons. "Melba Roy—Female Computer." *Flickr* (blog), Last accessed January 1, 1964. https://www.flickr.com/photos/nasacommons/9467783474/.

ncecire. "Melba Roy Mouton." *Tumblr* (blog), Last accessed March 10, 2013. https://ncecire.tumblr.com/post/45081525352/melba-roy-mouton.

Nelsen, R. Arvid. "Race and Computing: The Problem of Sources, the Potential of Prosopography, and the Lesson of *Ebony* Magazine." *IEEE Annals of the History of Computing* 39, no. 1 (2017): 29–51.

Nelson, Sue. "The Harvard Computers." *Nature* 455, no. 7209 (September 2008): 36–7.

Shetterly, Margot Lee. *Hidden Figures: The American Dream and the Untold Story of the Black Women Mathematicians Who Helped Win the Space Race*. William Morrow, 2016.

vintageblackglamour. "Vintage Black Glamour by Nichelle Gainer." *Tumblr* (blog). Last accessed February 13, 2025. https://vintageblackglamour.tumblr.com/post/43006851970/melba-roy-nasa-mathmetician-at-the-goddard-space.

Washington Post. "William Davies, Retired U.S. Geological Official, Dies." June 29, 1990.

Welther, Barbara L. "Pickering's Harem." *Isis* 73, no. 1 (March 1982): 94.

Chapter 10: Tear Down, Rise Up

98 Acres in Albany. "Our Name Means Shoemaker." *98 Acres in Albany* (blog), November 30, 2015. Last accessed May 12, 2024, https://98acresinalbany.wordpress.com/2015/11/30/our-name-means-shoemaker/.

Albany Riverfront Collaborative. "Together We Can – I-787 Study Opens New Paths to Reconnection." Last accessed 12 Nov 2024, https://www.albanyriverfrontcollaborative.com/together-we-can.

City of Mechanicville Archives. Mechanicville Urban Renewal Agency Records, Mechanicville, NY.

Eno, David. "Washington Park Area Fights to Retain 'Fashionable' Quality." *Albany Times Union*, June 22, 1968.

Fried, Marc. "Grieving for a Lost Home: Psychological Costs of Relocation." In *Urban Renewal: The Record and the Controversy*, edited by James Q. Wilson. MIT Press, 1966.

Fullilove, Mindy. *Root Shock: How Tearing Up City Neighborhoods Hurts America, and What We Can Do about It*. One World, 2004.

Hartman, Chester W. "The Housing of Relocated Families." *Journal of the American Institute of Planners* 30, no. 4 (1964): 266–86.

Jette, Aaron. "Accounting for Federal Highway Displacement from 1956 to 1976," unpublished paper. US Department of Transportation Volpe Center, 2021.

Kennedy, Bill. "Shameful Slums of Albany – A Study in Human Misery." *Albany Times Union*, August 1, 1965.

Legislative History, Public Law 91–646, S. 1, 1971.

Malley, Chuck. "Group Seeks Crosstown Arterial Veto." *Albany Times Union*, June 21, 1968.

Malley, Chuck. "Mid-Crosstown Arterial Hit by Residents." *Albany Times Union*, March 9, 1968.

Malley, Chuck. "Washington Park Urges Arterial Elimination." *Albany Times Union*, March 6, 1968.

New York Department of City Planning. "Transcript of Public Hearing before the City Planning Commission in the Matter of the Lincoln Square Urban Renewal Plan and Project." September 11, 1957.

New York State Archives. Empire State Plaza Construction Progress Photographs and Department of Transportation Commissioner's Correspondence and Subject Files.

Pfau, Ann, Kathleen Lawlor, David Hochfelder, and Stacy Kinlock Sewell. "Using Urban Renewal Records to Advance Reparative Justice." *RSF: The Russell Sage Journal of the Social Sciences* 10, no. 3 (June 2024): 113–31.

Pfau, Ann, David Hochfelder, and Stacy Sewell. "How the Albany Residential Security Map was Created." In Robert K. Nelson, LaDale Winling, et al., "Mapping Inequality: Redlining in New Deal America." *American Panorama: An Atlas of United States History*. Edited by Robert K. Nelson and Edward L. Ayers. 2023. Last accessed November 8, 2024, https://dsl.richmond.edu/panorama/redlining/map/NY/Albany/context.

Report of the National Advisory Commission on Civil Disorders. US Government Printing Office, 1968.

Rockefeller, Nelson. Speech, June 21, 1965. New York State Temporary Commission on the Capital City, New York State Archives.

Rose, Mark H. and Raymond A. Mohl. *Interstate: Highway Politics and Policy since 1939*. University of Tennessee Press, 2012.

Sam Dubois Cook Center on Social Equity. "The Plunder of Black Wealth in Chicago: New Findings on the Toll of Predatory Housing Contracts." Duke University, 2019.

US Commission on Urban Problems. *Building the American City: Report of the National Commission on Urban Problems to the Congress and the President of the United States*. Government Printing Office, 1968.

US Congress. House. Committee on Public Works. "Study of Compensation and Assistance for Persons Affected by Real Property Acquisition in Federal and Federally Assisted Programs." 88th Cong., 2nd sess. Committee Print No. 31, December 22, 1965.

US Congress. Senate. Committee on Public Works. "Urban Highways: Hearings before the Subcommittee on Roads." 90th Cong., 1st sess. Government Printing Office, 1968.

US Department of Housing and Urban Development. *Statistical Yearbook*. Government Printing Office, 1972.

Wales, Mike. "Van Dyke Says Brothers Dedicated to Peace." *Albany Times Union*, July 28, 1967.

Chapter 11: They Don't Own Us

Dotter, Earl. Interview (unpublished). By Grace Elizabeth Hale. March 2, 2023.

Eldridge, Betty. Interview. By Sally Ward Maggard. Nunn Center for Oral History, University of Kentucky Libraries. July 23, 1986.

Nolan, Irene. "The Brookside Women." *Louisville Courier-Journal and Times,* September 1, 1974.

Rainey, Nannie. Interview. By Sally Ward Maggard. Nunn Center for Oral History, University of Kentucky Libraries. September 23, 1986.

Terkel, Studs. "The New Left: A Trucker Speaks Out." *New York Times*, December 28, 1973.

Widner, Mary. Interview. By Sally Ward Maggard. Nunn Center for Oral History, University of Kentucky Libraries. October 9, 1986.

"Women and Collective Protest Oral History Project." Louie B. Nunn Center for Oral History, University of Kentucky Libraries.

Chapter 12: "Very Strong Women You Don't Mess With"

Anonymous. "SNCC Position Paper, November 1964." *Civil Rights Movement Archive.* Duke University Archives. Last accessed December 22, 2024, https://www.crmvet.org/docs/snccfem.htm.

Berkeley Barb. "Herrick Injury Reports." May 23–29, 1969.

Berkeley Barb. "Medic amidst Madness." May 23–29, 1969.

Berkeley Daily Gazette. "Students Accuse State Worker." September 20, 1969.

Berkeley Daily Gazette. "UC Cripples Score Cut of Monies." September 20, 1969.

Cash, Jon David. "People's Park: Birth and Survival." *California History* 88, no. 1 (2010): 8–55.

Catalyst. *Historical List of Women CEOs of the Fortune Lists: 1972-2023.* June 22, 2023. Last accessed August 7, 2025, https://www.catalyst.org/insights/2023/historical-list-of-women-ceos-of-the-fortune-lists-1972-2023/.

Cohen, Robert. *Freedom's Orator: Mario Savio and the Radical Legacy of the 1960s.* Oxford University Press, 2009.

Cone, Kitty. Interview. By David Landes. Disability Rights and Independent Living Movement Oral History Series. Bancroft Library, University of California, Berkeley, 1998.

Cone, Kitty. Interview. Paul K. Longmore Institute on Disability Collection, San Francisco State University, 2014.

Cone, Kitty. "Patient No More: Kitty Cone's Victory Speech." Paul K. Longmore Institute on Disability YouTube Channel. Last accessed December 22, 2024, https://youtu.be/HQ3kcSgAX-w?si=7–1iL61ZSUBsvAS.

Crenshaw, Kimberle. "Demarginalizing the Intersection of Race and Sex: A Black Feminist Critique of Antidiscrimination Doctrine, Feminist Theory and Antiracist Policies." *University of Chicago Legal Forum* 1, no. 8 (1989): 139–67.

Daily Ledger. "They Fought Disabilities and Won." May 2, 1982.

Danforth, Scot. "Becoming the Rolling Quads: Disability Politics at the University of California, Berkeley, in the 1960s." *History of Education Quarterly* 58, no. 4 (2018): 506–36.

Davis, Flora. *Moving the Mountain: The Women's Movement in America since 1960*. Simon and Schuster, 1991.

D'Lil, HolLynn. *Becoming Real in 24 Days: One Participant's Story of the 1977 Section 504 Demonstration for Disability Rights*. Hallevaland Productions, 2015.

Donald, James. Interview. By Cathy Cowan. Disability Rights Independent Living Movement Oral History Series. Bancroft Library, University of California, Berkeley, 1998.

Draper, Hal. *Berkeley: The New Student Revolt*. Grove Press, 1965.

Faderman, Lillian. *The Gay Revolution: The Story of Struggle*. Simon and Schuster, 2015.

Heumann, Judith, with Kristen Joiner. *Being Heumann: An Unrepentant Memoir of a Disability Rights Activist*. Beacon Press, 2020.

"History of Women in the US Congress." Center for American Women and Politics. Last accessed December 22, 2024, https://cawp.rutgers.edu/facts/levels-office/congress/history-women-us-congress.

Lembke, Darle E. "Oakland War Protest Quelled." *Los Angeles Times*, October 18, 1967.

Lembke, Darle E. "Third Day of Oakland Antiwar Protests Results in 91 Arrests." *Los Angeles Times*, October 19, 1967.

Lester, Mary. Interview. By Susan O'Hara. Disability Rights Independent Living Movement Oral History Series. Bancroft Library, University of California, Berkeley, 1998.

Los Angeles Times. "Newsmen Groups Protest Oakland Police Tactics." October 18, 1967.

MacPherson, Myra. "Newly Militant Disabled Waging War on Discrimination." *Washington Post*, May 9, 1977.

Margolis, Jon. "Protest for Guaranteed Rights Isn't Handicapped by Disabilities." *Chicago Tribune*, April 10, 1977.

Newton, Jim. *Man of Tomorrow: The Relentless Life of Jerry Brown*. Little, Brown, 2020.

Oka, Bruce. Interview. Paul K. Longmore Institute on Disability Collection, San Francisco State University, 2014.

O'Toole, Corbett. Interview. By Denise Jacobsen. Disability Rights Independent Living Movement Oral History Series. Bancroft Library, University of California, Berkeley, 1998.

O'Toole, Corbett. Interview. By Scot Danforth. May 15, 2019.

Parker, Ally Karen. Interview. Paul K. Longmore Institute on Disability Collection, San Francisco State University, 2014.

Pfaff, Timothy. "A Conversation with Ed Roberts: California Q & A." *California Monthly*, February 1985.

Rorabaugh, W.J. *Berkeley at War: The 1960s*. Oxford University Press, 1990.

Rosen, Ruth. *The World Split Open: How the Modern Women's Movement Changed America*. Penguin, 2000.

Ryan, Barbara. *Feminism and the Women's Movement: Dynamics of Change in Social Movement Ideology and Activism*. Routledge, 1992.

Sommer, Robert and Robert L. Thayer. "The Radicalization of Common Ground People's Park, Berkeley: An Unnatural History." *Landscape Architecture Magazine* 67, no. 5 (November 1977): 510–4.

Uzeta, Ray and Connie (Soucy) Uzeta. Interview. Paul K. Longmore Institute on Disability Collection, San Francisco State University, 2014.

Washington, Ron. Interview. Paul K. Longmore Institute on Disability Collection, San Francisco State University, 2014.

Whitaker, Joseph D. "Handicapped Protest Turned Away at HEW." *Washington Post*, April 23, 1977.

White, Evan. Interview. Paul K. Longmore Institute on Disability Collection, San Francisco State University, 2014.

Chapter 13: *Documerica*: Picturing Pollution in the 1970s

Arnold, Taylor and Lauren Tilton. "Digital Documerica: Exploring Environmental Photography from the 1970s." 2025. Last accessed http://www.digitaldocumerica.org.

Barnes, A. James, John D. Graham, and David M. Konisky, eds. *Fifty Years at the US Environmental Protection Agency: Progress, Retrenchment, and Opportunities*. Rowman & Littlefield, 2021.

Business Week. "Ammonia's New World: More Plant, Less Crew." November 13, 1965.

Business Week. "Lake Charles' Deep-Water Port … Keeps Warbuilt Plants Humming." June 12, 1948.

Clare Kelsey, "Life in Mossville, Louisiana: Policy Implications of Toxic Waste Exposure and Environmental Racism" (MS thesis, Rochester Institution of Technology, 2022), 23.

Colten, Craig E. "Mississippi River." In *History in Dispute, Volume 7: Water and the Environment since 1945*, edited by Char Mille, Mark Cioc, and Kate Showers. St. James Press, 2001.

Corrado, Frank. Interview (unpublished). By Mia Lazar. May 2023.

DeLaune, Jonathan Zachary. "Unwelcome Neighbors? Industrial Growth and Water Pollution in Lake Charles, Louisiana, 1940–1960." MA thesis, Louisiana State University, 2007.

Dunway, Finis. *Seeing Green: The Use and Abuse of Environmental Images*. University of Chicago Press, 2015.

Estabrook, Thomas. *Labor-Environmental Coalitions: Lessons from a Louisiana Petrochemical Region*. Baywood Publishing, 2007.

Fortune. "Port of Lake Charles." August 1, 1970.

Frankland, Peggy, with Susan Tucker. *Women Pioneers of the Louisiana Environmental Movement*. University Press of Mississippi, 2013.

Hampshire, Gifford Dean. *My American Heritage: A Genealogy*. Fairfax, 1997.

Jeannine Cahill-Jackson, "Mossville Environmental Action Now v. United States: Is a Solution to Environmental Injustice Unfolding?," *3 Pace Int'l L. Rev. Online Companion* 173 (2012).

Johnson, Rebecca O. "A Lot Like War: Petrocapitalism, 'Slow Violence,' and the Struggle for Environmental Justice." *Social Justice* 46, no. 1 (2020): 105–18.

Johnson, Timothy. "Nitrogen Nation: The Legacy of World War I and the Politics of Chemical Agriculture in the United States 1916–1933." *Agricultural History* 90, no. 2 (Spring 2016): 209–29.

Kline, Benjamin. *First along the River: A Brief History of the U.S. Environmental Movement*, 2nd Edition. Acada Books, 2000.

"Louisiana Rankings." *US News and World Report*. 2024. Last accessed https://www.usnews.com/news/best-states/louisiana.

Olson, James S., with Shannon L. Kenny. *The Industrial Revolution: Key Themes and Documents*. Bloomsbury Press, 2015.

Records of the United States Environmental Protection Agency. Documerica: Photographers' Correspondence and Assignment Folders. RG 412-P. National Archives and Records Administration, College Park, Maryland.

Rothstein, Richard. *The Color of Law: A Forgotten History of How Our Government Segregated America*. Liveright, 2017.

Smith-Howard, Kendra. "Absorbing Waste, Displacing Labor: Family, Environment, and the Disposable Diaper in the 1970s." *Environmental History* 26, no. 2 (April 2021): 207–30.

Stanfield, Frank E. "Project Documerica in the Southeast: The Use of Documentary Photography by the Environmental Protection Agency to Publicize Environmental Problems in the 1970s." MA thesis, The University of Georgia, 1980.

Travel Magazine. "Good-Time Charlie's Lake." August 1, 1971.

US Department of Justice. "CITGO Petroleum Corp. Will Pay over $19 Million for Injuries to Natural Resources Resulting from Its Oil Spill at Its Refinery in Lake Charles, Louisiana." Press Release, June 17, 2021. Last accessed March 12, 2025, https://www.justice.gov/archives/opa/pr/citgo-petroleum-corp-will-pay-over-19-million-injuries-natural-resources-resulting-its-oil.

US News and World Report. "Louisiana Rankings." 2024. Last accessed March 12, 2025, https://www.usnews.com/news/best-states/louisiana.

Wellum, Caleb. "The Ambivalent Aesthetics of Oil: Project Documerica and the Energy Crisis in 1970s America." *Environmental History* 22, no. 4 (October 2017): 723–32.

Chapter 14: The *Enola Gay* and the Culture Wars

Alperovitz, Gar. *Atomic Diplomacy: Hiroshima and Potsdam. The Use of the Atomic Bomb and the American Confrontation with Soviet Power*. Simon & Schuster, 1965.

AP Archive. "USA: Washington: Enola Gay Exhibition Causes Protests." June 28, 1995. Last accessed January 29, 2025, https://www.youtube.com/watch?v=ls1NC6qKQQY&t=2s.

Barnes, Harry Elmer. "Hiroshima: Assault on a Beaten Foe." *National Review* (May 1958): 441–3.

Barson, Michael and Steven Heller. *Red Scared! The Commie Menace in Propaganda and Popular Culture*. Chronicle Books, 2001.

BBC News. "Enola Gay Display Angers Victims." December 16, 2003.

Biden, Jr., Joseph R. "Remarks by President-Elect Joe Biden on the Electoral College Vote Certification." December 14, 2020. Wilmington, DE.

Blumenthal, Les. "20 Arrests at Smithsonian Protest." *The Press Democrat*, June 29, 1995.

"Boeing B-29 Superfortress *Enola Gay.*" National Air and Space Museum, Smithsonian Institution. Last accessed June 9, 2025, https://airandspace.si.edu/collection-objects/boeing-b-29-superfortress-enola-gay/nasm_A19500100000.

Boghosian, Joyce Naltchayan. Interview (unpublished). By Rebecca S. Wingo. May 21, 2025.

Bordner, Autumn S., Danielle A. Crosswell, Ainsley O. Katz, Jill T. Shah, Catherine R. Zhang, Ivana Nikolic-Hughes, Emlyn W. Hughes, and Malvin A. Ruderman. "Measurement of Background Gamma Radiation in the Northern Marshall Islands." *Proceedings of the National Academy of Sciences* 113, no. 25 (June 2016): 6833–8.

Buchanan, Patrick J. "Address to the Republican National Convention." August 17, 1992. Houston, TX.

Copp, Tara, Lolita C. Baldor, and Kevin Vineys. "War Heroes and Military Firsts Are among 26,000 Images Flagged for Removal in Pentagon's DEI Purge." *AP News*, March 6, 2025. Last accessed March 13, 2025, https://apnews.com/article/dei-purge-images-pentagon-diversity-women-black-8efcfaec909954f4a24bad0d49c78074.

Correll, John T. "Air Force Association Special Report: The Smithsonian and the *Enola Gay.*" *Air Force Magazine*, March 15, 1994.

Correll, John T. "The Activists and the *Enola Gay.*" *Air Force Magazine*, September 1995.

de Witt, Karen. "Smithsonian Scales Back Exhibit of B-29 in Atomic Bomb Attack." *New York Times*, January 31, 1995.

Dias, Elizabeth. "Biden and Trump Say They're Fighting for America's 'Soul.' What Does That Mean?" *New York Times*, October 17, 2020.

Du Mez, Kristin Kobes. *Jesus and John Wayne: How White Evangelicals Corrupted a Faith and Fractured a Nation*. Liveright, 2020.

Harwit, Martin. *An Exhibit Denied: Lobbying the History of the* Enola Gay. Copernicus, 1996.

Herken, Gregg. "The Smithsonian's Decision to Exhibit the 'Enola Gay'." *Public History Weekly* 10, no. 7 (2022).

Hunter, James Davidson. *Culture Wars: The Struggle to Define America*. Basic Books,1991.

Kingsbury, Kathleen, W.J. Hennigan, and Spencer Cohen. "The Last Survivors Speak. It's Time to Listen." *New York Times*, August 6, 2024.

Land, Charles E., Andre Bouville, Iulian Apostoaei, and Steven L. Simon. "Projected Lifetime Cancer Risks from Exposure to Regional Radioactive Fallout in the Marshall Islands." *Health Physics* 99, no. 2 (August 2010): 201–15.

Leahy, William D. *I Was There: The Personal Story of the Chief of Staff to Presidents Roosevelt and Truman, Based on His Notes and Diaries Made at the Time*. Whittlesey House, 1950.

Linenthal, Edward T. "Anatomy of a Controversy." In *History Wars: The* Enola Gay *and Other Battles for the American Past*, edited by Edward T. Linenthal and Tom Engelhardt. Henry Holt, 1996.

Linenthal, Edward T. and Tom Engelhardt, eds. *History Wars: The Enola Gay and Other Battles for the American Past*. Henry Holt, 1996.

Livingston, Steven and W. Lance Bennett, eds. *The Disinformation Age: Politics, Technology, and Disruptive Communication in the United States*. Cambridge University Press, 2021.

Mohan, Uday and Sanho Tree. "Hiroshima, the American Media, and the Construction of Conventional Wisdom." *The Journal of American-East Asian Relations* 4, no. 2 (1995): 141–60.

Morley, Felix Muskett. "The Return to Nothingness." *Human Events*, August 29, 1945.

Nafeesa, Seyed Ismail. "Japanese Atomic Bomb Survivor Warns Nuclear Taboo Is at Risk in Nobel Peace Prize Speech." *NBC News*, December 11, 2024. Last accessed December 30, 2024, https://www.nbcnews.com/news/world/japanese-atomic-bomb-survivor-nobel-peace-prize-speech.

Narayanan, Vasudha. "Oppenheimer Often Used Sanskrit Verses." *The Conversation*, August 16, 2023. Last accessed February 4, 2025, https://theconversation.com/oppenheimer-often-used-sanskrit-verses-and-the-bhagavad-gita-was-special-for-him-but-not-in-the-way-christopher-nolans-film-depicts-it-211253.

Newsweek. "Ike on Ike." November 11, 1963.

Overy, Richard. *Why the Allies Won*. W.W. Norton, 1995.

Parker, Lonnae O'Neal. "*Enola Gay* Exhibit opens to Protest." *Washington Post*, June 28, 1995.

Reid, T.R. "*Enola Gay* Exhibit Angers Japan." *The Press Democrat*, June 29, 1995.

S.Res. 257 - 103rd Congress (1993–1994). "A Resolution to Express the Sense of the Senate Regarding the Appropriate Portrayal of Men and Women of the Armed Forces in the Upcoming National Air and Space Museum's Exhibit on the *Enola Gay*." September 23, 1994.

Storrs, Landon R.Y. *The Second Red Scare and the Unmaking of the New Deal Left*. Princeton University Press, 2013.

Tampa Bay Times. "Trio Douses 'Enola Gay' with Blood, Ashes." July 3, 1995.

Walker, J. Samuel. "The Decision to Use the Bomb: A Historiographical Update." *Diplomatic History* 14, no. 1 (Winter 1990): 97–114.

Wellerstein, Alex. "Counting the Dead at Hiroshima and Nagasaki." *The Bulletin of the Atomic Scientists*, August 4, 2020.

White House. Executive Order. "Restoring Truth and Sanity to American History." March 27, 2025.

Wolfson, Richard and Ferenc Dalnoki-Veress. *Nuclear Choices for the Twenty-First Century: A Citizen's Guide*. MIT Press, 2021.

Wright, Jennifer. "Exhibiting the *Enola Gay*." Smithsonian Institution Archives, June 25, 2020. Last accessed January 30, 2025, https://siarchives.si.edu/blog/exhibiting-enola-gay.

Yelson, Rich. "What New Left History Gave Us." *Democracy* 35 (Winter 2015): 24–40.

Chapter 15: Selfie as Self-Love

ACLU. "Mapping Attacks on LGBTQ Rights in U.S. State Legislatures in 2024."
    Last accessed December 22, 2024, https://www.aclu.org/legislative-attacks-
    on-lgbtq-rights-2024.

Amore, Sorelle. *Take Your Selfie Seriously: The Advanced Selfie and Self-Portrait
    Handbook*. Laurence King Publishing, 2021.

Bal, Mieke. "Visual Essentialism and the Object of Visual Culture." *Journal of
    Visual Culture* 2, no. 1 (2003): 5–32.

Barthes, Roland. *Camera Lucida: Reflections on Photography*. Hill and Wang,
    2010.

BBC. "BBC World Service—World Update, Lighting Dark Skin for Screen."
    November 30, 2017. Last accessed March 3, 2025, https://www.bbc.co.uk/
    programmes/p05pmwjn.

Bhabha, Homi K. *The Location of Culture*. Routledge, 1991.

Bright, Susan. *Art Photography Now*. Thames & Hudson, 2011.

Brilliant, Richard. *Portraiture*. Reaktion Books, 1991.

Campany, David, ed. *Art and Photography*. Phaidon Press, 2012.

Cotton, Charlotte. *The Photograph as Contemporary Art*. Thames & Hudson,
    2020.

Dean, Carolyn. "The Trouble with (the Term) Art." *Art Journal* 65, no. 2 (June
    2006): 24–33.

Eler, Alicia. *The Selfie Generation: Exploring Our Notions of Privacy, Sex,
    Consent, and Culture*. Skyhorse Publishing, 2019.

FASHION Magazine (blog). "Here's How the Woman behind the Camera on
    Insecure Properly Lights Its Black Actors." June 16, 2020. Last accessed
    December 23, 2024, https://fashionmagazine.com/flare/insecure-lighting/.

Harding, Xavier. "Keeping 'Insecure' Lit: HBO Cinematographer Ava Berkofsky
    on Properly Lighting Black Faces." *Mic*, September 6, 2017. Last accessed
    March 3, 2025, https://www.mic.com/articles/184244/keeping-insecure-lit-hbo-
    cinematographer-ava-berkofsky-on-properly-lighting-black-faces.

Inquire Publication (blog). "'Black Boys Look Blue under Moonlight': The
    Importance of Humanizing Dark Skins in Cinema." March 30, 2017. Last
    accessed March 3, 2025, https://inquirepublication.com/black-boys-look-blue-
    under-moonlight-the-importance-of-humanizing-dark-skins-in-cinema/.

Jones, Amelia. "Ethnic Envy and Other Aggressions in the Contemporary 'Global'
    Art Complex." *Journal of Contemporary African Art* 48 (2023): 96–110.

Jones, Amelia. *Seeing Differently: A History and Theory of Identity and the Visual
    Arts*. Routledge, 2012.

Jones, Amelia. *Self Image: Technology, Representation, and the Contemporary
    Subject*. Routledge, 2006.

Jones, Amelia. "Who Is an Artist? Identity, Individualism, and the Neoliberalism
    of the Art Complex." *Arts* 12, no. 6 (2023): 234.

Kasperson, Katie. "Illuminating Diversity." *Definition Magazine*, November 3,
    2023.

Krawec, Patty and Nick Estes. *Becoming Kin: An Indigenous Call to Unforgetting
    the Past and Reimagining Our Future*. Broadleaf Books, 2022.

Latif, Nadia. "It's Lit! How Film Finally Learned to Light Black Skin." *The Guardian*, September 21, 2017. Last accessed March 3, 2024, https://www.theguardian.com/film/2017/sep/21/its-lit-how-film-finally-learned-how-to-light-black-skin.

Lehner, Ace, ed. *Self-Representation in an Expanded Field: From Self-Portraiture to Selfie, Contemporary Art in the Social Media Age*. MDPI, 2021.

MacLeod, Adam J. *The Age of Selfies: Reasoning about Rights When the Stakes Are Personal*. Rowman & Littlefield, 2020.

Merriam-Webster.com Dictionary. Last accessed March 3, 2025, https://www.merriam-webster.com.

Murray, Derek Conrad, ed. *Visual Culture Approaches to the Selfie*. Routledge, 2022.

O'Falt, Chris. "Moonlight Cinematography: Bold Color, Rich Skin Tone, High Contrast." *IndieWire*, October 26, 2026. Last accessed March 3, 2025, https://www.indiewire.com/awards/industry/moonlight-cinematography-color-barry-jenkins-james-laxton-alex-bickel-1201740402/.

Oxford Online Dictionaries. Last accessed March 3, 2025, https://www.lexico.com.

Park, Coyote. "About." Last accessed March 3, 2025, https://coyotepark.format.com/about.

Sealy, Mark. *Decolonising the Camera: Photography in Racial Time*. Lawrence & Wishart, 2019.

Sekula, Allan. "The Body and the Archive." *October* 39 (Winter 1986): 3–64.

Smith, Shawn Michelle. *At the Edge of Sight: Photography and the Unseen*. Duke University Press, 2013.

Solomon-Godeau, Abigail. *Photography at the Dock: Essay on Photographic History, Institution, and Practices*. University of Minnesota Press, 1991.

Sontag, Susan. *On Photography*. Picador, 2001.

Storr, Will. *Selfie: How We Became so Self-Obsessed and What It's Doing to Us*. Abrams Press, 2019.

Sturken, Marita and Lisa Cartwright. *Practices of Looking: An Introduction to Visual Culture*. Oxford University Press, 2001.

Tiidenberg, Katrin. *Selfies: Why We Love (and Hate) Them*. Emerald Publishing, 2018.

TRNK. "Coyote Park." Last accessed May 15, 2024, https://trnk-nyc.com/collections/coyote-park.

Weheliye, Alexander G. *Habeas Viscus: Racializing Assemblages, Biopolitics, and Black Feminist Theories of the Human*. Duke University Press, 2014.

Index

abolition 36–7, 39, 65
advertising 21, 51, 80–1, 83, 86–8,
    90–1, 228–9, 263–4
African Americans 3, 7, 9, 11, 32–42, 52,
    63–73, 103, 106, 135, 139–42,
    148, 160–7, 170–4, 179–90, 202,
    208, 210–11, 215–16, 223, 232–3,
    249, 257, 261
    activism 9, 33–7, 40–2, 65–6, 72–3,
        106, 141–2, 161, 164–7, 170–4,
        180–90, 208, 210–11, 215–16,
        223, 232–3, 257, 261
    photographers 3, 9–10
agrarian vision 66–7, 73
agribusiness 11, 136, 147–9, 155–7
agriculture 57, 63–73, 99, 135–41,
    147–57, 224–5, 227–8
agrochemicals 146–9, 151–3, 155–6,
    223–5, 227–8, 230–1 (*see also*
    DDT)
Air Force Association (AFA) 243–6
amateur photography 4–5, 8–9, 34,
    36, 79–85, 89–90
American Coalition for Citizens with
    Disabilities (ACCD) 208–9,
    214–17
American expansion 11, 20, 27–8,
    49–58, 63, 66, 117–18
anthropology 7, 97, 106–7
Appalachia 11, 195–204
archives 13, 19–21, 86, 106–7, 122–4,
    151, 162, 171–2, 181, 208–9,
    213
art
    aesthetics and beauty 8, 80–2,
        84–6, 101, 133–4, 139–41,
        256–64
    art history 8–9, 81–7, 91, 106–7,
        133–5, 255–8, 259–64

as western canon 255–6, 259–64
Asians and Asian Americans 28–9,
    112–24, 131, 135, 141–2,
    143 n.4, 155, 211, 237–46, 248,
    254–66
assimilation policy 97–104, 107
atomic weapons, *see* nuclear
    warfare

Baldwin, Marie Bottineau (Turtle
    Mountain Chippewa) 7, 11,
    96–9, 101–8, 110–11
Barthes, Roland 6, 8, 10
Biden, Joseph R. 108, 249
Black Panthers 9, 174, 208, 215
boarding schools 57–8, 97–100
Bockscar 237, 251 n.19
Boghosian, Joyce Naltchayan 236,
    247–8
Bonnin, Gertrude, *see* Zitkala-Ša
    (Yankton Dakota)
Boomers, *see* Sooners
boosterism 11, 39–40, 117, 227–9
bracero program 11, 146–59
    DDT 146–9, 151–3
Brady, Mathew 7–8, 26
Bureau of American Ethnology 106–8
Bureau of Indian Affairs (BIA), *see*
    Office of Indian Affairs (OIA)
Bush, George H.W. 247, 249
Butcher, Solomon 62–4, 68, 70–2,
    74 n.1

Califano, Joseph A. 208–10, 214–17
calling cards, *see cartes de visite*
camera clubs 8, 57, 81–2, 86
cameras 1–6, 9, 12–13, 24, 50, 78–84,
    118, 134, 223–4, 247, 260–1,
    263–4

capitalism 4, 11, 27–8, 69, 75–6 n.16,
79, 84–7, 149, 154–7, 162, 183–4,
187–9, 224, 227–9
captions 21–2, 27, 53–4, 88, 101, 119,
122, 124, 134–5, 138–9, 144 n.18,
162, 172, 202, 229–30, 264–5
Carson, Rachel, *see Silent Spring*
cartes de visite 51, 116, 119–21, 257
Carter, Jimmy 12, 207–10, 214–17, 231
Center for Independent Living (CIL)
211–15
Char, Yew 112–14, 121–4
Cherokee Outlet Land Rush 11,
48–54, 56–8
child labor reform 9, 132, 140–1
children 5, 140–1, 144 n.18, 200–3
Chinese and Chinese Americans 29,
119, 122
cinematography 4, 9, 261
citizenship 33, 35–7, 65–8, 72–3, 98–9,
101–3, 107, 116, 150, 154, 173,
190
City Beautiful movement 33–4, 39–42
(*see also* urbanism)
civil rights movements, *see* social
justice movements
Civil War (postbellum) 2, 7, 10–11, 26,
29, 34–40, 52, 64, 72–3, 98,
163–7
Clean Air Act (1970) 223–5, 227
Clean Water Act (1972) 223–4, 227,
231–2
coal, *see* mining
Cold War 11, 156, 161, 164, 166–9,
174, 181–2, 211, 237–43, 247
colonialism 56–9, 100–2, 111, 117–18,
121–2, 124, 255–6, 259–66 (*see
also* decolonialism)
communism 156, 161, 239–40 (*see
also* Soviet Union (USSR))
computers
electronic 160–4, 167–71, 174
human 11, 160–7, 170–2
computing 5, 11, 14, 160–77
Cone, Kitty 206–18
confederacy 2, 11, 32–42, 52, 65, 165
conservatism 38–9, 135, 173, 237,
239–41, 243–5, 248–50, 258
consumerism 38–9, 51, 79–81, 83–7
cortito (short handle hoe) 153–4

counterculture 12, 207, 210–14, 240–1
cropping, *see* photographic elements
culture wars 12, 176, 237–9, 243–50
Curtis, Edward S. 56, 60, 100–1

D'Lil, HolLynn 206, 208–9, 215–18
Daguerre, Louis 3, 5–6, 12, 260
daguerreotypes 3, 6, 12, 260
DDT (dichloro-diphenyl trichloroethane)
146–9, 151–3, 157, 224–5 (*see
also* agrochemicals)
decolonialism 255–6, 263–6 (*see also*
colonialism)
deportation 147, 149–50, 155–7
desegregation (*see* segregation)
diptychs 255, 258–60, 264–6
disability 7, 12, 134, 137, 199–200,
202, 206–18
disability rights movement 12,
207–18
documerica 9, 12, 222–32
Dotter, Earl 194, 196–8, 201–4
Du Bois, W.E.B. 39, 43 n.6
Duke Power 195, 199, 202–4
Dust Bowl 131, 137–8

East and West Shaking Hands 18–22,
24–9
Eastman, George (Kodak) 4, 88–9
Eastover Mining Company 195,
198–200, 202–3
Eickemeyer, Jr., Rudolph 80–6, 88
Eisenhower, Dwight D. 155, 167, 169,
240
Enola Gay 12, 236–50
Environmental Protection Agency
(EPA) 9, 12, 153, 223–7, 230–2,
242
environmental justice movement 12,
146, 149, 152–3, 223–33
environmentalism 131, 135–8, 147,
152–3, 195, 197, 199, 223–33
eurocentrism 98, 100, 116–17, 121,
259–66

families 28, 57–8, 62–7, 70–3, 99, 104,
115, 130–3, 139–41, 143 n.4,
150, 154, 201–3, 213
Farm Security Administration (FSA) 9,
58, 131–2, 135, 140, 225–7

fashion 80, 83–5, 87–8, 98, 107–8,
    207, 259, 263–4
femininity 81, 87–91, 101, 141, 258–9
feminism 87–91, 101–8, 113–18,
    121–4, 207, 210–15, 263
Fiorito, Eunice 206, 208–10, 214, 216,
    218
framing, *see* photographic elements
Free Speech Movement (FSM) 210–11
    (*see also* student activism)
Furlong, Harold 178–83, 189–90

Galarza, Ernesto 150–1, 154, 156
gender 11, 79, 81, 86–91, 99, 101,
    119–21, 124, 128 n.35, 162–4,
    170, 174, 200–4, 212–14, 256–66
General Allotment Act (1887) 97,
    99–100
Gibson Girls 81, 87–91 (*see also*
    Kodak Girls)
Gilded Age 69, 79–81, 84–7, 91
Golden Spike Ceremony 20–2, 24–9
    (*see also* railroads; *East and
    West Shaking Hands*)
Great Depression 9, 113–14, 123, 131–
    42, 149–50, 169, 184, 196, 226
Great Migration 63, 72–3, 179–89
Great Plains 27–8, 62–4, 66–73,
    100, 113–14, 123, 131, 135,
    137–8
group portraiture 11, 24, 113–15, 118–22

health and disease 64, 114, 150,
    152–3, 188–9, 199–200, 213–15,
    225, 229, 231–2, 238
Heumann, Judy 206, 208–10, 212–18
hibakusha 242–3, 248
Hidden Figures (film) 162–3, 166–7,
    173 (*see also* computers:
    human)
higher education 2, 10, 38, 83,
    90, 98, 102, 140, 163–4, 167–8,
    210–14
Hine, Lewis 6, 9, 132–3, 205 n.3
Hiroshima (Japan) 12, 237–40, 242–6
historical revisionism 33, 35–9, 237,
    240–1, 243–6, 249–50 (*see also*
    culture wars; Lost Cause)
homesteading 11, 52–4, 63–73, 75 n.13

IBM (company) 169–74
immigration 27–9, 52, 66, 69, 115–16,
    122–3, 135–7, 146–57, 226
Indian Removal Act (1830) 49, 52–3,
    59 n.4, 66, 69, 75–6 n.16
Indigenous peoples 7, 11, 28, 51–3,
    55–8, 66, 69, 75–6 n.16, 96–108,
    109 n.2, 113–14, 121, 124, 142,
    182, 254–7, 264–6
    activism 15, 27–8, 36, 49–53, 56–60,
        69, 75, 97–111, 121, 182, 264–6
    delegation portraits 57, 102–3, 106
    dispossession 11, 27, 52, 59, 69,
        76, 117, 125, 188
    regalia and clothing 40, 98, 100–1,
        103–8, 124, 162, 258–9
    reservations 49, 58, 98–100, 107
    sovereignty 28, 49–52, 54, 57,
        97–9, 102–3, 107–8, 265–6
industrialization 28, 40, 79–80, 84–6,
    100, 113, 148–50, 155–6, 169,
    199–201, 223–4, 227–33
internationalism 11, 113–24
intersectionality 97, 102–3, 121, 207,
    213–14, 255–6
interwar period 11, 113–16, 122–4
isolationism 113–16

Japanese and Japanese Americans
    113, 121, 123, 131, 135, 141,
    143 n.4, 155, 182, 237–46, 248
    internment 131, 141, 143 n.4
Jim Crowism 11, 33–40, 63, 73,
    161–2, 165–7
Johnston, Frances Benjamin 81,
    88–91

Kennedy, John F. 170, 173, 212
Kodak (cameras) 4, 6, 79–81, 84
Kodak (company) 4–5, 8, 12–13,
    79–83, 85–8, 90 (*see also*
    Eastman, George)
Kodak Girls 11, 78–81, 83–91 (*see
    also* Gibson Girls)

labor reform 9, 11–12, 15, 27–9, 35,
    63, 67–8, 85, 123–4, 135–7,
    139–41, 147–57, 161–3, 167–70,
    195–204, 228–30

Lancaster, Robert A. 32, 34–6, 38, 40–1
Lange, Dorothea 9, 11, 57–8, 130–42, 226
League of Nations 113, 116–17, 121
leisure 11, 80, 83–4, 86, 90–1, 151, 153–4, 224, 229–30
LGBTQIA+ rights 215–16, 256–60, 261–6 (*see also* trans rights)
liberalism 117–18, 167, 197, 205, 207, 210–14, 216, 237, 239–41, 243, 246–50
Lincoln, Abraham 7, 38, 65–6
Lost Cause 33, 35, 37–9, 41–2

manifest destiny, *see* American expansion
masculinity 36, 54, 87–8, 99, 101, 115, 148, 164–5, 170, 203, 208, 212–13, 258–9, 265–6
Mexicans and Mexican Americans 11, 30, 72, 109, 135–8, 143, 147–51, 154–9, 211, 227, 266
Migrant Mother 11, 58, 60, 130–2, 135, 142, 226
migrant workers 11, 122, 131–2, 135–41, 143 n.4, 146–57
mining 11, 85–6, 194–204
morality 161–2, 238–44, 248
motherhood 130, 132–3, 140–1, 165, 184, 212
Mouton, Melba Roy 11, 160–3, 167, 169, 171–4
museums 2, 50, 56, 86, 106, 121–2, 236–50

Nadel, Leonard 146–51, 153–4, 156–7
Nagasaki (Japan) 237–8, 240, 242–5, 248
National Aeronautics and Space Administration (NASA) 11, 160–74
National Air and Space Museum (NASM) 237–9, 241–8
National Organization for Women (NOW) 213
nationalism 11, 113, 116–17, 119, 123
Native Americans, *see* Indigenous peoples
negatives, *see* photographic negatives

neoliberalism 195–7
Nixon, Richard 173, 214, 225
nuclear warfare 12, 154, 167–9, 212, 237–48, 250, 253

Obama, Barack 7, 173
Office of Indian Affairs (OIA) 98–9, 102–6
Operation Wetback 147, 155
Organization of Petroleum Exporting Countries (OPEC) 223, 231

Pan-Pacific Women's Association (PPWA) 112–24
Park, Coyote 254–60, 264–6
Parks, Gordon 9, 205 n.3
petrochemicals 3, 223, 228, 230–1, 234–5
photo albums 51, 85–6, 116, 119–24, 128 n.35
photographic elements
    background 1, 7, 10, 23–5, 35, 41, 64, 141, 162, 202, 224, 229, 231–2, 258–9
    cropping 1–2, 9–10, 23, 104–5, 149, 258–9
    digital editing 1–2, 5, 9–10, 258–9
    exposure 3–4, 25, 50–1, 86, 103, 118
    framing 7, 23–5, 41, 54, 63–4, 80, 83–4, 87–9, 100–1, 105–7, 113–14, 118–19, 132–8, 141, 143 n.7, 144 n.18, 149, 161–2, 169, 180–1, 203–4, 208, 218, 224, 226, 229–30, 232–3, 246–8, 258–60, 264–5
    staging 7–8, 81–2, 105–7, 132–4, 141
photographic negatives 3–5, 8, 12, 24, 52, 72–3, 80–3, 86, 134, 180–1, 223, 260–1
photography, and ...
    bias 4–6, 9–10, 56–8, 133–4, 149, 244, 260–2
    circulation 5, 7–8, 10–11, 13, 83–7, 98, 104–5, 119–21, 124, 135, 149–51, 162, 169, 201–3, 215, 226, 256–7, 262–4
    colonialism 50–3, 100–2, 259–62

exclusion 13, 28–9, 35–6, 50–4,
57–8, 72, 121–2, 124, 135–7,
140–1, 150–1, 232–3, 256–7,
261–5
innovation 1–6, 9–10, 13, 24, 27,
50–2, 79–81, 82–6, 118–19, 134,
163, 196, 223–4, 259–61
reform 8–10, 65, 80, 90–1, 100–1,
104–6, 113–15, 117–18, 131–42,
148, 151–6, 205 n.3, 224–8,
231–2
stereotypes 97, 100–3, 135–41,
162–3, 174–5, 216, 256, 260–2
photography, history of 3–10, 81–7,
259–62
photojournalism 6–8, 49–51, 53–6,
104–5, 119–20, 181, 201–3,
205 n.3, 208–9, 215–16, 225–7,
247–8
pictorialism 8, 56, 81–2, 84–7, 133–4
Polaroid (company) 3, 5, 12
pollution 12, 84–5, 187, 198–9,
222–5, 227–34 (*see also*
environmentalism)
portraiture 3, 6–8, 11–12, 24–5, 51,
81, 85–6, 88–90, 96–7, 105–7,
113–16, 118–22, 132–41, 160,
171–3, 181, 254–66
Prettyman, William S. 48–58
Progressive Era 8–9, 40, 79, 87–8, 91,
97, 101–8, 113–15
propaganda 133, 147, 166, 240, 246

railroads 20–2, 24–9, 52–3, 55, 148
Reagan, Ronald 12, 196, 211, 237,
243
Reconstruction Era 2, 33–6, 39, 63,
65, 165
Rehabilitation Act (1973) 207–9, 211,
214 (*see also* disability rights
movement)
respectability politics 97, 103–9,
161–3
Riis, Jacob 8–9, 132–3
Rolling Quads 211–12 (*see also*
disability rights movement)
Roosevelt, Franklin D. 7, 132–4, 166,
239–40

root shock 188–9
Russell, Andrew J. 18–22, 24, 26–9

scrapbooks, *see* photo albums
secession 27, 35, 38–9
Second World War 11–12, 79–80, 114,
123, 135, 141, 143 n.4, 147–8,
152, 154, 156, 161, 164–9, 182,
189, 207, 212, 223, 226–8,
236–49
Section 504 sit-ins 206, 208–10,
211–17 (*see also* Rehabilitation
Act (1973))
segregation 11, 33–42, 161, 164–6,
170, 172–3, 179, 182–3, 185–6,
227, 232
selfies 7–8, 12, 254–60, 262–6
self-portraiture 51, 88–9, 256, 259–60
self-representation 3, 7–8, 10, 12, 57,
88–91, 97–8, 101–8, 113–14,
118–22, 255–9, 262–6
sharecropping 63, 65, 70, 131, 135,
139–41, 143–4
Silent Spring 152, 224–6
slavery 29, 33, 35–9, 52, 65–7, 71–3,
157, 162, 165
smartphones 1–3, 5, 12–13, 82, 171,
258, 263–4
social justice movements 9, 11–12,
33–7, 40–2, 65–6, 72–3, 97,
102–7, 113–18, 121–2, 133–5,
141–2, 147–51, 156–7, 161,
164–7, 170–4, 180–90, 195–204,
207–18, 223–33, 240, 255–9,
261–6
social media 1, 7–13, 80, 162, 255–9,
262–6
Sooners 49–53
Soviet Union (USSR) 161, 166–7, 170,
237–9, 247, 250
St. Gil, Marc 222–33
Stieglitz, Alfred 8, 82–3
student activism 102–4, 196, 210–14
Student Nonviolent Coordinating
Committee (SNCC) 210, 212
studio photography 3–4, 7–8, 51, 55,
70, 105–6, 122–3, 132–4, 137,
143 n.7

suburbanism 34, 40–1, 154, 167, 179,
        186–7, 223, 227–8 (*see also*
        urbanism)
suffrage 11, 36, 97–8, 101–5, 113–15

trains, *see* railroads
trans rights 12, 255–60, 262–6
transnationalism 112–18, 123–4, 147,
        154
transportation systems 22, 85,
        187–90, 209
Truman, Harry S. 166, 239–40, 246
Trump, Donald J. 249–50

undocumented workers 147, 151,
        154–6
Union Pacific Railroad Company 18,
        20–2, 24–9
unions and unionization 29, 79–80,
        115, 117, 123, 136, 148–51, 185,
        194–204, 216
United Mine Workers Association 195,
        199–204
urbanism (*see also* suburbanism)
    discrimination 40–2, 46, 63, 179–84,
        188–90, 214–15, 232–3
    infrastructure 39–40, 179–90,
        227–9, 232–3
    planning 35, 39–42, 178–90, 224,
        227–9, 232–3
    reform 8–9, 33–4, 39–42, 114–15,
        131–2
    renewal 11, 40–2, 178–90

US Department of Agriculture (USDA)
        132, 137–8, 228
US Department of Health, Education,
        and Welfare (HEW) 208–10, 212,
        214–17
US Department of Labor 149–51,
        155–6

veterans 29, 38–9, 148, 237, 239,
        241–5
Vietnam War 7, 173–4, 195–6, 208,
        210

white supremacy 37–42, 52, 73,
        165–6, 261–2
Wilson, Woodrow 104, 106, 117,
        126 n.13, 165–6
women 9, 11–12, 37–9, 54, 79–81,
        83–4, 87–91, 97–8, 101–8,
        112–24, 131–5, 139–42, 150,
        161–6, 168–74, 194–7, 200–4,
        207–18, 249
women's rights 87–91, 97,
        102–4, 113–18, 121–4,
        141–2, 194–204

xenophobia 113, 116, 150

youth culture 1–2, 7–8, 13, 80–1,
        83–4, 87–91, 210–11, 213–14,
        225, 256, 262–3

Zitkala-Ša (Yankton Dakota) 57, 103